The role of the hospital in medieval England

The role of the hospital in medieval England

Gift-giving and the spiritual economy

SHEILA SWEETINBURGH

FOUR COURTS PRESS

Set in 10.5 pt on 12 pt Bembo for
FOUR COURTS PRESS LTD
7 Malpas Street, Dublin 8, Ireland
e-mail: info@four-courts-press.ie
http://www.four-courts-press.ie
and in North America by
FOUR COURTS PRESS
c/o ISBS, 920 N.E. 58th Avenue, Suite 300, Portland, OR 97213.

A catalogue record for this title
is available from the British Library.

ISBN 1–85182–794–3

Printed in Great Britain
by Antony Rowe Ltd, Chippenham, Wilts.

Contents

To Ralph and Mary Sweetinburgh

Acknowledgments

This book has grown out of my study of Kent's medieval hospitals, research that was aided by the help I received at a number of county and national libraries and record offices. In particular, I owe a great debt to the staff at Canterbury Cathedral Archives and Library and to their colleagues at East Kent Archives. I have benefited from the knowledge and dedication of Mark Bateson, the archivist at Canterbury, who was always prepared to track down obscure leads and who located references to hospitals that I would not otherwise have found. My search for Kent's hospitals took me to St John's College, Cambridge, where I received considerable help and hospitality from Malcolm Underwood, the college archivist. He has also very kindly allowed me to cite his unpublished catalogue of the archive of St Mary's hospital, Ospringe.

During the time I have spent investigating medieval hospitals I have gained considerably from being part of the Canterbury Centre for Medieval and Tudor Studies at the University of Kent. It would be difficult to single out particular members (past and present) of the group because so many have given of their time, knowledge and special expertise. Most are cited at least once in the footnotes and/or under the unpublished papers, and to them and to others who have helped me I extend my warmest thanks. However, I feel Catherine Richardson, Claire Bartrum, Miles Banbery, Paul Lee, Mark Merry, Rob Lutton, Lynne Bowdon and Veronica Craig-Mair should be mentioned for their unstinting support. Similarly, Dean Bubier has been of immense help over the last few years, including willingly taking photographs of hospital artefacts.

Andrew Butcher was the supervisor of my doctoral thesis and I gained much from discussing the historiography of the medieval hospital with him. The depth and breadth of his knowledge and his enthusiasm for an inter-disciplinary approach offered new ways of seeing and for that I am extremely grateful. Moreover, he and Peter Brown have kindly provided the space for me to move from thesis to book.

David Birmingham generously agreed to read the whole manuscript and, as well as offering valuable comments and suggestions, he has provided moral support along the way. Consequently when I found myself getting too close to the subject he was able to get me to stand back and see the wider picture. For this and much more I owe him a great debt of gratitude.

I should like to register my appreciation of Shirley Sackman who very kindly acted as a preliminary editor. Her prompt action saved me from making a considerable number of grammatical errors. Imogen Corrigan similarly extended the bounds of friendship way beyond normal limits by volunteering to index the book and to both I extend my warmest thanks.

The county maps were drawn by John Hill and those of Dover and Sandwich by Barry Corke and I should like to thank them both. Charles Wanostrocht was extremely helpful regarding the photographing of the St John's hospital mazer at Sandwich. Gill Cannell, sub-librarian at Corpus Christi, Cambridge, and Ken Reedie, curator of Canterbury Heritage Museum, provided useful assistance concerning slides in the two collections.

Max Satchell, Mary Dixon and Pat Cullum very generously allowed me to draw on material from their unpublished theses, and Max Satchell's gazetteer of leper hospitals in England was exceptionally useful. I am grateful to them all.

Finally, I should like to thank my parents without whose unfailing support this book would never have been written and to whom it is dedicated.

Abbreviations

Arch. Cant.	*Archaeologia Cantiana*
BL	British Library
Cal. Inq. Misc.	*Calendar of Inquisitions Miscellaneous*
Cal. Inq. PM	*Calendar of Inquisitions Post Mortem*
Cal. Pap. Let.	*Calendar entries Papal Registers: Papal Letters*
Cal. Pap. Pet.	*Calendar entries Papal Registers: Papal Petitions*
CCAL	Canterbury Cathedral Archive and Library
CChR	*Calendar of Charter Rolls*
CCR	*Calendar of Close Rolls*
CLibR	*Calendar of Liberate Rolls*
CPR	*Calendar of Patent Rolls*
CKS	Centre for Kentish Studies
EKA	East Kent Archives
LPL	Lambeth Palace Library
L and P Henry VIII	*Letters and Papers, Henry VIII*
MA	Medway Archives
PR	*Pipe Rolls*
PRO	Public Record Office
Valor Eccl.	*Valor Ecclesiasticus*
VCH Kent	*Victoria County History: Kent*

EXPLANATORY NOTE

The dating has been standardized so that years run from 1 January to 31 December. Modern spellings have been used for Christian names.

Illustrations

Introduction

When, in 1514, Giles Love of Dover set out in his last will and testament his final gift exchanges with the master and brothers of St Mary's hospital, he was seeking to maintain his place among the honoured members of the hospital's community.[1] He wished to be buried in the hospital's chapel, and for this privilege he bequeathed to St Mary's six, part gilt, silver spoons with the image of St John the Baptist and twenty bushels of bay salt. These objects, if later returned to the market place, were probably worth about 25s., but in this exchange their importance was in their singularity.[2] The spoons and salt were gifts, and as special, symbolic items their value would be understood in terms of religious affiliations. In the case of the spoons, St John possessed gifts of the spirit and, like Mary, was a member of the holy family. Salt too had biblical significance because of its intrinsic nature but, like the spoons, its symbolism extended to its potential use at the hospital. As a preservative, the salt offered the brothers a way of continuing to provide hospitality; they could maintain their charitable role as feeders of the poor and of needy pilgrims. The silver spoons would become part of the hospital's treasury, joining other items invoking the devotional life of the house and the place of honoured benefactors like Giles.[3] Thus, through his burial in the church and his desire to aid a pres-

---

1 CKS, PRC 32/12, 172. 2 I. Kopytoff, 'The cultural biography of things' (1986), pp. 73–4. It is difficult to establish a likely price for the salt in early-sixteenth-century Dover, but from the few Kent inventories which mention salt later in the century it may have been worth about 13s. 4d. The inventory references: one wey of bay salt (140lbs) valued at 26s. 8d. in 1580 (Dover), two bushels of bay salt (7lbs) valued at 10d. in 1568 (Sandwich) and five weyes of bay salt valued at £8 6s. 8d. in 1567 (Faversham); CCAL, PRC 21/4, f. 197; PRC 10/3, f. 105v; PRC 10/4, f. 129. Catherine Richardson kindly supplied these references. The average price for salt nationally in the 1490s was about 10s. for twenty bushels; E. Miller (ed.), *The agrarian history of England and Wales* (1991), p. 467. The spoons are equally difficult. The price of silver from the late sixteenth-century east Kent inventories was between 4s. 4d. and 4s. 10d. per ounce, but the quality of the spoons was also important. For the purposes of this calculation they might have been worth between 1s. 6d. and 2s. each. 3 In an inventory of the hospital's possessions drawn up in 1535, the silver items included three dozen spoons and a cruet; M. Walcott, 'Inventories of (i) St Mary's hospital or

tigious charitable institution, Giles was strengthening his links with the hospital in terms of time and space, which had important implications with respect to commemoration and memory. Moreover, through his good works, Giles would expect to be allowed to stand with Christ's sheep on the Day of Judgement.

Other gift exchanges between Giles Love and the master and brothers were designed to further his relationship with St Mary's, and he gave 16s. for them to sing a trentall of masses for his soul. Though primarily indicating his concern about purgatory and about his spiritual well-being, the bequest also underlined his belief in the brothers as good advocates. He thus publicly acknowledged that the masses would be well performed, a declaration that would be heard and understood by his contemporaries. He wished to have his obit celebrated forever at the hospital church in the likely event of his son not reaching his majority, such services similarly highlighting the hospital community's value as worthy intercessors. Under these circumstances, Love's executors were to give St Mary's hospital all the plate left to his son and also the house in Bygon Street. In exchange, the brothers would celebrate six masses by note for his soul, for that of Johanna his wife and for those of the departed faithful. The six priest brothers were to be given 2s. and the thirteen poor men and women would each receive a penny dole. The master and brothers were to spend 2s. on fresh cakes and the act of eating them was to be accompanied by their remembrance of his soul.

Like the gift of his amber beads to his son-in-law, Giles' bequest of a silver drinking cruet to Sir John, the master at St Mary's, was a pregnant reminder of divine love, and the more humble attributes of human love and friendship. Sir John was to oversee Giles' will, which might explain the gift as a recompense for his services, but the personal nature of the item and its Eucharistic symbolism seem to indicate the strength of feeling between the two men. It is possible that both men saw themselves in some ways as outsiders in Dover society. As master of the hospital Sir John was on the margins, a reflection of the somewhat ambiguous position of the hospital *vis-à-vis* the town, while Giles Love appears to have had some role with regard to Dover castle, the other royal institution. Their relationship may have developed over several years, fostered by a mutual understanding of the other's place in Dover and possibly by a series of gift exchanges, which culminated in Giles' post-mortem benefaction.

Even though certain historians have cast doubts on the validity of using testamentary materials to investigate medieval ideas about piety and charity, these documents remain one of the best sources available, provided their inherent problems are acknowledged in the analysis.[4] This example concentrates on the

Maison Dieu, Dover' (1868), 274.   **4** Works on this subject include: C. Burgess, 'A fond thing

relationship between Giles Love and his local hospital to illustrate how he seemed to express his spirituality at an important time during his life. Giles' actions, and the connections he sought to initiate and maintain with the personnel at St Mary's, indicate his concerns for the salvation of his soul, through prayers and good works, but also the role of the hospital in the furtherance of his desire for commemoration and remembrance. Such an assessment of a single testament provides valuable indicators regarding that individual's pious and charitable devotions, and when the testaments and other documents left by Giles' contemporaries are similarly examined, it is possible to provide ideas about the perception of piety and charity in late medieval Dover.

Ideas about piety and charity in the late middle ages have been debated by a number of historians in recent years. Of particular interest here is the debate between Miri Rubin and Patricia Cullum regarding the level of charitable provision in England in the century after the Black Death. Basing her assessment primarily on the evidence from Yorkshire, but drawing also on other work, Cullum believes that people continued to aid the poor through the support of charitable institutions. She cites the large number of 'maisonsdieu' founded during this period, suggesting that charitable giving did not decline until the late fifteenth century in England.[5] Rubin, from her work on the Cambridge hospitals, disagrees with this analysis, seeing a marked decline in the provision of institutional care and a shift by donors towards aiding those who were seen to be like them.[6] One interesting aspect of the debate, introduced by Rubin, is the concept of the 'language' of charity and how this may have changed over the late middle ages to accommodate the different notions and concerns of potential benefactors.[7] Linked to this has been the idea that charity should be seen as an inclusive construct, where aid for poor scholars, for example, was perceived to be as meritorious in the sight of God as alms given to the poor.[8]

Many recent studies on medieval hospitals in England and continental Europe have addressed the issue of charitable provision and what it meant in medieval society.[9] These works are extremely diverse, ranging from national

vainly invented' (1988), pp. 56–84; C. Burgess, 'Late medieval wills and pious convention' (1990), pp. 14–33. Robert Lutton has devoted two sections of his doctoral thesis to the advantages and problems of using testamentary sources for the study of late medieval piety and many of his observations are relevant here; R. Lutton, 'Heterodox and orthodox piety in Tenterden' (1997), pp. 3–18. **5** P.H. Cullum, 'Hospitals and charitable provision in medieval Yorkshire' (1990), pp. 439–42, 444–6; P.H. Cullum, 'For pore people harberles' (1994), pp. 38, 43–4. **6** M. Rubin, *Charity and community in medieval Cambridge* (1987), pp. 54–98, 254–8, 292–3; M. Rubin, 'Development and change in English hospitals, 1100–1500' (1989), pp. 52–7. **7** M. Rubin, 'Imagining medieval hospitals' (1991), pp. 16–18. **8** P. Horden, 'A discipline of relevance: the historiography of the later medieval hospital' (1988), 369–74. **9** For example, historians like Carole Rawcliffe and Margery McIntosh have examined the development of the Norwich hospitals and

assessments to the history of an individual institution, and include a number of
regional studies and investigations of the hospitals of a single town.[10] Although
certain historians are still primarily concerned to ascertain the chronology of
the hospital's development, others have looked more widely, viewing the hospital through the roles it undertook in society. The latter approach has been
adopted here, the hospital seen through its inter-relationships with benefactors, patrons and beneficiaries, and how these changed over time. The study
has focused primarily on these inter-relationships in terms of the spiritual economy, where, following Robert Swanson, this economy was taken to involve
three categories of religious participants – the parish, parishioners and their
priest; the sub-parochial, like fraternities; and the extra-parochial, including
the hospitals.[11]

Gift exchange offered a way of looking at the inter-relationships involving
the hospital in the spiritual economy. As a theoretical concept, gift exchange
first came to prominence in the early twentieth century through the works of
Mauss and Malinowski, and since then anthropologists and, to a lesser extent,
historians have employed it in their analyses.[12] With regard to this assessment
of the hospital, the theoretical ideas concerning gift exchange that are seen as
especially significant relate to what constitutes a gift. The gift is thought to be
different from a commodity; it is a singular object which has been removed
from the market-place, though it may return there in a subsequent exchange.
Consequently, what is envisaged as appropriate as a gift is important for both
the donor and the recipient because it provides meaning about the relation-

---

the founding of almshouses in England, respectively; C. Rawcliffe, *The hospitals of medieval Norwich*
(1995); C. Rawcliffe, *Medicine for the soul* (1999); M. McIntosh, 'Local responses to the poor in
late medieval and Tudor England' (1988), 209–45. John Henderson and Katherine Park have investigated the hospitals of certain Italian cities; J. Henderson, *Piety and charity in late medieval Florence*
(1997); K. Park, 'Healing the poor' (1991), pp. 26–45. **10** See bibliography for regional and local
studies. Works on English hospitals include: R.M. Clay, *The medieval hospitals of England* (1909,
reprinted 1966); M.A. Seymour, 'The organisation, personnel and functions of the medieval hospital' (1946); B. Bailey, *Almshouses* (1988); E. Prescott, *The English medieval hospital* (1992); N.
Orme and M. Webster, *The English hospital, 1070–1570* (1995); M. Satchell, 'The emergence of
leper-houses in medieval England, 1100–1250' (1998); M. Carlin, 'Medieval English hospitals'
(1989), pp. 21–39. **11** R.N. Swanson, *Church and society in late medieval England* (1989), pp. 209–28.
12 The most recent English translation; M. Mauss, *The gift* (1990); B. Malinowski, *Argonauts of the
western Pacific* (1922). Recent anthropological works have developed and modified the theory: J.
Davis, *Exchange* (1992); C.A. Gregory, *Gifts and commodities* (1982); A. Appadurai, 'Introduction:
commodities and the politics of value' (1986), pp. 3–63; Kopytoff, 'Cultural biography of things',
pp. 64–91; P. Geary, 'Sacred commodities: the circulation of medieval relics' (1986), pp. 169–91;
M. Strathern, *The gender of the gift* (1988); M. Strathern, 'Qualified value' (1992), pp. 169–91; A.B.
Weiner, *Inalienable possessions* (1992); R. Lederman, *What gifts engender* (1986); A. Offer, 'Between
the gift and the market' (1997), 450–76; M. Godelier, *The enigma of the gift*, trans. N. Scott (1999).
See bibliography for recent historical works.

ship between the participants.[13] Also relevant is the notion of the counter-gift, the reciprocal act that fulfils the exchange, and the timing of this act, which is similarly meaningful as a way of expressing matters like hierarchy and the degree of obligation among the interested parties.[14] In addition, it is valuable to incorporate the idea of keeping for giving, where what is given is the alienable right of usage, but the inalienable ownership is kept.[15] By employing such refinements to the theoretical issues governing strategies and processes of gift-giving and reciprocity, and the inalienable relationship between gift and gift-giver, it has been possible to construct a history of individual hospitals from their involvement in the spiritual economy.[16]

The assessment of individual hospitals has been extended, through a number of local and regional studies, to gain a clearer picture of the changing roles of different hospitals in the religious life of the community. Through an exploration of the gift exchanges which individuals, groups, and secular and religious institutions undertook as participants in the spiritual economy, the various hospitals are perceived to be active in a number of roles that often change over time. This comparable analysis of the hospitals is extended to include other parties in the spiritual economy, in order to demonstrate the relative importance of particular hospitals, and of hospitals more generally as charitable institutions in medieval society. Thus, the hospital may be used as a sensitive indicator of contemporary attitudes regarding piety and charity, which may be considered along with religious establishments and others, like the crown, town officers, parish and craft fraternities, and individuals, all of whom might engage in processes of gift-giving and reciprocity. Furthermore, these regional and local case studies reveal ideas about how benefactors and beneficiaries perceived hospitals, highlighting notions of belonging or alienation which might have profound implications for the well-being and survival of certain houses. Nor were the implications of such ideas confined to the survival of the hospital, because at houses that continued to provide institutional care, levels and types of benefaction might indicate attitudes concerning the treatment of the poor and other disadvantaged groups in medieval society.

The gift exchanges examined in these local and regional studies were not solely concerned with the hospitals' charitable role, but also explored their activities in the secular life of the community.[17] Of particular interest were the hospitals under civic patronage, especially where founders and patrons were

---

13 Kopytoff, 'Cultural biography of things', pp. 73–6, 80–3, 89–90. **14** P. Bourdieu, *Outline of a theory of practice* (1977), pp. 6–7. **15** Godelier, *Enigma of the gift*, p. 36. **16** Geary, 'Sacred commodities', p. 186. **17** Two important recent books on the importance of gift exchange in late medieval and early modern society; V. Groebner, *Liquid assets, dangerous gifts* (2002); N.Z. Davis, *The gift in sixteenth-century France* (2000).

involved in complex gift exchange processes with the house, through which they sought to express ideas concerning lordship, hierarchy and good governance. Other patrons and benefactors are similarly seen to initiate reciprocal exchanges that were intended to have political and social implications, like the creation of rituals where the display of public gratitude by the beneficiaries was a fitting demonstration of their benefactors' largesse. These and other uses of the hospital indicate the complexity and significance of relationships among participants predicated on processes of gift-giving and reciprocity, which highlight the value of the hospital as an indicator of social and religious conditions in medieval England.

PLACING THE HOSPITAL

The book moves from the national picture of the medieval hospital in chapter 1 to a study of the hospitals in the Kent town of Sandwich in chapter 4. Using ideas explored in more detail later on, chapter 1 opens with a survey of the distribution and chronology of English hospitals in the middle ages to demonstrate the diversity of hospital provision nationally, and also the incidence of certain trends regarding foundation, founders and benefactors. The final part of this introduction looks at the nature of patronage nationally using the concept of gift exchange, which, together with the earlier components, forms an overview, providing a context for the regional and local studies that follow.

Initially, the investigation turns to the hospitals and religious houses, the other extra-parochial participants in the spiritual economy, of Warwickshire and Wiltshire. The comparable assessment illustrates many of the themes discussed in detail with regard to Kent in the remaining chapters. For instance, there were certain regional variations concerning the hospitals in the two counties, like the type and distribution of almshouses. Founders and patrons are seen to play an important part in such matters, their relationship with their chosen hospital articulated through processes of gift exchange. This is demonstrated more fully using evidence for the hospitals and religious houses of Kent and, as a way of providing a detailed picture, the hospitals are categorized by type. The resultant hospital models based on form and function – leper, poor, pilgrim, almshouse (subdivided into bedehouse-type and maisondieu-type) – allow the various hospitals to be investigated by looking at different types of gift exchange, like *in vitam* charters and testamentary bequests. Such an approach has certain advantages, not least the possibility of comparing a considerable number of houses and of envisaging their place in society, rather than seeing them as isolated entities.

In addition to employing county studies to examine the medieval hospital as an integrated establishment in terms of locality and region, the same method is applicable to towns, in this instance the Cinque Ports of Dover and Sandwich. Like the Kent assessment, those for the towns have drawn on a range of sources for the hospitals – documents like wills and testaments, town books and accounts, and the archives of various religious houses and parish churches. Such Kent records are generally of a good quality, though the testamentary materials, for example, have not survived in large numbers for the period before the late fifteenth century, and their distribution pattern across the county is extremely variable. However, materials for Dover, and particularly for Sandwich, are more abundant, offering the chance to produce a detailed analysis of the role of the hospital in a small provincial town. Of special importance with regard to Sandwich are the archives for St Bartholomew's and St John's hospitals, the latter including the house's admissions register.[18] The first surviving entry in this register is for 1397, comprising a list of the master, brothers and sisters present when the mayor and senior jurats, as patrons, visited the hospital. Thereafter many of the visitations are recorded, providing a detailed account of the brothers and sisters resident in the house over the fifteenth and sixteenth centuries. Other information is occasionally included, like the goods and bedding available for the sick-poor who stayed there, and notes concerning debts owed to and by people inside and outside St John's.

The quality of the Kent sources, therefore, provides a valuable opportunity to explore the social history of the medieval hospital locally and regionally. Such sources are investigated to demonstrate the range of inter-relationships various hospitals in Sandwich, Dover and Kent, more generally, developed with local people, town governments, members of the nobility, the crown and religious houses. Gift exchange is used as a way of looking at these relationships, especially gift-giving to and by hospitals when they were engaged in the spiritual economy, an economy which centred on the church's offer of salvation through good works and its need to provide for a priestly caste. Through an examination of the gift exchange strategies adopted by individuals, groups and institutions, it is possible to illustrate the role of the hospital in this economy. Moreover, the hospital's role was not confined to its religious activities. Some founders and patrons employed certain hospitals in the pursuit of their ideological objectives, perceiving gift exchange as a means of linking concepts like social responsibility and civic governance. This extended use of the hospital was an important feature at Sandwich, in particular, raising ideas about the place of the hospital locally, regionally, and possibly nationally. Thus this book, in moving from a broad overview of English hospitals to a detailed analysis of the hospitals of Sandwich, a place comparable to many in medieval

18 EKA, Sa/Ch 10J A1.

England, aids our understanding of these ubiquitous charitable establishments in medieval provincial society through an assessment of their political, religious and social roles.

CHAPTER I

Hospitals in medieval England

In medieval England there were a number of different types of hospital. Their form and their function were the product of a range of factors linked to the aspirations and desires of founders and patrons. Other factors included the proximity of pilgrimage sites, the perceived incidence of leprosy in the region, or the presence of urban settlements. As a result, many displayed differences regarding matters like the type of inmates accommodated, the numbers involved, the presence of a resident staff and/or clerics, and the distribution of alms. Furthermore, hospitals were rarely static institutions, but needed to adapt to changing conditions inside and outside, as hospital authorities sought to ensure the survival of their establishment within the increasingly competitive confines of the spiritual economy. Such diversity has been recognized by historians of medieval hospitals, but in the national picture it seems feasible to use a simple classificatory scheme, a system which is sufficiently flexible to allow for further differentiation when considering a detailed regional analysis.

Any national assessment, however, must take account of the uneven nature of the evidence. Although the list of medieval hospitals produced by David Knowles and Neville Hadcock is an extremely valuable starting point, recent regional studies and Max Satchell's evaluation of English leper houses have highlighted certain discrepancies.[1] This is hardly surprising, considering that Knowles and Hadcock were primarily using the Victoria County History series and material provided by R.M. Clay.[2] As the name implies, the series had its beginnings

---

1 D. Knowles and R.N. Hadcock, *Medieval religious houses: England and Wales,* 2nd edn (1971), pp. 250–324; Knowles and Hadcock, 'Additions and corrections to [hospitals]' (1957), 76–85; Satchell, 'Leper-houses in medieval England'. Regional studies of the medieval hospitals of Cambridgeshire, Cornwall and Devon, Cumbria, Kent, London, Middlesex, Norfolk and Suffolk, Norwich, Oxfordshire and Yorkshire have been produced respectively by Rubin, *Charity in Cambridge;* Orme and Webster, *English hospital,* pp. 169–266; W.G. Wiseman, 'The medieval hospitals of Cumbria' (1987), 83–100; S. Sweetinburgh, 'The role of the hospital in medieval Kent, *c.*1080–*c.*1560' (1998); C. Berridge, *Almshouses of London* (1987); C. Rawcliffe, 'The hospitals of later medieval London', (1984), 1–21; M.B. Honeybourne, 'The leper hospitals of the London area' (1967), 1–61; E.M. Phillips, 'Charitable institutions in Norfolk and Suffolk *c.*1350–1600' (2001); Rawcliffe, *Hospitals of Norwich;* M. Markham, *Medieval hospitals in Oxfordshire* (1979); Cullum, 'Hospitals in Yorkshire'.
2 Knowles and Hadcock, *Medieval religious houses,* p. 250.

in the late nineteenth century, and many of the volumes covering medieval hospitals were produced prior to 1930.[3] Some hospital accounts were written by distinguished historians who knew the field well, but others were less thoroughly researched.[4] Since the mid-twentieth century the collection has grown, though the histories of hospitals for a few counties have yet to be produced.[5] Furthermore, as Satchell has commented, the identification of certain hospitals may rest on a single reference, some of which are extremely obscure, making it very difficult if not impossible to produce a comprehensive gazetteer.[6] Even though this is applicable broadly, it is particularly significant with respect to the small ancient leper houses and the late medieval maisondieu-type almshouses, some of the former disappearing before the Black Death and the latter characterized by their ephemeral nature. In addition, the editors of the Victoria County Histories predominantly adopted a descriptive approach, which, though useful as collections of 'facts' about particular, sometimes selected, hospitals, does little analytically to place the hospital either locally or regionally. As a consequence, the quality of information known and assessments made about the medieval hospitals of the various counties is uneven, which means that any analysis on a national scale must take account of these factors, though it does not invalidate the attempt.[7]

This survey of the English medieval hospital, which forms the first section of the chapter, is divided into three parts. The first comprises an estimation of the numbers of hospitals of all kinds and an assessment of their distribution regionally and nationally. This leads to a consideration of the chronology of their provision, again seeking to ascertain whether regional patterns are duplicated at the national level. The third sub-section addresses the nature of patronage nationally, looking at the whole range of foundations, whether monastic, episcopal, aristocratic, royal, civic or of individual townsmen, in terms of the relationship between patrons and hospitals. By so doing, the survey highlights the characteristic variety of local and regional provision of hospitals, the significance of change and adaptation, and the role of patrons, themes central to this book.

Following the general survey, the second part of the chapter exemplifies the regional approach by conducting an examination of the changing networks of hospital provision based upon two counties. Such an analysis explores in outline issues later developed fully in consideration of medieval Kentish society in the remaining chapters.

---

3 W. Page et al. (eds), *The Victoria History of the Counties of England* (1900–); surveys of hospitals published before 1930; for details, see Bibliography.   4 Orme and Webster, *English hospital*, p. 7; Satchell, 'Leper-houses in medieval England', pp. 77–8.   5 For counties for which *VCH* surveys have now been produced see Bibliography under W. Page et al.   6 Satchell, 'Leper-houses in medieval England', pp. 79–84.   7 Orme and Webster outline the problems of trying to produce a national history of English medieval hospitals; Orme and Webster, *English hospital*, pp. 1–12.

NATIONAL SURVEY

Hospital number, type and distribution

When Truth spoke of repairing 'mesondieux' in Langland's *The Vision of Piers Plowman,* and the Lollards and certain knights of parliament referred, in 1395 and in 1410 respectively, to 'alms houses', and the latter also to 'spittles', they were alluding to institutions which today we might call medieval hospitals.[8] The term 'hospital' with regard to the middle ages is now often used inclusively to cover a variety of establishments (but not houses that were integral parts of monasteries) which might broadly be termed charitable, involving a relationship between benefactors and beneficiaries predicated in some way on the seven works of mercy.[9] They ranged in size and complexity from the use of a single room given to a poor person to massive, well-endowed institutions.[10] At these, the resident staff of clergy, brothers and sisters were engaged in the liturgical life of the house, as well as administering to the needs of paupers, the sick and poor travellers. Such diversity was in part a product of the absence of restrictions concerning their foundation, which meant that anyone could establish a hospital, providing it did not impinge on the local parish, though should this occur there were ways of alleviating the situation.[11]

To describe these disparate establishments, contemporaries used a nomenclature that changed over the middle ages, included a degree of regional variation, but was flexible. A particular institution might be referred to in a number of ways. The term 'hospital' was widely used nationally, but it might also refer to the religious military order of the Knights of St John of Jerusalem. Some hospitals, frequently those founded in the twelfth and thirteenth centuries, were under the rule of St Augustine, and their resemblance to religious houses meant that they might be described as priories or hospitals. Similarly, there was a degree of fluidity with respect to some hospitals which by the late medieval period were

8 A.V.C. Schmidt (ed.), *William Langland's The Vision of Piers Plowman,* 2nd edn (1995), VII, 26; A.R. Myers (ed.), *English historical documents 1327–1485* (1969), pp. 849, 669; Orme and Webster, *English hospital,* pp. 132–6. **9** Rawcliffe, *Hospitals of Norwich,* pp. 16–17. **10** The largest hospital in terms of resident personnel was St Leonard's, York. At its peak in the fourteenth century there were eighteen clergy, sixteen sisters and female servants, thirty choristers, ten corrodians and between 144 and 240 poor sick people (cremetts); Cullum, 'Hospitals in Yorkshire', pp. 156–60, 178; Orme and Webster, *English hospital,* pp. 35–6; *VCH Yorkshire,* vol. 3, pp. 338–40. It was one of the few English hospitals which housed orphans, possibly from a very young age; Cullum, 'Hospitals in Yorkshire', pp. 191–2. **11** Rubin, *Charity in Cambridge,* p. 103. The parochial rights of St Michael's church, Lichfield, were protected following an agreement drawn up in the early thirteenth century between the prior and brethren of St John's hospital and the prebendary of Freeford, who held the advowson of the parish church. Among the provisions was one which allowed the parishioners to worship at the hospital's chapel on holy days, the hospital using a small bell to summon them, provided the hospital staff received the sacraments at the parish church on major festivals; *VCH Staffordshire,* vol. 3, p. 279.

little more than chapels. These might be referred to as 'the free chapel or hospital of —', a practice that at times means it is difficult to assign a precise status to the institution concerned.

According to Orme and Webster, the Latin *domus dei*, in French and English *maisondieu*, was another common term, but in Kent, few hospitals were so described; the term was principally used in the county for the royal hospitals at Ospringe and Dover.[12] In contrast, as Cullum noted, 'maisonsdieu' were small ephemeral almshouses in late medieval Yorkshire, for which often the only reference was in the will of the founder, or occasionally a later benefactor.[13] 'Almshouse' (from the earlier Latin *domus elemosinarie*) is found in late fourteenth-century England, its use becoming increasingly common from the fifteenth century onwards. At about the same time, as Orme and Webster remarked, the term 'spittle' or 'spital' was employed to describe a more basic place, possibly for beggars, though it might also be used for houses which had formerly been called hospitals.[14] Houses for lepers, even more than those for beggars, were likely to be referred to differently, and in addition to Latin and French terms, the most common English forms were 'lazar house' and 'maldry' (from the French *maladerie*).[15]

Yet, even though contemporaries acknowledged the diversity of hospital forms, and the multifunctional nature of some hospitals, there seems to have been a number of broad categories – leper houses, non-leper houses and almshouses. Modifications to this simple scheme might include the division of the latter into 'bedehouses' and Cullum's 'maisonsdieu', and the non-leper houses according to the principal type of inmate.[16] This differs from the classification adopted by Knowles and Hadcock; it sees the almshouse as a late medieval phenomenon, concurring with the findings of Orme and Webster who, while acknowledging that there were similarities between the earlier hospitals and the post-Black Death almshouses, believed that 'there *were* new features [in the latter] and the mixture of elements was often different from before'.[17]

Using this simple classification, and taking due note of the problems outlined above of identifying hospitals in the literature, there were about 310 leper houses, a similar number of non-leper houses, and 225 almshouses founded in medieval England.[18] With regard to the degree of accuracy, the leper house figure is based on Satchell's gazetteer of 299 documented houses most probably founded before

---

12 Orme and Webster, *English hospital*, pp. 39–40. 13 Cullum, 'Hospitals in Yorkshire', pp. 318–20, 328–30. 14 Orme and Webster, *English hospital*, pp. 39–40, 138. 15 Ibid., p. 40. 16 Some of the Yorkshire maisonsdieu were founded in conjunction with chantries. This does not appear to have been the case in Kent, where the broad distinction was between endowed bedehouses and unendowed maisonsdieu; Cullum, 'Pore people harberles', p. 37. 17 Knowles and Hadcock, *Medieval religious houses*, p. 250; Orme and Webster, *English hospital*, pp. 138–9. 18 With regard to the number of leper houses, Rawcliffe believes there was 'a bare minimum of 320 *leprosaria*' (including ten run by the various military orders); C. Rawcliffe, 'Learning to love the leper' (2001), p. 231 and n. 3.

1250 and about a dozen known later leper house foundations.[19] As he states, this is a minimum figure, because some leper colonies were sufficiently informal that they may never have been recorded, and certain leper houses, particularly those which disappeared in the early to mid-fourteenth century, may remain forever elusive.[20] However, the almshouse figure is the most approximate, providing a minimum number that would probably be significantly increased if a national survey of the testamentary records was compiled as a means of locating references to maisondieu-type almshouses in particular.[21] Such a survey would, in addition, uncover evidence of the existence of other unknown hospitals, and also might aid our knowledge of the longevity of certain houses.[22]

Examined on a county basis, there was a considerable range in terms of the total number of hospitals and the balance among the different groups, even when the size of the county was taken into consideration. In the neighbouring counties of Nottinghamshire and Leicestershire, for example, there were nineteen hospitals and eight hospitals respectively, and in Nottinghamshire the largest category was the leper house; in Leicestershire it was the non-leper house.[23] Certain counties had few hospitals at all, like the northern, predominantly upland, sparely populated counties of Westmoreland and Cumberland, but also Worcestershire in the west midlands. Conversely, hospitals abounded in some counties: Northumberland and Yorkshire (even allowing for the size of the county) in the north, Gloucester and Norfolk in the midlands, and Devon and Kent in the south. To provide some idea of the number of hospitals that might be found in any given county, the average figure was just over twenty, though almost half had between ten and twenty hospitals.

This variation was similarly found within the counties, a product in part of particular heavy concentrations of hospitals in certain towns, like the thirty-five hospitals at York, sixteen at Bristol, fifteen at Norwich and ten at Exeter.[24] Yet some major towns, including certain cathedral cities, were apparently poorly supplied. Worcester may have had no more than four (though the total number of beds was considerable) and Chichester a similar number, in a county where there was a minimum of twenty-six hospitals.[25] Additionally, in some towns, particular hospital types were not present; for example there is no known leper hospital at the ancient town of Sherborne, Dorset. Such apparent omissions are difficult to understand.[26] Like the county distribution pattern, this may reflect

19 Satchell, 'Leper-houses in medieval England', pp. 251–399 (appendix 1). **20** Ibid., pp. 69–112. **21** Cullum, 'Pore people harberles', p. 39. **22** For example, the only known reference to a spital house called the 'Bekyn' at Faversham, Kent, occurs in a will, dated 1516, made by a testator from Deal; CKS, PRC 32/12, f. 33. **23** These assessments are based primarily on the *VCH* surveys, supplemented using evidence from individual hospital, town and regional studies. **24** Orme and Webster, *English hospital*, p. 37. **25** In 1294, it was reported that the hospital of St Wulstan, Worcester, had twenty-two sick persons in the infirmary; *VCH Worcestershire*, vol. 2, p. 175. **26** It is possible the town did have a leper hospital for which no records survive, or the leprous may have entered the

the considerable variation in the local balance of different hospital types. At Bury St Edmunds, Suffolk, for example, the town was encircled by several small leper houses, while at Hull, in the late fourteenth and fifteenth centuries, there had been a period of extensive almshouse provision.[27]

Looking more closely at this variation in terms of numbers and types of hospital, it may be possible to say something more about the non-leper houses, especially their role as multifunctional institutions, and changes to the form and function of certain hospitals over time. First, it is worth mentioning that probably a small proportion of the leper houses nationally did not exclusively accommodate lepers from their foundation, a consequence, maybe, of the founder's desire to aid others among the poor and sick-poor, but also an inability to endow separate institutions. However, it was the non-leper houses which from their foundation were most likely to cater to different groups. The poor and impotent formed the most important category of person aided, whereas the level of provision nationally for needy travellers and the sick-poor was far less, and varied considerably across the country. Very few houses specifically aided either group, moreover, preferring instead to care for them as one of several categories given sustenance at these multifunctional institutions. Yet there appear to have been a few counties, like Westmoreland, Cornwall and Derbyshire, which offered little or nothing to travellers or the sick.[28] Elsewhere the relative number of houses providing such support did vary, but was rarely more than two or three houses per county; in addition, the number aided at any particular hospital was usually small. There were a few notable exceptions, however; for instance, the great hospital of St Leonard in York, which had around 225 beds, and St Bartholomew's hospital, Gloucester which accommodated ninety sick persons in the fourteenth century.[29] Furthermore, Gloucestershire was exceptionally well endowed with houses providing assistance for travellers and the sick, the former at possibly three hospitals and the latter at up to seven houses. The scale of such provision in Hampshire was apparently similar. As a group the London hospitals provided the greatest concentration of places for the sick, especially after the establishment of the Savoy by Henry VII's executors in 1515, the inmates receiving attention from trained medical practitioners, a luxury of dubious worth and generally unavailable elsewhere.[30]

hospital of St John the Baptist and St John the Evangelist; Knowles and Hadcock, *Medieval religious houses*, p. 305. There are problems, however, regarding the latter idea because the house was founded for the sick-poor and is well documented. Only once is it referred to as a leper house, in a late record of 1547; Satchell, 'Leper-houses in medieval England', p. 76. **27** J. Rowe, 'The medieval hospitals of Bury St Edmunds' (1958), 253–63. Cullum, 'Hospitals in Yorkshire', p. 321; Cullum, 'Pore people harberles', pp. 37, 38. **28** In Cornwall, if there was any such provision it was at St John's hospital, Helston; Orme and Webster, *English hospital*, pp. 193–5. **29** Cullum, 'Hospitals in Yorkshire', p. 193. Orme and Webster, citing the 'Register of Thomas Charlton', state that there were perhaps ninety poor inmates in 1333, a figure somewhat higher than the fifty-two quoted by Fullbrook-Legatt from a petition of 1558–1603; Orme and Webster, *English hospital*, p. 36; L. Fullbrook-Legatt, 'Medieval Gloucester: hospitals' (1946–8), 229. **30** By the late middle ages there

Although some hospital authorities were prepared to aid the sick, excluding the leprous who were expected to seek aid at the lazar house nearby, others were far more discriminatory. Particular examples are frequently cited, like the statutes for St John's hospital, Bridgewater, where those prohibited from entering the house included lepers, lunatics, persons with the falling sickness or any contagious disease, pregnant women or any 'intolerable person' even if poor or infirm.[31] Yet it is difficult to know what proportion of the country's hospitals adopted such policies, or whether they were commonly in force throughout the life of the house. Some were introduced in the form of revised ordinances, suggesting that in certain cases people suffering from these specific complaints might previously have entered the hospital, and it is rarely clear how strictly the rules were followed.

Another factor might be the presence of complementary institutions in the neighbourhood, providing opportunities for those excluded elsewhere. Although this is easiest to measure with regard to the local provision of leper and non-leper houses generally, in certain places it is clear there were potentially places for a wide range of needy people. Such provision was an urban phenomenon – in broad terms, the larger the town, the more comprehensive the aid supplied. But it is worth noting that before 1350 several counties had only one town where there was a leper and a non-leper house, whereas others had considerably greater provision.[32]

Conversely, some hospital authorities adopted a positive discriminatory policy. In addition to the leper houses themselves, founders and patrons of non-leper houses might stipulate the type of inmate to be accommodated. Hospitals catering for travellers, pilgrims and the sick have already been mentioned, and from among the broad category of the poor and infirm some institutions sought to aid men or women, the elderly, clerics, orphans or scholars.[33] The latter possibly were provided with an education at or in association with the hospital, or with accommodation from whence they might pursue their studies nearby.[34] The use of such criteria may have occurred throughout the medieval period,

were a few references to medicine or medical practitioners regarding hospitals, but the Savoy statutes are exceptional; Rawcliffe, 'Hospitals of London', 9. On the provision of medical treatment nationally; Orme and Webster, *English hospital*, pp. 59, 62; Carlin, 'Medieval English hospitals', pp. 29–31. **31** Orme and Webster, *English hospital*, p. 58. **32** Counties apparently having this limited provision: Cornwall (Helston), Cumberland (Carlisle), Essex (Colchester), Huntingdonshire (Huntingdon), Lancashire (Lancaster), Leicestershire (Leicester), Worcestershire (Worcester). For comparison six towns in Berkshire – Abingdon, Hungerford, Newbury, Reading, Wallingford and Windsor – had this complementary provision. **33** Orme and Webster, *English hospital*, pp. 64–6, 111–12, 115. **34** According to the Merton College statutes drawn up in the thirteenth century, the college was to maintain St John's hospital, Basingstoke. The statutes included a provision whereby members of the college might reside there if need arose; *VCH Hampshire and the Isle of Wight*, vol. 2, p. 209. St John's hospital, Cambridge, provided accommodation for poor scholars in the early 1280s, and then again from the early fourteenth century; *VCH Cambridgeshire and the Isle of Ely*, vol. 2, pp. 304–5.

but appears to have become more common from the later middle ages when matters like gender, life-cycle stage, occupation, social and economic status were commonly employed in the selection of inmates.[35]

In addition to their use at the non-leper houses, selection criteria were employed at the almshouses. This was presumably deemed necessary at both types of house. At the bedehouses the resident inmates were expected to engage in some form of intercessory activity for the benefit of founders and benefactors, their good estate while living and the salvation of their souls after death, a task for which the worthy poor were especially suited.[36] For those seeking entry to maisonsdieu, suitability was presumably still important because they were the living embodiment of the donor's charitable action, a recognition that might enhance the donor's status in this world and the next. A majority of the almshouses identified so far apparently belonged to the former type, their distribution nationally far less patchy than the maisonsdieu, but this is primarily a reflection of the small number of county hospital studies completed where most of the latter have been identified. Furthermore, the bedehouse-type almshouses were generally endowed, unlike the poor maisonsdieu, which meant that most, unlike their ephemeral neighbours, were able to survive the disruption of the sixteenth century, though sometimes requiring a degree of adaptation, or refoundation.[37]

The need for adaptation in the quest for survival became increasingly important from the fourteenth century, though some leper and non-leper hospitals had previously extended their spiritual roles, mainly in response to the wishes of benefactors but possibly also as a means of staving off institutional poverty. For the leper houses, in particular, the general decline in the incidence of leprosy required them to find an alternative *raison d'etre,* which was either the accommodation of other needy persons or an extension of the intercessory services offered at the hospital's chapel, however some houses used both strategies.[38] As a consequence, by the later middle ages the distinction between leper

---

35 With regard to gender, for example, Cullum indicated that in late medieval Yorkshire women were apparently more commonly found as inmates, an observation not endorsed by Orme and Webster, who considered an earlier male bias was probably still applicable during the later period; P.H. Cullum, 'And hir name was charite' (1992), pp. 199–200; Orme and Webster, *English hospital*, pp.109, 117. 36 Degory Watur, a wealthy draper, founded an almshouse at Shrewsbury in association with the churchwardens and parishioners of St Mary's church in the mid-fifteenth century. Many of the thirteen inmates were local parishioners selected on Watur's advice. He seems to have lived in the hall of the almshouse and regularly joined the almsfolk at their prayers in the Lady Chapel of St Mary's church; *VCH Shropshire*, vol. 2, pp. 111–12. 37 Of the seven almshouses in Exeter, one appears to have disappeared in the 1530s, and at Wynard's almshouse the chaplain's salary was confiscated by the crown in 1548, but otherwise it appears to have suffered little at the Reformation. The other five also survived, possibly aided by the absence of a chapel at three of them and the involvement of the corporation in the management of four of the city's almshouses, at least by the late sixteenth century; Orme and Webster, *English hospital*, pp. 240–8. 38 At St Leonard's hospital, Peterborough, for example, the poor had replaced the lepers by the early fif-

and non-leper houses had frequently disappeared in terms of the personnel sup-ported, yet some, especially the hospitals around London, and in the south west and north of England continued to house a sizeable number of leprous persons.[39]

Another feature of many of these hospitals and the almshouses was a rise in the number of fee-paying inmates, or corrodians, a development which reduced the accommodation available to the poor and sick, though some hospitals may have used this device from their foundation.[40] Like the offering of chantry facil-ities, the taking of corrodians might provide a valuable source of revenue, but the high proportion of houses claiming poverty underlines the financial weak-nesses of these schemes, especially at badly managed establishments. The many poorly endowed leper houses were especially vulnerable, and the devastation of the Black Death was too much for some. Thereafter such houses continued to disappear, but some retained a precarious existence as free chapels until the six-teenth century, while others became indistinguishable from bedehouses.[41] Local circumstances presumably largely dictated the fate of particular early hospitals, but regional factors may have played some part in the histories of a town's or a region's hospitals.[42]

From her study of the Yorkshire hospitals, Cullum believes that there was a correlation between early borough status and the likelihood that a town would have a leper hospital.[43] Her assumption appears to have validity nationally,

teenth century. The poor inmates were expected to attend the abbey church on certain feast days to pray for the souls of the abbey's founders and benefactors; W.T. Mellows, 'The medieval hos-pitals and alms of Peterborough', (1917–18), 290–1.   **39** At Norwich, lepers were still being admit-ted to the city's *leprosaria* in the early sixteenth century, but the majority of the inmates at this time were sick and infirm paupers; Rawcliffe, *Hospitals of Norwich*, p. 53.   **40** Possibly one of the earli-est cases of a 'corrody' was at Rochester. The prior in about 1100 entered into a gift exchange with a local woman whereby she gave the priory her house and received in return food and clothing for life and the prayers of the monks, as though she was a nun, after her death. As Hirokazu Tsurushima maintains, this agreement apparently linked what would become known as a 'corrody' with the gift of confraternity; H. Tsurushima, 'Women and corrody in twelfth-century Kent' (2002), pp. 93–4. The leper house of St Margaret, Gloucester, offered corrodies in the fifteenth century to local men and women. The hospital's priest and the brothers and sisters attended the chapel daily, where they prayed for all the house's living and dead benefactors; S.E. Bartlett, 'The leper hospi-tals of St Margaret and St Mary Magdalen, by Gloucester' (1895–7), 134–6. See also; I. Keil, 'Corrodies of Glastonbury abbey in the late middle ages' (1964), 113–31; B.F. Harvey, *Living and dying in England 1100–1540* (1993), pp. 179–209.   **41** One of these hospitals was St Leonard's, Northampton, which began life as a leper house in the mid-twelfth century. The hospital survived the problems of the fourteenth century, but suffered in the late fifteenth century when the corpo-ration leased the hospital and its assets to lessees who were responsible for paying the chaplains and the inmates. As a way of increasing their profits, the lessees kept the number of inmates to a min-imum, an abuse which the civic authorities attempted to rectify in 1505 when they decided to manage the hospital themselves. Thereafter, the hospital accommodated a few persons until the house was closed in *c.*1549; *VCH Northamptonshire*, vol. 2, pp. 159–60.   **42** From her study of the Yorkshire hospitals, Cullum noted a number of reasons for the failure of some of the early hospi-tals; Cullum, 'Hospitals in Yorkshire', pp. 280–313.   **43** P.H. Cullum, 'Leperhouses and borough

because many regional centres had a leper house in the vicinity and most of these places were urban, even if they subsequently lost this status. Furthermore, as others have noted, leper houses were frequently sited alongside main roads, often in the suburbs or close to town gates or bridges, thereby providing ample opportunities to collect alms.[44] As a result, several leper houses might be found on the outskirts of a provincial town, though Norwich and York were unusual with regard to the larger numbers associated with these two cities.[45]

Non-leper houses were also predominantly urban, their distribution pattern similarly linked to the landholdings of founders. For some hospitals created by members of the aristocracy, this meant their site was in the vicinity of the founder's patrimony or near to one of his major estates. Monasteries also frequently sited their daughter hospitals close by; in some instances the hospital buildings abutted the monastic establishment.[46] Others were even more closely tied to the monastery and could be considered extensions of the main house, their inmates living as lay members of the institution.[47] Townsmen, too, intended their hospital should be built locally, sometimes using the founder's own premises, though others apparently purchased land specifically.[48]

The various groups of almshouse founders were equally concerned to perpetuate connections between themselves and their institution. Like their predecessors' houses, these almshouses were most likely to be found in towns, but not necessarily the same towns. Although there was some overlap in terms of distribution, the relatively scattered pattern of urban hospitals, a product possibly of the proliferation of small market towns nationally in the thirteenth century, was far less evident with regard to the almshouses. Many of these were in provincial centres, some in expanding towns, like Bristol, but also at towns in decline, like Hull, as well as in small towns, including those associated with the burgeoning cloth trade.[49]

status in the thirteenth century' (1991), pp. 37–46. **44** St Mary Magdalene's hospital with its chapel was sited at the Newnham end of the bridge over the Thames at Wallingford; *VCH Berkshire*, vol. 2, p. 101. **45** According to Satchell, there were five (Rawcliffe lists six) leper-houses by Norwich and six around York; Satchell, 'Leper-houses in medieval England', pp. 346–8, 397–9; Rawcliffe, *Hospitals of Norwich*, pp. 163–4. By the late middle ages there was a ring of leper hospitals around London; Honeybourne, 'Leper hospitals of London', 5. **46** The relief of the local poor and travellers at St John's hospital outside the gates of Reading abbey seems to have been seen as an integral part of the abbey's role by Henry I, who ratified the abbey's foundation charter; *VCH Berkshire*, vol. 2, p. 97. **47** Under such circumstances the hospital often became almost indistinguishable from the monastery. At Partney, the hospital of St Mary Magdalene was considered part of Bardney abbey; *VCH Lincolnshire*, vol. 2, p. 232. **48** St Bartholomew's hospital, Gloucester, was sited close to one of the city's bridges; M.H. Ellis, 'The bridges of Gloucester and the hospital between the bridges' (1929), 171, 173, 176, 181. **49** Parker considered there were about ten almshouses in Bristol; G. Parker, 'Early Bristol medical institutions' (1922), 157. Cullum has evidence for over fifteen almshouses in Hull; Cullum, 'Hospitals in Yorkshire', p. 321. Wealden towns in Kent acquired their first almshouses in the mid-fifteenth century; Sweetinburgh, 'Hospital in Kent', pp. 22–3.

Consequently, with regard to the national pattern, hospitals, including almshouses, were primarily established in the lowlands, the more densely populated areas, rather than the upland regions, like the Pennines, Lake District, or the moors of south-west England.[50] Furthermore, there remained a considerable number of small towns without a hospital; equally hospital provision was extremely sparse in the countryside, apart from a relatively few rural leper houses (or possibly leper colonies).[51] Even within counties where hospital provision was widespread, the distribution pattern was far from random; instead, there were clusters of hospitals, along regionally or nationally important pilgrimage routes, for example, or in areas where there was a locally or regionally recognized need, like the populous market towns of Berkshire.[52] Moreover, hospitals were only one type of religious institution within the spiritual economy, which meant that founders and benefactors envisaged their gift exchange with these houses as part of their charitable strategy. This suggests that any assessment of the place of the hospital in medieval England should take account of other participants in this economy, a proposition considered later in the chapter, and in more detail with regard to Kent.

Chronology of foundation

With regard to the chronology, there were two main phases of hospital foundation: an early period, from the late eleventh to the early fourteenth century; and a later period comprising about two hundred years from the mid-fourteenth century. During the first phase, the most active period was the twelfth and early part of the thirteenth centuries. However, it is impossible to produce an accurate national chronology or even a chronology by county because of the problems of dating. Only a minority of foundation dates are known for the hospitals from this period; instead, the historian is forced to rely on 'first known dates', which in a few cases were probably several hundred years after the institution's foundation.[53] Even with these restrictions trends are apparent; fortunately, this is less of a problem for the later hospitals or almshouses. Evidence for these later houses comes from a wide range of sources, and, with respect to timing, possibly the most problematic are testamentary sources where it may not always be clear when, or occasionally whether, the testator's wishes were implemented.[54]

Turning to the early period, during the reigns of the first two Norman kings, a small number of hospitals was established, beginning with Archbishop Lanfranc's

---

50 One of these few upland hospitals was St Mary's in the Peak in Derbyshire, bordering the Castleton to Hope road; *VCH Derbyshire*, vol. 2, p. 86. 51 These leper houses or colonies were found in remote rural areas, like parts of Cornwall, the Wirral peninsula in Cheshire and the upland valleys of Cumberland. 52 A.D. Brown, *Popular piety in late medieval England* (1995), p. 187. 53 Satchell discusses the problems associated with establishing a chronology of the leper houses; Satchell, 'Leper-houses in medieval England', pp. 136–45. 54 Some may have been established during the life of the testator, but most were apparently post-mortem foundations; Cullum, 'Pore people harberles', pp. 36–7, 40.

twin foundations of St John's and St Nicholas' hospitals at Canterbury. A few Norman magnates and senior churchmen seem to have followed his example. William de Warenne founded a leper house at Lewes; Gundulf, bishop of Rochester, provided a house for leper and other needy people at Chatham; and St Wulstan's hospital for the poor and sick appears to have been established at about this time by the bishop of Worcester.[55] Like Lanfranc, their establishments were sited close to the centre of their patrimony, proximity presumably enhancing the ties between benefactors and beneficiaries. Other, slightly later, documented leper house foundations listed by Satchell are for a house dedicated to St Mary Magdalene on the outskirts of Bath and for a house at Launceston, Cornwall.[56] Possibly also established during this period was a leper house to the north of Norwich, which is said to have been built by Herbert Losinga, bishop of Norwich 1090–1119; and another at York, credited to Stephen, abbot of St Mary's, though both houses may post-date 1100.[57] The same period saw even fewer non-leper house foundations, though St Nicholas' hospital, Nantwich, may be contemporaneous and there seems to have been a small house adjoining Battle abbey for the care of the poor and travellers. Furthermore, the great hospital of St Leonard at York was established during the late eleventh century at the latest, but it is possible that at least some kind of house pre-dates the Conquest.[58]

Henry I's reign saw a rising tide of new leper house foundations, a phenomenon that continued during the turbulent years of Stephen's kingship and the decades of stability and economic expansion under Henry II, though by the time of his second son, John, there were fewer new houses. The decline in the number of new foundations continued, which meant that by the mid-thirteenth century this movement had virtually ceased, but there are rare examples of new leper houses from the early fourteenth century.[59] Foundations of non-leper houses followed a similar but much more gradual rise over the first part of the twelfth century. Thereafter, their numbers continued to climb, reaching a peak of newly established hospitals during the first half of the thirteenth century. The following century witnessed a fall in the number of new foundations, a decline that had increased in velocity by the early fourteenth century.[60]

Though widespread, this expansion in terms of the total number of hospitals over the twelfth century was not uniform. Within two or three generations of the Conquest, hospitals catering for a variety of needy persons had been established in and around London, York, Norwich and Winchester, and at some other important provincial centres. For the whole period, growth appears to

---

55 Satchell, 'Leper-houses in medieval England', pp. 119–20, 303–4, 328, 359. *VCH Worcestershire*, vol. 2, p. 175.   56 Satchell, 'Leper-houses in medieval England', p. 120.   57 Ibid., pp. 348, 397. 58 Cullum, 'Hospitals in Yorkshire', pp. 71, 78.   59 Satchell, 'Leper-houses in medieval England', pp. 121–7.   60 Assessment based primarily on the *VCH* surveys and Knowles and Hadcock, *Medieval religious houses*, supplemented with evidence from individual hospital, town and regional studies.

have been greatest in East Anglia; parts of the south-east including London and the counties bordering the Thames valley; a few midland counties like Northamptonshire and Gloucestershire; and Yorkshire to the north. In these counties, especially, episcopal towns often had several hospitals and certain regional centres had one, or more rarely two houses. A primary reason for this dramatic rise in the number of new hospitals was the growth in the number of groups prepared to fund hospital building. Religious houses, especially Benedictine institutions, joined bishops and Norman aristocrats as founders of leper hospitals from the first half of the twelfth century and Henry I and his queens also showed a limited interest.[61] From the later twelfth century townsmen and members of knightly families became increasingly involved in the establishing of a variety of hospitals. Their interest, like that of the great magnates earlier in the century, was part of the strong revival in religious expression, which had seen the founding of Augustinian monasteries and houses of the new orders, the Cluniacs, and later the Cistercians and Carthusians.[62] This revival was spearheaded by leading churchmen on both sides of the English Channel, who through various exchanges of contacts and personnel produced a rich cross-fertilization of ideas about piety and charity, of which the hospitals were one result. Contemporary attitudes towards the leprous were also significant, and, as Satchell has indicated, the Vatican's stance on this issue can be gauged from canon twenty-three of the Third Lateran Council of 1179. This stated that lepers were not to dwell with the healthy, nor attend the same church. As a consequence, they were to have their own churches and cemeteries, a pronouncement that implies such matters were already in place but required clarification in order to safeguard the rights of parochial churches.[63] Thus by the last quarter of the twelfth century, the church saw the need to separate the leprous from others as given, suggesting that the provision of leper houses by this time was commonplace. The foundation and support of such places was a pious act whereby the donor believed he was imitating the actions of Christ and the godly; but he might also see himself as aiding Christ, who, in sermons and *exempla*, was said to visit the world in the guise of a leper.[64]

From the early thirteenth century, the shift in emphasis towards the founding of non-leper hospitals was due to the involvement of laymen who, as the largest group, played a major role in this movement. The resulting chronology

---

61 Their concern for the leprous may have provided a model of pious action for contemporaries and future generations. Yet it is interesting that Aelred of Rievaulx, in his account of Queen Edith-Matilda's piety, recorded her kissing lepers, not founding hospitals; Satchell, 'Leper-houses in medieval England', pp. 25–6, citing Aelred of Rievaulx, *Genealogia Regum Anglorum*, p. 386b. **62** Cluny's influence was at its strongest in the late eleventh century, thereafter it was challenged by the Cistercians, who sought a return to an ancient and authoritative past; R.W. Southern, *The making of the middle ages* (1953), pp. 159–62. **63** Satchell, 'Leper-houses in medieval England', pp. 30, 33. **64** Ibid., pp. 24, 27; Rawcliffe, 'Learning to love the leper', pp. 237–40, 242–7.

by county again saw the greatest increase in hospital numbers in East Anglia, Yorkshire and Gloucestershire, but there were also significant rises in North-umberland and Durham in the north, Shropshire in the midlands, and Kent and Wiltshire in the south. This continuing pattern of growth in the number of new non-leper houses founded in eastern England and Gloucestershire was a prod-uct of the relatively large number of medium-sized towns, including important episcopal centres. Some of these towns were of long standing, where townsmen and other lay landholders were willing to fund new hospitals individually or jointly.[65] In contrast, ecclesiastical founders, bishops and monasteries were more active in Wiltshire and County Durham.[66]

However, this growth was not sustainable from the mid-thirteenth century onwards, and during the reigns of the three Edwards there were far fewer new foundations. New leper hospitals were extremely rare nationally, and non-leper houses were only slightly more common, the rate of new institutions probably similar or below that of the early twelfth century before the advent of their pop-ularity among potential founders.

Although many leper hospitals founded throughout the early phase had been poorly endowed, small houses, probably often catering for up to twelve or thir-teen inmates, a few of those established by the Benedictine houses or by mem-bers of the Norman aristocracy, clerical or secular, had been houses of consid-erable wealth and status.[67] During the later part of this phase (the thirteenth century), non-leper houses became the favoured option, and the growing pre-ponderance of local laypersons as founders meant that these houses frequently were small institutions.[68] Having modest assets, they too were heavily reliant on casual alms and other forms of reciprocity within the spiritual economy.

Very limited assets, and thus the need to engage in reciprocal exchange, was also characteristic of the maisonsdieu and some of the bedehouse-type almshouses, though most of the latter were moderately well endowed, and certain houses, like Hosyer's almshouse, Ludlow, were more prosperous.[69] These almshouses, along with a handful of leper houses, were founded during the second phase

65 Laymen may have founded three non-leper houses at Bristol: St Mark's, St Katherine's and St Bartholomew's hospitals; *VCH Gloucestershire*, vol. 2, pp. 114, 118; *VCH Somerset*, vol. 2, p. 153. 66 At Gateshead, for example, Bishop Farnham united Holy Trinity hospital to his new founda-tion of St Edmund, bishop and confessor in 1248, and in 1272 the bishop of Durham founded the hospital of St Mary and St Cuthbert at Greatham; *VCH Durham*, vol. 2, pp. 117, 121. For Wiltshire see below.   67 One of the largest leper hospitals was the episcopal foundation at Sherburn for sixty-five poor lepers, but more typical was another leper house in County Durham at Witton Gilbert which supported five lepers; *VCH Durham*, vol. 2, pp. 114–15.   68 The hospital of St James, Tamworth, seems to have received little from its founder, Sir Philip Marmion, in or around 1274. Nor did he manage to provide it with any further assets, and the hospital may have become little more than a free chapel within a short time; *VCH Shropshire*, vol. 2, p. 295.   69 John Hosyer's almshouse comprised thirty-three rooms, each with its own wall fireplace in 1486; Bailey, *Almshouses*, p. 70.

from the mid-fourteenth to the mid-sixteenth centuries. The first decades of this period, however, witnessed very few new establishments; rather, as a result of high death rates and/or poverty, it was a time of loss and the disappearance, amalgamation or change in function of a number of hospitals.[70] Furthermore, by Richard II's reign there was a perception, which extended outside Lollard circles, that clerical abuses had adversely affected the role played by the nation's hospitals, but that hospitals were fundamentally useful institutions.[71] Although subsequent parliamentary petitions, concerning the establishment of an additional hundred almshouses from assets currently wasted by various churchmen, were probably considered outrageous by some contemporaries, the need for more charitable institutions was recognized.[72]

Thus, such ideas and the knowledge that there had been a decrease in the total number of hospitals, even if the significance of this decline varied across the country, apparently resulted in a growing desire to found almshouses during the final decades of the fourteenth century. Of the known houses, perhaps up to a third were established in Yorkshire, and possibly almost half of the English counties had none at all, but it was an important development nationally, and even more so regionally and locally.[73] In Yorkshire many of these new houses were called 'maisonsdieu', York itself seeing the greatest number, the founders primarily prosperous townsmen or, more occasionally, their wives.[74] Such people may have been responding to the problems faced by the city's great hospital of St Leonard, where poor administration and abuses had led to the sale of infirmary places as a means of generating revenue and thus the need to provide compensatory opportunities for the poor.[75] Nevertheless, the prevalence of maisondieu-type almshouses in Yorkshire, the evidence principally found in testamentary sources, might suggest that such houses were present in towns elsewhere in England, where testators were similarly concerned to provide at least some kind of short-term provision for the local poor.[76] York itself was experiencing economic growth during this period, which may also have contributed to the upsurge in the number of almshouses, a phenomenon that seems to find limited parallels in other, though smaller, urban centres, like those in Wiltshire and Berkshire.[77]

According to Cullum, almost all of the maisonsdieu had been established in York by the end of the first decade of the fifteenth century, but in other Yorkshire towns only a few pre-date 1410, and most in these towns were cre-

70 Orme and Webster believe there was a peak of at least 541 recorded hospitals before the Black Death; Orme and Webster, *English hospital*, p. 35. 71 Ibid., pp. 131–4. 72 Ibid., pp. 134–6; Myers, *English historical documents, 1327–1485*, p. 669. 73 New establishments do not appear to have been founded in the late fourteenth century in Cumberland, Westmoreland and Durham in the north; Derbyshire, Northamptonshire and Nottinghamshire in the midlands; and Somerset, Surrey and Cornwall in the south. 74 Cullum, 'Hospitals in Yorkshire', p. 331. 75 Cullum, 'Pore people harberles', pp. 44–5. 76 Ibid., p. 39. 77 Brown, *Piety in the diocese of Salisbury*, p. 187.

ated over the next hundred years.[78] In terms of total numbers, however, the dominance of York meant that fewer almshouses were established per decade in the county during the early fifteenth century compared to the 1380s and 1390s; and this slight fall was mirrored in the numbers nationally. Looking at the national figures, the provision of new houses did not increase dramatically over the fifteenth and early sixteenth centuries in England, and the numbers involved per county generally remained small. Many of these were bedehouse-type almshouses, a number founded by members of the aristocracy, but increasingly by guilds and most commonly by leading townsmen.[79] The founder's choice of this type of almshouse was dependent largely on a desire for specific intercessory services to be undertaken daily by the inmates, whose prayers would be expected to ease his soul through purgatory. From the early fifteenth century, such houses were sometimes linked to collegiate churches or chantries, thereby extending the intercessory and commemorative aspects to include the prayers of professionals. Elsewhere from the mid-century these almshouses might include schools as part of the growing provision of education in England, both in terms of grammar schools and university colleges at Oxford and Cambridge, yet the latter often included the appropriation of earlier hospitals.[80]

Nonetheless, as McIntosh has indicated, the founding of almshouses during the late middle ages was strongly connected to concerns about the deserving poor in society.[81] Although a few new leper hospitals were established and some of the early houses continued to accommodate the sick and pilgrims, there appears to have been a desire among certain groups in society, particularly townsmen, to extend the places available for local poor or poorer people. Consequently, while recognising that poverty was endemic, potential founders wished to include almshouses among their good works.[82] The timing of the greatest number of new foundations, the late fourteenth and early fifteenth centuries, apparently corresponded to a period of relative economic buoyancy, a feature mirroring that found by Paul Slack for the early modern period when there was a similar rise in charitable giving.[83] However, the apparent willingness of certain wealthy townsmen, and more occasionally members of the aristoc-

78 Cullum, 'Hospitals in Yorkshire', pp. 330–1. Certain York families seem to have been especially concerned about the plight of the poor during this period, and brothers Thomas and Robert Howm each founded a maisondieu in the city; *VCH Yorkshire*, vol. 3, pp. 351–2. 79 Orme and Webster, *English hospital*, pp. 141–4. 80 Ibid., pp. 144, 146. 81 She noted that the number of new almshouse foundations per decade for England (excluding London and the eight counties) did not alter greatly over the second half of the fifteenth century when compared to the average taken for the period 1400 to 1459 (an average calculated using data from most English counties). However, in eight counties in the south east and midlands there were considerably more almshouse foundations during the second half of the 1460s, the 1470s and the 1500s; McIntosh, 'Responses to the poor', 220–1. 82 For the debate between Rubin and Cullum concerning the charitable nature of late medieval society; Rubin, 'Imagining medieval hospitals', pp. 22–4; Cullum, 'Pore people harberles', pp. 38, 43–4. 83 P. Slack, *Poverty and policy in Tudor and Stuart England* (1988), p. 5.

racy, to continue to create almshouses after the mid-century slump may suggest ongoing charitable concerns, as well as the significance of local and regional circumstances. Even though fears about the rise in the number of 'sturdy beggars' were becoming more widespread from the late fifteenth century, such people were not welcome at the new almshouses, patrons preferring members of the 'shame-faced' poor, who were seen as worthy of largesse. This group was also becoming more numerous in Tudor England, which may help to explain the continuing foundation of new houses, at least in some counties like Devon, Kent, Northumberland and London, but even Henry VII's great hospital at the Savoy made little impression on the problem, except on a personal basis.[84] This was a perception shared by founders and patrons nationally and over time, who were principally concerned about the place of their institution locally, and more rarely regionally, rather than its capacity to sustain the needs of all the poor. Consequently, even the crown did not envisage its hospitals as part of a national policy of poor relief, except in the broadest terms; instead, the chronology of foundation, like the pattern of hospital distribution in medieval England, was dependent on local, and perhaps regional factors.

Nature of patronage

Patrons, like founders, might be deeply concerned about the place of their institution and its role within the local and regional spiritual economy. As powerful figures in the life of their hospital, the type of relationship they developed with their institution had a profound effect on its role and on its viability. In order to investigate the nature of patronage, this sub-section will assess the relationship between patrons and hospitals by considering a series of questions: were patrons always founders, who were patrons, what were patrons seeking from the relationship, how was the relationship sustained between patron and hospital, and what were the implications of such patronage on the hospital's survival?

Before examining the relationship between founders and patrons, it is worth noting the complexities surrounding the use of the term 'founder'. Satchell, in his work on leper houses, has highlighted the difficulties at certain hospitals of deciding who exactly was the founder.[85] As he points out, a variety of individuals or groups might be implicated in the creation of a hospital, including the giver of the site, major early benefactors, those giving permission for its construction, and the master. Depending on the particular circumstances, any of these might claim the role of founder, making it extremely difficult to decide who had the right to be so named, even when there appears to be a foundation

---

84 At the time of its construction, the population of London may have been somewhere between 40,000 and 50,000; C.M. Barron, 'London 1300–1540' (2000), pp. 396–7. The Savoy was by far the largest of the city's hospitals, including almshouses, of which there were about thirty-four in the late middle ages; Rawcliffe, 'Hospitals of London', p. 17. **85** Satchell, 'Leper-houses in medieval England', pp. 118–19.

charter. For many of the early leper and non-leper houses, this problem is compounded by the lack of knowledge about their early history, and even where later patrons are known, the knowledge may be of only limited use because often patrons changed over time, making it impossible to follow earlier connections.[86]

Yet founders and patrons were inextricably linked, either through descent or through transference, a choice dependent on the type of founder involved and individual circumstances.[87] Founders were drawn from a number of groups – monastic houses, bishops and other churchmen, the crown, members of the nobility, townsmen, guilds and civic corporations – all of whom might seek to retain control over their hospital, but with varying degrees of success. Even though precise numbers are unobtainable regarding the early leper and non-leper houses, monasteries were important founders and patrons. Nor were all the hospitals under their patronage monastic foundations, because founders, often members of the nobility but also others, wished to see their institution governed by a local religious house.[88] Such a strategy offered founders continuity and longevity on behalf of their hospital, though sometimes in the fourteenth and fifteenth centuries this transfer of the patronage was detrimental to the hospital because it was done to bolster the new monastic patron. For example, in 1316 the crown gave the patronage of St John's hospital, Chester, to Birkenhead priory, which was suffering from financial difficulties. Unfortunately neither house appears to have benefited from the transfer, and the crown took back its patronage of the hospital in 1341.[89]

In addition to acting as founders and patrons, kings became patrons through escheats or through the confiscation of a traitor's property. Such a change might benefit the hospital in terms of stability, especially if it subsequently received royal favours and was sited close to a royal manor or other crown estate. Bishops, too, might acquire hospitals, while others established leper and non-leper houses themselves, often near the centre of their see or on episcopal landholdings.[90] The remaining institutional founders and/or patrons, town corporations and guilds, were less important numerically with respect to the leper and non-leper hospi-

---

86 For example, in 1343 the townsmen of Cirencester stated that St John's hospital in the town had been founded by Henry I, a claim refuted by the local abbot, who said his house had established the hospital and it was under the abbey's patronage. Edward III confirmed the abbey's jurisdiction in this case, but his decision may reflect political expediency rather than an accurate knowledge of the early history of the hospital; *VCH Gloucestershire*, vol. 2, pp. 122-3. The crown claimed the foundation and patronage of Holy Innocents' hospital, Lincoln, in the fourteenth century, though there was a strong tradition that it had been founded by Bishop Remigius; *VCH Lincolnshire*, vol. 2, p. 230. 87 Orme and Webster, *English hospital*, p. 75. 88 Gospatric son of Orm is said to have given the small hospital of Caldbeck, with the church there, to Carlisle priory in the twelfth century; *VCH Cumberland*, vol. 2, p. 204. 89 *VCH Cheshire*, vol. 3, p. 180. 90 Though said to have been founded by Robert de Wateville in the mid-twelfth century, the hospital of the Holy Spirit, Sandon, was for most of its existence under the patronage of the Winchester see; *VCH Surrey*, vol. 2, pp. 118–19.

tals, but were significant with regard to the late medieval almshouses. For burgess and other lay founders, these civic institutions were in the hands of men like themselves who could offer local knowledge and continuity for the benefit of their almshouse, though some used feoffees for similar reasons. Yet when lay founders, especially members of the nobility, did seek to retain the patronage in the family, they were on occasion thwarted by a lack of male heirs. In these cases the hospital was transferred out of the family's hands through marriage via the female line, or possibly to the king in the absence of adult heirs. Far more serious was the loss by attainder to the crown.[91] Nonetheless, in some instances hospitals were apparently seen as saleable assets, part of the family's manorial holdings, and as a result of this or loss through misfortune, patronage might not even rest with a single family. At St Lawrence's hospital, Nantwich, founded by a member of the local Norman baronial family of Wich Malbank, two-thirds of the advowson was held by the Audley family and the rest by the Lovells during the late fifteenth century, when all that remained was a free chapel.[92]

The transfer of patronage was not always a matter of co-operation, however; on occasion it became a contested issue, especially when the parties believed their rights were being infringed. For example, the king successfully challenged the bishop of Carlisle's patronage of St Nicholas' hospital, Carlisle, in 1292, saying that the crown had held the right to appoint the master until the reign of Henry III.[93] Further disputes took place around 1300. The inmates claimed that Henry II had given this privilege to Aethelwold, bishop of Carlisle (1133–c.1157), while the cathedral canons stated that the hospital had been theirs by royal grant until the bishop took it from them in the early thirteenth century.[94] Such disputes highlight the importance of patronage and the perception that it was a position offering considerable advantages.

Patrons benefited from a variety of rights and privileges, counter-gifts provided by their institution, which may be divided into two broad categories: temporal and spiritual. The former related to matters like hospitality, selection of appointees and political advantages, and the latter to the provision of intercession and commemoration. Although these were generally enjoyed by patrons throughout the middle ages, the nature of these privileges did change over time, leading to a more contractural arrangement between the parties concerned in terms of the provisions sought by patrons. Yet, this was not a simple development and some patrons had made very precise demands in the thirteenth century. The wardenship or mastership was one of these rights, it provided opportunities to reward servants and others, retain the services of valued subordinates,

---

91 Edward, duke of Buckingham, suffered the loss of his possessions to the crown following his attainder in 1521. His property included St Leonard's hospital, Stafford, which was finally recovered by his son a decade later; *VCH Staffordshire*, vol. 3, p. 294. 92 *VCH Cheshire*, vol. 3, p. 186. 93 *VCH Cumberland*, vol. 2, pp. 200–1. 94 Satchell, 'Leper-houses in medieval England', pp. 276–7.

gain or repay favours, and aid family members.[95] Furthermore, such rights might be extended to the appointing of inmates, allowing some monasteries, the crown and, more rarely, members of the nobility to provide accommodation for those who developed the disease in their own institution or household.[96] Similar provisions may also have been implemented with regard to the sick, infirm and elderly at the non-leper hospitals from their inception, but the best evidence for the use by patrons of hospitals in this way comes from the late medieval period, and for the almshouses.[97] Corrodies were seen as an abuse of the charitable ethos of the hospital by some patrons, but for others they provided opportunities and were increasingly tolerated during the middle ages.[98] Nonetheless, the correlation between their widespread employment and the growing poverty of certain hospitals was seen as particularly pernicious.[99]

The related provision of hospitality was seen as a valuable counter-gift by patrons, especially the crown, and a rough estimate of the use made of this provision may be judged from the calendars of the various royal rolls. Civic authorities too, may have seen the advantages of using hospitals for the housing of important guests, an alternative to the hiring of space at friaries, for example.[1] Similarly, other patrons may have employed hospitals as guest houses on occasions, or found other ways of using the hospital's assets.[2]

The presence of the patron's charitable institution nearby was considered advantageous for a number of reasons. In particular, it allowed ecclesiastical patrons to provide neighbouring hospital accommodation for leprous or possibly other

95 At St John's hospital, Burford, in the fifteenth century, the right of nomination to the mastership was in the hands of the local burgesses. They were apparently prepared to offer this right as a favour to others and in 1456 the earl of Warwick sought their permission to put forward one of his chaplains at the next vacancy; *VCH Oxfordshire,* vol. 2, pp. 154–5. **96** According to the statutes drawn up in 1344 for St Julian's hospital, a leper house under the governance of St Alban's abbey, preference was to be given to the monks or persons born under the abbey's jurisdiction; *VCH Hertfordshire,* vol. 4, p. 465. **97** The earl of Arundel established Holy Trinity hospital close to his seat of power in 1395. He intended twenty poor, elderly or infirm men would reside there, with preference given to his servants and tenants; *VCH Sussex,* vol. 2, pp. 97–8. **98** In his will, Roger Thornton (died 1430), the founder of St Katherine's hospital, Newcastle, instructed his executors to provide John Felton with a corrody at his hospital; J.C. Hodgson, 'The 'Domus Dei' of Newcastle' (1917), 198. **99** The commission appointed to examine St Bartholomew's hospital, Gloucester, in 1357 found that the granting of a number of corrodies had caused the hospital severe financial difficulties, which meant it was no longer able to fulfil its charitable obligations; *VCH Gloucestershire,* vol. 2, p. 120. **1** In late fifteenth-century Canterbury, the civic authorities paid for board and lodging at the Austin friary for an important delegation from London, who were to adjudicate in a dispute between the city and St Augustine's abbey; CCAL, CC/FA2, ff. 180–v. **2** When Richard II granted the hospital of St Giles-in-the-Fields, Holborn, to the abbey of St Mary Graces on Tower Hill he caused the hospital community severe problems. The abbot, the new patron, apparently considered the hospital's property belonged to the abbey and, at an enquiry in 1391, it was reported that he had removed livestock, grain and other possessions to a value of over £1,000; *VCH Middlesex,* vol. 1, p. 207.

infirm members of the monastic community. Moreover, the location might be seen to reinforce the charitable nature of the patron. Hugh de Vere, the earl of Oxford, and his successors, as members of the aristocracy, sited and maintained the family's hospital outside the gates of their castle at Castle Hedingham, a reminder that they did not leave the poor man starving at their gate.[3] The physical proximity of the hospital may have been sufficient for the de Veres, but the hagiographical *exempla* of the washing of lepers' feet and kissing them attributed to Henry I's queen may have occurred at the leper hospitals she is thought to have founded, thereby underlining her charitable disposition.

Presumably, such recognition was as important for institutions as it was for individuals. As founders and patrons of hospitals, monasteries might anticipate that certain benefactors, at least, would appreciate the spiritual merit of aiding both houses in pursuit of their own salvation. Furthermore, in agreeing to take on the patronage of hospitals founded by others, monasteries and bishops were extending their charity, a meritorious deed which might bring further recognition in financial as well as spiritual terms.[4] In certain cases this brought more tangible rewards, allowing the monastery to safeguard its parochial rights in the spiritual economy put at risk by the encroachment of the hospital into the parish. Civic corporations also understood the value of patronage in lordship disputes, and in the thirteenth century a number of towns tried to establish their rights over local hospitals, moves frequently rebuffed by others who similarly sought to use the house as a marker of authority.[5]

In spiritual terms too, the charitable nature of patronage was important, providing patrons with the opportunity to organize often specific intercessory services at their hospital and possibly further services elsewhere. Nor were these spiritual benefits available only to current patrons, because those who gave the patronage of their hospital to a monastery might also expect commemoration at both institutions.[6] By the later middle ages, the financial plight of many of the

---

3 *VCH Essex*, vol. 2, p. 184. **4** The attraction of such a gift may be seen from the reaction of the prior of Christchurch, Twyneham, when he realised that the grantor and his son were attempting to reclaim the lordship of St Leonard's hospital, Tarrant Rushton. Following an enquiry the jury found in the prior's favour, and the hospital was restored to the priory in 1333; *VCH Dorset*, vol. 2, pp. 105–6. **5** The use of the hospital chapel by the local inhabitants for the sacraments of baptism and burial became a source of dispute in 1281 between the local vicar, whose church was under the jurisdiction of the neighbouring priory, and the mayor and burgesses of Northampton, patrons of the hospital. The townsmen cited the myth that the hospital had been founded by William I, who had conferred the patronage of St Leonard's hospital on the town; *VCH Northamptonshire*, vol. 2, pp. 159–60. Though slightly later, the statement made by the townsmen of Cirencester in 1343 demonstrates how hospitals might become battlegrounds over lordship. In this instance, the townsmen attempted to show that the local abbey was not the patron of either St John's hospital or St Lawrence's hospital; *VCH Gloucestershire*, vol. 2, pp. 122–3. **6** Patrons might also seek intercessory services for one of their ancestors, as John de Warenne sought to do in 1335. He assigned the family hospital of Domus Dei, Thetford, to the more prosperous priory of Holy Sepulchre in

ancient hospitals led to other strategies, patrons privileging the maintenance of the hospital's liturgical life. At St John's hospital, Lechlade, the duchess of York in 1472 obtained a licence from Edward IV to found a chantry of three priests in Lechlade parish church, the chaplains funded from the assets of the hospital. The priests were also to maintain the hospital chapel, holding services there on the vigil and feast day of St John the Baptist.[7]

Many of the founders and patrons of the bedehouse-type almshouses, however, adapted the example of some of the early hospital founders and chose to combine a chantry with a house for the poor. Such houses were living testimony of their largesse, providing founders/patrons, in addition, with intercessory prayers from professionals and from the poor, whose efforts on their behalf would enhance their reputation on earth and be expected to reduce the perils of purgatory.[8] Consequently, intercession and commemoration, together with temporal advantages, were seen as extremely valuable counter-gifts by patrons, who sought to perpetuate their relationship with their chosen institution through a variety of methods.

For the founder, his initial gift exchange with his hospital saw the transfer of part of his wealth to the new house for its use. In return, he received spiritual rewards, sometimes more tangible benefits, and the expectation that the relationship he had established would continue. Patronage was one of these ways, especially where it was passed on by descent either within the family or institution. For some patrons, this linking of a named family or institution and the hospital required strengthening through further reciprocal exchanges, possibly as a means of producing a more personal relationship. For example, John de Bakepuze increased his father's endowment of the family leper hospital at Alkmonton in the mid-twelfth century, enhancing his own position as benefactor, and also helping to secure his family's position as honourable members of the Derbyshire nobility.[9] The family, as patrons, presumably continued to retain this status until the late fourteenth century, when the last male heir died and the family's Derbyshire estates were bought by Sir Walter Blount, a local landholder. Sir Walter's second wife refounded the hospital and his grandson provided further gifts in 1474, on condition that a priest should pray for his soul, for those of his ancestors, wives, children and others he named, and also for the souls of the ancient lords of the hospital.[10] His concern for the ancient lords' souls highlighting his recognition of their place in the early history of the hospital, a posi-

an attempt to ensure his ancestor, the founder of the hospital, would be well served through the masses undertaken by two chaplains supplied by the priory; *VCH Suffolk*, vol. 2, p. 140.   **7** *VCH Gloucestershire*, vol. 2, p. 126.   **8** In 1485, the executors of John Gardiner of Bailrigg established his chantry in the parish church and his hospital for four poor people on land adjacent to the church. The poor people were to join the chantry priest/master of the hospital in prayer for the benefit of their benefactor; *VCH Lancashire*, vol. 2, p. 166.   **9** Satchell, 'Leper-houses in medieval England', p. 252.   **10** *VCH Derbyshire*, vol. 2, p. 80.

tion which his family had acquired and which they were fulfilling in the same honourable tradition.

Some patrons employed other forms of gift-giving to cement their ties with the hospital. Regular doles were provided by certain monasteries and towns, like Carlisle, or the abbey almoner might supply all the requirements of its daughter house.[11] The latter pertained at Reading abbey where, during their early history, the almoner may have furnished the needs of both St John's hospital and St Mary Magdelene's in the town.[12] Such ongoing charity highlighted the benevolence of the parent institution in its care of lepers and other unfortunates, a public demonstration presumably witnessed by the townsfolk and which would become part of the common knowledge of the locality. Action of this kind was likely to enhance the status of the donor institution, possibly encouraging potential benefactors to support both it and the recipient hospitals.

At another Berkshire town a special form of gift-giving was also intended to reinforce the link between the parties. Like many early hospitals, the founder of St Bartholomew's hospital, Newbury, is unknown, though the commonalty of the town apparently held certain privileges in relation to the house because they presented the warden to the bishop of Salisbury for institution. In addition to this right, the role of the townsfolk in the maintenance of the hospital was expressed through a ritual involving the wives of Newbury citizens. These women, on the morning after their churching, visited the hospital chapel with their midwives, offering wax, candles or money to the use of the house, the gift restating symbolically the town's commitment to the charitable and devotional work of the hospital.[13]

In addition to providing gifts themselves, patrons might encourage others as a means of aiding their hospital, a strategy that extended the network of connections between the house and the community outside its gate. For the hospital, this might bring certain advantages, not least additional assets, and a growing awareness of the place of the hospital locally, and possibly regionally. A group of local landholders founded the hospital of St John the Baptist and St Thomas the Martyr in Stamford during the reign of Henry II. They may have assigned the patronage of their house to the abbot of Peterborough, but the main supporters of the place seem to have been the local palmers' guild, whose members gave alms for its maintenance. This connection with the palmers of Stamford provided the hospital with a continuous, and perhaps, expanding corporate body of benefactors.[14]

---

11 For taking all the lepers sent to it by the mayor and commonalty of Carlisle, St Nicholas' hospital received weekly a 'pottle' of ale from each brew house in the town and a loaf from each baker; *VCH Cumberland*, vol. 2, p. 200. Lay founders and patrons, especially of bedehouses and early hospitals that resembled such institutions, might similarly aim to supply the needs of the residents. In the late fifteenth century, the inmates at St Leonard's hospital, Alkmonton, received food, clothes and firewood. They were not allowed to beg; rather, they were expected to attend the chapel daily, saying two psalters of Our Lady for the benefit of their benefactors; *VCH Derbyshire*, vol. 2, p. 81. 12 *VCH Berkshire*, vol. 2, pp. 97, 99. 13 Ibid., p. 96. 14 *VCH Northamptonshire*, vol. 2, p. 164.

The physical linking of patron and recipient took place in a number of ways in addition to positioning the hospital close to the patron's property, described above. Shared use of facilities provided a constant reminder of the relationship between the parties, as at St John's hospital, Winchester. Founded in the thirteenth century, the hospital was under the patronage of the civic authorities by the fifteenth century, which used the place to hold their assemblies.[15] In other instances, the townspeople were particularly aware of the devotional life of the hospital community through their sharing of the hospital's liturgical space.[16] Similarly, the presence of the inmates in the parish or guild church emphasized the inter-dependency of the exchange partners, and the continuing role of the inmates in society, who daily re-entered the world outside the house gates. At Abingdon, St Helen's church was at the centre of the life of the guild of Holy Cross, and of the guild's almsfolk. The almspeople regularly attended services in the church, and guild meetings for the selection of the inmates were held in a room over the north porch there.[17]

Like the selection of potential inmates from among members of a guild, prosperous townsmen and others recognized the value of aiding those like themselves who, through no fault of their own, had fallen on difficult times. Some self-help groups were of an informal nature, like parochial or fraternal give-ales, but almshouses were also established, their inmates chosen from the membership. This system was likely to be self-perpetuating, provided it retained the support of its patrons. Roger Smith apparently considered he could aid the leading civic officers of Chester in this way in 1508. He intended that after his death his house should be used as an almshouse for infirm and impoverished aldermen, members of the common council, or their wives, under the patronage of the mayor and corporation. The almsfolk were to pray daily for his soul. Initially, the town authorities supported the proposal, converting the old Mote Hall into a chapel, but even though the almshouse survived, interest in its role as a bedehouse seems to have been short-lived.[18]

In addition to their powers of selection, whether of the master or inmates, patrons might also be involved in regulating their hospital through visitations or inquiries, and the provision of ordinances, either produced by themselves or at their instigation. Such measures demonstrated their concern for the good governance of the house, and were most frequently enacted following periods of maladministration or the wrongful use of the house's assets. They might, therefore, lead to a renewed interest in the institution, but in most cases were

15 *VCH Hampshire and the Isle of Wight*, vol. 2, p. 201.   16 At St John's hospital, Wallingford, the town held the patronage, and on certain occasions the townsfolk also worshipped at the hospital's chapel; *VCH Berkshire*, vol. 2, pp. 99–100. Similarly, at St John's hospital, Lichfield, the chapel was used by the townspeople, though the bishop, as patron, had made an agreement with the prebendary of Freeford, who held the local parish church; *VCH Staffordshire*, vol. 3, p. 279.   17 *VCH Berkshire*, vol. 2, p. 92.   18 *VCH Cheshire*, vol. 3, pp. 183–4.

probably more significant in terms of the hospital community's financial and spiritual welfare.[19]

In some instances, however, patrons might take more drastic action and assign the hospital and its assets to another religious house in an attempt to safeguard at least part of the hospital's charitable role. St Julian's hospital, Southampton, had come under royal patronage by the late thirteenth century, and in 1343, five years after the hospital had been burnt in a French raid, the king granted it to the provost and scholars of Queen's Hall, Oxford. The gift was made on the understanding that the provost would maintain the original role of the house, and he could then use the surplus to aid the scholars.[20] Interestingly, founders occasionally used the same strategy, like William Fetyplace, who assigned certain lands to the same Oxford college in 1526 on condition that the college paid the salary of a chantry priest at Childrey, who was to give doles to the three poor men who lived in the almshouse adjoining the priest's dwelling.[21] Like the chantry priest, the almsmen were expected to pray daily for William and others he named; the provision of such counter-gifts sustaining the link between benefactor and beneficiary. This type of relationship was articulated even more vividly at Lambourn, where the bedesmen at John Isbury's almshouse daily said their devotions on behalf of his soul while kneeling around his tomb in the Holy Trinity chapel at his parish church.[22] Yet this apparently symbiotic relationship was at some hospitals distorted by the demands of the patron, whose expectations caused the hospital considerable difficulties; a situation that might have serious implications for its well-being and even, perhaps, its survival.

The level of endowment and subsequent benefaction by the founder and patron was a significant factor in the financial state of the house and consequently its viability. Even though hospitals attempted to gather alms from a range of sources, benefactors apparently preferred to aid a successful institution on the assumption, probably, that the spiritual return would be longer lasting. Furthermore, the absence of restrictions on the number of hospitals in any given locality, there would, of course, be no lack of recipients for this institutional largesse, meant that founders probably took little note of the presence of earlier foundations, thereby introducing further competition into an already competitive spiritual market.[23] Thus the poorest hospitals were generally likely to survive for the shortest time, unless their outgoings were also contained within very strict limits, a feature of certain small leper houses or colonies. A few small leper houses created in the twelfth century apparently did not survive into the thir-

---

19 For example, by 1429 the ancient episcopal hospital of St Lazarus, St Martha and St Mary, Sherburn, had fallen into decay, a situation which the bishop sought to rectify when he issued new statutes in 1434. A hundred years earlier his predecessor had considered similar measures following a visitation to the equally ancient episcopal hospital of St Giles, Kepier; *VCH Durham*, vol. 2, pp. 115, 111–12. **20** *VCH Hampshire and the Isle of Wight*, vol. 2, p. 203. **21** *VCH Berkshire*, vol. 2, p. 93. **22** Ibid., p. 95. **23** Orme and Webster, *English hospital*, p. 37.

teenth, a time when many others were seeking grants of protection to beg. For some of these, such grants were seemingly insufficient, and though they continued to function during Henry III's reign, they had disappeared by the time of his grandson.[24]

The inadequate funding of hospitals was not confined to the leper houses. Hospitals of all types suffered this fate, but the other category most likely to be poorly endowed and to experience low levels of support from patrons was the maisondieu. Yet the frequently ephemeral existence of these houses, possibly no more than the lifetime of the initial recipient, seems to have been envisaged by some founders and patrons, who saw themselves as providing limited aid against a background of endemic need.[25] It is conceivable, moreover, that certain founders and patrons from the earlier period similarly believed their houses should be thought of essentially as providing for their neighbour in the Biblical context. Such an *exemplum* would then be followed by others, regardless of whether they supported these particular hospitals.

Elsewhere, the hierarchical power relationship between patrons and hospitals seems to have contributed to the difficulties experienced by certain houses, which in turn may have hastened their demise. Following his annexation of the earldom of Chester and his becoming patron of St Giles' hospital, Chester, in 1237, Henry III generously supported his new hospital, but this royal beneficence was short lived because his successors did nothing beyond confirming Henry's grants.[26] The house survived the Reformation, but the crown's involvement in the selecting of the hospital personnel caused problems at times, circumstances which were familiar to the inmates at St Leonard's hospital, Lancaster, where the crown usurped the inmates' right to elect their own master on more than one occasion.[27] In 1356 the inmates' weak position was particularly apparent when the patron, Henry of Lancaster, gave the hospital and its possessions to the nuns of Seton in Cumberland to relieve their poverty, a move that prematurely ended its existence.[28]

Neglect also characterized the relationship between some patrons and their hospitals, a feature that might be expected to be especially prevalent where the

---

24 The leper house of Holy Cross, Woodstock, received two grants of royal protection in 1231 and 1232, and thereafter it disappears from the known records but it may have survived for a few decades; *VCH Oxfordshire*, vol. 2, p. 160. Another casualty in the thirteenth century was St Mary's hospital, Cannok, which seems to have disappeared at about the same time; *VCH Staffordshire*, vol. 3 p. 274. **25** Alice Neville of Leeds intended that her son should maintain two houses for poor women for the duration of his life. He was to ensure that each woman received 13s. 4d. annually, their obligation to Alice fulfilled through their prayers for her and for 'all [her] good doars'; Cullum, 'Pore people harberles', p. 48. **26** *VCH Cheshire*, vol. 3, pp. 178–9. **27** *VCH Lancashire*, vol. 2, p. 165. **28** One of Henry's servants at the time was Sir Robert Lawrence, a kinsman of the prioress, a connection that was said to have contributed to his generosity to the nuns. It is not clear when the nuns ceased their care of the hospital as part of the exchange, but at an enquiry in 1531 it was noted that the house had been demolished and the chapel was in ruins; ibid.

patron had few or no interests in the vicinity or surrounding region. Yet some local patrons, including a number of monastic houses, were prepared to let or unable to stop the hospitals under their authority from decaying, especially during the later middle ages. For example, in 1499 it was reported that at St John's hospital, Shaftesbury, under the patronage of the local abbey, the poor had received nothing for the last twenty years, and divine service was no longer conducted.[29] A similar fate seems to have befallen St Mary Magdalene's hospital, Partney, a century earlier, the hospital, a dependency of Bardney abbey, having become little more than an occasional retirement home for abbots by the fourteenth century.[30]

These cases appear to suggest that patrons considered the requirements of their own household first, particularly during periods of economic hardship. The desire to subjugate the hospital, possibly as a way of neutralizing its place as a competitor in the spiritual economy, was tried some times. As a consequence, conflicts of interest became even more pronounced, leading to disputes over patronage or between the patron and inmates, which frequently caused problems for the hospital concerned. In the early fourteenth century, the inmates at St Mary Magdalene's hospital, Colchester, complained to the king that Colchester abbey was not paying them certain tithes which it was due to pay them as patron.[31] Even though the abbot was able to answer all the allegations, relations between the two sides remained difficult. Relations were also strained at another Essex hospital. At Ilford in the fourteenth century the crown attempted to send corrodians on several occasions to the hospital, a right reserved to the patron, the abbess of Barking. She resisted this incursion in 1374, but the abbey's own conduct towards the hospital was similarly questionable because in 1397 it was found that it took most of the hospital's revenue, merely supporting one chaplain and one poor man.[32]

Overt exploitation of the hospital by its patron was a factor in the loss of a number of hospitals in later medieval England, though it is important to remember that evidence of this kind is likely to be especially visible in visitations, inquiries and petitions. Abuses might relate to the mastership, where candidates were pluralists or absentees, the housing of corrodians or the purloining of part of the house's revenue or assets. Members of all the groups of patrons might engage in such activities, but the crown seems to have been a significant culprit, especially at hospitals it had acquired through attainder and escheats. During its early history, St John's hospital, Stafford, enjoyed mixed relations with its patrons, members of the Stafford family, but when the crown held the mastership in the late fifteenth century, it was bestowed on pluralists and absentees. Nor when it returned briefly to the family were conditions any better because the next master,

---

29 *VCH Dorset*, vol. 2, p. 103. **30** *VCH Lincolnshire*, vol. 2, p. 232. **31** A former abbot was said to have asked to see the hospital's charter referring to this agreement and then to have thrown it into the fire; *VCH Essex*, vol. 2, p. 184. **32** Ibid., p. 186.

an absentee, arranged for the hospital and its revenues to be leased to his kin who, though apparently maintaining it as a hospital, allowed many of the buildings to become ruinous.[33]

Rather than allowing their hospital to fall into decay, some patrons sought to change its role, most commonly from a house caring for the poor or other needy persons to a chantry-type institution. In part this might be instituted on pragmatic grounds, the hospital's revenue seen as insufficient to sustain its charitable and liturgical activities; but for many this shift may denote a desire for intercessory counter-gifts. Edward IV, in 1462, intended to increase the religious services at St Julian's hospital, Southampton, of which he was patron, by granting it the alien priory of Sherborne. In addition to their liturgical duties, the priests at St Julian's were to say perpetual masses for the souls of Edward's father and grandfather.[34] However, the hospital was able also to maintain its charitable activities, a position not open to Holy Trinity hospital, Gateshead.[35] Because of its poverty, this house had been joined to the hospital of St Edmund, bishop and confessor, in 1248 and, almost two hundred years later, the place was given with all its possessions to the nuns of St Bartholomew's, Newcastle. The resulting agreement between the bishop and the nuns saw the hospital becoming little more than a chantry chapel, staffed by two chaplains.[36]

In other instances, the appropriation of the hospital meant that it was completely absorbed by the other institution, the fate of a growing number of poor hospitals in the fifteenth century as part of the foundation of colleges at Oxford and Cambridge, and elsewhere.[37] For the founders and patrons of these new establishments, hospitals were particularly valuable because they already held property, thereby removing or reducing the need to acquire further grants in mortmain. William Waynflete, bishop of Winchester, annexed a number of ancient hospitals to his new foundation of Magdalen College, Oxford, including St James and St John's hospital, Aynho. Two years earlier in 1483 the patron, William, earl of Arundel, had granted the hospital to him for this purpose on the understanding that a mass should be said daily at the Arundel altar for members of the family by the college's president and fellows.[38]

For those hospitals that had survived until the early sixteenth century, the extensive political and religious changes produced large numbers of casualties.

---

33 *VCH Staffordshire*, vol. 3, pp. 290–1. Bishops could equally exploit their position, as happened at God's House, Portsmouth, in the fourteenth century when there were a number of absentee masters holding multiple beneficiaries; *VCH Hampshire and the Isle of Wight*, vol. 2, p. 207.   34 *VCH Hampshire and the Isle of Wight*, vol. 2, p. 204.   35 According to the *Valor,* the hospital was still aiding twelve poor brothers and sisters, seven beggars and giving a daily dole to other needy persons; ibid.   36 *VCH Durham*, vol. 2, p. 118.   37 These educational establishments at Oxford and Cambridge continued the idea of the hospital's charitable role by aiding poor scholars and providing an educated clergy, though at the hospital, itself, the only survivor may have been a serving priest.   38 *VCH Northamptonshire*, vol. 2, p. 150.

Factors like wealth and function were important criteria on which royal and ecclesiastical officials based their assessment, but patronage was also taken into consideration. Consequently, those under monastic control were particularly at risk, whereas those seen as secular establishments, often in civic or lay hands, were more likely to be considered worthwhile charitable houses. Yet local conditions and the individual circumstances of particular houses also appear to have been significant, certain towns losing many more hospitals than others. Similarly, regional factors need to be considered in any assessment of the Reformation period, because there appear to be striking differences among the counties. It seems appropriate at this point, therefore, to investigate more fully the role of the hospital over time in terms of a regional perspective, and to examine its changing place in the spiritual economy, employing the county as the unit of analysis.

REGIONAL SURVEY OF WARWICKSHIRE AND WILTSHIRE

As noted earlier, this section extends the analysis through an investigation of two contrasting counties, demonstrating the importance of interconnections developed in the processes of reciprocal exchange between benefactors and their associated institutions, and established by founders and patrons within their spheres of influence. As appropriate, these domains are described geographically regarding their spatial relationship with the mother house, the diocese or the patrimony, but elsewhere are seen as a reflection of patronage networks and political influence, or the encouragement of piety or learning. Important as such concerns seem to have been for hospitals and benefactors throughout the middle ages, this comparative regional analysis highlights the significance of changes in emphasis of the expectations of all those concerned, and how they might relate to local, regional and national factors. To achieve these objectives, the analysis is subdivided into two subsections (preceded by a brief description of the ecclesiastical institutions in the two counties). The first contrasts the nature of hospital provision and the place of the hospital during the period from the Conquest to the end to the thirteenth century. The second subsection considers the same counties during the later middle ages. This was a time of substantial economic, demographic and social change, a situation mirrored in the histories of many of the hospitals described here, and in the type of new foundations characteristic of the later period. For simplicity, the hospitals are divided into two groups: leper and non-leper hospitals, to provide a clear comparative assessment of the two counties. It was not considered necessary to assess separately those houses primarily accommodating the sick or poor travellers/pilgrims within the non-leper hospitals, though the latter sub-group is employed for the Kent hospitals in the next chapter.

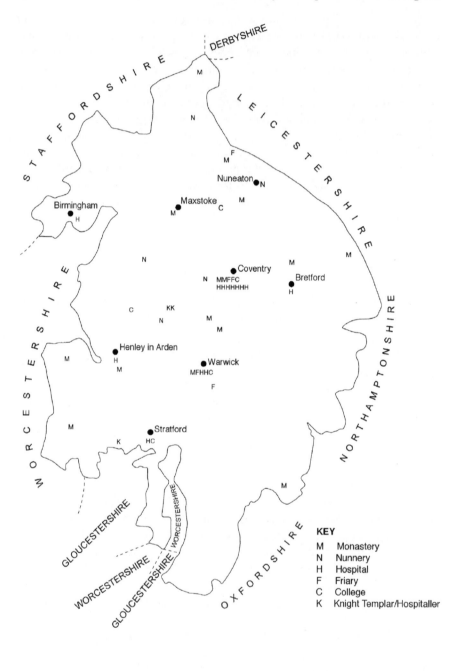

Figure 1 Warwickshire's medieval hospitals

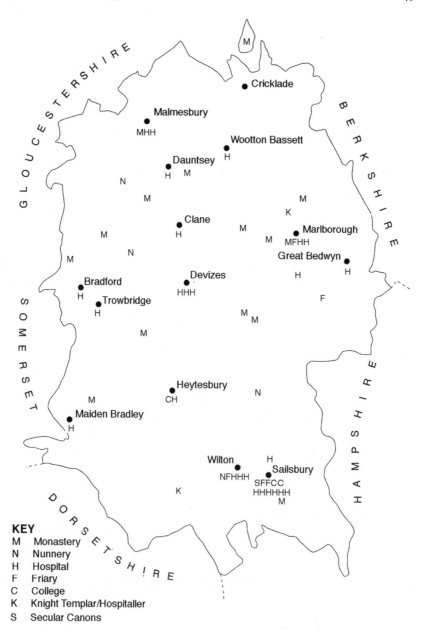

Figure 2 Wiltshire's medieval hospitals

The two counties selected for this regional analysis are Warwickshire and Wiltshire. There are a number of hospital histories associated with particular institutions, though many of these are the product of antiquarian investigations. One of the few exceptions is Michael Hicks' interesting assessment of the late medieval almshouse at Heytesbury.[39] Furthermore, the hospitals of both counties have been the subject of investigation within the remit of the Victoria County History series, but to date the hospitals have not been analysed on a regional basis, nor have they been assessed regarding their place within the spiritual economy. The two counties are, therefore, suitable for this regional study of the medieval hospital, because their histories display significant differences.

A survey of participants in the spiritual economy

The survey is important because it provides an indication of the range of those involved in the spiritual economy, especially the extra-parochial participants, and how this changed over time. Consequently, it supplies a context that allows the place of the hospital to be perceived in terms of others: donors, patrons, recipients, competitors, who were similarly active in processes of gift exchange and reciprocity for their spiritual and temporal benefit.

Unlike Wiltshire, which was encompassed within the diocese of Salisbury, the county of Warwickshire was shared between the diocese of Coventry and Lichfield, to the north-east, and that of Worcester, to the south-west.[40] This arrangement was a consequence of changes to the ecclesiastical structure in the eleventh century. In Warwickshire, the Norman preference for urban sees led initially to a move from Lichfield to Chester and thence to Coventry where, in 1095, the bishop also took the title of abbot of Coventry.[41] In Wiltshire the uniting of the dioceses of Sherborne and Ramsbury in 1058 led to the foundation of a new see at Old Sarum.[42] Though an urban settlement, the opportunities at Old Sarum were extremely limited, but it remained the episcopal centre for over a century, before its relocation to Salisbury in the river valley below in 1219, a move welcomed by the cathedral canons.[43] The diocesan structure of archdeaconries, deaneries and parishes seems to have been virtually in place by 1200, providing opportunities for the appropriation of parish churches by the growing number of religious houses. In Wiltshire the greatest culprit was the cathedral chapter, and though the bishop sought to control such acquisitions from the thirteenth century onward, by the early sixteenth century few remaining rectories were worth appropriating.[44] Warwickshire appears to show a similar pat-

39 M. Hicks, 'St Katherine's hospital, Heytesbury' (1984), 60–9. **40** For an assessment of the different counties and the regional variations within them for the diocese of Salisbury; Brown, *Piety in the diocese of Salisbury*, pp. 1–25. **41** *VCH Warwickshire*, vol. 2, pp. 3–4. **42** T.R. Slater, 'The south-west of England' (2000), p. 593. *VCH Wiltshire*, vol. 3, pp. 150, 156–7. **43** J. Barrow, 'Churches, education and literacy in towns 600–1300' (2000), p. 141. **44** *VCH Wiltshire*, vol. 3, pp. 1–3, 6–7.

tern, but lay holders were also involved, especially in the deaneries of Coventry and Kenilworth, where parochial livings were on average larger than elsewhere in the diocese.[45] As a consequence, in both counties many incumbents received very little revenue from their parishes because even the rectories were often burdened with pensions.

In addition to the parish clergy, others involved in the spiritual economy in the towns and villages were chantry priests and stipendary chaplains. The growing interest in the doctrine of purgatory from the thirteenth century and its particular potency for late medieval society, produced opportunities for unbeneficed clerics to become providers of intercessory services. The length of tenure enjoyed by these priests varied considerably, but such positions did offer a degree of stability, particularly for those associated with perpetual chantries, either for named individuals or linked to guilds. The latter were prevalent in Warwickshire, in towns like Birmingham, Stratford upon Avon, Warwick and especially Coventry, their priests providing additional services as well as on occasion serving alongside the parish clergy, valuable additions within the diocesan structure.[46]

As head of this diocesan structure, the bishops were in turn subordinate to York, Canterbury, and ultimately Rome. Archbishops occasionally exercised their jurisdiction through visitations.[47] The installing of suitable candidates at the various sees was also within their remit, though patronage played a part in the selection process. Many of the Salisbury bishops had held royal office, receiving the pallium in recognition of their services to the crown. A small proportion from the later medieval period were local men, who had been senior members of the cathedral chapter, a change in part due to the nature of the monastic community because, unlike the Benedictine house at Coventry, Salisbury was staffed by secular canons.[48] This situation may have led to a closer relationship between the bishop and his cathedral at Salisbury. However, among members of the local laity, episcopal authority over the town resulted in a number of clashes concerning lordship, the most serious occurring in 1302–6, 1465–74 and during the early sixteenth century.[49]

The laity were also involved in the spiritual economy with regard to the religious houses of Warwickshire and Wiltshire, though in neither county were these houses particularly numerous, nor were there many of more than local significance. In total, there were a similar number of establishments in both counties, but a greater variety of monastic orders were present in Wiltshire. Interestingly,

45 *VCH Warwickshire*, vol. 2, pp. 4–6. **46** Ibid., pp. 28–9. Guilds, both parish and craft, were also found in Salisbury, and parish and town guilds were a feature of life in the small Wiltshire towns; Brown, *Piety in the diocese of Salisbury*, pp. 63, 132–80. **47** The Worcester see received exemption from the jurisdiction of York in 1072; W. Dugdale, *Monasticon Anglicanum* (1817), p. 571. **48** *VCH Wiltshire*, vol. 3, pp. 13–15, 159–61, 165. **49** Ibid., pp. 19–20. A further indication of the distance between town and cathedral may be the small proportion of lay benefactors and the few chantries founded in the cathedral by laymen; Brown, *Piety in the diocese of Salisbury*, pp. 51, 53.

female Benedictine houses outnumbered male houses in Warwickshire and Wiltshire, and in each county there was one further female religious institution.[50]

Looking at these religious establishments in terms of their foundation date, a far larger number survived in Wiltshire from the pre-Conquest period. These comprised the great Benedictine houses at Malmesbury and Wilton, which both had extensive temporal and spiritual holdings, the lesser Benedictine house at Amesbury, and the new cathedral under construction at Old Sarum, served by secular canons.[51] In contrast, Poleworth abbey was a small Benedictine nunnery, though the other Warwickshire house, Coventry priory, had been extremely well endowed by its mid-eleventh-century aristocratic founders.[52] Consequently, under the early Norman kings, potential donors in Wiltshire had a greater choice of extra-parochial recipients, and the wealth and fame of these institutions attracted gifts from members of the royal family and the aristocracy. Malmesbury abbey, in particular, may have gained from the efforts of its second Norman abbot, who translated the bones of his seventh-century predecessor, Abbot Aldhelm, to a magnificent new shrine in 1078.[53] Miracles occurred within two years, and Aldhelm's consequent elevation to sainthood provided the abbey with a rich source of funds. Fortunately for the cathedral priory of Coventry, it too was blessed with an important relic, the arm of St Augustine, bishop of Hippo, whose splendid shrine similarly attracted devotions from the faithful.[54]

The pace of this eleventh-century reorganization and expansion of the church increased dramatically over the next hundred years as the Anglo-Norman aristocracy sought to establish monastic houses. Founders in Warwickshire continued to favour the old religious order of St Benedict (monks at Alcester abbey, and Alvecote priory, nuns at Henwood priory, Nuneaton priory and Wroxall priory), possibly a response to the loss of most of the pre-Conquest houses. Others among the aristocracy preferred the Cistercian order (monks at Combe abbey, Merevale abbey and Stoneleigh abbey, nuns at Pinley priory), and an equal number wished their houses to follow the rule of St Augustine (canons at Kenilworth abbey, Arbury priory, Studley priory and St Sepulchre's priory, Warwick). In addition, the Knights Templar established a preceptory at Balsall, and four priories or cells of French Benedictine houses were founded prior to

---

50 The Benedictine nunneries of Warwickshire were Polesworth abbey and the priories of Henwood, Nuneaton and Wroxall. The other female house was the Cistercian priory of Pinley; *VCH Warwickshire*, vol. 2, p. 50. In Wiltshire, Benedictine nuns were at Wilton and Amesbury abbeys and Kingston St Michael priory, and there was a house of Augustinian canonesses at Lacock abbey; *VCH Wiltshire*, vol. 3, p. 155. **51** *VCH Wiltshire*, vol. 3, pp. 210–20, 231–5, 243–7. **52** *VCH Warwickshire*, vol. 2, pp. 52–5, 62–3. **53** *VCH Wiltshire*, vol. 3, pp. 210, 215. **54** *VCH Warwickshire*, vol. 2, p. 52. Salisbury cathedral was dedicated to Our Lady, bringing pilgrims to the place, but the bishop and cathedral also sought the canonization of Bishop Osmund. They were ultimately successful in 1457, though the cost may have outweighed any financial advantages; Brown, *Piety in the diocese of Salisbury*, pp. 58–64.

1200. Henry de Newburgh, earl of Warwick, also created the collegiate church of St Mary in Warwick, a work of piety completed by his son in 1123.[55] The earls of Warwick were major benefactors during this period, supporting the nunneries at Nuneaton and Pinley, and the Augustinian canons at Kenilworth and at St Sepulchre's, Warwick.[56]

New foundations in Wiltshire were far more sparse. The sole new Benedictine house in Wiltshire was a nunnery, the only female monastic institution founded in the county between the Conquest and 1200.[57] Of the other new establishments associated with the major orders, there were three houses for Austin canons (Bradenstoke priory, Ivychurch priory, Maiden Bradley priory), a Cluniac priory (Monkton Farleigh) and a Cistercian abbey (Stanley). The only exclusively male English Gilbertine house was also founded at this time, St Margaret's priory, Marlborough. The Knights Templar were able to form a preceptory at Temple Rockley and a number of prebendaries were established at St Peter and St Paul's church, Heytesbury, to form a collegiate church. Furthermore, certain continental religious houses also attempted to develop links with Wiltshire, resulting in the establishment of alien priories at Avebury, Charlton, Corsham, Ogbourne and Upavon. Like their counterparts in Warwickshire, most founders and early benefactors were members of the aristocracy and/or of the royal family, whose endowment of their favoured institutions varied considerably in total value and type of assets. This variation was especially marked in Warwickshire, from the poorly endowed Benedictine priory at Alvecote to the extremely rich Augustinian abbey at Kenilworth. During the same period, a number of hospitals were established, which will be investigated later in this chapter.

The thirteenth century was marked by the appearance of the mendicant orders, leading in both counties to the foundation of a number of friaries. In Wiltshire, the Franciscans were the first to settle in Salisbury, the Dominicans creating their first house in Wilton about fifteen years later, but it was not until 1281 that they also had a house in Salisbury.[58] The Franciscans were similarly the first to found a house in Warwickshire, on the south side of Coventry.[59] The Dominicans were also able to secure aristocratic patronage and in their case significant royal aid as well, allowing them to settle in Warwick, probably in the 1260s.[60]

Wiltshire also witnessed the establishment of several other religious houses; in particular, the well endowed Augustinian nunnery at Lacock, the creation of Ela, the daughter and sole heiress of William, earl of Salisbury, and the wife of William Longespee.[61] As a consequence of the endowment it received and subsequent royal

---

55 *VCH Warwickshire*, vol. 2, p. 124. **56** Ibid., pp. 67, 82, 86, 97–8. **57** Kingston St Michael priory was founded before 1155, possibly by the family of Robert Wayfer of Brimpton; *VCH Wiltshire*, vol. 3, p. 259. **58** Ibid., pp. 329–32. **59** *VCH Warwickshire*, vol. 2, p. 103. **60** Ibid., pp. 101–2. **61** *VCH Wiltshire*, vol. 3, pp. 303–5.

gifts, Lacock abbey was one of the few institutions in the county of more than local significance, a privileged position that brought heavy responsibilities. Many of its temporal holdings were subject to military obligations and it was also expected to find accommodation for royal corrodians at its own expense.[62]

The other Augustinian foundation in Wiltshire was Longleat priory, a small house for canons established by and under the patronage of the Vernon family.[63] Another newly created institution was the preceptory at Ansty, which was under the Knight Hospitallers, and in both counties a Trinitarian house was founded, at Easton in Wiltshire and at Thelsford in Warwickshire, the latter probably a house formerly under the order of the Holy Sepulchre. In addition to the friaries already mentioned, a further two religious institutions were created in Salisbury, De Vaux college and St Edmund's college, though, unlike the friaries which were significantly aided by the crown, the colleges were the work of various bishops. Both colleges seem to have been involved in the flowering of scholastic learning at Salisbury in the thirteenth century, but episcopal ambitions to establish an alternative to Oxford were never fully realised. Consequently, they predominantly functioned as chantries.[64]

It has been noted elsewhere that by 1300 enthusiasm among the laity for founding religious houses had declined considerably, a situation which also had implications for the type of institution founders and benefactors were prepared to support and the gift exchanges they were prepared to adopt. In Wiltshire, only three new houses (discounting hospitals) were created in the fourteenth century: a priory of Gilbertine canons at Poulton, a Carmelite friary at Marlborough and a house of Bonhommes at Edington (one of two such houses in England).

Warwickshire, in contrast, saw the founding of nine religious establishments during the same period. Of these new houses, two were friaries, the Carmelites at Coventry and the Austins at Athelstone. There was also Maxstoke priory for Augustinian canons, founded by Sir William de Clinton, a member of the aristocratic family whose forebear had established the wealthy Augustinian house at Kenilworth.[65] For the founders and certain benefactors involved with these houses, their choices may reflect attitudes and ideas prevalent in the twelfth and thirteenth centuries, whereas those associated with the other five new institutions seem to display a greater concern for more precise intercessory provisions. The reputation of the Carthusian monks as a strict, reformed order may have persuaded Lord Zouch to found St Anne's priory in Coventry, thereby placing the welfare of his soul in the hands of a pious community.[66] The other institutions were collegiate churches, the founders in two cases using (and rebuilding) their local parish church as a basis for their collegiate church, a device employed

62 Ibid., pp. 306–7. 63 Ibid., p. 302. 64 Ibid., pp. 369–70. 65 *VCH Warwickshire*, vol. 2, p. 91. His ancestor was Godfrey de Clinton, chamberlain and treasurer to Henry I; *VCH Warwickshire*, vol. 2, p. 86. 66 The house also received royal support from Richard II and Queen Anne; ibid., p. 83.

by Sir Thomas de Astley at Astley and by John Stratford, bishop of Winchester, at Stratford upon Avon.[67] Seeking similar counter-gifts in terms of chantry services, the founders of Bablake and Knowle colleges built separate chapels for their colleges. The former by 1400 provided intercession and commemoration for members of several Coventry guilds and the royal family, while the priests at Knowle served the needs of the living and the dead.[68]

No further religious houses were founded in either county during the fifteenth and early sixteenth centuries. Rather, some of those established in the earlier centuries were lost, while others, like the Warwickshire Benedictine houses of Alvecote and Henwood were in a poor state, the result of high mortality rates and a lack of interest by potential benefactors. The ability to adapt to serve the needs of later benefactors saved some institutions. Amesbury priory in Wiltshire, for example, provided corrodies, though chantries were apparently not a significant feature there, whereas for some of the early, wealthy houses their considerable assets enabled them to continue their liturgical and other duties as they had done for generations.[69]

Hospitals in the high middle ages

The enthusiasm displayed by the Norman nobility in twelfth-century Warwickshire for the creation of monastic houses was also evident, though somewhat muted, regarding hospital foundations. In addition to the nineteen monastic houses established between the Conquest and 1200, three leper hospitals and at least two (possibly as many as five) non-leper hospitals were constructed.[70] Although piety may have been foremost in the minds of the founders, the small number of surviving Anglo-Saxon monastic houses may also have influenced their choice of institution. This upsurge in foundations was not sustained, and the thirteenth century brought very few new monastic houses (all were friaries), and a further two leper hospitals and three non-leper hospitals.[71]

The chronology of foundation was different in Wiltshire. Like the number of new monastic establishments (eight), there were slightly fewer hospitals (four) created in the twelfth century, and of these all except one were leper hospitals.[72] Although the problem of 'first known' rather than foundation date is particularly

67 Ibid., pp. 117, 123. **68** Ibid., pp. 120–2. **69** *VCH Wiltshire*, vol. 3, p. 254. **70** The leper houses of St Edmund, Bretford, St Mary Magdalene, Coventry, and St Michael, Warwick; Satchell, 'Leper-houses in medieval England', pp. 268–9, 286–7, 387. The two non-leper houses were St John's, Coventry, and St John's, Warwick; *VCH Warwickshire*, vol. 2, pp. 109, 115. **71** St Leonard's hospital, Coventry, and St Laurence's, Warwick, housed the leprous; Satchell, 'Leper-houses in medieval England', pp. 287, 387–8. The three non-leper houses of St Thomas, Birmingham, Holy Cross, Stratford upon Avon, and one at Henley in Arden; *VCH Warwickshire*, vol. 2, pp. 108, 112–13. **72** The leprous were housed at St Mary the Virgin and St Matthew's hospital, Maiden Bradley; St John and St Anthony's hospital, Old Sarum; and St Giles and St Anthony's hospital, Wilton; Satchell, 'Leper-houses in medieval England', pp. 336, 350, 390–1. The non-leper house was also at Wilton, dedicated to St John the Baptist; *VCH Wiltshire*, vol. 3, p. 364.

acute for Wiltshire, there was a considerable expansion in the number of new hospitals in the thirteenth century, between thirteen and fifteen, which was accompanied by a slight rise in the number of monastic house foundations (nine). Most founders wished to help the poor, and sometimes sick people or travellers, apparently establishing nine new non-leper hospitals, and an additional four houses for the leprous.[73] As a consequence, the distribution pattern of the two types of hospital differed considerably between the two counties.[74] In Warwickshire, over half the hospitals were either in Coventry or Warwick. Each had at least two leper houses and one non-leper hospital, while the remaining leper house and non-leper hospitals were thinly scattered across the county in a small number of urban settlements. The Wiltshire hospitals were more evenly distributed; four small towns each had a leper and a non-leper hospital, and Old Sarum and Salisbury were together similarly served. The rest were widely distributed across the county, and all except the leper hospital of Maiden Bradley were urban institutions.

Like almost all the founders of religious houses in Warwickshire in the twelfth century, those involved in establishing hospitals were predominantly members of the Norman nobility. Some were great lay landholders, like the earls of Warwick, whose considerable interests in the county, especially in the area around Warwick, resulted in the foundation of two hospitals. The first, a leper house dedicated to St Michael, was the creation of Roger, earl of Warwick, and within a few decades Henry had founded the hospital of St John the Baptist for the poor and wayfarers.[75] Henry de Newburgh, Roger's father, had been the first to establish such a connection between the family and the town when he founded a priory of regular canons dedicated to the Holy Sepulchre (which may initially have accommodated poor travellers), and St Mary's college.[76] The latter foundation was completed by Roger, who was also a major benefactor of the Augustinian abbey at neighbouring Kenilworth, a house founded by another Warwickshire magnate, Godfrey de Clinton.[77] The earls and the de Clintons were presumably responding to the spiritual revival of the twelfth century, but on occasions founders were motivated by personal considerations, like the earl of Chester's establishment of a leper hospital at Coventry, which he is said to have created for the benefit of a leper knight in his household.[78]

It is difficult to compare the two counties because few founders of twelfth-century Wiltshire hospitals are known, but members of the local nobility were

73 The non-leper houses of St John, Great Bedwyn; St John and St Anthony, Calne; St John, Cricklade; St John, Devizes, St John, Malmesbury, St John, Marlborough, St Nicholas, Salisbury, St Mary Magdalene, Wilton, St John, Wootton Bassett; *VCH Wiltshire*, vol. 3, pp. 334–7, 340–50, 367–9. The four leper houses were St Margaret's, Bradford on Avon; St James and St Denys', Devizes; St Mary Magdalene's, Malmesbury; and St Thomas', Marlborough; Satchell, 'Leper-houses in medieval England', pp. 268, 290, 337, 338. **74** See maps 1 and 2. **75** *VCH Warwickshire*; vol. 2, pp. 115–16. W. Dugdale, *The antiquities of Warwickshire*, 2nd edn (1730), vol. 1, p. 459. **76** *VCH Warwickshire*; vol. 2, pp. 97, 124. **77** Ibid., p. 86. **78** Ibid., p. 111.

involved. Manasser Biset and his wife established the only rural leper hospital in the county, later a house of Augustinian canons, possibly on her land.[79] In addition, members of the royal family were also active in Wiltshire, a consequence perhaps, of the degree of royal landholding there, especially the extensive royal forests of Savernake and Braden.[80] Moreover, donors like Adela of Louvain, the second wife of Henry I, who probably founded the leper hospital of St Giles at Wilton, may also have been responding to contemporary charitable attitudes that sometimes regarded the leprous as fitting spiritual recipients.[81]

The only known ecclesiastical foundation of a hospital in either county during the twelfth century was the Coventry hospital of St John the Baptist, a non-leper house established by Coventry priory at the request of Edmund, archdeacon of Coventry. The priory literally and symbolically sustained its connection with the hospital through the daily gift of two monks' portions to feed the poor there, a three-way ongoing reciprocal relationship that brought together the priory, hospital and the poor until the Dissolution.[82] Interestingly, two of the wealthy Wiltshire Anglo-Saxon monastic foundations seem to have had similar relationships with hospitals in the local town (though both hospitals may date from the early thirteenth century). The first record of St Mary Magdalene's hospital in Malmesbury is a charter commemorating a donation of a 'monk's corrody' to the infirm brothers at the hospital, the gift of Abbot Walter of Malmesbury (1208–22).[83] A hospital of the same dedication apparently stood close to Wilton abbey, but little is known about the early history of the place, except that in the mid-thirteenth century the abbey granted the brothers and sisters the reversion of a house in the town.[84] As noted earlier, links of this kind between wealthy and often ancient Benedictine houses and hospitals were found elsewhere in England, monasteries founding houses for the benefit of their own community and the local populace.

The thirteenth century saw some changes to hospital foundation patterns, not least the apparently large increase in the number of new hospitals in Wiltshire. Even though foundation charters rarely survive from this period, it appears that the nobility continued to establish many of the hospitals, yet knightly and ecclesiastical foundations are not unknown, and the crown may also have been involved. The most important ecclesiastical hospital was St Nicholas', Salisbury, probably the creation of Bishop Poore who also began the construction of a new cathedral at Salisbury. His successor, Bishop Bingham, was particularly involved in the development of the city, building a bridge and neighbouring chapel, both

79 *VCH Wiltshire*, vol. 3, p. 295. **80** Henry III gave the lepers of St Thomas', Marlborough, timber for building from Savernake, and he also granted the hospital of St John, Cricklade, the right to collect timber and fuel wood from the forest of Braden; ibid., p. 342, 335. **81** Ibid., p. 362. **82** *VCH Warwickshire*, vol. 2, pp. 109–10. **83** *VCH Wiltshire*, vol. 3, p. 341. **84** The hospital apparently became part of the abbey later in its history, possibly ultimately becoming a house solely for women; ibid., pp. 367–8.

of which were associated with the hospital. Such good works were important parts of Poore and Bingham's charitable strategies, but Poore also provided his hospital with the services of a chantry chaplain, whose duties included celebrating daily for the bishop's soul and for other named souls, including those of certain early benefactors.[85]

Unfortunately, little is known about the thirteenth-century founders of Warwickshire hospitals, but, like their counterparts in Wiltshire, most were probably members of the nobility. There was one unusual exception, however. At Stratford upon Avon, the Holy Cross guild petitioned the bishop, as holder of the manor of Stratford, for a licence to found a non-leper hospital there. Initially at least, many of the recipients of this fraternal largesse were poor unbeneficed priests, who were presumably expected to provide their benefactors with intercessory services in the guild chapel as part of the reciprocal exchange process.[86]

Such acts were important aspects of the relationship between the hospital and its patron, who was frequently the founder, or later his heirs and successors. Patrons also expected to be involved in the election of hospital officials, especially the master or warden, a role exercised by the earls of Warwick at the family's hospital of St Michael, Warwick, and possibly by the de Bermingham family at St Thomas' hospital, Birmingham.[87] Equally, lay founders in Wiltshire sought to exercise their right as patrons, a role the king seems to have adopted at St Thomas' hospital, Marlborough, but at times such rights and privileges, like the choice of appointees, were contested, leading to considerable friction and acrimonious disputes.[88] In addition to those directly implicated in the reciprocal relationship between patron and recipient institution, these disputes might also concern others involved in the spiritual economy. For example, in mid-thirteenth-century Malmesbury, the local vicar at St Paul's accused the master and brethren of St John's hospital of encroaching on his rights. The situation was made more complicated by the involvement of Malmesbury abbey, the hospital's landlord and the holder of St Paul's parish. Following the intervention of Bishop Walter and his official, the disagreement was resolved: the hospital community were seen as part of the parish, paying a proportion of the parish dues to the incumbent, though they were allowed to worship in their own church.[89]

Links among founders, patrons and benefactors were probably more common than surviving records suggest. In Warwickshire such connections are known for only a minority of the twelfth- and thirteenth-century hospitals, but these illustrate various relationships. Descendants in the male line were apparently willing to help maintain their ancestors' hospital, usually through the gift of further land grants or rents, some continuing to donate such assets after the enactment of the Statute of Mortmain. William de Bermingham was one of three men who

85 Ibid., pp. 343–5.   **86** *VCH Warwickshire*, vol. 2, p. 113.   **87** Ibid., pp. 116, 108; Dugdale, *Antiquities of Warwickshire*, vol. 2, p. 903.   **88** *VCH Wiltshire*, vol. 3, p. 343.   **89** Ibid., p. 340.

donated land to St Thomas' hospital, Birmingham, as part of a licence granted by Edward I in 1286.[90] Similarly, the earls of Warwick continued to support Earl Roger's hospital of St Michael in Warwick, of whom two of the early donors were family members, Waleran (died 1203) and Margaret.[91] Occasionally, the female line was important concerning matters of patronage and benefaction. At St Mary Magdalene's hospital, Coventry, Sir Roger de Montalt and Cecily, his wife, the niece of Ralph Blundeville, earl of Chester, reserved the patronage of the hospital to themselves and their descendants when they donated the manors of Coventry and Cheylesmore to Coventry priory.[92] Yet it is interesting that in the same grant they donated a weekly load of wood to be delivered by the priory's foresters to the other Coventry hospital of St John.[93]

Although the links were fraternal rather than familial, Holy Cross guild members continued to support their hospital and chapel through the giving of dues and other alms. Probably many of the guild members were from Stratford itself or its environs, a catchment area possibly enjoyed by most hospitals, like St Thomas' hospital, Birmingham, where local and regional benefactors were the norm. Yet, like some other hospitals in Warwickshire, the house at Stratford apparently received very few *in vitam* grants, relying instead on casual alms, its endeavours aided by the gift of an episcopal indulgence in 1270.[94] These counter-gifts were given to the faithful who visited or aided the hospital, an incentive that may have become increasingly important in the competitive world of the spiritual economy, particularly after the appearance in the county of the friars in the early thirteenth century.

Many of the known benefactors of the Wiltshire hospitals were also laymen. Local and regional connections and knowledge were presumably significant factors in the choices made by these donors. Such factors may also have influenced certain members of the aristocracy, like William Longespee, who supported two Wilton hospitals, St Giles and St Anthony's, and St John's, as well as the leper hospital near the castle at Old Sarum. Although many of these *in vitam* grantors were not seeking specific counter-gifts, a few extended the value of the good work to gain spiritual advantages, like the provision of confraternity.[95]

With regard to other groups of benefactors, the picture did vary between the two counties. Ecclesiastical donors, either local monastic houses or various bishops, were slightly more numerous in Wiltshire. St Nicholas' hospital, Salisbury, enjoyed the greatest support receiving a considerable endowment from its episcopal patrons, and the manor of Guston from the abbess of Wilton.[96] However, the level of royal benefaction was more variable, and a number of Wiltshire hos-

---

90 *VCH Warwickshire*, vol. 2, p. 108. **91** Satchell, 'Leper-houses in medieval England', p. 387; Dugdale, *Antiquities of Warwickshire*, vol. 1, p. 458. **92** *VCH Warwickshire*, vol. 2, p. 111. **93** Ibid., p. 109. **94** Ibid., p. 113. **95** Walter and Emma Bodmin gave the hospital community of St John's, Malmesbury, two messuages in 1247, thereby providing them and their heirs with all the spiritual benefits of the house; *VCH Wiltshire*, vol. 3, p. 340. **96** Ibid., pp. 343–5.

pitals received royal grants, in addition to protection grants. Of particular significance were Henry III's gifts of timber, for building and firewood, which were given to the leper hospitals of St Thomas, Marlborough; St John and St Anthony, Old Sarum; and St Giles and St Anthony, Wilton.[97] Many of the non-leper hospitals similarly received such royal largesse, like St John's, Cricklade; St John's, Wilton; and especially St John's, Marlborough.[98] For the hospitals, this munificence was exceedingly valuable because of the almost constant requirement for firewood and the need to repair and, where possible, extend their premises.

The seeking of royal protection grants may imply that several of the Wiltshire hospitals were suffering from poverty in the thirteenth century, a product perhaps, of a meagre endowment, but possibly also a result of increasing competition. By 1300, therefore, even though a few hospitals in both counties were continuing to receive *in vitam* grants, for most houses new acquisitions were becoming increasingly rare, and certain hospital authorities were adopting a more pro-active approach to alms collection.[99] Yet, probably all the hospitals founded in the previous two centuries were still serving the charitable aims for which they had been established, though it is not clear when the leper hospital of Maiden Bradley became an Augustinian priory.

Hospitals in the later middle ages

Andrew Brown, in his assessment of the relationship between the hospital, almshouses and charity in the late medieval diocese of Salisbury, highlighted three differences he saw compared to the earlier period: a fall in the number of new hospitals created in the fourteenth and fifteenth centuries; the different nature of such institutions, which might be labelled almshouses; and the corollary that the clientele accommodated at these new houses, and at some of the old hospitals, had changed.[1] Nevertheless, he was not prepared to see this solely as a reflection of hardening attitudes towards the poor in the later middle ages; rather, he considered attitudes to the poor, even if they could be assessed from the chronology of hospital foundations, were more complex.[2]

Taking these three changes as a starting point, in broad terms the hospitals of Warwickshire display a similar pattern, though there are differences between the two counties. Warwickshire, too, saw fewer hospitals founded from the fourteenth century onwards, but the almost complete absence of fifteenth-century foundations does not follow the Wiltshire pattern, where that century produced the highest number of new establishments compared to the preceding and sub-

---

97 Ibid., pp. 342, 361, 362. **98** Ibid., pp. 335, 365, 341–2. **99** The collection of alms was a common device used by hospitals, and St Thomas' hospital at Marlborough received royal letters of protection in 1260, 1267, 1269 and in 1340; ibid., p. 342. This strategy was also used by Holy Cross hospital, Stratford upon Avon, in 1270, when it also received an episcopal indulgence of forty days for those penitents who contributed to the hospital; *VCH Warwickshire*, vol. 2, p. 113. **1** Brown, *Piety in the diocese of Salisbury*, pp. 182–5. **2** Ibid., pp. 186–7, 200–1.

sequent periods. This is partly a reflection of Brown's work on the Salisbury testamentary sources, in which he found a number of previously unknown
almshouses (not recorded in Knowles and Hadcock).[3] Some of these houses
appear to be maisondieu-types, and a systematic search of the Worcester and
Coventry diocesan testamentary materials would probably also reveal the presence of at least a small number of this kind of establishment. Yet, even in the
absence of comparing like with like, the distribution pattern of late medieval
hospitals is very different. The Warwickshire hospitals were concentrated in
Coventry, whereas under half (five) of the Wiltshire houses were in Salisbury;
the rest were in small towns scattered across the county.[4] Brown has suggested
that their presence may be linked to the relative proliferation of urban settlements in Wiltshire, places that attracted those seeking work in the market centres and in the cloth industry.[5] However there is little to suggest founders and
patrons envisaged migrants among the beneficiaries of their institutional largesse,
apparently preferring instead those belonging to the town.

   The local nature of this charitable provision in terms of the recipient clientele (see below) was similarly mirrored in the type of founder. For certain leading citizens, the founding of a small hospital in their home town was an attractive proposition, their work of Christian charity providing them with spiritual
merit. There too, they might expect specific intercessory services, as James
Terumber intended at his almshouse at Trowbridge, where the inmates prayed
twice daily in the local parish church for the benefit of his soul, the site of his
chantry.[6] Such a charitable act was also likely to bring prestige, enhancing the
founder's social standing among his fellow townsmen, especially for those associated with civic government.

   Similarly, in Warwickshire, founders were drawn from the mercantile elite,
like William Ford, a merchant of the Staple. In 1529, he established an almshouse
in Coventry, seeking specific intercessory provisions on behalf of his own soul
and a number of others, including William Pisford, his executor, a considerable
benefactor of his friend's almshouse. Pisford's will survives, providing insights
into his charitable concerns and perceptions, ideas that may mirror those of Ford
and others among the leading citizenry. Pisford gave nothing to Coventry cathe-

---

3 For Wiltshire, he noted three first known or founded in the fourteenth century, six for the fifteenth century and two for the early sixteenth century (up to 1545); ibid., p. 182.   **4** The new
Coventry houses were Bond's or Trinity hospital and Ford's hospital, both early sixteenth-century
foundations; *VCH Warwickshire*, vol. 2, p. 112. There may have been others: Walssh's and a second
cited by Knowles and Hadcock (from Clay), dating from the fourteenth century; Knowles and
Hadcock, *Medieval religious houses*, p. 266. The Salisbury houses were the late fourteenth-century
Holy Trinity hospital, an earlier hospital at Harnham, a third (early fifteenth century), St Edmund's,
another fifteenth-century hospital and almshouse tenements for five people (*c.* 1530); *VCH Wiltshire*,
vol. 3. p. 357; Brown, *Piety in the diocese of Salisbury*, pp. 182, 189.   **5** Brown, *Piety in the diocese of
Salisbury*, p. 187.   **6** Ibid., p. 183.

dral, preferring to direct his pious bequests towards St Michael's church, his desired place of burial; and to two local friaries. The recipient categories of his charitable provision were carefully selected; he wished to aid poor householders, especially those who were ashamed to ask for help. His concern for the respectable and deserving nature of his recipients was similarly reflected in his gifts towards the marriages of poor maidens and the giving of the means of honest labour to other poor women. His linking of civic and personal responsibility within his charitable strategy appears to be exemplified by his bequest to the common box in St Mary's hall, an almsbox he himself had installed for the benefit of the 'Common wealth'; and his numerous gifts to various Coventry craft guilds to aid their upholding of the city's 'laudable custom'.[7]

This emphasis on the guilds, as part of a complex web of reciprocal relationships within the spiritual economy, seems to have become more apparent during the later middle ages. And for certain almshouse founders, the guilds offered opportunities for the securing of the future of their institutions, an alternative or a supplement to their use of feoffees or the town officers as patrons. Though not widely used in either county, this strategy was employed by Thomas Bond in Coventry, where he linked his almshouse to the Trinity guild there. Bond intended that the patronage of his institution should be in the hands of the city corporation, but as a means of ensuring its long term future as a prestigious urban institution he instructed his executors that the inmates should be indigent members of the Trinity guild. In addition, these recipients of his, the guild's and the corporation's charity were to repay their benefactors' largesse through their daily prayers, their place in the hierarchical reciprocal exchange process symbolized through their annual receipt of a black gown bearing a device of the Trinity on the front and back.[8]

The situation regarding Holy Trinity almshouse in Salisbury was more complicated, but again suggests the importance of charitable provision as a binding agent among the various fraternal organizations of parish, craft and town. After the death of John Chandler, one of Agnes Bottenham's executors, her almshouse came under the patronage of the mayor, remaining in municipal hands throughout the fifteenth and sixteenth centuries.[9] Its place as a town hospital in Salisbury was presumably significant in terms of the support it received locally, a favoured position which was enjoyed by relatively few charitable institutions during this period. One of its benefactors was William Ashleigh, whose gift of several tenements to the mayor and commonalty was intended to sustain the prestigious St George guild and the Holy Trinity almshouse.[10] Unlike the Coventry house, the linking of guild and almshouse in the minds of benefactors was not mirrored in the selection of the recipients. Some were chosen because they were of the

7 Dugdale, *Antiquities of Warwickshire*, vol. 1, pp. 184–5. 8 Ibid., p. 194; *VCH Warwickshire*, vol. 2, p. 112. 9 *VCH Wiltshire*, vol. 3, p. 357. 10 Brown, *Piety in the diocese of Salisbury*, pp. 181, 192.

town and, at various times, those with even more tenuous links with Salisbury were allowed to seek temporary shelter at the house. Nevertheless, such institutions do highlight the broad shift in the type of founder in these counties, from the involvement of senior churchmen, religious institutions, the crown and the nobility during the earlier period, to the pre-eminence of leading townsmen during the later middle ages. Through the local infrastructure of fraternal institutions, men were able to provide, at least in some instances, a degree of permanence for their charitable establishments, constructing a fiction of constancy at a time of familial fragility and social instability.

These shifts in the type of founder and his creation were reflected in the sort of person aided. The new houses in Warwickshire and Wiltshire rarely provided shelter for the sick or poor travellers; instead, founders and patrons directed their benevolence towards the local poor or their elderly servants and retainers. For founders like Margaret Hungerford, the choice of recipient was under their control, allowing them to dispense largesse in the form of an almshouse place to those whom they deemed worthy; an assessment based on local knowledge and conversation.[11] This selection process was especially important with regard to the bedehouse-type almshouses, of which Heytesbury was one, because the fate of the founder and patron's souls were, at least in part, in the hands of the bedesfolk. Thus, it was imperative for benefactors that patrons and hospital authorities acted responsibly in the selection and policing of those undertaking the prescribed intercessory services, as well as ascertaining their moral worth to do so. At the maisondieu-type almshouses, of which there were a few in fifteenth-century Wiltshire, the burden of intercession may have been lighter, allowing patrons to employ a less rigorous selection process. Yet the authorities presumably wished to maintain such houses as worthy charitable institutions, which meant that the character of the inmates remained subject to scrutiny.[12]

Such choices and changes in emphasis with respect to the relationship between benefactors and recipients might have been expected to have implications for the early hospitals, especially in providing them with a survival strategy. A few of the non-leper houses in both counties were able to or perceived the advantages of adopting this device, but nationally the practice was far more common. At the hospital of the Holy Cross, Stratford, the inmates were said by the early fifteenth century to be living in the almshouse tenements, apparently attending divine service at the guild chapel under the guidance of the guild priests.[13] Though possibly restating rather than initiating a new code of practice at St John's hospital, Coventry, it was noted in 1426 that the brothers and sis-

11 Ibid., pp. 184–5; Hicks, 'St Katherine's hospital', 66. Heytesbury was an unusual foundation (one of six nationally) which comprised an almshouse, chantry and school, ibid., 65. 12 As Brown noted, founders took pride in their almshouses as part of the communal effort on behalf of their towns; Brown, *Piety in the diocese of Salisbury*, p. 189. 13 *VCH Warwickshire*, vol. 2, p. 114.

ters were expected to partake in the liturgical life of the house for the spiritual benefit of their benefactors, their involvement dependent on their degree of learning.[14] The sisters were also expected to administer to the infirm, but their role as carers for the dead as well as the living may have meant they were seen and saw themselves as primarily fulfilling an intercessory role.

At St Nicholas' hospital in Salisbury the house similarly seems to have become more like a bedehouse-type almshouse over the late fourteenth and fifteenth centuries. Rather than serving the poor and sick through their religious and nursing duties, the hospital staff gradually became the recipients when they became too old or too ill to work, their needs supplied through the provision of board, lodging, and occasional items of clothing. By 1478, when Bishop Beauchamp revised the hospital statutes, the brothers and sisters were described as almsfolk, who lived in separate rooms, though married couples were allowed to share. The master seems to have been a secular chaplain. He was supposed to sing or say divine service daily, the inmates joining him in the chapel to say two psalters of Our Lady.[15]

This shift in the role of the early hospital to one of accommodating often fee-paying inmates, local poorer people rather than the poor, provided patrons with another source of revenue at a time when benefaction had for some houses all but ceased. Although it is impossible to monitor casual almsgiving except in terms of the gaining of episcopal or other indulgences or protection grants, it is clear that *in vitam* grant giving had declined markedly since the thirteenth century and testamentary bequests (in Wiltshire) followed a similar pattern.[16] Nonetheless, a few potential benefactors continued to value the early hospitals, but most sought a more contractual relationship with their favoured institution, their choice influenced by matters like its reputation and status, personal connections and the presence of alternative establishments. In 1444, for example, John Blakeman and his wife entered into a tripartite agreement with St John's hospital, Coventry, and the members of Corpus Christi and St Nicholas guild whereby they, for the love and benefit shown to the house, could nominate the occupant of a bed in the hospital. They retained this privilege for life on the understanding that the nominee was a suitable person. Thereafter, the guild received the right of nomination and in recompense agreed to intercede annually on behalf of John and Margaret for a century.[17]

Other hospitals, particularly the leper houses in both counties, had been less successful in drawing support from the early fourteenth century onwards, resulting in their demise from poverty, probably exacerbated by recurrent mortality crises. Some, like Bretford in Warwickshire and Great Bedwyn in Wiltshire, disappeared completely, though a greater number became wayside or free chapels,

14 Ibid., p. 110. **15** *VCH Wiltshire*, vol. 3, p. 348; Brown, *Piety in the diocese of Salisbury*, p. 190.
16 Brown, *Piety in the diocese of Salisbury*, pp. 188–94. **17** *VCH Warwickshire*, vol. 2, pp. 110–11.

often served by a single priest, the sole survivor of the hospital community, or a chaplain whose wages were paid by the master from the hospital's income.[18] In the spiritual economy these hospital chapels were extra-parochial, which occasionally led to disagreements with the local parochial incumbent when he felt his rights and/or income were threatened. The bishop of Salisbury, in the early fourteenth century, instructed the prior at St John's hospital, Devizes, to ensure that the rector received all the offerings when his parishioners frequented the hospital chapel. At this time there was still a community at the hospital, but at some point over the next two centuries the hospital was reduced to a chapel, though whether the townspeople still attended services there is unclear.[19]

Such chapels, however, might retain the name of hospital, and a few exchanged their charitable role for the benefit of the living to care exclusively for the dead. As an alternative survival scheme, this employment of the hospital chapel as a chantry had several advantages for those involved, including cost. Edward IV, as patron, was able to set up intercessory provisions forever for himself, his wife and son when he granted the free chapel or ancient leper hospital of St Mary Magdalene, Coventry, to Studley priory on payment of £12 in the hanaper.[20] Yet the founders of chantries in both counties generally preferred religious houses, parish churches or cathedrals to hospital chapels, which may indicate perceptions concerning the different spiritual roles of various institutions and their efficacy as places of intercession and commemoration. Similarly, the parish church appears to have been favoured by benefactors who wished to initiate other forms of pious gift exchanges, like the setting up of lamps or the donation of vestments or other commemorative markers.[21]

At a local level, therefore, certain houses remained favoured beneficiaries, but generally hospitals were considered marginal participants in the spiritual economy by most in both counties during the late medieval period. Using the Salisbury testamentary records as a guide, Brown found that Holy Trinity received the greatest support, while only a few benefactors named the ancient hospital of St Nicholas, and the other hospitals there received almost nothing. Furthermore, of those testators who wished to aid the poor, most found other methods, like doles at the three funeral days.[22] These findings indicate that testators discriminated regarding hospitals, their choices perhaps a reflection of the importance of local connections among benefactors, patrons, hospital authorities and the resident inmates. Nevertheless, even the new almshouses were rarely well supported, including those known to be providing places for poorer people

18 Ibid., p. 109; *VCH Wiltshire*, vol. 3, p. 334. **19** *VCH Wiltshire*, vol. 3, p. 337. **20** *VCH Warwickshire*, vol. 2, p. 111. **21** One of few who did want to be commemorated at his local hospital was William Chitterne of Wilton. In 1403, as a consequence of his gift of twelve and a half acres, he wished a lamp to burn daily at high mass in the chapel of St Giles and St Anthony's hospital, Wilton; *VCH Wiltshire*, vol. 3, p. 363. **22** Brown, *Piety in the diocese of Salisbury*, pp. 188–99.

from the locality. However, the presence of a number of small almshouses, as well as Holy Trinity in Salisbury, may suggest a growing concern by the local leading citizens about the problems of poverty.[23]

Such ideas were expressed more forcibly from the early sixteenth century, nationally, regionally and locally, leading to policies which aimed to curb the evils of vagabondage and to aid those seen as deserving alms. These discriminatory policies presumably affected those managing the hospitals and almshouses because, unless the house was well endowed, it remained dependent on casual alms. Consequently, unlike the masters or wardens who served the free chapels at the ancient hospitals of Wiltshire and Warwickshire whose primary concern may have been the collection of rents due to the hospital/chapel, a sum frequently sufficient to maintain the sole incumbent, their counterparts at the hospitals and almshouses had to find additional ways of raising revenue. Growing social and economic difficulties from *c.*1500 increased the problems faced by many of the hospitals and almshouses, a position exacerbated by the political and religious upheavals of the 1530s and 1540s. As a result, relatively few of these establishments were still functioning as houses for the poor during the late sixteenth century, and most of the survivors were late medieval foundations, like Holy Trinity, Salisbury and Bond's hospital, Coventry. For these houses, their survival was dependent on matters like patronage, prosperity and the perceived role of the house. Its worth was measured in terms of function, but also in prestige and status, factors of overwhelming concern to the local citizenry, and at times to a wider audience. In Wiltshire for example, St John's hospital, Marlborough, may almost have ceased to function as a house for the poor by the mid-sixteenth century, but its worth as an adaptable town institution was recognized by the mayor and burgesses who successfully campaigned for it to become the town's grammar school.[24] For the leading townsmen of Stratford, the guild hospital of Holy Cross was similarly seen as a worthy establishment, though in this instance the almshouse and chapel were retained for the use of the town. They were also able to endow

---

23 For a selection of the literature on the subject: Brown, *Piety in the diocese of Salisbury*, pp. 194–201; McIntosh, 'Responses to the poor', 209–45; Cullum, 'Hir name was charite', pp. 182–211; P.H. Cullum and P.J.P. Goldberg, 'Charitable provision in late medieval York' (1993), 24–39; P.W. Fleming, 'Charity, faith and the gentry of Kent 1422–1529' (1984), pp. 36–58; P. Heath, 'Urban piety in the later Middle (1984), pp. 209–34; J. Kermode, 'The merchants in three northern English towns' (1982), pp. 7–48; M.G. Vale, 'Piety, charity and literacy among the Yorkshire gentry 1370–1480' (1976), 26–7; C. Burgess, 'By quick and by dead' (1987), 837–58; C. Burgess, 'The benefactions of mortality' (1991), pp. 65–86; W.K. Jordan, *Philanthropy in England 1480–1660* (1959); Rubin, *Charity in Cambridge*, pp. 54–98, 237–88; Rubin, 'Imagining medieval hospitals', pp. 14–25; J. Thomson, 'Piety and charity in late medieval London' (1965), 178–95; N.P. Tanner, *The Church in late medieval Norwich, 1370–1532* (1984), pp. 130–40, 222–3; Rawcliffe, *Hospitals of Norwich*, pp. 135–61; Rawcliffe, *Medicine for the soul*, pp. 8–18, 162–76; P.J. Lee, 'Monastic and secular religion and devotional reading in late medieval Dartford and west Kent' (1998), pp. 179–84. 24 *VCH Wiltshire*, vol. 3, p. 342.

a grammar school for sons of the local citizenry, an even more prestigious charitable institution and a source of civic pride.[25] Such relatively rare survivors highlight the fragility and complexity of the processes of reciprocal exchange within the spiritual economy. In addition, these examples demonstrate the hospital authorities' need to manipulate such processes to try to secure the future of their institution, a task which defeated a considerable number in Warwickshire and Wiltshire during the later middle ages.

Patrons in Wiltshire and Warwickshire were not alone in the difficulties they experienced in seeking to maintain their hospitals during the fifteenth and sixteenth centuries. Prior to the Reformation period, a number of houses had disappeared completely or survived solely as appropriated appendages of religious and educational institutions. Further losses were inevitable as a consequence of national policies, though a number of establishments were able to survive or were reconstituted as almshouses or schools, often through the efforts of the local citizens. Consequently, like the history of the place of the hospital during the reigns of the Norman and Angevin kings, factors that primarily influenced the hospital's later history were local, though regional and national matters were not insignificant. It seems appropriate, therefore, to turn now to studying the role and place of the hospital regionally and locally by looking at the institution in Kent.

---

25 *VCH Warwickshire*, vol. 2, p. 115.

CHAPTER 2

Kent's medieval hospitals

This chapter builds upon the general survey and the methods of regional analysis developed in the preceding chapter to provide a detailed social history of hospital provision in medieval Kent. Kent was selected for a number of reasons, not least the presence of a number of ancient towns, which were important centres of secular administration and self-regulation. Nonetheless, ecclesiastical lordship was very strong; the considerable number of religious houses and the two national and internationally important sees of Canterbury and Rochester heavily influenced the development of the county. Relations with London and continental Europe provided important cross-cultural connections within the county, affecting the character of Kentish institutions and, in addition, there were relatively large numbers of hospitals and almshouses. The majority were to be found in one of two regions *viz.* (1) east Kent: the areas in and around Canterbury and the Cinque Ports, and (2) north Kent: the towns and vills close to Watling Street from south-east London to the area around Faversham. The remainder comprised a small group in central Kent, especially those at Maidstone, and a few late-medieval almshouses in the Weald. The quality of the surviving evidence is not sufficient to allow the history of hospital provision to be assessed separately for the two regions with respect to the different hospital types, though it is possible in terms of Kent as a whole. In some instances, however, there were certain regional characteristics with respect to hospital provision; for example, the high proportion of hospitals for the poor under civic patronage in the Cinque Ports. Where possible, these characteristics are demonstrated.

The Kent study illustrates the changing role of the different types of hospital over time within provincial society. In order to provide a context for the study the first section comprises a general description of the whole county to illustrate the diversity and range of participants in the spiritual economy. Following this there are sub-sections on each of the four main types of hospitals: leper houses, pilgrim hospitals, houses for the poor, and almshouses, where the development of the hospital is assessed with respect to the processes of reciprocity as part of the spiritual economy. The final part of the chapter considers early founders and patrons, the difficult fourteenth century, and benefaction in the later Middle Ages, as a means of exploring critical episodes and significant trends. Such an analysis provides ideas regarding chronology and causation of

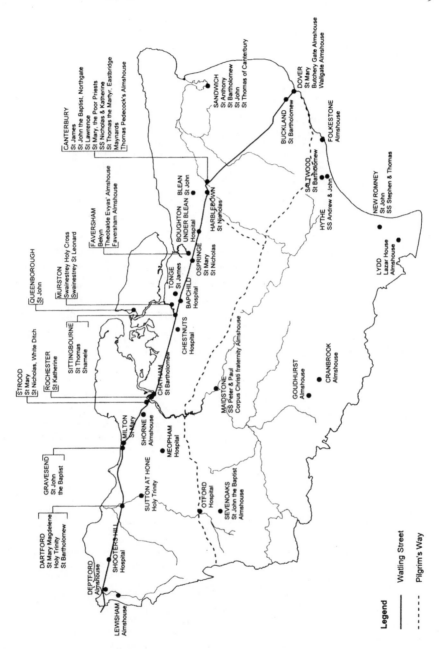

Figure 3 The medieval hospitals of Kent, reproduced from T. Lawson and D. Killingray, *Historical atlas of Kent* (2004)

change and adaptation of all the various hospital types to be found in Kent, from the substantially endowed hospital to the poorest almshouse.

GENERAL SURVEY OF KENT

Participants in the spiritual economy

Archbishop Lanfranc's ambitious ecclesiastical building programme, as part of his strategy to raise the profile of the archiepiscopal see of Canterbury, included the construction of two large hospitals in *c.*1080.[1] Even though charity and hospitality had been offered by some Anglo-Saxon monastic houses, the hospitals of St John, for the poor and infirm, and St Nicholas, for the leprous, were the first in Kent, and possibly the first in England.[2] His lead was followed by Bishop Gundulf who, as part of his building programme for the see of Rochester, founded a single, smaller hospital, thereby reflecting on a more modest scale the work of his friend and superior.[3] St Bartholomew's hospital at Chatham housed the poor and infirm, and lepers, and like many later hospitals in the county accommodated between thirteen and fifteen brothers and sisters.[4]

During the first half of the twelfth century, several monasteries followed this episcopal initiative and founded their own hospitals, in part for the benefit of their own institution but often including provisions for the wider community.[5]

---

1 Besides the two hospitals, Lanfranc's building programme included rebuilding Canterbury cathedral after the fire of 1067, the construction of a new archbishop's palace, and the foundation of a house of priests at St Gregory's. The priests' house was sited on the opposite side of the road from St John's hospital and they were to administer to the spiritual needs of the hospital inmates. It was traditionally said that Lanfranc had formed St Gregory's priory in 1087 from a guild of clerks found within the city and recorded in Domesday under the entry entitled 'the land of the Archbishop of Canterbury'. Recent research has clarified the situation, and it appears Lanfranc's priests were replaced by Augustinian canons in 1133 when Archbishop William of Corbeil founded a priory there, the canons coming from Merton priory; M. Hicks and A. Hicks, *St Gregory's priory, Northgate, Canterbury: excavations, 1988–1991* (2001), p. 371. The construction of the new palace required the demolition of twenty-seven dwellings, a factor that may have been influential with respect to the archbishop's charitable acts; P. Morgan (ed.), *Domesday Book, Kent* (1983), 2, 16.   2 As Satchell indicates, there is no evidence of any pre-Conquest leper hospital foundations; Satchell, 'Leperhouses in medieval England', pp. 119–20.   3 The hospital comprised a chapel and parallel hall on a site outside Rochester city walls; J. Hayes, D. Williams and P. Payne, 'Report of an excavation in the grounds of St Bartholomew's chapel, Chatham' (1982), 177–89. Gundulf also rebuilt Rochester cathedral, modelling it on Canterbury, and a number of ancillary buildings for the monastery. Other building projects in which he was involved included replacing Rochester's wooden castle in stone and constructing a convent at Malling; M. Ruual, 'Monks in the world' (1989), p. 248.   4 It seems likely there were up to fifteen brothers and sisters accommodated at the hospital (in 1382 there were nine brothers and seven sisters), which means that in comparison with Lanfranc's institutions there were four times as many places offered at Canterbury as in Rochester, though the catchment area was presumably far larger for Canterbury; *CCR 1341–1343*, p. 408.   5 Two of these hospitals were founded by wealthy Benedictine houses (the pre-Conquest

The apparent concentration, by the mid-twelfth century, of the early hospitals at Canterbury, and to a lesser extent at Dover and Rochester, may have been of increasing concern to the townspeople outside these urban centres, who may also have wished to provide for the leprous, in particular, in their own communities.[6] Thus, it is possible that during the second half of the century a number of small leper houses were established close to the Cinque Port towns and also in the vicinity of the various urban settlements bordering the main road between Canterbury and London.[7] The period was also marked by a growth in foundations for the poor and for pilgrims, some, like Bishop Gilbert's hospital at Strood near Rochester, providing aid for a number of groups.[8]

As elsewhere in England, one of the results of the revived interest in spiritual matters during the late eleventh and twelfth centuries was a dramatic increase in the founding of monastic institutions by members of the nobility.[9] These men often favoured the reformed new orders rather than houses under the Rule of St Benedict, and the growth in the number of hospitals during the later twelfth century may also have been part of this revival.[10] Consequently, few new

Canterbury abbey of St Augustine and Dover priory, which had been refounded as a Benedictine house in the early twelfth century under the patronage of Christchurch priory, Canterbury), probably a necessary prerequisite and one that may have been well understood following the financial problems encountered by St Bartholomew's hospital at Chatham; E. Greenwood, *The hospital of St Bartholomew, Rochester* (1962), pp. 11–12. St Laurence's hospital at Canterbury (founder St Augustine's abbey) housed six brothers, six sisters, a chaplain and a clerk; St Bartholomew's hospital at Dover (Dover priory) may initially have accommodated twenty inmates; CCAL, DCc/Lit. MS. C20, p. 34; Bodleian, Rawlinson MS. B.335, f. 2. Although not founded by Christchurch priory, St James' hospital at Canterbury did come under the priory's jurisdiction from the late twelfth century; A. Hussey (ed.), *Kent chantries* (1932), p. 80. **6** Cullum, 'Leperhouses and borough status', p. 46. **7** There is evidence for at least one leper hospital in both regions and it is likely that these were not isolated examples. The earliest known charter for the leper hospital at the Cinque Port of New Romney may date from *c.*1180, and by 1182 there was a leper hospital dedicated to St James at Tonge to the north-west of Sittingbourne; Satchell, 'Leper-houses in medieval England', pp. 344, 381; A.F. Butcher, 'The hospital of St Stephen and St Thomas' (1980), 18 n. 6; Hussey, *Kent chantries*, p. 313. The hospital at Saltwood, near Hythe was said to be for the 'Infiimis de Salt Wuda' in the Pipe Rolls of 1168–9, but it seems likely that this too housed lepers; *PR* 15 Henry II, p. 111. **8** Consequently, Gervase's total of eight hospitals in Kent by 1200 is too low. He listed four (or five because he counted St Gregory's priory) in Canterbury (St Laurence's, St James', St Nicholas', St Thomas') and one each at Bapchild (Bakechilde), Blean (St John's), Dover and Rochester; W. Stubbs (ed.), *The Historical Works of Gervase of Canterbury* (1880), p. 418. According to the foundation charter, St Mary's hospital at Strood was founded for the liberation of King Richard and 'for poor and infirm persons, whether neighbours or strangers'; J. Thorpe (ed.), *Registrum Roffense* (1769), p. 1. **9** Southern, *Making of the middle ages*, pp. 157–62. **10** Hospitals probably founded in the last quarter of the twelfth century: Shooter's Hill (founded 1170s); Sandwich: St Bartholomew's (1st known *c.*1180); New Romney: St Stephen and St Thomas' (1st known *c.*1180); Canterbury: St Thomas' (1st known *c.*1180), St Nicholas and St Katherine's (1st known *c.*1195): Tonge: St James' (1st known 1182); Strood: St Mary's (founded 1192). Bapchild: hospital (1st known *c.*1200); Canterbury: Maynard's (1st known *c.*1200); Sutton at Hone: Holy Trinity (1st known *c.*1200).

Benedictine monasteries were added to the list of pre-Conquest houses.[11] Instead, most male lay establishments were Augustinian or Premonstratensian priories, and there was a Cistercian abbey at Boxley and a Cluniac priory at Monk's Horton.[12] Other new institutions included four new Benedictine nunneries. The house at Malling was under episcopal patronage, Highham was a royal foundation and St Sepulchre's, Canterbury and the priory at Davington had been established by laymen. In addition, there were the three alien houses at Folkestone, Throwley and Patrixbourne.[13] This multiplication of potential participants in the spiritual economy was not confined to exchanges within the institution itself but, as at the older houses, benefactors might donate gifts to specific obedientaries; the almoner, for example, was especially favoured at the Dover and Rochester priories.[14]

In addition to the growth in the number of extra-parochial participants, papal directives in Lateran IV had highlighted the centrality of the Eucharist in the lives of the laity and the need for parishioners to articulate this reciprocal relationship between themselves and their parish priest through their offerings.[15] Parish priests were, therefore, significant local participants in the spiritual economy, but other religious persons might also become involved. Though difficult to gauge, there were large numbers of unbeneficed clergy, hermits, anchors and anchorites in the county, some of whom were to be found serving at chapels of ease, private chapels or in parish churches.[16] To provide some idea of scale,

---

11 By 1200 only Faversham abbey (founded by King Stephen and his queen in 1148) and Dover priory (refounded *c.*1140) had been added to the surviving male Benedictine houses of St Augustine's abbey, Christchurch priory and Rochester priory.   **12** Of the Augustinian priories Leeds (early twelfth century), Combwell (initially a Premonstratensian house), Lesnes and Tonbridge (late twelfth century) were founded by laymen, the episcopal foundation of St Gregory's at Canterbury being the one exception. Later, Bilsington priory was founded in 1253. The two Premonstratensian houses near Dover were St Radigund's abbey and West Langdon abbey (late twelfth century). The two military orders had also founded houses in Kent by the late twelfth century, the small preceptories of Ewell and Swingfield.   **13** These houses joined the surviving pre-Conquest nunnery of Minster in Sheppey and the alien priory of Lewisham.   **14** In the index of the Dover priory register matters relating to the almonry were listed under a separate heading; LPL, MS. 241, ff. 94–5v. Of the surviving deeds for Rochester priory for the period 1200–84, the almoner was the most frequent recipient with twenty-six; A. Oakley, 'Rochester priory, 1185–1540' (1996), p. 47. Consequently, as the recipient in the gift exchange, the official/department was seen by the donor as responsible for the well-being of the gift. According to *Thorne's Chronicle*, for example, the royal gift of Northborne church to the almonry at St Augustine's abbey required the almonry to 'hold and keep it properly and peacefully, freely and honourably, as the charter of the abbot and convent testifies'; A. Davis (trans.), *William Thorne's Chronicle of St Augustine's abbey* (1934), p. 127.   **15** M. Rubin, 'What did the Eucharist mean to thirteenth-century villagers?' (1992), pp. 50.   **16** Although he did not study either of the Kent dioceses, Townley's assessment is useful. He believes this significantly large body of people was influential among the laity concerning issues like charity and piety, whereby they might initiate a series of reciprocal exchanges, possibly including themselves, their own chapels, their patrons and the poor; S. Townley, 'Unbeneficed clergy in the thirteenth century' (1991), pp. 38, 55–60.

Everitt has estimated there were 500 parishes and 300 chapels in Kent before the Black Death, which formed part of the diocesan structure for the sees of Canterbury and Rochester.[17] At the apex of this ecclesiastical pyramid was the archbishop of Canterbury, while his less wealthy neighbour, the bishop of Rochester, was his subordinate within the southern province, both seeking to operate independently of their monastic institutions, Christchurch priory and Rochester priory respectively, of which they were the titular head. The archbishop, moreover, was answerable to the pope who, as head of western Christendom, was active in the county as an exchange partner in matters of patronage, jurisdiction, arbitration and almsgiving. Like the papal curia, the archbishop and bishop required an episcopal staff of chaplains and clerks and they, with the diocesan staff of the archdeacon and rural deans, were active participants in the spiritual economy on the church's behalf.

A further group of participants entered Kent in the early thirteenth century. The first friars to settle there were the Franciscans in 1226 and, like the Dominicans, their first friaries were in Canterbury, both houses receiving episcopal support, though only the Dominicans were favoured by the crown.[18] Thereafter, friaries from the different orders were established in seven towns in the county, predominantly during the thirteenth and fourteenth centuries, including one house of Dominican nuns at Dartford.[19] The thirteenth century also saw the foundation of a number of hospitals, but very few new monastic houses.[20]

---

17 A. Everitt, *Continuity and colonization: the evolution of Kentish settlement* (1986), p. 206. Though discussing the ecclesiastical courts of the diocese of Canterbury, Woodcock provides a valuable indicator of the roles of the diocesan staff; B. Woodcock, *Medieval ecclesiastical courts in the diocese of Canterbury* (1952). **18** C. Cotton, *The Grey Friars of Canterbury, 1224–1538* (1924), pp. 6, 44–5, 47; C.F.R. Palmer, 'The Friar-Preachers or Black Friars of Canterbury' (1880), 81–6, 88–9. **19** At Canterbury there were also the Friars of the Sack (short lived, disbanded by 1314) and the Augustinian friars; there were Carmelite friaries at Aylesford, Sandwich and Lossenham; New Romney had a Franciscan friary (also short lived), and there were Trinitarian friars at Mottenden. **20** Hospitals founded or first known in the thirteenth century: Canterbury: Eastbridge (the amalgamation of St Thomas', and St Nicholas and St Katherine's seems to have occurred *c*.1200), St Mary's or the Poor Priests' (founded *c*.1218); Chestnuts: leper hospital (1st known 1256); Dartford: St Bartholomew's (1st known 1315), St Mary Magdalene's (1st known 1256); Dover: St Mary's or the Maison Dieu (founded *c*.1203); Hythe: St Bartholomew's (1st known 1276); Maidstone: St Peter and St Paul's (founded 1260); New Romney: St John's (1st known 1315); Ospringe: St Mary's or the Maison Dieu (possibly refounded *c*.1230), St Nicholas' (1st known 1247); Otford: leper hospital (1st known 1228); Swainestrey in Murston: Holy Cross (1st known 1225), St Leonard's (1st known 1232); Sittingbourne: Shamele (1st known 1216), St Thomas' (1st known *c*.1255); Sandwich: St Antony's (1st known 1315), St John's (1st known 1287); Strood: St Nicholas' (1st known 1253). The history of hospital foundation during the first half of the thirteenth century appears to represent a continuation of the previous century with possibly a rising frequency of foundation, though there are still problems dating some of the hospitals. Such problems were similarly noted by Cullum in her study of Yorkshire hospitals but the broad pattern looks very similar for the two counties; Cullum, 'Hospitals in Yorkshire', p. 51. In part this phenomenon was presumably the result of rising prosperity in these urban settlements, which provided the leading citizens and members of

Although difficult to assess from the surviving evidence, the mendicant lifestyle of the friars may to some extent have channelled benefaction away from some neighbouring hospitals, while other participants in the spiritual economy were similarly continuing to seek gifts from local benefactors and those from further afield.[21] For example, by the late thirteenth century in Canterbury there were four monastic houses, three friaries, seven hospitals, twenty-two parish churches and the internationally important shrine of St Thomas. This 'competition' may partly explain the general pattern of benefaction seen with respect to the hospitals, where most received the highest level of *in vitam* grants during the first century of their existence. Thus, by the time the Statute of Mortmain was enacted in 1279, nearly all of the county's hospitals (excluding the late medieval almshouses) had received the majority of their endowment. Relatively few Kent hospitals received royal licences to alienate land and property during the late middle ages, but it is not clear how effective the Statute was in curbing such giving to the church more generally, and Raban considers those who wished to found ways of circumventing the restrictions.[22]

A small number of hospitals were created in Kent during the fourteenth century, the majority founded by laymen, including two which were expected to aid lepers and other unfortunate persons.[23] The exceptions were Bishop Hamo's two hospitals for the poor in his natal town of Hythe.[24] It is possible a number of small, ephemeral maisondieu-type almshouses were also created during the late fourteenth century, but the absence of surviving testamentary materials from the period means the idea cannot be substantiated.[25] However, the testamentary records from the fifteenth and sixteenth centuries do indicate the formation of

the local knightly families with sufficient assets to be able to support the hospitals, in particular, as part of their charitable strategies in life and at death; R. Britnell, *The commercialisation of English society, 1000–1500* (1993), pp. 79–90, 102–8. It has also been noted, though primarily for post-Reformation society, that the level of aid to the poor is higher when the general living standard is higher; Slack, *Poverty and policy,* pp. 5–6. **21** It is worth remembering that reciprocal exchange networks did not stop at the county, nor at the national boundary. For example, Christchurch priory's connections were principally with mainland Europe, but it was also involved in exchanges relating to its Irish lands. In 1245 an exchange was implemented between the priory and the monks of Tynterne who, in exchange for the priory's Irish lands, were required to provide Christchurch with an annual sum. They also agreed to fulfil all the episcopal demands by supplying certain churches with efficient priests and to execute the obligation previously placed on the priory by the benefaction of the late Herveius de Monte Mauricio, for whom they were to say masses in the church of Bredanus Banarwe; *Royal Commission on Historic Manuscripts,* 5th Report and Appendix, pt I, p. 445. **22** S. Raban, 'Mortmain in medieval England' (1987), pp. 205–7, 224–6. **23** The two late leper houses were at Rochester (founded 1316) and at Boughton under Blean (founded 1384); Thorpe, *Registrum Roffense,* p. 546; *CPR 1381–1385,* p. 448. Other hospitals known to have been founded in the fourteenth century: Sandwich: St Thomas' (founded 1392). **24** Hythe: St Andrew's, later St John's (founded 1336), St Bartholomew's (founded/refounded 1342); C. Johnson (ed.), *Registrum Hamonis Hethe Diocesis Roffensis, 1319–1352* (1948), p. 393; *CPR 1340–1348,* p. 427. **25** Cullum, 'Hospitals in Yorkshire', pp. 318–20, 322–31, 334–44.

a considerable number of these almshouses. Those identified to date provide an idea of the minimum number in Kent because will-survival rates are relatively poor in the Canterbury diocese before the later decades of the fifteenth century, and for the Rochester diocese the only extant wills are from the Consistory court. Interestingly, the almshouses were not confined to the areas in which the older hospitals had been founded. There were a few in the west Kent towns of Lewisham and Lullingstone, and in several of the Wealden towns, like Cranbrook and Goudhurst.[26] Support for the majority of these houses was confined to the founder but very occasionally the almsfolk might receive further small testamentary bequests. Consequently, the formation and support of these almshouses probably did not impinge greatly on the giving of alms generally to the poor.

Looking at the spiritual economy more broadly, the loss of most of the alien houses under Henry V and the decline in the number of parish churches, a consequence of demographic, economic and other factors, was offset by the arrival of other participants.[27] The creation of several colleges of secular canons, the first at Wingham in the late thirteenth century and the last at Ashford in the late fifteenth century; the growing establishment of chantries, in parish churches, hospitals and at religious houses; and the founding of strict Observant (Franciscan) friaries at Greenwich and Canterbury, produced alternative choices by and for benefactors.[28] Even though these initiatives might be considered to relate to piety, in particular to the doctrine of purgatory, the associated idea of salvation through good works remained a cornerstone of orthodox Catholicism. In terms of the spiritual economy, such ideas were important for the individual Christian, but were also significant for groups. Parish fraternities and, from the mid-fifteenth century, craft guilds were involved in pious and charitable activities, though only the Corpus Christi guild at Maidstone appears to have had its own almshouse, and the only guild known to have been associated with a Kent hospital was the Corpus Christi guild at St Thomas' hospital in Canterbury.[29] Civic involvement, however, was far more widespread, especially at the Cinque Ports, where a number of hospitals were under the patronage of the mayor and jurats.[30]

The other important secular institution was the crown, of which the greatest participant was the king either directly or through one of the departments of the royal household, like the exchequer.[31] In addition, other members of the royal

26 Sweetinburgh, 'Hospital in Kent, pp. 22–4. **27** At New Romney, for example, the town's economic problems and the fall in population meant that the townsfolk were no longer able to support all the parish churches. Even though there were still four in 1500, St John's was in a particularly poor state, and St Nicholas' had become the town church by 1530. **28** The other colleges were at Cobham (founded mid-fourteenth century), Bredgar (founded late fourteenth century), Maidstone (founded from the assets of the hospital of St Peter and St Paul in 1395) and Wye (mid-fifteenth century). Ashford college was in existance during the late fifteenth and early sixteenth centuries, but it is difficult to establish its history. **29** J. Russell, *The history of Maidstone* (1881), p. 165; CKS, PRC 17/15, f. 101. **30** See, in particular, chapter 4. **31** See the history of St Mary's

family engaged in almsgiving on their own behalf, for example when they travelled through the county between London and mainland Europe; their staff were similarly active establishing networks of reciprocity. This same pattern of large numbers of participants with the king at the apex and royal servants at the bottom was applicable for foreign royalty, like the king of France, but might also apply to the households of the English aristocracy, the wealthiest townsmen and certain knights.[32] For the Kent hospitals, the level and type of support they received from such benefactors varied considerably over time, few houses succeeding in maintaining links with their founder except those under royal, episcopal or civic patronage.[33] Yet, although continuity might have provided certain advantages, it appears that the welfare, or at least survival, of most hospitals before the Reformation was primarily a product of the level and type of benefactions they had received during their early history and the later management of the house.[34] For some of the small hospitals, which seem to have disappeared during the late fifteenth and early sixteenth centuries, their inability to survive was probably a product of meagre resources and lack of flexibility.[35] In a few cases, like St Mary's hospital at Ospringe, problems associated with poor management and difficulties over personnel left the house vulnerable to appropriation by founders of the new Oxford and Cambridge colleges, though often a single priest continued to serve at the old hospital.[36] Consequently, by the early 1530s a large proportion of the hospitals in the Rochester region had gone, in part replaced by the small

hospital in chapter 3. **32** In 1360, for example, the king of France on his way back to his realm after captivity in England donated alms to St Mary's hospital, Ospringe, while he was staying there; C. Drake, 'The hospital of St Mary of Ospringe commonly called Maison Dieu' (1914), 53. **33** The problems of a lack of long-term support from the founder and his family may be exemplified by the case of St Stephen and St Thomas' hospital in New Romney, where the de Charing family were apparently no longer supporting the hospital within a couple of generations of its foundation. As a consequence, it was appropriated by the Frauncey and Brenchley families, becoming little more than a chantry chapel until they too disappeared, allowing the house and its lands to become part of Bishop Waynflete's endowment for his new Oxford college; Satchell, 'Leper-houses in medieval England', pp. 192–4. **34** Although there were charges of mis-management brought against a number of houses in Kent, leading in the case of St Mary's hospital at Strood to its being placed under the jurisdiction of Rochester priory by Bishop Hamo of Rochester, the worst abuses appear to have taken place at St Mary's hospital, Ospringe; Johnson, *Registrum Hamonis,* vol. 1, pp. 4–5; Drake, 'The hospital of St Mary of Ospringe', 58–9. **35** This may have been especially true for the leper hospitals once the incidence of leprosy declined, but was also the case for other types of hospital. Although the earlier status of St Mary's hospital at Milton is ambiguous, it was refounded as a chantry for Sir Henry Wyatt in 1524 (an inquisition of that year reported that all the priests there had died), while St Thomas' hospital at Sittingbourne was recorded as a free chapel in the chantry certificates; *L. and P. Henry VIII,* vol. 4, 297 (1); Hussey, *Kent chantries,* p. 293. **36** After Magdalen College appropriated St Stephen and St Thomas' hospital at New Romney, it still seems to have made provision for a priest to serve at the chapel until at least the 1480s and possibly later; Butcher, 'St Stephen and St Thomas', 24. Similarly, St John's College, Cambridge apparently continued to maintain a priest at St Mary's hospital in Ospringe when it acquired the place because Richard Stukney, the priest there, made his will in 1543; CKS, PRC 17/23, f. 120.

almshouses, and these, with the few remaining earlier hospitals, were predominantly small houses accommodating the poor and infirm on a long-term basis.[37] Considerably more hospitals were still present in the Canterbury region, including most of the pre-Black Death foundations, though, as in the north west of the county, it was the small, early leper hospitals that had disappeared.[38] The hospitals at the two cathedral cities and at the Cinque Ports had almost all survived, but the Canterbury diocese visitation in 1511 indicated that there were significant problems at certain hospitals and these early warning signs of impending crisis may suggest that a number would have disappeared anyway.[39]

The loss of the monastic houses in Kent, Becket's shrine and the reformation of the two cathedral priories under a dean and chapter at Rochester and Canterbury were an inevitable part of the changes which took place during the 1530s and 1540s. However, it is more difficult to gauge the degree of support for such measures among the people of Kent, though Clark is probably correct in his assessment concerning the presence of anticlericalism in the county.[40] What is less clear is the degree of anticlericalism, the form it was likely to take and the prevalence of orthodox and heterodox belief in the different regions within the county.[41] Furthermore, with respect to the survival of the hospitals, the significance of lay, often civic, patronage seems to have been a decisive factor. Often relatively small, these poorly to moderately endowed hospitals were perceived to be valuable town assets by the local leading citizens. In part, their concern to preserve such local charitable institutions was a direct consequence of the new, as it had been of the old, Christian doctrine, but at a time of increasing economic and social difficulties the hospitals formed part of the official response, however inadequate, to deal with the growing numbers of poor people. Thus, even though there were a number of notable casualties, like the hospitals of St Mary at Dover and at Strood, St Bartholomew's hospital at Dover, and several

---

37 For example, there were at least three houses operating in Dartford at some point over the period: the old leper house of St Mary Magdalene, Milett's almshouse and the hospital near the bridge. **38** The Cinque Ports of Hythe and Sandwich seem to have lost their leper hospitals, while the late fourteenth-century leper hospital at Boughton under Blean had apparently disappeared. **39** St James' hospital at Canterbury was only housing the prioress and four sisters, the majority of whom were extremely old and no new members had been recruited for three years. Such a situation may not have been surprising, because the prioress was in dispute with the sisters, Christchurch priory was not supplying the hospital as it should, and the house was suffering from a poor reputation, which was not helped by the setting up of a beer stall in the precincts by Richard Welles' wife; K. Wood-Legh (ed.) *Kentish visitations of Archbishop William Warham and his deputies, 1511–12* (1984), p. 12. **40** P. Clark, *English provincial society from the Reformation to the Revolution* (1977), pp. 28–31. **41** Interest in religious matters did not stop at the hospital gate. At St Bartholomew's hospital in Chatham, Thomas Batman, the former prior, was twice accused of being a heretic (1524 and 1525), and on the latter occasion he was imprisoned in the bishop's palace; J. Davis, *Heresy and Reformation in the south-east of England, 1520–1559* (1983), pp. 41–2. According to investigators, in 1543 certain inmates at St John's hospital, Canterbury, had connections with well-known heretics, while others there witnessed against heretics; *L. and P. Henry VIII*, vol. 18, pp. 291, 312, 345, 366.

Canterbury hospitals, the distribution pattern of hospitals in the county did not alter dramatically between the fourteenth and sixteenth centuries.[42] In addition, the type of resident inmate probably did not change much either between the fourteenth century hospital and the Elizabethan almshouse.[43] Those who did lose their places were the priest brothers who, like the monks, nuns and friars, were no longer needed to fulfil intercessory roles. For the benefactors of Elizabethan Kent, therefore, their priorities with respect to the spiritual economy had changed, but a large percentage of the county's hospitals were able to bridge the gap between Catholicism and Protestantism.

KENT HOSPITALS

The leper hospitals

1	foundation	range late 11th–late 14th century; *12th century*
2	founders	*senior churchmen, religious houses, laymen*
3	foundation gift	variable; *relatively poorly endowed*
4	size	under ten to a hundred; *about thirteen to fifteen*
5	inmates	*laymen and women, priests,* monks
6	patronage	*archiepiscopal, monastic, lay*
7	own chapel	*yes*
8	*in vitam* grants	*small to moderate number, local, within century of foundation; lay donors*; few grants in late middle ages
9	diversification from the 14th century	*non-lepers* (including the sick-poor), *corrodians, chantry,* lepers
10	casual alms	*variable*; probably important at some hospitals
11	testamentary benefactors	*very variable, clusters over time, predominantly local, explicit reciprocity,* (masses, prayers, corrodies)

It is not clear from whence Archbishop Lanfranc drew his inspiration to found the large hospitals of St Nicholas and St John, but in seeking to help the disadvantaged, especially the leprous, he was extending his pastoral care to one of the most marginal groups in society.[44] Bishop Gundulf, his friend at Rochester, soon

---

42 Sweetinburgh, 'Hospital in Kent', pp. 64–8. **43** Inmates at the hospitals of St John, Canterbury, and St Bartholomew, Sandwich, continued to make wills throughout the sixteenth century, suggesting that such people were at least moderately wealthy townspeople. In an inquiry into St Bartholomew's hospital in 1587 it was stated that although most of the inmates were old and impotent, some were young, held property outside the hospital and had paid large entry fees; *VCH Kent*, vol. 2, p. 226. **44** The monk Eadmer, writing between 1095 and 1123, provides a valuable description of the two hospitals as well as an indication of their part in Lanfranc's plans for his cathedral city; G. Bosanquet (trans.), *Eadmer's History of recent events in England* (1964), p. 16. Satchell suggests that there were similar developments in parts of France, especially in Normandy, 'Leper-houses in medieval England', p. 243, n. 5.

followed his example, and Lanfranc's successors at the Canterbury see may subsequently have established a few leper hospitals.[45] During the twelfth century, this episcopal initiative was taken up by a second group of founders, members of monastic houses, who provided hospitals for those among the general populace suffering from leprosy and, more occasionally, for lepers from their own communities.[46] A few laymen are known to have become involved in the creation of leper houses during the same period, members of knightly families and possibly a number of townsmen, some of whom may have acted collectively.[47] By the early thirteenth century, the majority of the county's leper hospitals had been established and, even though the surviving records are far from complete, the foundation pattern where most towns had at least one leper hospital appears to have held true for both east and north Kent.[48] Thereafter, very few new leper hospitals were founded in either region, and none were said to be exclusively for lepers.[49]

As elsewhere in England, Kent's leper hospitals were located on the margins of urban areas, but there is little evidence of rural leper colonies like those found in Cornwall by Orme and Webster.[50] In terms of recent scholarship, it is not clear whether founders in Kent were seeking to isolate the leprous for the benefit of

---

45 R.A.L. Smith, 'The place of Gundulf in the Anglo-Norman church' (1943), 258–66; Satchell, 'Leper-houses in medieval England', p. 121. Although there is no evidence concerning the lepers of Otford before 1228, their house was close to an important archiepiscopal residence and they received payment from the archbishops of Canterbury as fixed alms, which suggests that the house was an archiepiscopal foundation; *CLibR* 1226–1240, p. 110. 46 In 1141, two brothers, monks at Dover priory, sought to establish a hospital nearby; Bodleian, Rawlinson MS. B. 335, recto of the second unnumbered folio at the beginning of the cartulary. At St Laurence's hospital, Canterbury, the foundation charter and other details were written up in the hospital's register and at St Augustine's abbey the foundation of the daughter hospital was recorded in the narrative history of the abbey compiled by William Thorne; CCAL, DCc/Lit. MS. C20, pp. 9–10, 34; Davis, *Thorne's Chronicle*, pp. 85–6. 47 According to the late fourteenth-century cartulary for St James' hospital, Canterbury, the land for the hospital site had been given by Godefrid of Malling. This grant must predate 1166 (and his death), because in that year his daughter held property in Canterbury; BL, Add MS. 32098, f. 1; W. Urry, *Canterbury under the Angevin kings* (1967), pp. 53–4. Of the leper houses at the Kentish Cinque Ports, laymen were probably founders or early benefactors at Hythe and New Romney. It seems likely that the reference to the sick of Saltwood, who had been given a grant of land worth 34s. 8d. per year by Robert de Vere in the time of Henry I (recorded in the pipe roll of 1168–9), concerns the leper community at Hythe, a community that may have been established (or aided) by one of Lanfranc's successors, close to the archiepiscopal castle of Saltwood; *PR* 15 Henry II, p. 111. The leper house dedicated to St Stephen and St Thomas at New Romney may have been founded by Adam de Charing, who also had property in Canterbury and had connections with Becket; Satchell, 'Leper-houses of medieval England', pp. 344–5; Butcher, 'St Stephen and St Thomas', 18–19; W. Urry, 'Two notes on Guernes de Pont Sainte-Maxence: Vie de Saint Thomas' (1953), 92–5. 48 See figure 3. 49 St Katherine's hospital, Rochester, was founded by Simon Potyn, a local leading citizen, in 1316, and the hospital dedicated to the Holy Trinity at Boughton under Blean, founded 1384, was the gift of Thomas atte Herst; Thorpe, *Registrum Roffense*, p. 546; *CPR* 1381–1385, p. 448. 50 Orme and Webster, *English hospital*, pp. 170–5.

the wider community, or to separate a group who were thought to have gained certain spiritual merit through their affliction.[51] Such considerations were presumably an important part of the decision-making process, but founders may also have wished to site their hospital nearby. In part, this was a consequence of the location of the founder's landholdings, but also may have been seen as a means of underlining spatially the link between donor and recipient.[52] For example, at Canterbury, Lanfranc's hospital was outside the city walls in the neighbouring village of Harbledown, and St Laurence's hospital was, like its parent institution St Augustine's abbey, in Canterbury's southern suburbs. The city's third leper house, St James' at Thanington, bordered the city's Worthgate ward and was on land given by Godefrid de Malling, whose family held and continued to hold land in the area. Moreover, the first master and reputed founder was Master Feramin, a local physician and member of the archbishop's household, who may have been instrumental in the transfer of the patronage of the hospital to Christchurch priory.[53] The situation was slightly different at Rochester. Although Gundulf's lazar house of St Bartholomew was close to his cathedral city, it was located just outside the walls in Chatham, and the later (early fourteenth century) lay founder of St Katherine's hospital was a local citizen. Nothing is known about the foundation of St Nicholas' hospital across the river at Strood.[54]

51 Satchell provides an interesting and balanced discussion concerning contemporary attitudes about lepers during the twelfth and thirteenth centuries; Satchell, 'Leper-houses in medieval England', pp. 22–39. Even though urban bye-laws against lepers and against begging were relatively common this may in part reflect the inability of the local civic authorities to remove them from the town and its suburbs which suggests the leper with his begging bowl remained a feature of medieval society; P. Richards, *Medieval leper and his northern heirs* (1977), pp. 50–51, 55; Rawcliffe, *Hospitals of Norwich*, pp. 38–40, 52–53. The idea of confining the lepers as a way of protecting society was stated to be the purpose of St Nicholas' hospital, Canterbury, in 1276; *CChR 1257–1300*, p. 199.   **52** For Hugh, abbot of St Augustine's abbey, the establishment of a leper hospital close by might be perceived as a way to increase the standing and public awareness of his own institution, at a time when such long established monastic communities as St Augustine's were seeking to consolidate their social and economic ties with the local citizens. Even though the hospital's register was produced in the late fourteenth century, it seems likely both houses would have had a record of their relationship, a testimony of the pastoral and charitable actions of the Benedictine house; CCAL, DCc/Lit. MS. C20, pp. 9–10, 34; Davis, *Thorne's Chronicle*, pp. 85–6. M. Gibson, 'Normans and Angevins, 1070–1220' (1995), pp. 56–7.   **53** Master Feramin was named as the founder of the hospital in the late fourteenth-century cartulary, but this may not be strictly accurate, BL, Add MS. 32098, f. 1; Hussey, *Kent chantries*, p. 80. However, his close association with the house was well known, and when Feramin became involved in the dispute between Archbishop Baldwin and Christchurch priory over the archbishop's plans for a secular college at Hackington, the sisters at St James' were physically attacked by several pro-monastic Canterbury citizens; Urry, *Angevin kings*, pp. 158, 165–7.   **54** In his will dated 1316 Simon Potyn, the keeper of the Crown Inn at Rochester and a leading member of the town government, left a house to be used as a hospital for male and female lepers and 'other pouer mendicants' of Rochester; Thorpe, *Registrum Roffense*, p. 546. The first known reference to St Nicholas' hospital, Strood, is a grant of protection dated 1253; *CPR 1247–1258*, p. 194.

The form of the foundation gift varied considerably, being linked to a number of factors, but in most instances founders provided a site and presumably a minimum of some shelter for the lepers, though others were able or wished to be more generous. In such cases they provided a number of buildings, often including a chapel, more occasionally a specialist staff to care for the spiritual and physical needs of the lepers, and an income.[55] Consequently, most leper hospitals in both regions probably had a chapel, even though the majority predate the Lateran Council directive of 1179, where it was stated that leper houses were expected to have their own chapel and burial ground, as long as they did not impinge on the rights of the local parish church.[56] Land, in addition to the hospital site, was a common endowment gift, but a few founders appear to have provided rights or goods, and Lanfranc gave £70 annually from the revenues of the Canterbury see.[57]

Patronage was frequently held by the founder and his successors, a position that brought responsibility as well as power. In addition to the selection of the inmates, patrons also chose the master and other officers at the hospital, providing them with the opportunity to aid clients, return favours and receive gifts on behalf of the hospital or themselves, as at St James' hospital, Canterbury, in *c.*1280.[58] Moreover, their power might similarly be expressed through the withholding of places, especially when those petitioning were of high status.[59] Such

---

[55] Few, if any, founders could match Lanfranc's endowment of St Nicholas' hospital; Bosanquet, *Eadmer's History*, p. 16. Gundulf's much more modest endowment of St Bartholomew's hospital, Chatham, meant that the house was dependent on the munificence of Rochester priory from early in its history; Greenwood, *Hospital of St Bartholomew*, pp. 11–12. [56] Satchell, 'Leper-houses in medieval England', pp. 29–31. [57] During vacancies, St Nicholas' hospital did sometimes experience difficulties in gaining its annual award of revenue from the archbishop's estates. To try to remedy the situation Archbishop Kilwardy, in 1276, granted Reculver church to Lanfranc's two hospitals, but this was seen as unacceptable by the parishioners, who were unwilling to be put under the lepers. The resulting disagreement was prolonged and acrimonious, forcing Archbishop Peckham to revoke the grant, though it is likely that the dispute was not forgotten by the parishioners, who were presumably loath to enter into any form of gift exchange with the hospital in the future. Unfortunately little documentary evidence survives, but from the fragments it appears that the real grievance was monetary. The parishioners found themselves supporting the hospital and maintaining the whole fabric of Reculver church, at a time when the spiritual services available to the parish were severely reduced; *CChR* 1257–1300, p. 199; R. Graham, 'Sidelights on the rectors and parishioners of Reculver from the register of Archbishop Winchelsey' (1944), 1–3. [58] In this case the archdeacon wrote to Thomas, prior of Christchurch, on behalf of Denis de Yldallegate for a place to be found at St James' hospital, Canterbury for the daughter of John de Somery, possibly his ward, and even though the letter does not detail the provision of any gifts it was presumably implicit in the terms of the petition; CCAL, DCc/EC IV/74. There seems to be considerable confusion about the processes involved in the diagnosis of leprosy and the likelihood that the person involved would enter a leper hospital, though it is generally agreed that by the later medieval period physicians were more likely to examine those accused of having the disease; Richards, *Medieval leper*, pp. 40–1, 48–53, 59; L. Demaitre, 'The description and diagnosis of leprosy by fourteenth-century physicians' (1985), 340–3. [59] Queen Philippa's attempt to gain a place for her nominee at St James' hospital, Canterbury may suggest she considered such favours were available at a price

instances may also indicate the types of petitioners favoured by patrons, and the relationship between those seeking places and the perceived needs of the hospital in terms of a viable and sustainable community.

Occasionally, founders or their successors provided further gifts, but most *in vitam* grants the leper hospital received came from other benefactors. The level of benefaction differed considerably between hospitals, and there seems little correlation with the size of the original endowment. Instead, the particular circumstance of the hospital appears to have been the decisive factor, probably because the majority of the donors were from the local town or its hinterland, or had some other connection or knowledge of the house. Even though the records of some leper houses are poor or non-existent, it seems likely that few were as generously supported as St Laurence's hospital at Canterbury.[60] Rather, the twenty grants the hospital of St Stephen and St Thomas at New Romney received might represent a more typical level of benefaction.[61] For most hospitals, the vast majority of this gift-giving took place within the first century of their existence, which meant that in most cases houses received few grants after the mid-thirteenth century.[62] As elsewhere, national circumstances were impor-

from the prior of Christchurch. On this occasion, however, he was apparently unwilling to enter into this form of exchange, which may imply that he judged her offer was insufficient. It is possible others were also seeking the place, candidates whom he may have felt, for a variety of reasons, were more deserving; J.B. Sheppard (ed.), *Literae Cantuarienses*, vol. 2 (1888), p. 282.   **60** According to the late fourteenth-century cartulary, the hospital acquired about seventy grants of land, rents and other gifts. Most concerned land and property in the city itself and the surrounding area of Wincheap, Thanington and Sturry; CCAL, DCc/Lit. MS. C20, pp. 72–3, 76–7, 87–90. St Bartholomew's hospital at Dover, another house under monastic patronage, received about fifty grants, most were rents or small plots of land in the countryside to the north of Dover; Bodleian, Rawlinson MS. B. 335, ff. 11v–95v. Lanfranc's leper hospital was also well supported, though it is difficult to trace when it received its holdings. The most accurate records are at Lambeth Palace library and in Duncombe and Battely, but even these are incomplete (comparing the witnesses, the early undated charters appear to date from the early thirteenth century); LPL, Lambeth MSS 1131 and 1132; J. Duncombe and N. Battely, *The history and antiquities of the three archiepiscopal hospitals* (1785), pp. 204–9, 236–40, 241–9.   **61** Charters relating to the New Romney hospital are now held by Magdalen College, Oxford, the college received the hospital's muniments when the house's assets were transferred by Waynflete, bishop of Winchester, to his new foundation; Satchell, 'Leper-houses in medieval England', pp. 189–96. St Leonard's hospital at Swainestrey appears to have received very little support in the form of *in vitam* grants (at least before 1232), though its location in the vicinity of the main route from London to Canterbury may have meant casual alms was its primary source of income; CChR vol. 1, p. 168. However, its apparently precarious financial state may have resulted in its early demise and its amalgamation with the neighbouring hospital of Holy Cross, a house which had slightly greater assets and seems to have been under the patronage of the local manorial lord of Murston; R. Griffin, 'The lepers' hospital at Swainestrey' (1920), 62, 67–78.   **62** The practice of housing the leprous and non-leprous in the same hospital (though with a degree of segregation) appears to have been seen as acceptable by hospital authorities throughout the medieval period which may have influenced some potential benefactors. For example, a grant of 1249 addressed those at St Bartholomew's hospital, Chatham, as 'pauperes et leprosi santi

tant, like the Statute of Mortmain of 1279.[63] But for the Canterbury leper hospitals, for example, the founding of two friaries in the city during the 1220s and the subsequent establishment of other mendicant houses in the region may have had a detrimental effect on the aid these hospitals received.[64] Initially, however, support for the leper houses was relatively high, most received their first grants shortly after the house's foundation.[65] Early benefactors will be considered later in the chapter, but it is worth noting here that the pattern of benefaction saw clusters of grants linked by location, possibly a consequence of the influence of the hospital authorities, others associated with the house or previous benefactors.[66] Unfortunately, unlike the east Kent region, there are few surviving sources for the leper hospitals in the Rochester diocese, but there may have been considerable similarities between the benefaction patterns of the two regions.

Yet even those few leper hospitals which had received relatively substantial assets were pleading poverty by the early fourteenth century.[67] Again, the particular circumstances of the hospital were important with regard to the chronology of the house's financial problems, but by this period most were seeking tax exemption or permission to send out proctors to gather alms.[68] Others adopted more radical measures in an attempt to counter the detrimental conditions, conditions that probably became increasingly difficult after the Black Death. As a consequence,

---

Bartholomei extra Roffam'; F. Smith, *A history of Rochester* (1928), p. 457. Furthermore, even those leper hospitals which continued to house only the leprous were suffering from a fall-off in support, like St Nicholas' hospital, Canterbury; *CChR* 1257–1300, p. 199. Though looking at monasteries, not hospitals, Thompson's observations on the changes in perception of what donors expected from their recipient institution may also be applicable here; B. Thompson, 'Monasteries and their patrons at foundation and dissolution' (1994), 108. **63** Some hospital benefactors appear to have tried to ignore the Statute of Mortmain in order to save the fee and the problems of seeking royal approval which meant, for example, that the prior at St Nicholas' hospital, Canterbury, was required to seek a royal pardon for the hospital in 1412 with respect to a considerable number of property and land grants it had received; *CPR* 1408–1413, p. 406. **64** It is possible the hospitals at Sandwich were affected similarly; *VCH Kent*, vol. 2, pp. 177, 190; See chapter 4. **65** Even though there was considerable variation among the hospitals, both within each region and between the regions, in broad terms it appears the leper hospitals were more likely to receive a larger number of *in vitam* grants compared to the hospitals for the poor. **66** S. Sweetinburgh, 'Supporting the Canterbury hospitals' (2002), 237–58. **67** St Nicholas' hospital, Canterbury, sought tax exemption from the crown because of the poor state of the house; *CPR* 1334–1338, p. 184. In 1342 an inquiry was held at St Bartholomew's hospital, Chatham, where it was stated that the hospital had three acres near the hospital, one and a half acres of salt marsh in Chatham, half an acre of wood at Boxley, various rents in cash and kind, and gifts of specific alms from three religious houses. Yet after it had paid dues to certain religious houses its income was insufficient to sustain the charitable work of the house; Greenwood, *Hospital of St Bartholomew*, pp. 16–19. **68** Interestingly, the main cluster of royal letters of protection was in the 1250s: St Nicholas', Canterbury (1251), St Nicholas', Rochester (1253), St Leonard's, Swainestrey (1232 and 1253), St Mary Magdalene's, Dartford (1256 and 1263), leper hospital at Chestnuts (1256), and St Nicholas', Ospringe (1247), St James', Canterbury (1231), St Stephen and St Thomas', New Romney (1232).

the move to accept poorer people, paying guests and pensioners sent by patrons (corrodians), and/or the expansion of chantry facilities may have preceded the second, even smaller, cluster of *in vitam* grants received by a few leper houses.[69] Where such grants occurred, they seem to have begun in the early/mid-fourteenth century and continued into the following century. In terms of exchange and reciprocity, the grants may have reinforced the viability of the hospital rather than initiated it, which was claimed in some refoundation charters.[70] These later donors apparently made more explicit demands on the recipient hospital compared to their earlier counterparts, a reflection of changing attitudes towards the three-fold obligations – to God, to one's neighbour and to oneself – where there was a growing emphasis on the duty to oneself.[71] In part, this was a response to the growing influence of the doctrine of purgatory and the consequent desire for greater intercessory services; services that the leper hospital might provide, but which previously may primarily have been provided by other religious institutions.[72] The other adaptation, the supplying of corrodies, became increasingly important at certain hospitals, especially once the incidence of leprosy began to decline.[73]

Testamentary benefactors and the later *in vitam* grantors apparently attempted to develop similar relationships with their chosen leper hospital, the timing of

---

69 However, at certain hospitals such changes were not always easy to impliment. As late as the early fifteenth century, the continuing presence of lepers at the hospital might cause considerable tension between the various exchange partners when patrons wished the hospital to adopt a new role. For example, in 1402 the authorities' desire to appoint a chantry priest at St Nicholas' hospital, Canterbury, was thrawted because potential candidates were concerned about the presence of lepers; CCAL, U39/2/K. **70** The absence of lepers at the New Romney hospital in the mid-fourteenth century was cited as the reason for its decay; *CPR* 1361–1364, p. 481. Yet, if Butcher's analysis of the later history of the Romney hospital is correct, other factors were probably more important, an assessment which may be applicable more widely with regard to the chronological changes in hospital function; Butcher, 'St Stephen and St Thomas', 25. **71** Clay identified this three-part spiritual duty in the charters benefactors made with their chosen institution and it provides a useful simple division when considering gift exchange in the spiritual economy; Clay, *Hospitals of England*, p. 85. **72** The presence at St Nicholas' hospital, Canterbury, of a mazer (probably early fourteenth century) with a silver medallion showing Guy of Warwick (the Beauchamp arms are on his shield) slaying a dragon suggests that it was given to the house by a member of the Beauchamp family; V.B. Richmond, *The legend of Guy of Warwick* (1996), pp. 91, 106. The family held land in Kent, and Sir John de Beauchamp, in 1368, had sought to establish a chantry for his soul, those of his parents and brother at Canterbury cathedral (the prior at Christchurch considered Sir John's gift was insufficient to warrant the assignment of one of the monks, who was to wear vestments decorated with the family arms, to sing mass at the altar of Our Lady in the crypt of the cathedral); Sheppard, *Literae Cantuarienses*, vol. 2, pp. 485–7, 489. However, the mazer may form part of a gift exchange between St Nicholas' hospital and the earl of Warwick, Sir John's nephew, who intended to make other arrangements on behalf of his uncle's soul if the prior of Christchurch was unwilling to undertake the commission; ibid., pp. 487–9. **73** According to the hospital register (compiled in 1373), new inmates at St Bartholomew's, Dover, were expected to provide an entry fee; Bodleian, Rawlinson MS. B. 335, f. 2v. Though considerably later, there is evidence to suggest that St Katherine's hospital, Rochester, was housing corrodians in the fifteenth century; DRb/Pwr5, f. 169v.

most will-making, close to death, adding a greater urgency to secure spiritual rewards and services in this world for the benefit of the testator's soul in the next. As one provider of such services amongst many, leper hospitals faced severe competition, the more prestigious houses frequently receiving greater support, especially when additional intercessory services were offered.[74] This is most clearly seen by examining the experiences of the Canterbury hospitals and those in the Medway towns, but St Bartholomew's hospital at Hythe is a rare example of a leper hospital in a small town which was relatively successful, possibly a consequence of its refoundation in the mid-fourteenth century.[75]

The provision of accommodation for either potential donors or their dependants was another counter-gift offered by certain leper hospitals. The decline in the incidence of leprosy meant some leper houses were increasingly looking to house the poor and the not-so-poor as a way of producing revenue, the corrodian or his sponsor paying an entry fee. Although such transactions had been forbidden at St Nicholas' hospital, Canterbury, in Archbishop Winchelsey's revised statutes of 1299, these regulations were apparently being disregarded by the fifteenth century (if not earlier), a position that may mirror the experience of leper hospitals more generally.[76] Thus men like Richard Wekys of Canterbury

---

[74] The bequests in William Benet's will suggest that he was aware of these considerations. He gave 100s. to the hospital at Harbledown for the provision of a good priest to sing and pray for a number of named souls, including his own, at the hospital's chapel, and bequests of 2d. to each of the brothers and sisters there. In addition, the brothers and sisters (as poor people of God) were to receive linen shirts and smocks; CKS, PRC 17/1, f. 114. His will is undated but his death was recorded by John Stone in his chronicle for 1463. He was a wealthy citizen and leading member of the corporation (he had held office as bailiff on six occasions and was the city's second mayor in 1450). He was a parishioner at St Andrew's, one of the city centre churches, and in his will he sought to be remembered there through the performance of his obit on the morrow after the feast of St Edmund, king and martyr. Several other acts of commemoration and intercession for his soul were to be performed in the city's churches, other churches and religious houses. He also sought to be remembered and commemorated as a consequence of his aid to the city, including the paving of the street from St Andrew's to the pillory; C. Cotton, 'Churchwardens' accounts of the parish of St Andrew, Canterbury, AD 1485–1509' (1917), 188–91. **75** The later history of St Bartholomew's hospital is difficult to trace. The leper hospital was said to be in existence in 1336, the year Bishop Hamo founded his first hospital in the town and it received an indulgence from Archbishop Langham in 1368; A.C. Wood (trans. and ed.), *Registrum Simonis Langham* (1956), p. 192. However, by this date Hamo had founded a second hospital in Hythe, which appears to have taken the dedication to St Bartholomew at some point in its early history, thereby appropriating the place of the old leper hospital. From the Hythe town archive it appears that the new or refounded hospital was far better supported (there are thirty-five grants dated between c.1320 and c.1500) than its neighbour, St John's hospital, though the latter does seem to have held a relatively large acreage to the north-west of the town (see Hythe hospital map, dated 1684); EKA, hbarth 22d, 27, 30–1, 34, 37–8, 40–8, 50–1, 53, 56, 58, 60–1, 63–9, 71 [transcription provided by A.F. Butcher]; G.M. Livett, 'West Hythe church and the sites of churches formerly existing in Hythe' *Arch. Cant.*, 30 (1914), 259. **76** R. Graham (trans. and ed.), *Registrum Roberti Winchelsey* (1956), p. 831; Duncombe and Battely, *Three archiepiscopal hospitals*, pp. 211–13. Those ignoring the ruling

were able to provide for their servants by bequeathing a sum of money sufficient to gain them a place at St Nicholas' hospital.[77] These entry fees were useful
additional funds, but for the hospital authorities at most of the old leper hospitals, the house's financial viability in the long-term remained marginal, being
dependent on a range of complex issues.[78] In addition to internal factors, like
the ratio of fee-paying to non-fee-paying residents, the life expectancy of the
different groups of inmates, the type and value of the hospital's assets and the
number and employment of the priest brothers, external factors, though completely outside its control, were similarly significant. As a result, the leper hospital needed to maximize, where possible, all potential sources of income to meet
the house's various commitments.

The collection of casual alms, therefore, may have been essential for the survival of certain leper hospitals, but for most remained a valuable but erratic source
of income. In addition to having almsboxes at the hospital gate and in the chapel,
possibly in association with the relics or shrines there, most hospital authorities
adopted a pro-active approach. This might simply be the employment of the
brothers to solicit for alms actively from passers-by, a probably particularly lucrative approach where the house was sited alongside a pilgrimage route or main
thoroughfare.[79] Other methods included the promise of an indulgence to those
who visited and gave alms to the hospital and the sending out of proctors or the
hospital brothers, a device used by St Bartholomew's hospital, Dover, to gather
alms locally and more widely.[80] These men were able to offer indulgences and

included Winchelsey' successors and the prior at Christchurch when the see was vacant. Corrodians
who entered St Nicholas' hospital through the patronage of the prior have been listed by Hussy
from the Christchurch registers; A. Hussey, 'Hospitals of Kent' (1909), 417–8.   **77** He does not
appear to have had any connections with the hospital at Harbledown, but he believed his maidservant, Alice, could become a sister at the hospital if he provided 33s. 4d. for her place; CKS,
PRC 32/2, f. 238.   **78** Mismanagement was also an issue, though the evidence of such problems
is relatively limited. One hospital which did suffer in this way was St James', Canterbury. In 1415
the prior at Christchurch issued new ordinances to try to halt the house's financial difficulties.
These included the provision that the hospital chest should have three locks. The prioress was to
hold one key, the other two were to be held by the cellaress and another of the sisters; the prioress was to appoint a deputy if she was away from the house for as much as a day; she was not
to spend more than 20s. without consulting the brothers and sisters; and these and the other rules
were to be read to the community six times a year; Duncombe and Battely, *Three archiepiscopal
hospitals*, pp. 431–4.   **79** Nicholas Glover was recorded as 'custodian of the gate' at St Nicholas'
hospital, Canterbury, in 1479; CKS, PRC 32/2, f. 465. He may still have been there when Colet
was stopped on his way to Becket's shrine and was expected to give alms and kiss a stone reputed
to have come from the saint's shoe, one of the hospital's prized relics; J.G. Nichols (trans.), *Desiderius
Erasmus' pilgrimages to Saint Mary of Walsingham and Saint Thomas of Canterbury* (1875), pp. 53–4;
Orme and Webster, *English hospital*, p. 47.   **80** For example, St Bartholomew's hospital at Dover
had received grants from Archbishop Theobald (an indulgence of twenty days) and from Richard
bishop of Chichester in 1252 (an indulgence of twenty days); Bodleian, Rawlinson MS. B.335, ff.
5v, 7v.

the intercessory prayers of the grateful hospital community to potential benefactors, which in the case of St Nicholas' hospital, in the late fourteenth century, meant the daily provision of 4,000 Pater Nosters, Ave Marias and Credos.[81]
For the donors their motives cannot be recovered but like the other forms of
giving, it seems likely their motives might be seen as political, charitable, and/or
devotional, where benefactors saw themselves entering into a moral contract
with the hospital.[82]

Yet for certain leper hospitals, the counter-gifts they were able to provide
were insufficient or did not attract the degree of support necessary to sustain the
life of the hospital. Consequently, by the late fifteenth century a substantial
number of the county's leper hospitals, especially those from north Kent, had
disappeared or had become little more than chantry chapels.[83] This fate too had
befallen some hospitals in the Cinque Port towns and in both regions the most
viable leper hospitals were in the two cathedral cities. This was a reflection of
their greater size and endowment, and their ability to adapt to changing social,
economic and religious conditions.[84] The hospitals of St James and St Laurence,
however, were unable to survive the Reformation, their links with the local
Benedictine abbeys probably ultimately led to their dissolution. The remainder,

---

81 A letter, dated 1398, stated that the eighty brothers and sisters at St Nicholas' hospital would
offer these prayers to any who provided a penny or its worth, or even a halfpenny; Duncombe and
Battely, *Three archiepiscopal hospitals*, pp. 203, 255.   **82** Such gift exchanges were not confined to
individuals and the hospital, but might also take place between institutions. St Bartholomew's hospital's subordination to Rochester priory was in part due to the alms-gathering activities of the
priory on its behalf. Through the priory's donation to the hospital of alms given at the altars of St
James and St Giles in the cathedral and pittances from their refectory, the priory was apparently
able to retain its power to select the new inmates to the hospital; Greenwood, *Hospital of St
Bartholomew*, pp. 14–15. Others provided the leper hospital with alms from their own resources,
thereby fulfilling part of their own charitable obligations and possibly in turn influencing the monasteries' own benefactors. Such alms might be supplied to the lazar house on a regular basis, often
annually like the four quarters of corn and four of rye given for the sake of charity to St
Bartholomew's hospital, Chatham by Boxley abbey; ibid., p. 18. Occasionally donors provided
alms at particular times to mark specific anniversaries or other times of commemoration. The bread
dole by Christchurch priory in 1315 to a large number of Kent hospitals was apparently given to
mark an anniversary associated with Archbishop Lanfranc, which seems to suggest that the timing
was not related to the precise needs of the hospitals concerned but was primarily a symbolic act of
importance to the priory. The surviving document does not appear to be complete but does include
several of Kent's leper hospitals: St Mary Magdalene's, Dartford (twenty-one breads), St
Bartholomew's at Hythe (thirty-three breads), St Bartholomew's, Dover (fifty-nine breads), the
lepers of Sandwich (twenty-five breads), the lepers of Harbledown (twenty-four breads), St
Nicholas', Canterbury (eighty-five breads), St Stephen and St Thomas', New Romney (forty-eight
breads); CCAL, DCc/DE 26.   **83** For example, the hospital of St James at Tonge may have become
little more than a chantry chapel for the Badelesmere family in the fourteenth century and, by marriage, was later under the patronage of the earls of March; *CCR* 1339–1341, p. 183; *CPR* 1405–1408,
p. 299.   **84** In broad terms the leper hospitals adapted in one of three ways: they became houses
for the poor, they became chantry chapels, they combined both roles.

of which the wealthiest and largest by far was St Nicholas' hospital at Canterbury, resembled the later hospital for the poor, a model adapted, only slightly, by most almshouse founders in late sixteenth- and seventeenth-century Kent.

The pilgrim hospital

1	foundation	*late 12th century*, early 13th century
2	founders	*aristocracy, crown*, townsmen, bishops
3	foundation gift	*very variable*
4	size	variable, *ten to twelve*
5	inmates	*priests, laymen* and women
6	patronage	*episcopal, crown*
7	own chapel	*yes*
8	*in vitam* grants	*variable, local, for a century from foundation*, founder's successors
9	diversification from the 14th century	*corrodies, chantry*, poor, fraternity
10	casual alms	*variable, probably important*
11	testamentary benefactors	*rare*, clusters over time, local, explicit reciprocity – masses

Although Becket's martyrdom was the spur for the foundation of the majority of the pilgrim hospitals in Kent, a few may pre-date 1170 and may have provided accommodation for those visiting other shrines at Canterbury, like the tomb of St Dunstan.[85] Most, however, were established in the late twelfth century, a response to the growing number of pilgrims flocking to Canterbury from continental Europe, via Dover and the other Kent ports, and from other parts of England, often via London. The north Kent region, which encompassed the pilgrimage route from London along Watling Street, may have had up to seven small hospitals where a few pilgrims might stay overnight, as at St Thomas' hospital in Sittingbourne, but few houses were dedicated solely to the care of pilgrims.[86] Initially, there may have been comparable houses at some of the Cinque Ports, like the hospitals dedicated to St Bartholomew at Sandwich and at Dover.[87]

---

85 The hospital of St Mary the Virgin at Milton by Gravesend (and St John's hospital at Blean) apparently pre-date 1170 and may have provided shelter for pilgrims on the road between London and Canterbury; *PR* 2, 3, 4 Henry II, pp. 16, 72, 132; *Curia Regis rolls of the reign of Henry III* (1952), p. 121. 86 Unfortunately, little is known about these hospitals; for example, the first reference to St Thomas' hospital is from the mid-thirteenth century; *CPR* 1247–1258, p. 397; 1258–1266, pp. 299, 571. Nonetheless, there is a late twelfth-century reference to a pilgrim hospital at Shooter's Hill; J.C. Robertson (ed.), *Materials for history of Thomas Becket, Archbishop of Canterbury*, vol. 1 (1875), p. 530. 87 Leland reported that there was a hospital outside the town of Sandwich that had been founded to care for 'maryners desesid and hurt', but as Boys noted he did not say on what authority he made the statement; L.T. Smith (ed.), *The itinerary of John Leland in and about the years,*

Yet neither aided pilgrims for long and, even though St Mary's hospital at Dover was apparently catering for such people by the early years of the thirteenth century, the pilgrim hospitals in the east Kent region were concentrated in and around Canterbury.[88] Consequently, even with the added accommodation provided by the religious houses, demand for places must have outstripped supply by a considerable margin, suggesting that those unable to afford the cheapest hostels would have sought shelter under hedges or in barns.[89]

The image of Christ the Pilgrim and the inclusion of aid for the stranger among the seven corporal works of mercy might have been expected to encourage the wealthy to found hospitals for the care of pilgrims. Members of the regional aristocracy and a few senior churchmen appear to have responded to this perceived need, especially in north Kent, and Henry III followed their lead in the early thirteenth century through his patronage of the hospital at Ospringe.[90] In contrast, interest among the county's prosperous townsmen was apparently muted, except in Canterbury itself, where Edward son of Odbold and William Cokyn each founded a hospital for pilgrims in the late twelfth century. A few of their contemporaries, however, were prepared to found hospitals for other groups among the disadvantaged, often those from the local area, which may indicate that part of their reluctance was due to the itinerant lifestyle of the pilgrims.

In terms of the hospital's endowment, there may broadly have been three tiers of wealth; the lowest were the small hospitals in north Kent that housed a few pilgrims on a daily basis, and possibly St John's hospital at Blean. The middle level comprised St Mary's hospital at Strood, an episcopal foundation, and the refounded hospital of St Thomas in Canterbury, following its amalgamation with the neighbouring house of St Nicholas and St Katherine *c.*1203.[91] The two most

1535–1543, vol. 4 (1964), p. 48; W. Boys, *Collections for an history of Sandwich in Kent, with notices of the other Cinque Ports and members and of Richborough* (1792), p. 5. Some of the earliest records relating to the Dover hospital were grants given for the sustenance of pilgrims and the poor at the hospital; Bodleian, Rawlinson MS. B.335, ff. 5v, 7v, 53, 64v. **88** In addition to St John's hospital at Blean there were two new foundations in Canterbury. The first, St Thomas' hospital, was established by Edward son of Odbold in *c.*1180; the second by another leading townsman, William Cokyn, whose hospital was dedicated to St Nicholas and St Katherine; E. Holland (trans.), *The Canterbury chantries and hospitals in 1546* (1934), pp. 8–9. St Mary's hospital at Dover was said to have been founded by Hubert de Burgh in *c.* 1203, Henry III's charter of 1227 confirms Hubert's earlier gift to the house; EKA, Do/ZQ 01. **89** The lucrative nature of the pilgrim trade may be gauged from Christchurch priory's programme of building large pilgrim hostels, a strategy it was still pursuing in the late fifteenth century; J. Zeiger, 'The survival of the cult of St Thomas of Canterbury in the later middle ages', unpublished M.A. dissertation, Kent University, 1997, pp. 16–17. **90** Henry III took the name of founder of St Mary's hospital *c.*1234, but seven of the hospital's charters pre-date 1234; the first is a lease dated 1215; M. Frohnsdorff, *The Maison Dieu and medieval Faversham* (1997), p. 12. **91** St Mary's hospital at Strood had been founded by Richard de Glanville, bishop of Rochester in 1193 'for the liberation of King Richard, ... for poor and infirm persons, whether neighbours or strangers'; Thorpe, *Registrum Roffense*, pp. 631.

lavishly endowed houses were St Mary's at Ospringe and St Mary's at Dover.[92] From the third decade of the thirteenth century, Henry III provided the hospitals at Ospringe and Dover with extensive foundation gifts in the form of land and property, judicial and taxation privileges, and other sources of income, like tithes and the advowson of various churches. Such gifts were sufficient to provide the hospitals with a staff of priests and a wide range of buildings, thereby signalling Henry's role as a generous donor, who, as a consequence, would visit his institution and stay in his own apartments.[93] He expected, furthermore, that the hospital would extend the counter-gift of hospitality to his officials travelling on royal business and to the royal corrodians; while spiritual counter-gifts for the welfare of his soul and those he named were to be provided in the form of costly obits forever, as well as other commemorative masses held daily and weekly.[94]

Although Henry III and, to a much lesser extent, his successors, provided further gifts for their hospitals, other benefactors also chose to support the pilgrim hospital through *in vitam* grants. Little is known about the level of such support received by most of the pilgrim hospitals, especially those in north Kent, but where records do survive, there were considerable differences between hospitals. The greatest contrast was between the two hospitals under royal patronage.[95] St Mary's at Dover received few additional grants, whereas the hospital at

92 The early history of the Ospringe hospital is difficult to trace, but it appears that Alexander of Gloucester (probably the founder of the Poor Priests' hospital in Canterbury) and William Gratian (later master of the hospital), were acting as feoffees in the accummulation of land in the early thirteenth century. This land was an important part of the hospital's endowment; M. Underwood, *Index of the archive of St Mary's hospital, Ospringe, held at St John's College, Cambridge* (unpublished), p. 1. As founder, Hubert de Burgh provided St Mary's, Dover, with substantial assets; see chapter 3.   **93** See chapter 3. Grants of Henry III to Ospringe hospital; St John's College, Cambridge, D8.33–5, D9.16, D9.220, D12.1–4; *CChR* 1226–1257, pp. 226, 238, 253–4, 294–5, 362, 391; 1257–1300, p. 70; *CCR* 1231–1234, p. 492; 1234–1237, pp. 98, 164, 250, 493, 495; 1237–1242, pp. 76, 305; *CPR* 1232–1247, p. 496; 1247–1258, p. 194. Archaeological excavations at Ospringe may have revealed the *Camera Regis* and it is known from the documentary evidence that various kings stayed at the hospital en route between London and the Channel ports; Frohnsdorff, *Maison Dieu*, pp. 12–13; G. Smith, 'The excavation of the hospital of St Mary of Ospringe, commonly called Maison Dieu', *Arch. Cant.*, vol. 95 (1979), 105–6.   **94** See chapter 3. Letters patent were sealed at Ospringe while Edward I was staying there in 1273, 1278, 1281, 1294, 1297, 1299, 1302 and 1305; *CPR* 1272–1281, pp. 25, 260, 454; 1292–1301, pp. 69, 252, 427; 1301–1307, pp. 38, 299, 300, 373–5. The master of Ospringe, in 1342, sought tax exemption on the grounds that if such relief was not forthcoming the hospitality, chantries and other works of charity incumbent on the hospital could not be maintained; *CPR* 1340–1348, p. 516. Though later, Froissart provides a description of his return to Canterbury, reporting that Richard II on his visit to Becket's shrine had stayed the night at Ospringe and had returned there the following night; G. Brereton (trans.), *Froissart's Chronicles* (1968), pp. 404–5.   The first royal corrodian was Andrew *clericus*, the nephew of Agnes de Everle, lady in waiting to Beatrice, the king's daughter, who was sent to the hospital in 1258; *CCR* 1256–1259, p. 337. Yet the king had been involved on two earlier occasions regarding the entry of blind Helen of Faversham and Adam, a chaplain; *CCR* 1234–1237, p. 48; 1242–1247, p. 44.   **95** In part, this may relate to the size of the initial endowment because Hubert de Burgh and Henry

Ospringe was the recipient of over ninety *in vitam* gifts.[96] Of the other pilgrim hospitals, St Thomas' hospital, Canterbury, was well supported, whereas St Mary's at Strood seems to have received comparably few grants after its foundation. From the surviving charters it appears local small landholders were the most numerous grantors, though the minor aristocracy provided some support, and a few religious houses were prepared to enter into gift exchanges with the hospitals.[97] This seems to imply that most donors selected their chosen institution as a result of personal connections with the hospital, its personnel or other benefactors; or as a consequence of their local knowledge of the institution.[98] Such factors are examined regionally and locally, the former later in this chapter, the latter in the Dover case study.

The four pilgrim hospitals at Canterbury, Dover, Ospringe and Strood received the majority of their *in vitam* grants during the thirteenth century, and even though a considerable number were made in free alms, certain benefactors at all the hospitals did seek specific spiritual or material counter-gifts.[99] Intercessory services were the favoured option, while others intended lights or other good works would act as commemorative aids for the benefit of their soul and for the souls they named.[1] For the hospitals, such requirements could be undertaken by

III provided the Dover hospital with several large landholdings in the region. Henry III was also generous at Ospringe, giving the hospital considerable assets, which, in this case, seems to have led to a greater willingness among landholders to support the hospital. However, the relationship between the initial endowment and the degree of later support is complex, involving factors concerning the hospital, its reputation locally and regionally, the presence of other religious houses in the area, and more general social, political and economic factors. **96** In addition to the grants recorded in the hospital's cartulary, the archive at St John's College, Cambridge, contains over 170 deeds (dated and undated) to the Maison Dieu at Ospringe; Underwood, *Index*, pp. 6–56; *CChR* 1226–1257, pp. 315–18; 1258–1300, p. 809. **97** All benefactors of St Mary's hospital, Strood, were to receive the counter-gift of confraternity according to the foundation charter; Thorpe, *Registrum Roffense*, p. 632; Johnson, *Registrum Hamonis*, vol. 1, p. 1. **98** The collection of grants and leases for St Mary's hospital, Strood; MA, DRc/T573–611A. The collection of grants and leases for St Thomas' hospital, Canterbury; CCAL, U24 A – H, J – N. **99** These grants illustrate a range of counter-gifts received by donors to Eastbridge hospital. In *c.*1200 Adam de Saringherst granted seven acres in the lordship of Westgate, next to Canterbury, to the brothers and sisters in free and perpetual alms for his soul, the souls of his parents, ancestors and the departed faithful; in 1269 John de Adisham granted two and a half acres in St Martin's parish, Canterbury, to the master and brothers, and in return John received the use of a chamber at the hospital for life, his food, drink, clothes and shoes, and an annual rent for the land of 0.5*d*.; in *c.*1225 Peter de Dene granted a messuage in Westgate to the brothers and in return he and his heirs were to receive 10*s*. annually; in the mid-thirteenth century John Holte, a citizen of Canterbury, granted a messuage and appurtenances to the master and brothers. In return they were to give annually a silver mark to the prioress and convent at Minster in Sheppy and 2*d*. to John Polre; CCAL, U24 A32, A19, A14, A24. **1** In an undated deed William the Palmer of Faversham granted to Ospringe hospital a rent of 3*d*., the hospital to provide an alms light for the upper chapel; St John's College, Cambridge, D8.225. Of the few Strood hospital benefactors none appear to have sought such provisions, though a later benefactor (1444) wanted one of the priest brothers from the hospital to celebrate divine service annu-

the staff of priest brothers and were unlikely to impinge on the financial well-being of the house.[2] However, the demands placed on the two hospitals under royal patronage were far greater, which indicates that some masters may have considered the crown's involvement a mixed blessing.[3] The wealth the hospitals gained was counter-balanced by the physical and spiritual obligations placed on them, acting as a heavy drain on their financial and human resources. By the early fourteenth century, partly as a result of this relationship, the hospitals of Dover and Ospringe were seeking royal tax exemption on the grounds of poverty.[4] Their predicament was matched by the other pilgrim hospitals, similarly suffering financial problems during this period, as the authorities sought to try to fulfil their obligations, including aid for poor pilgrims, at a time when the hospital's income was falling, or at best static.[5] As well as the sharp decline in new grants by the late thirteenth century and the agricultural disasters of the 1310s, certain pilgrim hospitals were also hit by disputes over contested rights and privileges.[6] For example, there was a long-running dispute between St Mary's hospital at Strood and Rochester priory concerning Bishop Gundulf's appropriation of the churches of Aylesford and St Margaret's, Rochester, from the priory to the hospital.[7] Changing local circumstances during the period adversely

ally in his manorial chapel; MA, T575/1. **2** For example, under its foundation charter two of the brothers at St Mary's hospital, Strood, were to be priests. They were to celebrate mass daily for the benefit of the hospital's living and deceased benefactors; Thorpe, *Registrum Roffense*, p. 631. At the Maison Dieu, Ospringe, the three professed brothers may have undertaken similar intercessory duties. It is not clear when the brothers disappeared to be replaced by priests, clerks and boys but it may have been *c.* 1480; Drake, 'Hospital of St Mary of Ospringe, pp. 56–7; but as Wood-Legh also noted a deed of 1508 was made by 'Robert gardianus et fratres', Wood-Legh, *Kentish visitations*, pp. 32–3 and n. 8. **3** For a detailed assessment of St Mary's hospital, Dover, see chapter 3. **4** The Ospringe and Dover hospitals were granted exemption from royal tax demands in 1325 and on several other occasions during the following decades; *CCR* 1323–1327, p. 421; 1327–1330, p. 255; 1330–1333, pp. 496, 520; 1333–1337, pp. 13, 275, 352, 566, 640; 1337–1339, pp. 198, 352, 502, 583; 1339–1341, p. 499; 1341–1343, pp. 185, 187, 220; 1343–1346 pp. 437, 619; 1354–1360, p. 477. **5** St Thomas' hospital, Canterbury first sought tax exemption on the grounds of poverty in 1341 and again in 1354; *CCR* 1341–1343, p. 305; 1354–1360, p. 35. **6** St Mary's hospital at Dover held several manors on Romney Marsh which required a high level of organization and maintenance with respect to the sea defences, in addition to regular manorial administration. The area was badly hit by the great storms of the 1280s, and in 1290 there was a case between the master of the hospital and the hospital's tenants concerning the maintenance of the local sea defences; *CPR* 1281–1292, p. 407. The loss of the manorial records from this and the other pilgrim hospitals means that it is difficult to assess the impact of the agricultural disasters of the early fourteenth century, but the much larger and wealthier religious institutions, like Christchurch priory, did suffer at this time; M. Mate, 'The impact of war on the economy of Canterbury cathedral priory, 1290–1340' (1982), 771–8. **7** This dispute finally resulted in an affray inside the hospital grounds between the monks and the hospital brothers. The brothers were successful in their battle with the monks on both counts, but the dispute presumably damaged the hospital's financial situation, and in the longer term alienated its larger and wealthier neighbour, Rochester priory, which in other circumstances might have been a valuable benefactor; H. Smetham, *History of Strood* (1899), pp. 130–2.

affected the same hospital when the new Rochester bridge was sited upstream from the old one and thus away from the hospital's bridge chapel. Chapel revenue, which had been used for the hospital's contribution for bridge maintenance, fell even further when a chapel was established on the Rochester side near the new bridge, though the hospital was still expected to provide money for bridge repairs.[8]

Generally, however, pilgrim hospitals in both regions were well placed to collect casual alms because they were sited in or near towns or vills, close to major routes, or occasionally bridges. Travellers and pilgrims were, therefore, encouraged to offer alms at the hospital's gate or chapel, especially when the chapel had particular relics or a special cult, while those staying overnight might attend services there, offering donations at one of the altars or to the image of a saint.[9] As examples of the potential value of casual alms for the hospital, it is worth looking at two hospitals, one in either region, which were sited close to a bridge. As noted above, St Mary's hospital was sited alongside the road between London and Canterbury, near the Strood end of Rochester Bridge and close to the chapel of St Mary, which was under its governance.[10] Though less hazardous than the ferry, the bridge crossing was notorious, and it seems probable that stories like the divine rescue of 'The harper of Rochester' were well known, thereby ensuring a good supply of alms to St Mary's until the new bridge was built.[11] In contrast, the Eastbridge at Canterbury was unlikely to generate revenue for St Thomas' hospital for the same reasons.[12] The hospital may, however, have received alms from grateful pilgrims who were now close to their destination, some of whom may have rested overnight and attended services in St Thomas' upper chapel before making their way to the shrine.

Yet, from the early fourteenth century, such offerings were frequently seen as insufficient by the hospital authorities, which applied a more pro-active approach to the collecting of alms.[13] The appointment of proctors to beg on

8 N. Brooks, 'Rochester bridge, AD 43–1381' (1994), pp. 44, 49–50, 71. 9 The presence of a piece of the true cross at Faversham abbey may have drawn pilgrims to St Mary's hospital, Ospringe, as the shrine of St William of Perth at Rochester cathedral may have drawn pilgrims to the Strood hospital; Frohnsdorff, *Maison Dieu*, pp. 9, 15; Oakley, 'Rochester priory', pp. 38 and n. 52, 40. The Ospringe hospital had had its own extensive relic collection until the early fifteenth century when the warden or master carried off many of the house's treasures, including its books and relics; *CPR* 1416–1422, p. 208. 10 Smetham, *Strood*, pp. 133–4. The relationship between the hospital and bridge was extended in the fourteenth century to include the crown because two masters, William de Basing and Thomas Bromelegh were at various times appointed master of the king's works, which included Rochester Bridge; *CPR* 1364–1367, p. 398; 1367–1370, pp. 43, 44; 1370–1374, pp. 286, 291, 302, 330, 429; 1374–1377, pp. 190, 199, 214; 1377–1381, pp. 213, 334, 540; 1381–1385, pp. 5, 221, 235, 240, 243, 308, 398, 506; 1385–1389, pp. 216, 295, 377. 11 Brooks, 'Rochester bridge', p. 36. 12 The hospital authorities were, however, expected to maintain the bridge from a number of rents they received for that purpose; *CPR* 1385–1389, p. 523. 13 Among the recipient institutions of the gift of breads distributed in 1315 to mark an anniversary associated with

behalf of the hospital was a valuable option at several houses in both regions. A measure of the success of this strategy may be gauged from the complaints made to the crown by the master of St Thomas' hospital about the activities of false proctors.[14] Occasionally, these hospitals appear to have adopted other methods of attracting offerings. For example, the establishment of a fraternity, like the fraternity of Corpus Christi at St Thomas' hospital, Canterbury, which drew its membership from the city's clerks; or the provision of daily and other services that might attract local people to particular cults at the hospital.[15] The provision of hospitality for guests at the two royal establishments, in particular, was part of their reciprocal relationship with the crown, but did occasionally produce further gift exchanges for the hospital.[16] Even though the monetary value of the exchange may frequently have been insufficient recompense for the entertainment provided, such acts of conspicuous consumption were an important part of the social process, through which the hospital was investing for the future. By providing hospitality, the hospital was enhancing its status and reputation to a number of audiences, who might consequently wish to be associated with the house through their own gift exchanges.

An alternative source of income was the provision of chantry facilities at the hospital, or at a chapel under its jurisdiction. In 1363, the archbishop of Canterbury gave permission for Dom. Bartholomew de Bourne to transfer the chantry established by his ancestor to St Thomas' hospital, the lands attached to the chantry being incorporated into the hospital's own neighbouring holdings in Bekesbourne. As a consequence, a small chantry chapel was built near the hospital entrance to be served by a chanty priest, thereby providing the hospital with another site for the collection of alms.[17] In addition, Thomas Newe, master of Eastbridge, founded a chantry at the hospital church of St Nicholas at Harbledown in 1372. He partly funded the enterprise, and it also received monies

---

Lanfranc were St Mary's hospital at Ospringe and possibly St Thomas' at Canterbury; CCAL, DCc/DE 26. Another episcopal gift was the provision of indulgences which were presumably valuable aids in the search for alms. St Thomas' hospital was the recipient of a number of papal indulgences and an indulgence from Archbishop Islip in 1350; *Cal. Pap. Let.* 1198–1304, p. 77; 1362–1404, p. 36; 1396–1404, p. 472; *Cal. Pap. Pet.* 1342–1419, p. 351; *Reg. Islip*; f. 18v. Similarly, the Maison Dieu at Ospringe received indulgences granted by several bishops between 1246 and 1348; Underwood, *Index*, p. 2. **14** The master of the hospital complained about false proctors in 1312, 1314, 1322 and 1323; Eastbridge also sought a letter of protection from the crown in 1230, in 1286 and on several occasions during the first half of the fourteenth century; *CPR* 1225–1232, p. 326; 1281–1292, p. 247; 1307–1313, p. 499; 1313–1317, p. 87; 1321–1324, pp. 122, 126, 345, 352; 1327–1330, p. 201; 1330–1334, pp. 527, 559; 1334–1338, pp. 306, 307; 1350–1354, p. 529. **15** It is not known when the fraternity was established at the hospital. Few apparently made post-mortem bequests to the guild, one of those who did was Master Robert Goseborne. He gave 6s. 8d. to it in 1522; CKS, PRC 32/13, f. 184. **16** For example, in 1360 the king of France, on his way back to his realm after captivity in England, donated alms to the hospital at Ospringe during his stay there; Drake, 'The hospital of St Mary of Ospringe', 53. **17** Hussey, *Kent chantries*, pp. 62–4.

from the master and inmates at St Nicholas' and from certain rents arising out of a number of properties in the area.[18] This arrangement was presumably beneficial to both hospitals, the chantry priest fulfilling his intercessory duties on behalf of the founder and other benefactors, as well as caring for the spiritual welfare of the inmates at St Nicholas'.

Some benefactors may have supported certain pilgrim hospitals through postmortem giving during the middle ages, but little testamentary evidence survives for either diocese before the late fifteenth century and, for this later period, it would appear such houses were rarely favoured. There were exceptions, however: St Mary's hospital at Strood received a comparable number of bequests as the hospitals of St Bartholomew at Chatham and St Katherine at Rochester, and St Mary's at Dover did receive a small cluster of bequests in the 1520s.[19] These bequests were almost exclusively directed towards the hospital, especially its chapel, or towards the priest brothers or more frequently the master; but only at St Thomas' hospital, Canterbury, were the poor pilgrims or their helpers named as recipients.[20] Yet even at these houses such gifts presumably had little effect on the institution's financial well-being during the late medieval period. Rather, the house's viability was a product of its resources and personnel, and the management of these assets.[21] As a result, donors and recipients probably saw the exchange in symbolic terms, the gift producing an explicitly sought response or possibly the prayers of the hospital's grateful personnel.[22] Thus, for the pilgrim hospitals of both regions, the testamentary support they received was principally from local benefactors and might occur as a cluster of bequests, implying the significance of personal connections and knowledge of the institution. The sole exception appears to have been St Mary's hospital at Dover where, in addition to some local support, its regional importance led to bequests from certain citizens from Canterbury and other Cinque Ports.[23]

Looking at the development of the pilgrim hospital in the two Kent regions, it appears that there were certain common themes, like the significance of royal and episcopal patronage and the implications of these relationships for the later history of the hospitals. Even though this analysis draws predominantly upon the development of four hospitals, it suggests that by the late middle ages pilgrim

---

18 Ibid., 136–7. **19** From the Consistory court register, St Mary's hospital, Strood, received bequests from eighteen testators; information kindly supplied by Paul Lee. **20** One of these few benefactors was Henry Newell (1475), who bequeathed a mattress, a red-and-white coverlet and a pair of sheets to Alice, the custodian of the paupers; and 6s. 8d. to repair the bedding of the poor there; CKS, PRC 32/2, f. 324. **21** Unfortunately little evidence survives for the management of these hospitals. A single rental concerning the Dover hospital's estates at River, Whitfield, Colrede and Little Pising is all that remains from its archive; BL, Add. MS. 62710, ff. 1v–6. **22** Master Thomas Clerke, a chaplain at Sandwich, bequeathed a number of books to the Maison Dieu at Dover in 1487, a gift which may mark a strong fraternal link with the master there; CKS, PRC 17/4, f. 123. **23** See chapter 3.

hospitals in Kent had adapted in a number of ways. The house possibly closest
to its original function was St Thomas' in Canterbury, where the poor pilgrims
continued to find respite until the destruction of Becket's shrine in 1538.[24]
Nevertheless, not all its resources were used for the care of the pilgrims, because
one of the priest brothers served the chantry and hospital of St Nicholas at
Harbledown and a second priest served at the chantry in Eastbridge hospital itself.
In contrast, the three hospitals dedicated to St Mary at Dover, Ospringe and
Strood had become chantry-like institutions, where the priest brothers were
principally engaged in services of intercession and commemoration for their
founders, patrons and benefactors.[25] Yet, unlike chantry chapels, the hospitals
were able to provide vocational opportunities for those seeking to enter the
priesthood. [26] Furthermore, the Dover hospital was also able to maintain its other
charitable roles, the distribution of aid to pilgrims and the poor.[27] This multifunctional approach may have aided the hospital's viability, at least until the mid-
sixteenth century, providing it with opportunities to engage in further reciprocal exchanges with potential benefactors, most of whom were interested in the
offer of spiritual counter-gifts from its professional staff as a worthy charitable
institution.

The hospital for the poor

1	foundation	range late 11th–early 14th century, *late 12th–13th century*
2	founders	*laymen, bishops*, towns, clerics
3	foundation gift	*variable*
4	size	six to a hundred, *mainly twelve to sixteen*
5	inmates	*laymen and women*, priests

24 As well as the accommodation provided for poor pilgrims, the hospital distributed wood, ale
and other things to the poor who came to its gate; Hussey, *Kent chantries*, p. 65. In addition, according to a papal indulgence of 1363, the hospital offered shelter to women in childbed; *Cal. Pap. Let.
1362–1404*, p. 36. Zeiger considers that Canterbury remained a pilgrimage centre into the 1520s;
Zeiger, 'Survival of a cult', pp. 39–40.   **25** At the Strood hospital this change may, in part, have
been a consequence of Bishop Hamo's new ordinances of 1330 (resulting from certain problems
there), in which he laid out in detail the daily routine to be followed by the priest brothers, including acts of worship; Johnson, *Registrum Hamonis*, vol. 1, p. 4.   **26** For example, brother Giles
Crouche of St Mary's, Dover, was presented as an acolyte on 7 March 1422, a subdeacon on 24
March 1425, a deacon on 22 December 1425 and a priest on 30 March 1426; E.F. Jacob (ed.),
Register of Henry Chichele (1947), pp. 350, 368, 374–5. Brother Warin de Suthflet of St Mary's,
Strood, was presented as a subdeacon on 8 April 1329, a deacon on 3 March 1330 and a priest on
7 April 1330; Johnson, *Registrum Hamonis*, vol. 2, p. 1166. Schooling was available at the Ospringe
hospital; Wood-Legh, *Kentish visitations*, p. 32.   **27** According to the *Valor*, the hospital spent £20
per year on the poor, £9 2s. 6d. on two messes daily of bread, meat and drink to two honest poor
persons and £8 on the wages, livery and board of two women who were to serve the poor people
staying there; *Valor Eccl.*, vol. 1, pp. 56–7.

6	patronage	*lay*, civic, episcopal
7	own chapel	*most*
8	*in vitam* grants	*small, local, lay donors*, from foundation to 15th century; founder's successors
9	diversification from the 14th century	*fewer poor, corrodies*, chantry
10	casual alms	*variable between hospitals*, possibly important
11	testamentary benefactors	*very variable between houses, clusters over time, mainly local, some explicit reciprocity* (corrodies, prayers)

Apart from Archbishop Lanfranc, none of the early hospital founders in either region were sufficiently wealthy to found separate institutions for the poor and leprous. Instead, as at St Bartholomew's hospital in Chatham, the two groups shared the same house, though they were segregated within the hospital precincts. For the purposes of this study, such hospitals have been classified as leper houses. Unfortunately the evidence regarding hospitals for the poor is severely limited for the north Kent region, which means this analysis draws principally on the hospitals of east Kent. Where the founders are known, most were prosperous townsmen, less frequently bishops or members of the nobility; and a number of early benefactors were members of local knightly families. In most instances, individual townsmen apparently acted alone in the creation of their institution, but particular circumstances might lead to the collective establishment of a town hospital, like St Bartholomew's at Sandwich.[28] These houses for the poor were founded during the late twelfth and thirteenth centuries, thereby frequently pre-dating the coming of the friars to Kent, though the ideas of St Francis and others may have been influential.[29] It seems more likely, however, that concern for the local poor was already a prime consideration among the leading citizens, who wished to demonstrate ideas about pastoral care and *noblesse oblige*, as well as their desire to maintain order through the application of measures designed to enforce morally correct behaviour.[30] Even though the numbers accommodated comprised a tiny proportion of the total population in terms of the lay brothers and sisters and the sick-poor, this concern for the disadvantaged may have been prompted by the contemporary spiritual revival and an awareness of the difficult economic conditions.[31]

---

28 See chapter 4.   **29** With regard to later foundations, Bishop Hamo's two hospitals in Hythe and Thomas Ely's hospital at Sandwich, these seem to share characteristics with the almshouses and are discussed in the next sub-section.   **30** For example, the revised ordinances of Archbishop Winchelsey (1299) for St John's hospital, Canterbury, included rules about what the brothers and sisters should wear and how they should conduct themselves in the hospital; Graham, *Registrum Winchelsey*, vol. 2, pp. 828–9. **31** Under John, there were considerable economic difficulties caused by high inflation and currency problems; P.D.A. Harvey, 'The English inflation of 1180–1220', *Past & Present*, 61 (1973), 3–30.

Unlike the leper hospitals, those for the poor were predominantly sited within the town, indicating the importance of viewing the hospital and its residents as being of the town.[32] Though many founders were wealthy citizens, they frequently confined their endowment to the provision of the hospital's premises, but often this did include a chapel. While cost was presumably a significant factor, some founders may have expected their fellow citizens to support the enterprise. Indeed, local townsmen had given considerable *in vitam* grants to the earlier leper houses, and it might have been assumed that they would similarly donate land, property, rents and other sources of income to the later town hospitals. The provision of a chapel, moreover, enhanced the value of the hospital with respect to the spiritual economy. Consequently, these later benefactors would be seen as the producers of meritorious deeds. They might, in addition, seek specific intercessory services for their souls from the hospital's priest. It is interesting, therefore, that the majority of these hospitals appear to have received relatively few *in vitam* grants. Nonetheless, unlike the leper and pilgrim hospitals, hospitals for the poor continued to receive such gifts during the later middle ages. Donors used a variety of forms. While grants in free alms did occur, most sought specific counter-gifts, like grants in frankalmoign, or in more precise spiritual or monetary terms. The lands and rents received frequently concerned properties in the vicinity of the hospital, suggesting the importance of local interest and the moderate scale of the hospital's resources.

The modest nature of these hospitals and the considerable involvement of the Cinque Ports' town officers as patrons were perhaps equally influential in attracting local benefactors. These donors were often prosperous townsmen, but some local knightly families were also involved. More occasionally, religious houses aided neighbouring hospitals. The gift, by St Augustine's abbey, of the advowson of St Margaret's parish church in Canterbury to the neighbouring Poor Priests' hospital provided the hospital with the opportunity to engage in further gift exchanges with parishioners and others. Furthermore, the same hospital aided the Franciscan friars when they arrived in Canterbury in 1226, and subsequently helped them to establish a friary close to the hospital. Such gifts, however, might also lead to disagreements, especially with respect to burial rights and the collection of tithes, a situation which faced St Peter and St Paul's hospital in Maidstone when the house was in dispute with St Augustine's abbey, Canterbury, over the tithes from the church at Sutton by Dover.[33]

The preponderance of hospitals under local patronage was apparently also significant with regard to the collecting of casual alms, especially for those hos-

---

32 One of the few known exceptions was Lanfranc's great hospital of St John, which was outside Canterbury's Northgate. However, Canterbury's topographical development was unusual because of the importance of the suburbs, like those outside this gate. These seem to have been relatively highly populated, at least alongside the main roads into Canterbury, from at least the reign of Henry II; Urry, *Angevin kings*, p. 186. 33 Graham, *Registrum Winchelsey*, vol. 2, p. 1086.

pitals under civic patronage. Even though the ordinances only survive for St John's hospital at Sandwich, it seems highly probable that its counterpart in New Romney was similarly allowed to collect alms from the local townspeople and receive produce which was considered sub-standard by the officers of the town markets. Elsewhere, as at St Peter and St Paul's hospital, Maidstone and Holy Cross hospital at Swainestrey, patrons provided aid for their hospitals in terms of the right to collect tolls at markets or fairs. The proximity of these activities to the hospital might, in addition, produce casual alms. Consequently, these hospitals, like the hospitals of St John at Canterbury and at Sandwich, presumably collected alms at the hospital gate and chapel.[34] The success of such strategies varied considerably, but the poor brothers were not shunned like their leper brethren, and the more able-bodied could travel around the diocese, or possibly further afield, gathering alms. As a result, even though many of the hospitals for the poor were at best only moderately well-endowed and subsequently received relatively few *in vitam* grants, their links with the local town, through patronage and the house's personnel, were an important part of their ability to survive adverse conditions. St John's hospital at Canterbury may have been exceptionally successful in this respect, because the hospital's proctors were able to offer a considerable number of indulgences.[35] During Edward III's reign most of the money raised was probably used to rebuild the hospital after a disastrous fire had destroyed the main building, and possibly part of the chapel, though subsequently the authorities may have had the opportunity to engage in other building projects.[36]

However, some hospitals for the poor were suffering from poverty by the fourteenth century, though generally not on the same scale as the leper hospitals.[37] In

---

34 The early sixteenth-century pittance book from St John's hospital, Canterbury, includes entries detailing the alms collected by the porter (the largest amount), from the box in the hall and the box in the church; CCAL, U13/1. Furthermore, a number of medieval almsboxes survive at the hospital, including one which was attached to St John's gate. Geremek found a similar pattern in the amount collected inside the hospital at the infirmary and at its gate for the Hotel-Dieu in Paris; B. Geremek, *The margins of society in late medieval Paris* (1987), p. 190. **35** St John's hospital apparently sent out proctors for a month before both the feast of the Nativity of St John the Baptist and Christmas, and for three weeks after the two feasts, to collect alms across the country. They were able to provide a large number of indulgences to the hospital's benefactors, which the hospital had received from several popes, archbishops and bishops. They also promised that the brothers and sisters would daily offer up 30,000 paternosters and Ave Marias on behalf of the benefactors; Duncombe and Battely, *Three archiepiscopal hospitals*, pp. 203, 253–5. **36** Although the standing hospital buildings suggest that they have suffered fire damage, the documentary evidence for the fire seems to rest on Somner's testimony that there was a letter under the hospital's seal recording the fire. However, Duncombe and Battely were unable to find this record, though they believed that they had located the correct letter and there was nothing else regarding the fire in the hospital chest; Duncombe and Battely, *Three archiepiscopal hospitals*, p. 203; W. Somner, *The antiquities of Canterbury* (1703), p. 50. **37** The Poor Priests' hospital, Canterbury, may have been a more extreme example, but its financial difficulties may have been exacerbated by the

part, the paying of entry fees by the brothers and sisters, possibly throughout the hospital's history, may have been a significant factor, especially for those houses that did not provide facilities for the sick-poor. Furthermore, the resident inmates were frequently capable of working the hospital's landholdings, and the production of victuals at certain houses may have significantly aided the institution's viability. Nevertheless, certain hospitals for the poor were expected to accommodate corrodians sent by patrons and, even though the numbers involved were far smaller than those aided by the pilgrim hospitals, such people may have placed considerable burdens on the host institution. Consequently, as well as seeking exemption from taxation, a few hospitals procured indulgences which they could offer to potential benefactors.

Thus by the late medieval period, if not before, hospitals for the poor were adopting similar schemes to those used by the leper houses, and possibly to a lesser extent by the pilgrim hospitals. For many hospital authorities, the shift from housing the poor to accommodating fee-paying residents may have been a very small step, especially at the hospitals under civic patronage, where a discretionary system was apparently employed, including the opportunity to pay by instalments. The other strategy practised by these hospitals was the provision of chantries, either in the hospital chapel itself or at a church under the hospital's control. The former was more frequently detrimental to the hospital's other function, care for the poor, but either might cause financial difficulties for the hospital if the chantry was insufficiently endowed.[38] Yet the presence of chantry chaplains in or associated with the hospital might have been expected to produce additional aid for the house. They could conduct further intercessory services on behalf of other donors, including the institution's own inmates.

This does not appear to have happened, instead, testamentary bequests were more frequently directed towards the hospital, or to the brothers and sisters. Of the different types of hospital, those for the poor were generally the most favoured, though there was considerable variation in the level of support individual hospitals enjoyed. Local rather than regional issues appear to have been the deciding factor, but the level of testamentary support received by certain hospitals also varied over time. Such houses gained the majority of these bequests during the late fifteenth century, before a gradual or steep decline (dependent on the particular institution) after about 1510. Testators predominantly aided local hospitals or those with which they had connections, through

authorities' ambitious rebuilding programme due to its decayed state; P. Bennett, 'The Poor Priests' hospital – the chapel' (1982), 219–20. **38** An example of the former was the fate of the hospital of St John, Sevenoaks. In 1354 Cecily, late wife of Gamelin atte Watre, was apparently following the lead of Peter de Crouland, when she organised the payment of a chaplain to celebrate at the hospital's chapel (at a time when there were no longer any poor inmates) for the king and for Cecily, and for their souls post-mortem; *CPR* 1338–1340, pp. 46, 411; *CPR* 1354–1358, pp. 14, 90, 246.

birth, kinship, previous residence or landholding, and most bequests were in the form of a lump sum for the house or a few pence to each inmate. A minority of these benefactors gave gifts in kind, or intended food, drink or clothes should be purchased; and where the counter-gift was designated, most sought the prayers of the inmates, not specific intercessory services. One remarkable exception was John Roper, a prosperous inmate at St John's hospital in Canterbury, who intended his executors should establish a perpetual chantry in the chapel of Our Lady in the hospital's chapel, for the benefit of his soul and others he named.

Although the brothers and sisters may have welcomed these testamentary gifts, especially when the testator named individual recipients, for the hospital itself, such bequests may have had little impact on the viability of the institution. Rather the gifts were presumably recognised for their symbolic value, a reflection of the 'economy of regard' between donor and beneficiary, whereby the value of the bequest was perceived in terms of public awareness and the hospital's status as a favoured charitable institution.[39] Yet, for some of these hospitals for the poor, the relationship between viability, reputation and status, and the level of testamentary support they received was extremely complex and fragile, a product of matters like the house's personnel, the interests and support of the local clergy, and others from the locality.

However, with regard to its long-term survival, the hospital for the poor appears to have changed relatively little over the medieval period. The presence of fee-paying brothers and sisters does not seem to have been exceptional by the early fourteenth century, and may have occurred from considerably earlier at a number of institutions. By widening their selection policy, patrons, particularly the civic authorities, were presumably increasing the appeal of the hospital to local benefactors. A strategy which appears to have been successful in most of the Cinque Ports and may similarly have appealed to some of the founders and patrons of the small hospitals for the poor in north Kent. Although fewer of these houses apparently survived as hospitals into the late middle ages, a greater number had become chantry chapels, a result perhaps, of their meagre endowment and consequent fragility. Moreover, there were significant differences between the north Kent towns as a group and the Cinque Ports, the latter having enjoyed a greater degree of self-regulation from at least the thirteenth century, mirrored in their control of many of the local hospitals. For the master, brothers and sisters, this meant they were involved in complex relationships with the civic authorities, other leading local citizens, the commonalty and, more occasionally, those from further afield, who, through a variety of means, sought to engage in gift exchanges as part of the spiritual economy.

39 Offer, 'Economy of regard', 450–7.

Almshouses	'bedehouse' type	'maisondieu' type
1 foundation	*mid-14th–c.1500*	*mid-15th–16th century*, ? from mid-14th
2 founders	*townsmen, bishop*, gentry	*townspeople*, parish clergy, civic
3 foundation gift	*reasonably well-endowed*	*poorly endowed*, reasonable
4 size	*about six to twelve*	*about one to five*, up to twelve
5 inmates	*laymen and women [long-term]*	*laymen and women [long-term]*
6 patronage	*lay, civic, lay+clergy*	*lay, civic, lay+clergy*
7 own chapel	*own/local parish church*	? *local parish church*
8 *in vitam* grants	*rare*, ? important locally	? *rare*
9 diversification	*aged, corrodies*, poor	*aged, poor*, corrodies
10 casual alms	? *little*, variable	? *little*
11 testamentary benefactors	*nil to rare, local*	*nil to rare, local*

As noted in chapter 1, Orme and Webster's idea that late medieval almshouses displayed certain different characteristics compared to the older hospitals was seen as a useful means of classifying these institutions. Kent's hospital provision appears to follow a similar pattern, though none of the county's almshouses matched the grandeur and scale of some late medieval English almshouses.[40] Instead, most Kentish almshouses were relatively small, apparently intended for the local poor or poorer persons, predominantly founded from the late fourteenth, though a few mid-fourteenth-century foundations were subsequently called almshouses. The founders were predominantly prosperous townsmen, though Hamo the bishop of Rochester, established two houses in his natal town of Hythe. One of the characteristics of these houses was the explicit intercessory role assigned to the almsfolk, who might be seen as the founder's bedesmen and women. As a consequence, the spiritual well-being of both exchange partners was of prime importance, suggesting that in terms of Clay's spiritual obligations, almshouse founders were seeking to fulfil all three duties but with a certain bias towards the obligation to oneself. This emphasis on the intercessory duties of the resident inmates seems to suggest that the almshouse resembled certain leper hospitals and those for the poor, where the brothers and sisters were similarly

40 In part this is due to the differences in the main groups of founders nationally and regionally. Nationally founders were often members of the aristocracy or gentry, archbishops or bishops, or wealthy merchants, whereas in Kent the county aristocracy apppear to have shown little or no interest in such projects, the archbishops favoured other parts of their province, and the leading merchants were less wealthy than their counterparts in London, Bristol, Coventry or any of the other major English towns.

expected to attend the hospital chapel daily. Interestingly, very few almshouses in Kent had their own chapel, most almsfolk attending to their devotions in the local parish church. For the inmates, their devotions comprised the extensive repetition of a number of prayers, often in the form of Our Lady's psalter, though at none of the Kent almshouses were the demands as great as at places like Ewelme.[41] Consequently, the ability and willingness of the inmates to repeat certain prayers was frequently part of the selection process, but at some houses allowances were made for those who agreed to learn or who were physically incapable of fulfilling this requirement. Possibly the first example of this type of house in Kent was Bishop Hamo's foundation in Hythe in 1336 for 'ten aged and infirm poor of both sexes, preferably such as have fallen into poverty from no fault of their own ... [who] must be able to repeat the Lord's Prayer, the Angelic Salutation and the Creed ... [they] shall regularly attend mass and other offices in the parish church until they can have a chapel of their own; and each of them shall say 300 Paters and Aves daily for founders and benefactors'.[42] The last example of this type appears to be William Milett's Holy Trinity almshouse founded in Dartford in 1500, a project that his late master, William Rotheley, had begun in 1452.[43]

As a means of highlighting the important relationship between the founder and his institution, it is worthwhile to examine briefly Milett's almshouse. His will, drawn up at a time of impending death, included instructions for his almshouse. Five poor men of 'good condition' were to be housed and each was to receive 4*d.* per week provided they did not beg. Though meagre, this allowance may have saved the recipients from destitution and thus generated feelings of gratitude towards Milett and those he nominated as patrons of the house. Milett may have been motivated by neighbourly considerations, but the provision of penny doles to the apostolic thirteen poor men and women, at his obit in Dartford parish church, seems to imply a deeper concern for the welfare of his own soul. This idea was given credence by his desire for the long-term provision of the saying of masses and prayers on his behalf by certain professionals at set times, and 'Christ's poor', the almsmen, on a daily basis. These demonstrations of his piety, including the almost constant stream of prayers from the grateful almsmen, were strengthened by the annual public display of the

---

41 C. Richmond, 'Victorian values in fifteenth-century England' (2001), pp. 224–41. **42** Johnson, *Registrum Hamonis*, vol. 1, p. 393; EKA, hbarth5 [transcription provided by A.F. Butcher]. **43** PRO, Prob 11/12, f. 138; *CPR* 1452–1461, p. 114. Although the religious changes of the sixteenth century necessitated modification of the devotional duties of the almsfolk, certain ideas regarding the relationship between the founder and his beneficiaries lived on. Roger Manwood, a prominent citizen of Elizabethan Canterbury and Sandwich, founded an almshouse just to the north of Canterbury in 1570. In his will he stipulated that his poor almsfolk were to attend at his tomb in the neighbouring parish church. I am grateful to Paul Lee and Claire Bartrum for bringing to my attention their work on Milett and Manwood, respectively.

bedesman at Milett's obit, when he went through the town ringing a bell and praying for the souls of a number of prominent citizens and other local bene-factors. Thus, the physical and public manifestation of Milett's charity, the almshouse, was visible to all in Dartford, who saw the almsmen passing to and from the parish church daily or who heard the bedesman's bell as he walked through the town on his annual progress. In addition, by placing the patronage of the house under the prominent, and presumably respected local religious, sec-ular and lay members of the town, Milett was able to demonstrate their public endorsement of his charitable institution, which was important in terms of its and his reputation, and so his long-term commemoration as a worthy, pious individual who stood well in the eyes of God and his fellow man.

As well as almshouses like Milett's, there were a few establishments display-ing some similar characteristics but which were different in probably significant details. For example, Simon Potyn's foundation of 1316 was said to be for the leprous and the infirm, but the regulations he imposed on the inmates, like the saying of two psalters of Our Lady daily, are closer in form to those found at the later almshouses than those at the earlier leper hospitals. In contrast, St Thomas' hospital at Sandwich, though well-endowed and resembling an almshouse, seems to have been different from those mentioned above. The three priests at Thomas Elys' chantry in St Peter's church appear to have undertaken all the intercessory services required by Thomas, leaving the almsfolk at his hospital without any prescribed devotional duties on his behalf. This seems to imply that Thomas envisaged his chantry and hospital as complementary establishments in his desire to fulfil all three aspects of his Christian duty.

However, the bedehouse was not the only almshouse found in medieval Kent. The maisondieu-type was more common, and such houses were in exis-tence from at least the early fifteenth century. These small ephemeral almshouses were not confined to north and east Kent, but were also present in a few of the Wealden towns. For the founders of such houses, their primary motivation may be seen in terms of neighbourly obligations, which suggests that the inmates' material welfare was their principal concern. Although a few of these houses were apparently established by the local civic authorities and others may have been created during the lifetime of the donor, most were post-mortem founda-tions, frequently forming a large part of the testator's charitable provision. Occasionally, these houses might be built specifically for the purpose, but most were either all or part of the founder's former home or another property he or she owned. For example, Henry Swerder (1504) of Canterbury intended that his executors should established post-mortem an almshouse consisting of three messuages for the use of three poor people.[44] These were sited next to that of Johanna Albert, who may similarly have been impoverished because Henry left

44 CKS, PRC 32/8, f. 68.

the messuage to her for life. His executors presumably held the patronage of his almshouse and selected the new inmates as necessary. The poor people were not explicitly requested to reciprocate through the saying of prayers for his soul, nor were they expected to attend his three funeral days. Instead, they were apparently allowed to live there, making a living as they saw fit. Consequently, even though his charitable provision may have been considered by his contemporaries and himself as an act pleasing to God, his priorities with regard to his almshouse seem to reflect more neighbourly concerns when compared to Milett's institution. It may be worth noting that the number of new foundations of this type of house apparently declined during the Reformation period, possibly a reflection of changing ideas regarding charitable provision and the poor. The greatest changes did not occur until later in the century, however, when the parish became the official agency for poor relief.

Nevertheless, at this earlier date a few parish clergy were involved as patrons. For example, Thomas Elys selected the vicar of St Mary's as a feoffee and patron of his hospital, and later clergymen were similarly involved with St Thomas' hospital in Sandwich.[45] Patrons of both types of almshouse were predominantly local leading townsmen, though where the founder chose his executors to oversee his almshouse, familial connections may have been of greater significance. This use of locally known, respectable and frequently prosperous individuals was presumably considered by founders to provide the greatest safeguard for the competent management of their institutions, and in cases where the founder was no longer from the locality, he seems to have believed the civic authorities would provide an adequate alternative. Such strategies were as important, therefore, for founders like Johanna Lull of Faversham, whose almshouse had been founded for five years, as for William Milett.[46] For both, reputation and status were inextricably linked to public perceptions of their charitable institutions.

For Milett and possibly for some other founders, this may explain the prohibition on begging by the inmates, whereas at certain almshouses, in particular some of the poorest maisonsdieu, the collection of alms may have been a necessity. With regard to alms-gathering generally, it is not clear how successful these houses were, but the testamentary records from north and east Kent suggest that few almshouses received any bequests. Of the few maisondieu type almshouses that did, most gifts were either cash or bedding, and donors hardly ever stipulated that they expected the recipients' prayers in return. For example, in 1523 Richard Wylkynson of Canterbury left 2*d*. to each of the poor

---

45 *CPR* 1391–1396, p. 109. 46 In her will, dated 1506, Johanna Lull directed her executors to make her house on the quey side at Faversham into an almshouse, under the management of her maidservant; CKS, PRC 17/13, f. 339. An interesting slant on aid for the local almshouse is to be found in Johanna Porter's will. In 1469 she intended that her executors should deliver her bedding, a mattress and other items to the first available almshouse in Faversham; CKS, PRC 32/2, f. 116.

women in the almshouse near the city wall.[47] Even though they may have remembered him in their prayers, they were not specifically requested to do so, unlike the canons at St Gregory's priory who were expected to commemorate him in their 'good prayers'. Furthermore, gifts of bedding might imply a greater interest in the material welfare of the almsfolk as a group; they might share the gift as they saw fit.

Testamentary gifts to the bedehouse-type almshouse were equally rare, and the scarcity of such houses meant that the total number of bequests was extremely small. It is very difficult, therefore, to assess the few known bequests, although at least in one instance it appears that the founder's successors wished to use his almsfolk as bedesfolk. However, with respect to the Kent almshouses more generally, the predominant response by testators in the early sixteenth century was one of indifference. For the minority of testators who did see a role for the almshouse, it was as a temporal haven for the poor to which they could contribute gifts as a means of fulfilling their neighbourly obligations in particular. They might receive the gratitude of the poor recipients, and possibly their prayers, while the main providers of intercessory services were the professionals, the parish and unbeneficed clergy, and more occasionally the friars. Moreover, the donors would gain satisfaction from giving to the less fortunate, local poor people who were suitable recipients and, as a consequence of their good works, would expect to receive spiritual favour in the next world, as well as recognition in this. Consequently, even though many of the late medieval almshouses in Kent, especially the maisonsdieu, failed to survive in the longer term, as a type of charitable institution the almshouse remained a popular charitable institution, albeit always in small numbers, over the Reformation period and into Elizabeth's reign.

THE PLACE OF THE HOSPITAL IN KENT

Early founders and patrons

The primary symbol of power and status was the possession of land. But for some members of the Kentish nobility the opportunity to engage in gift exchanges with local religious houses provided a number of spiritual and temporal advantages, a condition which appears to have been especially widespread during the twelfth and thirteenth centuries.[48] By studying the de Crevequer family, it is possible to illustrate the relationships such people developed through reciprocity with cer-

47 CKS, PRC 17/16, f. 40. **48** Wood briefly indicates these in her introduction before exploring them in the various chapters of her book; S. Wood, *English monasteries and their patrons in the thirteenth century* (1955), pp. 1–3. Southern, writing about the twelfth century, noted that it was a time when 'spiritual enthusiasm ... refashioned the forms of religious devotion' these forms included the founding of religious institutions which were more in tune with the new age; Southern, *Making of the middle ages,* pp. 162, 207–8, 241–4.

tain religious and charitable establishments and the significance of the regional and local networks of influence they were prepared to employ for the benefit of their chosen institutions. Robert de Crevequer apparently initiated these gift exchanges on the family's behalf when he founded the house of Augustinian canons at Leeds in the early twelfth century.[49] This establishment was at the heart of the family's patrimony based on the manor of Leeds, the rights of the founder and his heirs extending to such matters as patronage and lordship over the priory.[50] Yet, from an early date Robert appears to have relinquished his rights concerning governance of the house during vacancies, following the death or resignation of the prior, though he did retain his rights with regard to the election of the prior. Such a privilege may have proved a considerable asset for his family. More specific counter-gifts, however, like the provision of a priest to sing for his soul, were not included in Robert's charters, thereby implying that he believed the prior would respond appropriately, a situation Thompson believes provided a more informal relationship than that associated with secular tenure.[51] Possibly as a result of this relationship between Robert and the priory, his heirs and successors, his sons, grandson and other family members followed his example. This meant that the canons became involved in a growing number of relationships, all of which necessitated the provision of spiritual counter-gifts. In some instances the donors continued to employ the gift in free-alms form. But certain members of the family sought a more contractual type of exchange through their more explicit requirements regarding the spiritual act of reciprocity, and others directed the canons to use the donations for specific purposes, like aiding the poor.[52]

Even though the family continued to engage in a cycle of gift exchanges with their priory throughout the twelfth and thirteenth centuries, the acquisition of further estates, especially in the east of the county, and the family's rising wealth and status in the region apparently persuaded certain family members to extend their reciprocal exchanges to other religious houses. In particular, Hamo de Crevequer, Robert's grandson, seems to have targeted several different types of institution during the early thirteenth century in areas where he was a significant landholder. His support for a second house of Augustinian canons may reflect the strength of the bond between his family and that order. By aiding St Gregory's at Canterbury, he also was linking himself to the order's premier house in the county.[53] This connection might be seen as extending his family's interest in the

49 L. Sherwood, 'The cartulary of Leeds priory' (1951), 33; *VCH Kent*, vol. 2, p. 162. **50** Woods considers Austin canons normally formed a strong relationship with their patron, where his rights were well defined; Wood, *English monasteries*, p. 3. **51** Thompson, 'Monasteries', 107–8. **52** The late twelfth-century charters of Helyas de Crevequer included his desire that the acts of reciprocity should include rites for his soul and the souls of his family, while Hamo, son of Robert de Crevequer (the founder), intended one of his grants should be for the support of the poor and for the priory's guests; Sherwood, 'Leeds', 33. **53** A. Woodcock (ed.), *Cartulary of the priory of St Gregory, Canterbury* (1956), no. 85, 86, 88.

region and, for Hamo, allowed him to emphasize his links with Canterbury, a position he apparently wished to extend further through his exchanges with the local leading Benedictine house, Christchurch priory.[54] Although his gift-giving to both houses included grants made for his soul, he seems to have sought to develop his relationship with St Gregory's on both sides of the grave because he also wished for the counter-gift of confraternity from the prior there.[55] His greater regard for St Gregory's may relate to his family's extensive support for the order at Leeds. It may also suggest a preference for the less regimented regime of the Augustinians, who were more concerned to develop their charitable duties, compared to the older type of monastic house under the Benedictine order. Such an interest may have influenced his decision to support a number of hospitals, because these charitable institutions were nationally more likely to follow the Augustinian rule.[56] The most favoured was Eastbridge hospital, which received lands and rents from his manor of Blean and, in *c.*1206, his gift of the advowson of the local parish church. There is nothing in the charters to suggest why he supported Eastbridge hospital, but he may have wished to be associated with a prestigious new foundation linked to England's premier saint. It was, moreover, only a short distance from his landholdings at Blean.[57] Yet the names of the witnesses in his charters with the hospital do not indicate that he had any strong personal connections with the known masters or others at the hospital, though a few witnesses were prominent Canterbury citizens.[58]

---

54 Although he seems to have provided this ancient Benedictine house with a few grants over his lifetime, his long-term interest in Christchurch priory appears to have been relatively limited. His grants to the priory were not large, like the 20*d.* in annual rent it received from the hospital of St James in Canterbury (the result of an earlier grant from Hamo to that house), and his grants did not specify the counter-gifts he sought; CCAL, DCc/Reg. E, f. 228 no. 977. **55** Woodcock, *Cartulary of St Gregory*, p. 67. Wood suggests that members of the nobility saw this counter-gift and, the relationship it produced, to be extremely important for themselves as patrons and benefactors; Wood, *English monasteries*, pp. 122–3. **56** Although few hospitals in Kent appear to have followed this rule, it may not have been obvious during Hamo's life-time and it may have been the charitable function of the hospital which appealed to him. Unfortunately, the lack of extant documentation relating to the early friaries in Canterbury means it is impossible to ascertain whether he also supported these houses of voluntary poverty. **57** There is a tradition that *c.*1200 Ralph (the first master) was Becket's nephew; D.I. Hill, *Eastbridge hospital and the ancient almshouses of Canterbury* (1969), p. 4. **58** Even though some witnesses are difficult to identify, the majority listed on Hamo's charters seem to have been men from Blean, with only a few Canterbury citizens. In contrast, William Cokyn's grants, including the amalgamation of the two hospitals, were frequently witnessed by his peers from Canterbury, though occasionally local churchmen acted as witnesses for both men. However, such information may be misleading regarding their likely acquaintances, because it may merely reflect where these charters were drawn up (Hamo's manor at Blean, Canterbury); CCAL, U24 A4, A6, B1–8, B22–23, B25–27, B59–60, B66. Before Hamo's interest in the hospital, it does not appear to have held land in Blean, but it may have received a few grants of property and rents from outside the Westgate. This may indicate the importance of physical proximity between the hospital's interests and Hamo's, and thus the likelihood of personal connections between him and those at St Thomas', as well as the court officials in the hundred of

Hamo used a number of grant types in his dealings with Eastbridge, which seems to indicate that he was involved in a complex relationship with the house initiated through his almsgiving. About half of his grants were gifts in pure and perpetual alms, like the grant of an area of land with appurtenances between 'Nigrethe' and 'Mideldich', which he made to the hospital in free and pure alms for his soul and for the souls of his ancestors and successors.[59] The remainder of his grants used a range of forms wherein he sought various counter-gifts from the hospital. In another undated charter, he granted to the hospital six acres of woodland in his wood called 'Nigrede' for his soul, for the souls of his father, ancestors and successors in free, pure and perpetual alms, the hospital paying him five silver marks and 5s. 4d. for the woods.[60] The first of these two examples might be considered an act of charity; the recipient was under no obligation in law to provide a counter-gift. Yet both Hamo and the master of Eastbridge knew that such a gift would be expected as part of the moral economy. For Hamo, the prayers of his grateful beneficiaries would benefit him on both sides of the grave, binding him to the hospital forever as one of its worthy benefactors. The hospital too gained from the relationship; it was a welcome confirmation of Eastbridge's position as a worthy charitable institution. The latter example might also be seen as a charitable act because it was a public demonstration of his commitment to the hospital. For Hamo, and for the hospital, the counter-gifts of money and prayers were not morally mutually exclusive, both forms contributing to their relationship. Furthermore, such a relationship was ongoing, his role as an important benefactor given expression by the commemorative and intercessory actions of the hospital staff, which would be understood by his contemporaries and successors as the mark of a worthy and charitable nobleman.[61]

Nor was his special link with Eastbridge the result of his own grants alone, because he was apparently able to persuade some of his tenants to engage in similar exchanges, albeit often involving small grants. Michael, Lambert and John, the sons of Helye de Blen, granted to the hospital land and woodland in Blean, their charter confirmed by Hamo in a charter of his own and recorded in his court at Blean.[62] Under the terms of his grant, Hamo expected that the hospital would pay him 4s., a gift exchange in which he was able to demonstrate his role as a mediator between the hospital and the people of Blean. By so doing, he was illustrating the importance of the nobility in the promotion of such charitable acts, although it is not clear whether the small landholders in this area were seeking to emulate their lord or whether other factors were equally important.

Westgate, Canterbury city and St Gregory's which also had significant interests in these northern Canterbury parishes and suburbs; CCAL, U24 A2, A10, A44. Furthermore, Eastbridge hospital had apparently taken control of St John's hospital, Blean, before 1239, though whether this was a result of Eastbridge's property acquisitions in the area is unclear; St John's College, Cambridge D10.10. **59** CCAL, U24 B27.   **60** CCAL, U24 B25.   **61** Sweetinburgh, 'Supporting the hospitals', 241–7. **62** CCAL, U24 B39, B24.

Even though, unlike Leeds priory, the patronage of the hospital was not held by his family but by the archbishop of Canterbury, Hamo was apparently able to persuade his son Robert to support Eastbridge. As well as confirming his father's grants, Robert aided the hospital in his own right, but he seems to have been less generous than his father.[63] Patronage may have been a factor, but the level of benefaction to the hospital had also fallen, and Robert's support for Simon de Montfort may have prematurely curtailed his involvement with the hospital.[64] However, like his father, he may have influenced his tenants' attitudes towards Eastbridge, though fewer were involved and at least one may have supported the hospital as a consequence of his late master's ideas, rather than those of his late master's son.[65]

Hamo's mother and brother were also benefactors of Eastbridge hospital, yet whether as a consequence of his influence is difficult to ascertain, because all the relevant charters are undated. William, his brother, provided rents from his Blean lands, 40*d*. and three hens, and his widowed mother similarly provided rents from Blean.[66] Moreover, his sphere of influence may have extended beyond his immediate family and the small landholders of Blean. Giles de Badlesmere's gift to Eastbridge of land from the manor of Horton was confirmed by Hamo, both men employing the language of charity which suggests the importance of shared knowledge and ideas.[67] For Giles, his willingness to support a charitable house favoured by Hamo, a man of considerable local standing, may have been seen as a means of strengthening the ties between them and their families. Such bonds associated with patronage, marriage and political alliances apparently perceived by the local nobility as a means of maintaining their position in the county.

In addition to Eastbridge, Hamo supported three leper hospitals in east Kent, the Canterbury hospitals of St Laurence and St James, and St Bartholomew's at Dover. In his grants to the Canterbury hospitals he sought counter-gifts, which may indicate that he was not intending to develop a long-term relationship with these charitable institutions.[68] Instead, he apparently wished to develop closer relationships with religious houses in the Dover region, an area where he and his wife had strong connections. Interestingly, his gift to St Bartholomew's hospital was not directed towards the lepers; rather he intended the infirm brothers should be the recipients.[69] His use of the language of charity was not con-

---

63 CCAL, U24 B17, B9, B45, B48.   **64** The family fell from favour in 1263 after Robert joined Simon de Montfort which ended their role as noble benefactors; E. Hasted, *The history and topographical survey of the county of Kent*, 2nd ed., vol. 8 (1799), p. 526. Though speculation, if the family had survived his successors might have established a chantry at Eastbridge in the fourteenth century.   **65** One such was Robert Lupus, who appears to have been an old man when he made his grant to the hospital in 1245. The timing may imply that he was concerned to secure spiritual services through his grant to his late lord's chosen charitable institution; CCAL, U24 B33.   **66** CCAL, U24 B70, 72.   **67** CCAL, U24 D2, D4.   **68** His grant to St Laurence's hospital, for example, involved a quitclaim of an annual rent of 44*d*. for which he sought two marks; CCAL, DCc/Lit. MS. C20, f. 49.   **69** All his gifts were given in pure and perpetual alms, with no stipulation con-

fined to the hospital, but was extended to the neighbouring abbey of St Radigund. As holder of the barony of Folkestone and warden of the south coast ports, Hamo's interest in St Radigund's, in particular, also may have been linked to his contacts with the Crioil family who held the patronage.[70] Thus, through his various gift exchanges his soul, and the souls of his wife, ancestors and successors would be specially commemorated at two important religious institutions at Canterbury, two further establishments near Dover, and at Leeds priory. Through their complex charitable strategies, Hamo and his family sought to develop different relationships with the various religious and charitable establishments. Their place as one of the locally important noble families allowed them to influence the gift exchanges of others in the region, and they too were drawn to support particular houses as a consequence of marriage and other ties. For Eastbridge hospital, Hamo's support and influence were especially significant, leading to a relationship that lasted for several generations, and was possibly only broken because of the family's fall from favour, rather than a loss of interest in its chosen institution.

The place of burial might also be used to indicate links between the exchange partners, with implications with respect to such matters as patronage. This may be illustrated by an example from the de Clare family, the overlords of the de Crevequers. As a leading member of the aristocracy with royal connections, Richard de Clare, earl of Gloucester, was an extensive landholder nationally, whose family were patrons of Tonbridge priory and more especially Tewkesbury abbey, the burial choice of Richard's mother, his father's wishes being more ambiguous. Richard's own views similarly expressed the complexity of his exchange network, and this seems to have been resolved on his behalf by burial at three sites: his entrails in Canterbury cathedral, his heart at Tonbridge priory and his body at Tewkesbury abbey.[71] Although his tomb at Tewkesbury was sumptuous, the actual level of his benefactions to the house was not great. Instead, he seems to have favoured the Augustinian friars at Clare, which may represent the link with his ancient Clare ancestry before they gained the Gloucester inheritance.[72] His relationship with Tonbridge was linked to local landholding; the Clare family held the manor of Tonbridge and Richard's namesake had founded the priory there in the late twelfth century. This manor formed the basis for Richard's connections with Christchurch priory.[73] Interestingly, whereas Tonbridge and Tewkesbury invoked past generations and so memory with respect to the exchange process, the Canterbury gift and obligation process were designed

cerning the act of reciprocity, except that it should be for certain souls; Bodleian, Rawlinson MS. B.335, f. 95–5v; Rawlinson MS. B.336, ff. 19, 161. The wording of these grants suggests Thompson's earlier, less regulated form; Thompson, 'Monasteries', 108. **70** The witness lists provide evidence concerning connections between the two families. **71** C. Wilson, 'The medieval monuments' (1995), p. 507 n. 249. **72** B. Golding, 'Burials and benefactions' (1986), pp. 70–1. **73** *VCH Kent*, vol. 2, p. 167.

for the benefit of future generations; the earl's successors were to perform important offices at the enthronement of future archbishops in return for services rendered to the archbishop relating to the family manors.[74] Thus, such benefactors needed to balance their complex networks of exchange within the region and beyond, to provide the maximum spiritual and temporal benefit for themselves, for past generations of the family and where possible for those to come.

The difficult fourteenth century

By the thirteenth century, the major areas involved in the relationship between a religious house and its patron had been established. Though the relative and absolute importance of the different elements, for example elections, custody, exploitation, and/or confraternity, continued to vary, they were dependent on the type of patron and the power relationship between the two parties.[75] Initially, however, both partners may have considered the relationship advantageous, whatever the balance of power. By the early fourteenth century the situation had changed, and certain religious houses and a considerable number of hospitals in the county were said to be suffering from poverty, the patron's exploitation of the house being seen as a contributing factor.[76] Moreover, certain types of patron were thought to be more demanding than others and, although hospitals elsewhere in England appear to have suffered under their mother house, the main group implicated in Kent were the nation patrons, principally the crown and to a lesser extent the archbishop of Canterbury.[77] The areas most open to abuse were the choice of master, the selection of an incumbent for a benefice held by the house, the provision of hospitality, and the placing of corrodians at the institution.[78] The relative significance of these factors differed considerably

74 Wilson, 'Monuments', p. 507 n. 249.   75 Wood, *English monasteries*, pp. 40–136.   76 For example, the act of reciprocity whereby the house provided a corrody for those whom the patron nominated had been seen as a type of custom but in the fourteenth century, as Wood has indicated, this counter-gift was being claimed as a matter of right, thereby implying that the relationship between the parties was one of feudal tenure; ibid., pp. 114–15.   77 For Yorkshire, Cullum has found evidence that monastic patrons were prepared to exploit the assets of their hospitals, like Ellerton priory, which was failing to maintain its hospital by the late fourteenth century, against the express demands of Archbishop Neville; Cullum, 'Hospitals in Yorkshire', p. 310. In Kent the only known charge brought against a monastic patron by the head of the hospital concerned the failure of Christchurch to supply St James' in Canterbury as was customary in the early sixteenth century, though at times there must have been a thin line between the legitimate right of the patron and exploitation; Wood-Legh, *Kentish visitations*, p. 12. There does not appear to be any evidence that the bishops of Rochester used the hospitals in this way, though Bishop Hamo in the fourteenth century seems to have exploited his relationship with Rochester priory; Oakley, 'Rochester priory', p. 34.   78 As patrons of St Mary's hospital, Ospringe, Edward III, and earlier his father, were involved in the removal of certain brethren from Ospringe to its sister institution, St John's hospital in Oxford; and the crown seems to have appointed or ratified the appointment of various masters on the grounds that such appointments were during the king's pleasure; *CPR* 1247–1258, p. 185; 1258–1266, p. 284; 1266–1272, pp. 232, 707; 1292–1301, p. 148; 1307–1313, p. 285;

between institutions, being dependent on matters like the requirements of the patron and the facilities and assets of the house. With respect to Kent hospitals under royal patronage in both regions, the last two factors were the most significant, leading to considerable financial problems for the institutions concerned during the mid-fourteenth century, a situation which can be illustrated by looking at the use made of the latter privilege.[79]

Having taken the name of founder and benefactor for the Dover and Ospringe hospitals dedicated to St Mary, Henry III used this system of sending individuals to his religious institutions where they would receive board and lodging at the establishment's expense. He thereby implied that he considered that he had instituted a measure of regard between himself and the two hospitals, which would continue to operate through the ongoing cycle of gift exchanges.[80] Edward I and his son, however, did not share this outlook and seem to have been particularly ruthless exponents of the system of 'free' accommodation for their servants and others, an attitude resented across England.[81] Nor, as elsewhere, did the royal family confine its requirements to houses under royal patronage, because Queen Philippa sought a corrody for her maidservant at St James' hospital in Canterbury. Yet, on this occasion, the prior of Christchurch, the hospital's patron, refused her request on the grounds that it was not within his power.[82] His refusal may owe less to his powerlessness (he had previously assented to two others seeking corrodies there) than to his resentment about royal exploitation, because Christchurch had been pleading poverty and its inability to house royal corrodians from 1318, though this had not deterred the king from seeking such places at the priory.[83] Exploitation by the crown was one of the grievances voiced by

1313–1317, p. 105; 1317–1321, p. 321; 1327–1330, pp. 58, 500; 1330–1334, p. 425; 1348–1350, pp. 260, 286, 368; *CCR* 1313–1318, p. 55; 1318–1323, p. 62; 1327–1330, p. 53; 1330–1333, p. 551; 1333–1337, p. 347. **79** The choice of master may have been equally important with regard to Ospringe, but it is difficult, without further information, to know whether the apparently poor choices made in the late thirteenth and early fourteenth centuries were the result of the king as patron considering the needs of his retainers before the hospital, or whether it was principally bad judgement; Frohnsdorff, *Maison Dieu*, pp. 21–2. Certain archbishops and the king, during vacancies at Canterbury, do seem to have used the office of master as a means of advancing particular clerics and king's clerks, but the visitation evidence and the introduction of revised ordinances do not show a link between these appointees and mismanagement. However, during the fourteenth century three of the masters at the archbishop's hospital at Maidstone were pluralists (one of these was a king's clerk and appointed by the crown because the see was vacant), which was against the regulations and may have contributed to the halving in the number of poor accommodated there; A. Emden, *A biographical register of the University of Oxford to 1500* (1957–8), vol. 1, p. 257; vol. 2, pp. 1173, 1375; *CPR* 1348–1350, p. 308. **80** Frohnsdorff, *Maison Dieu*, pp. 10–12. **81** Seymour, 'Hospital in later middle ages', pp. 236–8. Harvey, *Living*, pp. 188–9. **82** He may also have been concerned about the well-being of the hospital and the problems such a corrodian would pose for the house; Sheppard, *Literae Cantuarienses*, vol. 2, p. 282. **83** Alice de Hertlip received her corrody in 1342, to be followed by her sister; ibid., vol. 2, p. 262. The priory's problems concerning poverty and royal corrodians; ibid., vol. 1, p. 42; vol. 2, pp. 122, 212, 234; vol. 3, p. 32.

the church in 1309, the clergy again raising the issue in 1315 at Edward III's first parliament.[84] Their concern emanated from the grievous financial problems experienced by some religious establishments, a consequence of the nature of the exchange process. For these houses the provision of corrodies failed to provide them with any form of compensation at entry, the patron believing that such gifts were unnecessary because he or his ancestors had supplied the initial endowment. Consequently, for the institution concerned there was a considerable imbalance between income and outgo in terms of these corrodies, a problem magnified by the immortality of the corrodian, because even though individuals did die their place was soon given to another. As a result, some houses were rarely free from this drain on their resources, which was especially difficult for those houses that were expected to provide for more than one corrodian or those with very limited assets. Certain religious houses, however, had been successful in lawfully establishing their right to give such corrodies by courtesy only, while others used any method available to try to delay their implementation.[85]

The relationship between St Mary's hospital in Ospringe and the crown exemplifies many of these problems. In about 1234, within a few years of his majority, Henry III appropriated the title of founder and patron of St Mary's, thereby providing him with a second institution where he might secure hospitality and other privileges. In turn, the hospital received valuable capital assets, protection and the likelihood of further benefaction from those of the royal household and local landholders who wished to be linked to a prestigious royal hospital and one of spiritual merit through its aid to poor pilgrims. As patrons, Henry and his successors expected to receive the right to hospitality for themselves. Henry also expected that this would be extended to his household and officials, a privilege that may have necessitated an expensive building programme and extensive provisioning arrangements for the hospital's guests. This alone presumably caused a severe drain on the hospital's resources, but was compounded by the king's insistence that his nominees should become residents there, the first royal corrodian arriving in 1258.[86] His grandson appears to have been especially ruthless in his exploitation of the hospital's facilities, placing three concurrent corrodians at Ospringe during the second and third decades of the fourteenth century.[87] There may have been six lay brothers and three chaplains at the hospital during this period, which meant the corrodians constituted a large proportion of the total number of persons dependent on the hospital's annual revenue. The situation was exacerbated by the king's requirement of hospitality when travelling between

84 Wood, *English monasteries*, p. 115; Harvey, *Living*, p. 189. 85 At Glastonbury the abbot appealed to the queen to intercede on behalf of the house when he attempted to thwart Edward III's nomination of a corrodian at the abbey; Keil, 'Corrodies', 116. 86 *CCR* 1256–1259, p. 337; *CCR* 1272–1279, p. 445; *CCR* 1288–1296, p. 250; *CPR* 1307–1313, pp. 9, 544; *CCR* 1313–1318, pp. 83, 90, 192. 87 S. Rigold, 'Two Kentish hospitals re-examined' (1964), 36.

London and Canterbury and the time needed to manage the hospital's scattered lands and property.[88] Apart from the need to supply the corrodians with food and clothing, the hospital may have had to build extra accommodation at a time when royal tax demands were becoming more common.[89] Unlike some institutions, which seem to have found ways of obstructing the king, the master at St Mary's hospital apparently had very little success in reducing the numbers of corrodians sent there, which meant that the fourteenth century was a difficult time for the house. Thus, even when the problems of its poverty were recognised by the crown in 1330, the king seems to have been loathe to relinquish his prerogative concerning such places except in the short-term, apparently believing that the crown's requirements were paramount.[90] There is little to suggest, moreover, that the king's frequent sight of the poor state of the hospital prompted him to investigate the situation, and nothing was apparently done until the early fifteenth century. In 1415, for example, the hospital's problems were said to have resulted from poor governance by the previous masters and the charging of great annuities, pensions and corrodies to the hospital.[91]

Although the crown was the prime user of this system in Kent, sending corrodians to the two pilgrim hospitals of Dover and Ospringe, to the hospital of St Peter and St Paul at Maidstone, and to certain Benedictine houses at Canterbury, Dover and Faversham, other patrons sought similar benefits.[92] As a result, patrons might become engaged in complex reciprocal exchanges with prospective corrodians, other patrons and the house itself, though in some instances patrons did refuse to grant corrodies which they believed were prejudicial for their institution. This apparent greater regard by the patron for his house, even if it did not extend to further gift-giving at the entry of the corrodian, may characterize the archbishop's gift of places at his hospitals of St John and St Nicholas in Canterbury. The archbishops were apparently very sparing

---

88 Rigold in Smith, 'Excavation of St Mary', 89. The surviving masters' accounts for the Maison Dieu suggest that guests were well fed. In the account for 1293–4 Prince Edward was provided with four gallons of wine during his visit. During the same year, when the sheriff of Kent was collecting royal dues, his visit cost the hospital 6s. 10d. in victuals; St John's College, Cambridge, D2/1/3b. **89** Smith, 'Excavation of St Mary', 102–5; Frohnsdorff, *Maison Dieu*, p. 20. **90** In 1330 Edward decreed that the master and brothers should be free from providing sustenance out of their house as had been done at the late king's request because Robert le Messenger was now dead; *CPR* 1327–1330, p. 494. However, in 1335, Gilbert de Sheffeld was sent to Ospringe and others followed; *CCR* 1333–1337, p. 503; *CCR* 1343–1346, p. 220; *CCR* 1360–1364, p. 133. **91** For example, the hospital claimed poverty in 1325, 1332, 1334, 1338, 1340, 1341; *CCR* 1323–1327, p. 421; *CCR* 1330–1333, p. 520; *CCR* 1333–1337, p. 275; *CCR* 1337–1339, p. 502; *CCR* 1339–1341, p. 499; *CCR* 1341–1343, p. 187; *CPR* 1413–1416, p. 364. Interestingly, Frohnsdorff considers that the king was keen to keep the ecclesiastical authorities out of the hospital at a time when he was apparently not prepared to deal with the problems there; Frohnsdorff, *Maison Dieu*, p. 22. **92** The king sent a corrodian to the Maidstone hospital during a vacancy at the Canterbury see; *CPR* 1374–1377, p. 81.

in their use of such privileges and, unlike the royal corrodians, the recipients were probably rarely aged or infirm servants from the archbishop's household, but were more often local people.[93] The situation did differ at St Peter and St Paul's hospital in Maidstone, however, where certain archbishops did exercise their rights much more extensively, possibly as a consequence of its changed status and function following its refoundation as a college in 1395.[94] Nevertheless, even for the Canterbury hospitals, such measures may have had a detrimental effect on their well-being, especially at a time when they were facing other financial difficulties, which led them to claim poverty and tax exemption, a condition that the crown was apparently willing to recognise.[95] As a way of overcoming these severe financial difficulties, the hospital authorities needed to seek further gifts, which meant they often found themselves engaged in the provision of various counter-gifts. In some instances such measures were sufficient to ensure the hospital's survival, but at St Mary's, Ospringe, financial problems were compounded by difficulties over personnel at the hospital. The resulting negative balance with the crown during this period may, therefore, have had repercussions for its long-term future, probably contributing to its subsequent demise at the beginning of the sixteenth century.[96]

Benefaction in the late middle ages

The diversity of exchange partners within the three parts of the spiritual economy: parochial, sub-parochial and extra-parochial allowed Everyman a degree of choice, but this latitude was tempered by the knowledge that some exchanges were considered compulsory, like tithes and mortuary payments, while society also placed restrictions on the freedom of the individual.[97] As a way of exploring ideas about choice with regard to the hospital, this sub-section concentrates

---

93 Many were from the area around Canterbury, like Walter Wenderton of Ickham who was to receive a place at St John's, and John Pette of Stodmarsh who was granted a corrody at St Nicholas'; Jacob, *Register Chichele*, vol. 1, pp. 189–190. During periods when the see was vacant, the prior at Christchurch nominated the corrodians at both hospitals; such people were said to be confrater and poor which may imply they had previously developed a relationship with the priory; CCAL, DCc/Reg. G, ff. 194v, 226, 285.   **94** Archbishop Winchelsey intended his servant, Stephen de Wengham would receive a corrody at the Maidstone hospital in 1306; Graham, *Registrum Winchelsey*, vol. 1, p. 507. Archbishop Islip was said to have given two concurrent corrodies there; *Cal. Inq. Misc.*, vol. 3, p. 361. Russell lists ten recipients who were admitted to the hospital between 1353 and 1380; Russell, *History of Maidstone*, p. 23.   **95** Both St John's and St Nicholas' hospitals were claiming poverty in 1338 and 1341, but it is not clear when corrodians were first admitted (fee-paying or the archbishop's nominees). The first known was in 1375, yet it seems likely there had been others before Robert Meller, though the giving of corrodies had been expressly forbidden in the ordinances of 1299 and the next known revision of the houses' statutes was in 1560; *CCR 1337–1339*, p. 502; *CCR 1341–1343*, p. 5; CCAL, DCc/Reg. G, f. 194v; *VCH Kent*, vol. 2, p. 211.   **96** In 1516 the hospital was granted to the college of St John the Evangelist, Cambridge; *L and P Henry VIII*, vol. 2, no. 1647; Underwood, *Index*, pp. 5–6.   **97** Swanson, *Church and society*, pp. 210–28.

on one type of reciprocal exchange, the testamentary bequest; allowing comparisons to be made in terms of regionalism and, more especially, localism. For example, taking the parish as a unit of analysis, the degree of testamentary support for the hospitals varied even within towns, but such differences became more marked when comparisons were made between towns, between urban and rural areas, and between rural parishes. On a broader scale there were also differences, like those between the hinterland of Sandwich and the hinterland of Dover, and between the Rochester and Canterbury regions. Looking first at the various towns in the two regions, a similar proportion of testators in the two cathedral cities made bequests to hospitals (Canterbury 15%, Rochester 14.6%), but there was a greater range of support found in the smaller towns, though the proportion never rose above one in five. The highest level of testamentary giving was recorded at Sandwich, where 17% of the town's testators made such bequests, and the lowest at New Romney and Dartford, where a mere 4% gave to hospitals (of the others, the figures for Hythe and Dover were 13.8%, and for Strood 14.7%).[98] Though figures for comparable provincial towns are only gradually becoming available, the level of support found in these north and west Kent towns seems closest to Cullum's figures for mid-fifteenth century York and those for London for the late fifteenth and early sixteenth centuries (about one in six testators).[99] Such diversity suggests that local conditions and ideas were perhaps more important than regional and national factors, a hypothesis that may also apply to differences over time. Even though the predominant trend in both the north and east Kent towns, as at London and Norwich, was a decline in the level

---

[98] Testamentary bequests for hospitals 1470–1530: Sandwich 57 bequests in 334 wills; Dover 21 in 152; Hythe 35 in 254; New Romney 5 in 128; Canterbury 135 in 898. Bequest for hospitals 1438–1537: Rochester 30 bequests in 206 wills; Strood 20 in 136. Figures for the Rochester diocese kindly supplied by Paul Lee. For the town of Faversham and its hinterland, including the Isle of Sheppey, testamentary bequests to hospitals were almost non-existant, though a few testators in Faversham either founded or supported maisondieu-type almshouses. Melanie Caiazza kindly provided this information. [99] For the period 1440–1459 17.5% of Yorkshire testators made bequests to maisonsdieu and hospitals; Cullum, 'Hir name was charite', p. 194. In Marche and Luffenam registers 23.4% of wills had hospital bequests, in Logge 17.8% and Jankyn 9.4% (1520s); Thomson, 'Piety in London', 187. Cullum also found that 40% of testators in Scarborough gave to the hospitals which seems closest to the figure for Norwich where, for the period 1370–1532, 38% gave to at least one of the sick-houses near the gates; Cullum, 'Hospitals of Yorkshire', p. 293; Tanner, *Church in Norwich*, p. 223. In contrast, there was very little support by the testators of Bury St Edmund's. Eleven testators in 559 wills (2%) left bequests to hospitals for the period 1451–1500. The town had at least seven hospitals and a higher proportion of the Bury testators had provided them with bequests during the late fourteenth and early fifteenth centuries, so it is not clear why they were apparently losing interest. They may have felt the hospitals were sufficiently well endowed, though it seems more likely the strong link between the hospitals and the abbey was a significant factor. However, it does show that the presence of several hospitals in a town did not necessarily produce support for such charitable institutions. Mark Merry kindly supplied the data for the Bury hospitals.

of testamentary support directed towards the hospitals, the situation at Dover differed considerably.[1] Bequests to St Mary's hospital, Dover, rose during the second half of the period, apparently associated with the master, Sir John Clerke, leading to a cluster of post-mortem gifts during the 1520s, following his actions on behalf of the town in the previous decade.[2] The reversal of trends seen elsewhere in Kent was probably primarily a consequence of the small number of testators involved, but is interesting and may imply that benefaction was linked to matters like the personnel at a particular hospital.[3]

Most hospitals in Kent were sited in or near a town, and proximity to these institutions was likely to produce testamentary support. In general terms, this seems to have been the case, and the greater the choice of hospitals within the locality the higher the proportion of testators engaging in such exchanges.[4] The reasons for this are likely to relate to a number of factors, some of which were interlinked, like the number of hospitals, the size of the town and the levels of wealth displayed in the testamentary materials. Thus Canterbury, the largest town in the county, may have had the most prosperous citizens and the highest proportion of these wealthier individuals in Kent, a situation apparently reflected in the figures, because the Canterbury testators were most likely to make bequests to extra-parochial recipients, though not the hospitals. These townspeople were sufficiently wealthy to be able to engage in a wide range of gift exchanges in the spiritual economy. The presence of prosperous potential donors, however, was not sufficient to guarantee support for a particular establishment or category of institution (the monastic houses, the friars and the hospitals), and the reputation, longevity and type of counter-gift on offer from the recipient institution was part of the decision-making process. At Canterbury, this seemingly resulted in a higher level of support for the monastic houses (almost one in three testators) compared to the rest of the county: the percentage for the Rochester diocese was 6.8% and for east Kent excluding Canterbury 2.5%. Yet, even though the monastic house was the favoured extra-parochial exchange partner for the leading Canterbury citizens, the friaries and hospitals were not completely neglected. This benefaction was in addition to the giving of parish and sub-parish bequests and may suggest that,

---

1 Although Tanner lists the hospitals singly or as part of a group, the downward trend in the number of testators supporting the hospitals was generally applicable. For example, for the period 1490–1517 32% of lay testators gave to St Paul's hospital in Norwich and between 1518–1532 the percentage had fallen to 22%; Tanner, *Church in Norwich*, p. 223; Thomson, 'Piety in London', 187. 2 See chapter 3. 3 Though negative evidence is notoriously difficult to use, it is possible that the almost total absence of bequests to St Thomas' hospital, Canterbury, may be linked to the apparent use of the mastership in the fifteenth century by various archbishops for their nephews, while the early sixteenth-century masters were pluralists; Emden, *Register of Oxford to 1500*, vol. 1, pp. 229, 412; vol. 2, pp. 1032, 1187; vol. 3, p. 2085. 4 However, as noted above, this was not always true, and in the north Kent town of Dartford the presence of three hospitals in the town did not lead to large numbers of bequests; Lee, 'Monastic and secular religion', p. 184.

unlike many other testators in the county, they were able to choose a wider range of exchange partners, most of which were local and so locally well-known.[5] With respect to the hospitals, as mentioned above, the level of testamentary support given by the townspeople of Canterbury was similar at Rochester, Strood and at three of the Cinque Ports. All had at least two hospitals, a factor that may have been significant with respect to choice, but the favouring of particular hospitals may have been equally important, like Lanfranc's two foundations at Canterbury or St Bartholomew's hospital at Hythe. Testators were most likely to aid more than one hospital when there were at least four in the town, and at Sandwich, Rochester and Canterbury the most frequent pairings were a leper hospital and one for the poor, each often receiving the same sized bequest.[6]

Conversely, the presence of a hospital(s) in a town was not sufficient to ensure any support, even when there were no other extra-parochial recipients in the locality. At Romney, the testators apparently showed little interest in the town's hospitals, even though one was still caring for local poor people. They were equally unwilling to help any of the monastic houses or friaries in the region, preferring instead to support the town's parish churches. This preference for the parish and the sub-parish as the focus for testamentary giving may be a characteristic of small Kentish towns (below 1000 persons) generally, though local and regional factors were presumably significant.[7] For the townspeople of New Romney, economic and demographic problems put a considerable strain on their resources regarding the upkeep of the town's parish churches, which meant few wished or were able to seek additional exchange partners.[8] Testators from the small towns of the Rochester diocese, for example Gravesend, demonstrated similar preferences for parochial and sub-parochial based religion and bequests

---

5 The Canterbury citizens were apparently willing to support the friars (26% of testators), similar to the proportion at Sandwich (29%), whereas for the rest of the eastern part of the diocese support was minimal (4.8%). **6** For example, John Dogett of Rochester in 1490 bequeathed 40*d.* to each of the two houses of St Bartholomew's next Rochester (Chatham) and St Katherine's, Rochester (he also gave 40*d.* to the third hospital in the locality: the hospital of the White Ditch at Strood); CKS, DRb/Pwr5, f. 130. John Plompton of Canterbury in 1501 bequeathed 3*s.* 4*d.* each to the hospitals of St John and St Nicholas and, as often occurred, a smaller bequest to Maynard's hospital, in this instance 12*d.*; CKS, PRC 32/7, f. 74. John Archer of Sandwich in 1490 left 20*d.* each to St John's hospital and the Maldry; CKS, PRC 32/3, f. 268. **7** There may have been a few exceptions, like Folkestone, but in this instance the local priory held the parish church, where its own staff presided. Throughout the period, more than 50% of Folkestone testators (eighty bequests in 155 wills for the period 1470–1530) supported the vicar (curate), but certain individual monks also received some support until 1506. Nicholas Baker was the last to mention them, which may imply that previously the wealthier townsmen had retained a degree of regard for the house. Similarly, though possibly to a more limited extent, this may also have occurred with respect to St Mary's parish church in Dover and the Maison Dieu; see chapter 3. **8** New Romney's existence as a port was curtailed by the effects of longshore drift and storm damage, the town becoming increasingly distant from the sea.

to hospitals were equally rare, their testamentary strategies apparently reflecting orthodox attitudes.[9] Areas known for Lollard connections and ideas, like the small towns of the Kentish Weald, also witnessed an absence of support for the very few local extra-parochial institutions.[10]

Furthermore, the concentration of hospitals in the urban communities meant that few rural testators in either east or north Kent were concerned to support the region's hospitals.[11] Of the few rural parishioners who did provide such bequests, most were apparently extending their links with the hospital rather than attempting to form a new relationship, their connections often a product of personal links with one of the inmates, either through family, friends or the parish.[12] Landholding offered another source of linkage, where the hospital, through its roles of landlord, tenant, tithe collector and receiver, provided opportunities for bonds to develop, a situation that may explain some of the bequests to St Mary's hospital at Dover.[13] One consequence of these links was the apparently haphazard geographical pattern of testamentary giving for certain hospitals, especially those which drew inmates from a wide catchment area, and which had widely scattered holdings.[14] Bequests might also appear haphazard over time, but occasionally there was a cluster of these gifts from a single parish, as at Deal in the first decade of the sixteenth century. Yet even here, although there were links between the individual benefactors and between individuals and Sandwich, it was not possible to identify the connection between any of them and St Anthony's hospital at Sandwich, the recipient institution.[15]

In terms of testamentary support, hospitals were generally aided by the local leading townspeople resident throughout the town. The only qualification concerns Kent's largest urban community where the likelihood and level of bequests

---

9 Paul Lee has provided valuable ideas relating to the religious convictions of those living in the Rochester diocese; Lee, 'Monastic and secular religion', pp. 145–98. **10** For example, the testators of Tenterden did not make any bequests to hospitals and only 5 or 6% of these will-makers mentioned religious houses; Lutton, 'Heterodox and orthodox piety', p. 153. **11** Support for the hospitals from the parishes in Sandwich's hinterland was low: 1.5% (22 bequests in 1354 wills for the period 1470–1530); and was not much higher from Dover's hinterland: 3.25% (14 bequests in 401 wills). Similarly, few rural testators from the Rochester diocese made such bequests, Lee, 'Monastic and secular religion', p. 184, n. 303. **12** It is possible Thomas Consaunt snr of Chislet had already entered St John's, Canterbury, when Thomas Dodd and Richard Knyght, also of Chislet, made their wills in 1479 and 1480, respectively, where each left a bequest to the same Canterbury hospital; CKS, PRC 17/3, f. 282; 17/3, f. 431. However, it is not clear what the connection was between Richard Chapman of Ash (1501) and St James' hospital, Canterbury, before he bequeathed cash to it in return for prayers for his soul; CKS, PRC 33/1, f. 87. **13** See chapter 3. **14** Knowledge about the reputatation and status of particular institutions was also disseminated across the region and beyond, a product of widespread migration and other forms of contact. For example, St Bartholomew's at Sandwich appears to have drawn inmates from a fifty-mile radius, while St John's at Canterbury drew people from the Romney Marsh area (about thirty miles from Canterbury), as well as those sent by the archbishop from London; CKS, PRC 32/15, f. 127; 17/3, f. 118; Jacob, *Register Chichele*, vol. 3, p. 105. **15** See chapter 4.

to the smaller Canterbury hospitals may have been influenced by proximity to the institution.[16] For example, the hospitals of St James and St Laurence were sited outside the southern town walls of Canterbury. Neither received any testamentary bequests from people in the western Canterbury parishes of St Dunstan and Holy Cross, nor from the northern parishes of St Mary Northgate and St Alphage. Rather, the majority of their benefactors lived in three of the southern parishes of St Mildred, St George and St Paul; and St James' also received a few bequests from the parish of Thanington, its own parish. In contrast, Canterbury's two largest hospitals, St John's and St Nicholas' drew post-mortem support from all the town's parishes except St Martin's in its eastern suburbs, as well as bequests (seven to St John's and two to St Nicholas') from a few rural parishioners in the area between Canterbury and Sandwich, and four more from testators in the Rochester diocese.[17] The regional and national importance of these two hospitals may partly explain even this small level of support from outside the Canterbury diocese, because very few testators in Kent appear to have shown any interest in hospitals more than fifteen miles away from their place of residence. Those testators, prepared to aid hospitals further afield, predominantly chose institutions from their natal parish or area, or from the place where they or their family were landholders.[18] Others sought special intercessory services or other commemorative acts, which may imply that at this critical point in their lives testators wished to develop a relationship with their chosen hospital based on a single symbolic act of charity, thus stressing their worthy intentions for the benefit of an equally worthy institution.[19] This more personal approach to the process of reciprocity by testators in Kent was the product of numerous and complex factors, but wealth, status and provincialism were presumably significant and may partly explain the exceptional nature of Edward Mynot's hospital bequests.[20]

---

16 The numbers involved are extremely small and Canterbury on a national scale was no more than a medium-sized town, but such differences are interesting.   **17** It seems highly likely that these hospitals also received testamentary gifts from other parishes in Canterbury's hinterland, but this has yet to be investigated.   **18** For example, Leticia Brent (1480) intended that if she died in London she was to be buried in the Trinity chapel at Whittington's college next to her first husband, the college receiving 20s.; CKS, PRC 17/5, f. 50. Her London lands and further connections may have influenced Jane Frogenhale, a gentlewoman, to seek masses 'at Scala Coeli' at the Savoy or Westminster abbey in 1516; CKS, PRC 17/13, f. 89; E. Duffy, *The stripping of the altars* (1992), p. 376. The career of Sir John Roo, the vicar at Hakington near Canterbury, can be followed through his bequests: he left 13s. 4d. to the house of poor men in Bodmin, the old leper hospital of St Lawrence, his natal town; certain books to Exeter college, Oxford, where he had been a scholar, and various bequests to religious houses in Canterbury, the three friaries, Lanfranc's two hospitals, the Corpus Christi guild at St Thomas' hospital in the city; the abbot of Faversham and his own church; CKS, PRC 17/15, f. 155.   **19** In 1511, John Osmundeston intended that those of the fraternity of St Thomas' hospital in Rome should pray for his soul, the preceptor receiving his bequest; CKS, PRC 17/12, f. 33.   **20** He was an exceptionally wealthy Canterbury citizen and major benefactor to the city. Moreover, in his position as town clerk and in his business affairs he had developed widespread contacts in the county and, more importantly, London. His extremely generous

Testators in both north and east Kent sought a range of counter-gifts from the hospital, which may be classified under concerns for the living and for the dead. For the living, the gift was valued as a charitable act, its merit seen by a wide audience of the hospital inmates, the hospital's patrons, the testator's family, friends and neighbours and, possibly of even greater importance, God and his saints. Presumably, most testators assumed the worthiness of the deed would be self-evident, but occasionally donors appear to have believed they ought to remove any chance of ambiguity, and the possible charge of simony, which might have nullified the spiritual value of the exchange process.[21] Others hoped for the gift of confraternity, a provision granted during life which the testator wished to confirm in death, so that he would remain among the hospital's community for all time, a recipient of the intercessory services provided by the living for the dead. Thus Joane Bakke, in 1500, intended that the brothers and sisters of St John's, Canterbury, would receive 3s. 4d. annually for three years in order to celebrate her obit as they would for a brother or sister who had died there.[22] The only fraternity in the county known to have had its own almshouse was the Corpus Christi guild at Maidstone, while the only hospital known to have housed a fraternity was St Thomas' hospital, Canterbury, at which the Corpus Christi fraternity met.[23] The apparent lack of fraternal links between hospitals and members of the local populace is interesting. It might have been expected that the hospital authorities would have seen this gift as a valuable means of strengthening the position of the hospital in its environs, especially as such gifts were available at certain monastic houses where they were apparently valued by the local leading citizens.[24] However, certain testators did seek a personal relationship

bequests (in his will dated 1487 he left 6s. 8d. to each lazar house in Kent) would appear to suggest that his ideas and aspirations were more in keeping with his peers in London, rather than his fellow Canterbury citizens. However, he also sought a more personal gift exchange with St John's hospital in Canterbury, including specified acts of intercession, which was more akin to the bequests of the wealthier Canterbury citizenry; CKS, PRC 17/5, f. 67. For comparison: John Bartilmewe (1526), a citizen of London, intended that each lazar house within 4 miles of London was to receive 6s. 8d. in bread and victuals to pray especially for his soul; PRO, Prob 11/22, f. 9v. Reference supplied by Paul Lee. **21** For example, John Bishop of Rochester (1497) bequeathed 20s. to the hospital of St Bartholomew at Chatham to be used for reparations and other good deeds in the same place, thereby informing his audience that he was engaged in a charitable gift exchange of special merit; CKS, DRb/Pwr6, f. 60v. **22** CKS, PRC 17/7, f. 213. Interestingly, the only testator from Canterbury known to have stipulated that he wished his name to be recorded in the bede-roll at a hospital was John Whytlok. He wished to be remembered at both St Nicholas' and St John's hospitals in Canterbury; CKS, PRC 32/7, f. 70. **23** Russell, *History of Maidstone*, p. 165. John Williamson, the parson at St George's, Canterbury, appears to have been a member of the Corpus Christi fraternity because he remembered them in his will of 1521 (he bequeathed 26s. 8d. to them); CKS, PRC 17/15, f. 101. **24** Christchurch priory offered the gift of confraternity to members of the royal family and aristocracy, leading members of the gentry in Kent, merchants from London, but apparently to only a few from Canterbury itself; Dobson, 'Canterbury', pp. 146–7. Yet, there were a few from Canterbury who sought this gift post-mortem, which suggests that some leading

between themselves and the recipient institution through the giving of bequests to a named inmate or the master. Such gifts might reflect links based on family or friendship or, in the case of the clergy, the confessional or other spiritual services, the testamentary gift marking the culmination of this relationship.[25] By so doing, the donor was increasing the value of his gift as a symbolic reminder of the relationship, thereby expressing the regard felt by both partners for each other through their exchange.[26] A few testators appear to have perceived the hospital as a valuable institution for the care of their aged relatives or servants. It allowed them to make future provision when they were no longer able to do so. At Canterbury, the two most frequently favoured hospitals were St John's and St Nicholas', though the placing of St John's first may imply that the conditions there were more favourable.[27] Other hospitals were presumably selected in this way, but the only hospital chosen by testators from the Cinque Ports and surrounding countryside was St Bartholomew's at Sandwich.[28] Though the evidence is severely limited, it appears some found other ways of providing for family members through their gift exchanges with the hospital. John Rygby of Strood, for example, sought to provide his wife and servant with a source of income that would also safeguard their possession of his mill and might, in addi-

townspeople did wish to develop bonds with the priory (and similarly other monastic houses in Canterbury). This situation may be a reflection of the high proportion of testators in Canterbury who supported their local monastic houses compared to testators elsewhere in the county. For example, Agnes Vyncent (1518), a widow from St Alphage's parish, Canterbury, bequeathed her best girdle to the prior and convent of Christchurch so that they would admit her as a sister to their chapter; CKS, PRC 32/12, f. 132. From at least 1519, the Canterbury guild of shoemakers, curriers and cobblers had established a link with the local Austin friars; CCAL, CC/Woodruff Bundle LIV/2. **25** Neighbourliness may have been significant for both William Laurence of St Paul's parish and Thomas Miller of Thanington. In 1506, William's hospital bequests concerned the nearby hospital of St Laurence, the three named sisters and the prioress; and Thomas' main gift was to a named sister at St James', the others at this local hospital receiving a smaller total amount; CKS, PRC 17/11, f. 298; 17/14, f. 179. This relationship might include more tangible acts by the recipient on behalf of the benefactor, like acting as an executor or overseer. In 1528, Thomas Marre of Canterbury bequeathed 6s. 8d. to Roger Hunt, a brother at St Nicholas' hospital, for his labour as the overseer of Thomas' will; CKS, PRC 17/13, f. 367. **26** Even though Isabel Payable (1513) did not state how Agnes Staple was to reciprocate, it was presumably well understood by the two women when Isabel, a widow and parishioner at St Mildred's, bequeathed her sanguine gown and black kirtle to Agnes, a sister at Maynard's hospital in the same parish; CKS, PRC 17/12, f. 526. **27** In 1526, William Tewkesbury stipulated that his wife, after his death, should provide sufficient monies to make his mother a sister at either St John's or St Nicholas' hospital. Furthermore, once she had been accepted his wife should furnish her with a bed, bedding and other necessaries; CKS, PRC 17/17, f. 213. **28** For example, William Gybbe (1527) of Hythe seems to have preferred St Bartholomew's at Sandwich for his daughter, rather than its namesake in his home town. He expected her to receive £10 from his estate which may have been about half of the highest entry fee charged. He was concerned about the reputation of the establishment because, if she was unable to gain a place there, his executors were to find her a place in another 'honest' hospital; CKS, PRC 32/14, f. 210.

tion, produce intercessory services for himself and possibly later for his wife. In his will of 1517, he stated that his malt mill should pass to his servant (John farmed the mill from the hospital of St Mary, Strood) on the condition that his servant would grind the hospital's malt 'by obligation'. John's wife was to continue paying rent for the mill to the master of the hospital.[29]

Provisions for the dead may have been even more important to the benefactor at this critical stage in his life, and for the hospital this seems to have produced a variety of gift exchanges. The likelihood that particular hospitals would become involved in these processes seems to have varied considerably, testators apparently considering such matters as the value of the exchange for the wellbeing of their soul and for their good name on earth, as well as the availability of particular counter-gifts. The first gift sought by a very small number of testators was burial in the hospital's chapel or churchyard, but most were former inmates, which suggests that the desire to remain physically within the hospital was primarily important only for those who had been part of the living community. Of the outsiders who did seek this reciprocal gift, the majority presumably had strong links with the hospital and its staff, especially the master, either through familial ties or those of friendship.[30] Intercessory services were considered a valuable counter-gift by some testators, who favoured certain hospitals over other religious institutions.[31] Inmates from the county's almshouses were rarely called upon to provide such services, donors preferring the brothers and sisters from the hospitals for the poor.[32] Some testators extended their desire for prayers to the inmates of the leper hospitals, but such people may have been poor rather than lepers, again indicating the worth placed on this group of recipients as spiritual intermediaries.[33] Yet this does not explain the lack of interest

---

29 CKS, DRb/Pwr7, f. 108v.   **30** See chapters 3 and 4. This desire was equally rare in the wills of the Rochester diocese. One of the few exceptions was Robert Shamell of Strood (1465) who sought burial at the hospital of St Bartholomew, Chatham. To facilitate this act he left 3s. 4d. to the hospital chapel; CKS, DRb/Pwr2, f. 277.   **31** From the Rochester diocese wills, the only hospitals receiving gifts for their chapel or explicitly asked to provide intercessory services were St Mary's at Strood, St John's at Sutton at Hone, St Nicholas' at Canterbury and two hospitals outside the county.   **32** Robert Clerke (1498) seems to have been unusual in his request for the brothers and sisters at St Bartholomew's at Hythe to pray for him, a hospital that might be classified as a bedehouse-type almshouse (but ideas about its longevity in the town may have been appropriated from its dedication to the same saint as Hythe's ancient leper house); CKS, PRC 32/4, f. 192. However, even with respect to the hospital for the poor, there seems to have been a considerable variation in such requests between hospitals in the same town, between towns and over time. For example, St Bartholomew's at Sandwich was rarely supported in this way at all, and the brothers and sisters were apparently not considered suitable spiritual intermediaries by the town's testators, whereas St John's hospital, Canterbury, another house that seems to have housed moderately prosperous corrodians, received 102 bequests from local testators, of whom thirty sought some form of intercessory service as a counter-gift.   **33** The proportion of bequests from local testators seeking intercessory services at St Nicholas' hospital, Canterbury, was less than at St John's 14 in 75 bequests), though it is unclear how many lepers were still at the hospital. It is more difficult to assess the

in the poor of the new almshouses, who might be poorer than their counterparts at the ancient hospitals, some of whom, at least, were moderately prosperous corrodians.[34] Consequently, the reputation of the house may have been
more significant, where longevity of existence, the identity of the patrons and
possibly the religious life of the hospital were important contributing factors.
For some testators the provision of additional religious counter-gifts, like a bede-
roll or specific commemoration and intercession, might have influenced their
willingness to support certain hospitals, both for their spiritual value and as a way
of publicly demonstrating their close links with a prestigious charitable institution. St John's hospital at Canterbury seems to have been one of the few houses
to offer such opportunities, though whether this reflects the favour shown St
John's by testators rather than an absence of opportunity elsewhere is unclear.[35]
The presence of priest brothers at most hospitals provided opportunities to engage
professionals, but the degree of interest varied considerably. Comparing St Mary's
hospital at Dover with the one at Strood, nineteen bequests were associated with
intercession from a total of thirty at the Dover hospital (it had a wider catchment area of about twenty miles), whereas St Mary's, Strood, received eleven
bequests associated with the hospital's church or for intercessory services from
a total of nineteen.[36] Furthermore, there seems to have been a difference in the
type of recipient targeted by testators, and thus the form of the counter-gift. The
principal recipients at Dover were the priest brothers, especially the master, while
at Strood the hospital church and its ornaments were the prime targets for bene-

position at Rochester. Testamentary benefactors there did not state a specific desire for intercessory services from the inmates at St Bartholomew's at Chatham or St Katherine's at Rochester
(their bequests were generally to the brothers and sisters or to the house), though St Mary's at
Strood did receive such bequests. This may suggest that at these Medway towns, testators considered the professional intercessors (the priest brothers of St Mary's) more valuable exchange partners for this type of counter-gift than the poor (probably neither St Bartholomew's nor St Katherine's
housed any/many lepers by this period).   **34** Certain inmates at St John's hospital, Canterbury,
seem to have been extremely wealthy which appears to make them a strange choice as providers
of intercessory prayers. Thus, John Swete's (1512) desire for the prayers of the bedeswoman of St
Clement's in St Mildred's parish in return for 6*d*. may have been perceived by many of his contemporaries as a more spiritual choice than Geoffrey Holman's (1478) much larger gift of 5*s*. to the
brothers and sisters of St John's for prayers for his soul; CKS, PRC 17/12, f. 239; 32/2, f. 414.   **35**
John Whytlok's (1503) testament seems to demonstrate the different types of counter-gift sought
by benefactors from the various hospitals. Yet all the inmates might be classified as poor and so
ought to have been seen as valuable exchange partners in their own right at the different institutions. The brothers and sisters at St John's and St Nicholas' were to set him in their bede-roll and
for this each house was to receive 5*s*.; Maynard's hospital was to receive 2*s*. 4*d* and the inmates
were to pray for his soul; while each of the poor bedesmen living in the almshouse of the old vicar's
gift was to receive 12*d*.; CKS, PRC 32/7, f. 70.   **36** Of the wills examined, only three testators
supported St Mary's at Ospringe, one from Faversham, a second from Hythe and a third from
Canterbury. The hospital archive contains the will of John Wellys of Ospringe (1465/6), who was
a generous benefactor; St John's College, Cambridge, D8.170.

factors. In contrast to the Dover hospital, which was expected to provide complex intercessory services, including the provision of obits or a temporary chantry,
donors of its counterpart at Strood merely sought the provision of prayers.[37] Yet
testators in neither of the Kent regions commonly saw hospitals as valued
exchange partners within their charitable strategy during the late middle ages.
Of those few who did, only a minority sought explicit reciprocal gifts, and for
these people their choices were a product of a complex range of factors, linked,
only in part, to the specific services available at particular hospitals.

37 See chapter 3. For example, at Strood Katherine Munde (1525), a widow, bequeathed her best
'kersche' to St Mary's hospital, her second 'curcher' to the high altar of the hospital's chapel and
from the sale of her house and lands a number of ornaments for the chapel 'as the master and his
brethren think most necessary'. For these they were to pray for her soul; CKS, DRb/Pwr7, f. 349v.

Dover's medieval hospitals

Chapters 3 and 4 move from national and regional surveys to the close consideration of particular hospitals in two specific communities, Dover and Sandwich. These towns were both head ports in the Cinque Ports Federation. Despite their importance as trading and strategic centres, neither developed to challenge the pre-eminence of the regional capital of Canterbury. In part this was due to historic institutional and geographical factors, in part their vulnerability to foreign depredations, and in part to later social and economic problems. Nonetheless, they were significant urban centres with distinctive cultural characteristics and complex populations possessing interests in extensive hinterlands.

The study of Dover's hospitals permits the detailed examination of both a pilgrim and a leper hospital, and provides the opportunity to assess the nature of monastic, lay aristocratic, and royal foundations. The presence of Dover priory, immediately to the north of the town, and St Radigund's abbey on the neighbouring higher ground, provide special local contexts for the operation of patronage and benefaction.

THE PLACE OF THE HOSPITAL IN MEDIEVAL DOVER

Consideration of the hospitals is undertaken first of all by division into significant time periods: 1) the mid-thirteenth century, the time of foundation and development of Dover's second hospital, 2) the mid-fourteenth century, a period of readjustment, and 3) c.1470–1530, when the town was beset by increasing economic, demographic, and social problems. The second part of the chapter explores the social history of the two hospitals for the whole period, examining their capacity to adapt as circumstances changed in late medieval provincial society. Each sub-section provides a brief description of the town during the chosen period, emphasizing the relevant developments of social structure. This is followed by an analytical description of the processes of exchange and reciprocity for the different institutional exchange partners and the townspeople. Even though the hospitals remain the focus of attention, other institutions, like the priory, are also examined to provide an assessment of the range of exchange partners active in the town and its hinterland. The identification of the diversity of

127

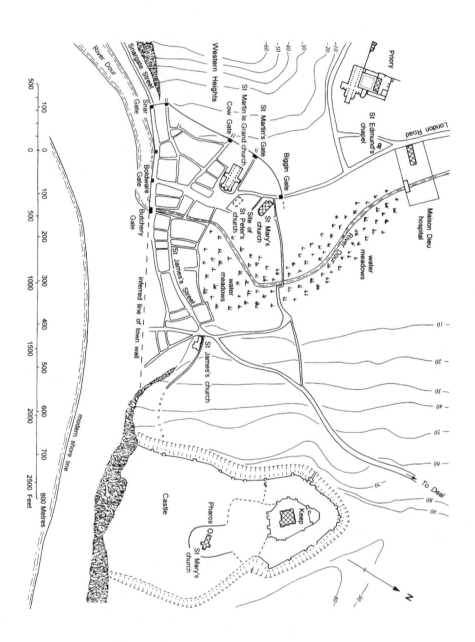

Figure 4 Map of Dover

available partners in benefaction and patronage and the range of processes by which exchanges are undertaken, permit the consideration of the peculiar factors at the local level governing charitable choice.

The mid-thirteenth century

By the thirteenth century, the massive castle works over shadowed the town and port of Dover, a physical reminder of royal jurisdiction which the king claimed through his official, the *praepositus* or bailiff, who received the fee-farm from the burgesses and, with the civic officers, presided over the town courts.[1] Dover's strategic importance in the defence of the realm and as an embarkation point for those crossing the narrow seas to France and other parts of continental Europe may indicate its main roles.[2] But the town also housed a thriving fishing community around St James' church, to the east of the river, and it was a significant port, both for coastal and international trade, especially with northern France and the Low Countries.[3]

The Benedictine priory of St Martin to the north of the town was a twelfth-century refoundation of the minster church of St Martin-le-Grand.[4] Initially staffed by secular canons, this community in the centre of the town had been suppressed by Archbishop Corbeuil, who intended to replace them with regular canons.[5] However, the prior at Christchurch, Canterbury, sought to staff the new priory with his own monks, beginning a long and bitter dispute between the two houses concerning Christchurch's wish to make Dover its daughter house. Following these changes, St Martin-le-Grand was accorded parochial status under the jurisdiction of the archbishop, who appointed the incumbent called the 'archipresbyter'. The parochial situation in Dover was extremely complicated because, in addition to the parish altar of St Martin, the church also housed the altars of the parishes of St Nicholas and St John the Baptist in its two apsidal chapels.[6] Nearby were the two parish churches of St Mary and St Peter,

---

1 According to Domesday, the burgesses had their own guild hall and were allowed to assess themselves with regard to the collective tax demand laid on the town; Morgan, *Domesday Book, Kent,* 1a–1a,b. They received further confirmation of their privileged status in a number of royal charters from successive Norman kings; K. Murray, *Constitutional history of the Cinque Ports* (1935), pp. 13–15. The Dover custumal details the duties and jurisdictions of the town officials and those of the crown; BL, Stowe MS. 850, ff. 133–42. 2 Henry II, his sons and grandson together spent in excess of £6,000 on the construction of Dover castle; R.A. Brown, H.M. Colvin and A.J. Taylor, *The history of the King's Works: the middle ages,* vol. 2 (1963), pp. 632–4. 3 The town's commercial activities were concentrated in an area between the church of St Martin-le-Grand and the harbour to the south, the fish market being held by the river. The annual St Martin's fair took place in the churchyard of the minster church, the royal grant for the fair dating from *c.*1160; J. Jones, *The records of Dover* (Dover 1907), pp. 16, 59. Archaeological evidence of the fishing community has been uncovered; K. Parfitt, personal communication. 4 In the Domesday record the land of the canons of St Martin's of Dover was listed separately; Morgan, *Domesday, Kent,* 1b,c–1d. 5 LPL, MS. 241, f. 2. 6 S. Statham, *The history of the castle, town and port of Dover* (1899), p. 176.

and to the east was St James' parish church. The church of St Mary de Castro was sited within the castle walls, the priest serving the castle garrison under the patronage of the constable of Dover castle.[7]

Two houses of Premonstratensian canons were in the town's hinterland, St Radigund's abbey at Bradsole to the north-west and West Langdon abbey to the north-east. Hugh, its first abbot, founded St Radigund's, apparently persuading several members of the regional nobility to provide gifts for the establishment and maintenance of the abbey.[8] There seems to have been some ambiguity about lordship and patronage, however, and, as Wood has indicated, this resulted in a redefining of the privileges linked to its foundation by Lord Poynings, its fourteenth-century patron.[9] Langdon was founded by a member of the nobility and continued to draw support from this same social group during its early history.[10]

Two matters of particular significance at this time were conflict and the increasing number of pilgrims. The priory, and probably the town, sustained considerable damage following the French invasion during 1216–17. The subsequent temporary halt to hostilities aided the town's recovery, its economy gaining from the growing numbers of foreign and local merchants who imported wine and luxury goods for resale in Canterbury and London.[11] But the resumption of war with France in the 1240s severely hindered international trade and similarly disrupted the fishing industry.[12] And in the early 1260s the citizenry supported Simon de Montfort against the crown, their defeat leading to a certain loss of autonomy, though the town was allowed to retain its privileged status.[13]

---

7 Ibid. p. 234.   **8** The cartulary for St Radigund's abbey; Bodleian, Rawlinson MS. B.336.   **9** Lord Poynings seems to have considered his holding of the advowson meant that the abbey had been founded by one of his ancestors; Wood, *English monasteries,* pp. 20–1.   **10** The foundation charter and a few others have been printed; Dugdale, *Monasticon Anglicanum,* vol. 7, p. 898.   **11** *CChR* 1226–1257, p. 50. The presence of foreign merchants, including Italians in the town, suggests the importance of international trade, though some trade was in the hands of local burgesses. For example, in 1229 several Dover merchants received a licence to trade in Gascony, and towards the end of this period there were Dover men listed among the wool merchants; *CPR* 1232–1247, p. 424; *CPR* 1247–1258, p. 379; *CPR* 1225–1232, pp. 277, 319; *CPR* 1266–1272, pp. 690, 699, 713.   **12** The town may have gained from the growing restrictions placed on merchants and others in 1264 when, for reasons of national security, entry and exit from the realm was restricted to Dover for most people; *CPR* 1258–1266, p. 361.   **13** The constable of Dover castle was given jurisdiction over the port; Statham, *Dover,* pp. 50, 52. It may have been considered necessary because of Dover's strategic importance against the French, though in the past the constable had organized the sea defences using the men of the Cinque Ports. This suggests that the king considered it was advisable to adopt a policy of co-operation and coercion, especially with respect to the men of Dover. Consequently, their earlier valuable service to the crown in terms of ship-service was rewarded with the recognition of the town's mayor in 1256 and the first single charter granting the liberties in common to the Cinque Ports in 1260. At the same time the constable, and later the warden of the Cinque Ports remained powerful royal officials locally and regionally; S. Statham (ed.), *Dover charters and other documents in the possession of the corporation of Dover* (1902), p. xvii, citing *Rot. Parl.,* 40 Henry III. Murray, *Constitutional history,* p. 11.

In 1220 the translation of Becket's bones to the new shrine gave new impetus to the cult, and Dover's virtual monopoly of the passenger traffic across the Channel brought many overseas pilgrims to the port.[14] Such people were drawn from a wide range of social groups, which meant that even though the poor pilgrims may have been a drain on the town's resources, others like the abbess of Fontevrault probably provided valuable revenue.[15] Consequently, the provision of board and lodging for pilgrims and others passing through Dover was an important part of the town's economy, providing work for the innkeepers and those engaged in associated occupations, like the hackneymen and the suppliers of victuals.[16]

St Mary's hospital or the Maison Dieu

Dover's second hospital, traditionally dating from 1203, provided hospitality for poor pilgrims and the poor. Hubert de Burgh, as founder, generously conferred on St Mary's hospital the manor and advowson of Eastbridge in Romney Marsh, the advowson of Ospringe church, land in London, and further manors and lands in south-east Kent.[17] His actions may have stemmed from his close association with the town as constable of Dover castle and his local knowledge about the rapidly growing number of pilgrims in need of shelter at the port. Though primarily concerned with military matters, his active defence of the town and role as leader of the portsmen may have created a strong bond between Hubert and the men of Dover that he wished to extend through his charitable benefactions. His choice of a hospital for the poor and pilgrims suggests his desire to demonstrate through this symbolic gesture and practical aid his concern for the spiritual poor, as shown by the image of 'Christ the Pilgrim', which was believed by contemporaries to provide additional merit to the pious gift.[18] In addition to such neighbourly concerns, the spiritual merits of his gift-giving were valuable for the salvation of his soul.[19] By the time of his death in 1243 he had established at several religious houses the specific counter-gifts of intercession and commemoration, of which the hospital at Dover was probably the second most important after his chantry-type foundation at Westminster.[20]

14 For example, in 1226 a letter patent directed to the Cinque Ports stated that foot passengers and those on horseback were only to leave the realm via Dover; *CPR* 1225–1232, p. 25. **15** Though in her case she had an ancient privilege regarding exemption from toll on her passage; *CPR* 1232–1247, p. 62. **16** Disagreements did occur between the townspeople and certain travellers, either concerning the Channel crossing or covering their stay in Dover. Disputes were usually linked to non-payment or particularly high prices charged by the portsmen, and such difficulties became even more common during the following century; *CPR* 1247–1258, pp. 610, 662. **17** *CChR* 1226–1257, pp. 78, 141, 315. J. Lyon, *The history of the town and port of Dover* (1813), pp. 44–5. **18** The image of 'Christ the Pilgrim', who was cold, hungry, thirsty and in need of hospitality, was used in sermons by the friars; Henderson, *Piety and charity*, p. 245. **19** Though not stated in any of the documents relating to his gift-giving to the hospital, it is possible that as founder he received the reciprocal gift of confraternity, which was apparently sought by some later benefactors; I. Churchill, R. Griffin and F. Hardman, *Calendar of Kent Feet of Fines* (1956), p. 309. **20** He was also a benefactor to two other

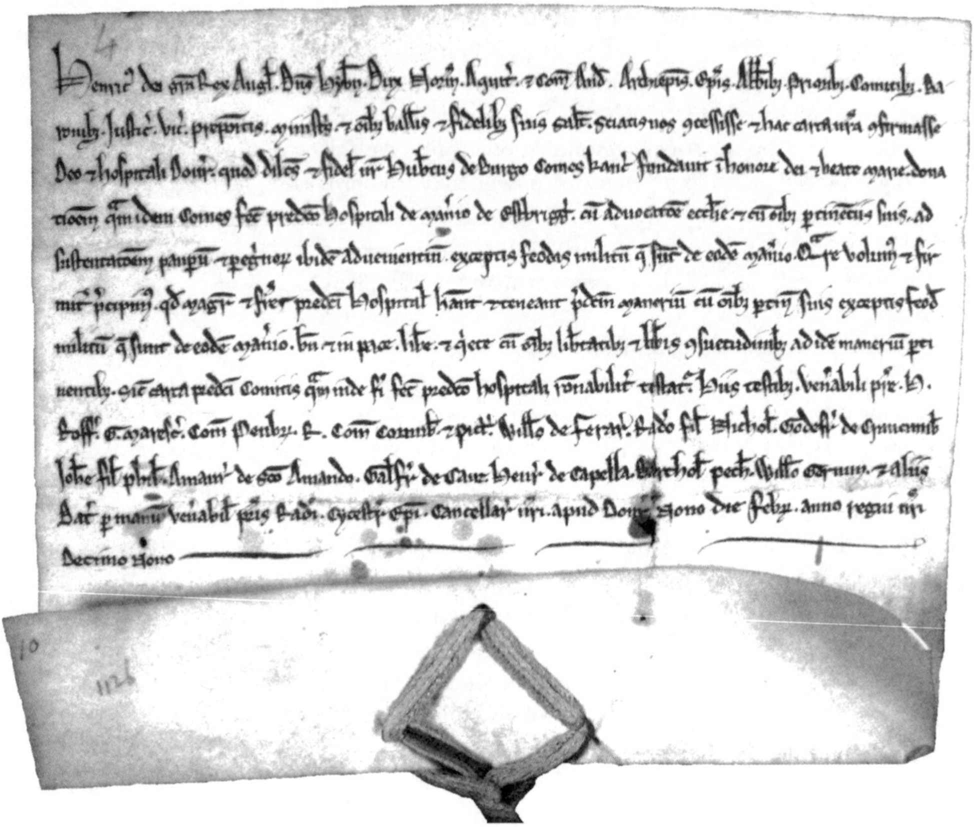

Figure 5 Royal charter re-confirming Hubert de Burgh's gift to
St Mary's hospital, Dover. EKA, Do/ZQ 3, courtesy Dover District
Council and East Kent Archives; photo: Kent County Council

Henry III's priorities, when he usurped the patronage and the name of founder
of St Mary's, seem to relate to his desire to establish his charitable concern for
the pilgrims. As a boy of twelve he was probably deeply affected by the splen-
dour and spiritual significance of the occasion when he witnessed the translation
of Becket's bones in 1220.[21] For Henry there was no ideological contradiction
between his support for Becket's cult and his own philosophy concerning king-

religious houses in Kent, the nuns at St Sepulchre's, Canterbury and the canons at St Radigund's
near Dover; C. Ellis, *Hubert de Burgh* (1952), pp. 176–7. There are no extant contemporary records
concerning the commemoration of Hubert at the Dover hospital, but the *Valor* lists an obit that was
still taking place in 1535; *Valor Eccl.*, vol. 1, p. 56. **21** R.B. Dobson, 'The monks of Canterbury in
the later middle ages, 1220–1540' (1995), p. 69.

ship, or his involvement in several disputes with senior English clergymen, which meant he believed it was fitting that he should bestow gifts for the glorification of the saint: a magnificent pavement at the shrine and a hospital for pilgrims at Dover.[22] Such gift exchanges suggest he saw himself as the special protector of this special group of his subjects, the pilgrims, so enhancing the prestige of the monarch as God's vicar through his role in initiating this benevolence. In particular, his provision of a chapel and his presence at its dedication marked his appropriation of the hospital and established the spiritual life of his new house.[23] Henry may initially have believed that his own prestige would be enhanced through association with Hubert, the renowned defender of Dover, but he soon publicly established his rights as patron through control of the mastership and the provision of hospitality, though in both cases he claimed fewer rights than he held at other religious institutions.[24] Yet Henry's generosity presumably resulted in a positive balance between income and outgo for St Mary's during the thirteenth century, his gifts shaping the development of the hospital.[25]

Initially the house was staffed by a number of brothers and sisters under a master who may not have been in clerical orders. The construction of a chapel and further buildings brought the introduction of priest brothers, like the chap-

---

22 Ibid. 70. M. Clanchy, *England and its rulers 1066–1272* (1993), pp. 222–30.   **23** He appears to have been present at the dedication of the chapel at which time he confirmed Hubert's gift to the hospital; Statham, *Dover charters*, p. 3; EKA, Do/ZQ 01. *CChR 1226–1257*, p. 142.   **24** For example, Henry's confirmation charter concerning the manor of River stated that the gift was given at the petition of Hubert de Burgh who founded the hospital. The hospital was to hold in pure and perpetual alms for the sustenance of paupers and pilgrims forever. It was dated 14 July 1228; BL, Add. MS. 6166, f. 215v. The grant of privileges concerning the election of the master was made by Henry in 1229; *CChR 1226–1257*, p. 101; Dugdale, *Monasticon.* vol. 6, p. 657. Lyon, *Dover*, p. 40. In 1230 Henry confirmed the election of John, vicar of Tenham as *custos* of the hospital, the archbishop agreeing; *CPR 1225–1232*, p. 331. Apart from his servants, who were sent to various religious houses for short or long periods, Henry sent his horses to such houses to receive forty days of fodder and stabling; Wood, *English monasteries*, pp. 65–7, 84–5, 106–7. *VCH Kent*, vol. 2, p. 218.   **25** His grants included Selling church for the sustenance of the poor in 1222; *CPR 1216–1225*, p. 339. In 1226 the right of free transport along the coast of things needed for the hospital; *CPR 1225–1232*, p. 31. In 1227 the tithe of the issues of the passage of the port; *CChR 1226–1257*, p. 48. In 1228 a grant of an annual fair at the hospital manor of Whitfield for three days from the feast of St Philip and St James, the manor of River, and certain confirmatory grants concerning the gifts of Hubert de Burgh and Simon de Wardon; *CChR 1226–1257*, p. 78. In 1229 a grant that the master and brothers should be quit of suit of shires and various other charges, that they might build a porch at the front of the house, and that the hospital might receive £10 annually out of the issues of the port; *CChR 1226–1257*, pp. 91, 98, 99; EKA, Do/ZQ 02. In 1231 a grant received in frankalmoin of the church of St James in Sheppey for the support of the brothers and the poor, that the master and brothers receive as dowry for the hospital church an extra £10 yearly out of the port issues for the sustenance of the brothers and the poor, a confirmation grant of land granted in Sheppey and elsewhere, and further gifts of Hubert de Burgh; *CChR 1226–1257*, pp. 130, 141, 142. In 1235 the gift of the advowson of Ospringe church, and further confirmations of previous grants; *CChR 1226–1257*, pp. 191, 192, 202.

lain financed by Henry's gift of 50s. from the issues of the port, who was to celebrate daily for the soul of Raymund de Burgh.[26] This and other gifts required the hospital to respond reciprocally through the provision of spiritual services for Henry, as patron, and those he nominated. The evidence from the *Valor* shows that the brothers commemorated their patron at his obit and annually on the feast days of St Edmund and the Annunciation of Our Lady, as well as saying intercessory masses for Henry's father at his obit.[27] In 1236 this shift in emphasis away from care for the poor and pilgrims concerned Pope Gregory IX sufficiently that he specifically forbade anyone to convert the place to any other use, but within three years, at the pope's command, the master and brothers were under the Augustinian Rule.[28] Although the commonest rule found at hospitals, it does suggests that within a decade of appropriating the hospital Henry had placed a greater emphasis on the recruitment of priest brothers, the poor and pilgrims delegated to the care of a few lay brothers or servants and the sisters.[29]

The loss of the hospital's muniments in the late sixteenth century is a severe handicap in assessing the gift-giving of other donors.[30] Of the few known benefactors, some gave land or rent in free alms, so conforming to Thompson's notion of free-alms tenure where donors did not place restrictions on how their gifts were to be used, which suggests that intercessory masses were not their first priority.[31] Others sought a definite return, either in monetary form or counter-gifts relating to the provision of intercessory services, or the gift of confraternity for themselves and their heirs during life and post-mortem.[32] Most of these *in vitam*

---

26 *CChR* 1226–1257, p. 126. Ellis, *Hubert*, p. 176, n. 5. **27** *Valor Eccl.*, vol. 1, p. 56. BL, Add. Ch. 16428. **28** *Cal. Pap. Let.*, 1198–1304, pp. 154, 181. **29** The sisters were still there in 1344; *CCR* 1343–1346, p. 301. **30** It is possible some charters may have been lost, but the details contained in the royal confirmation grants suggest that, unlike St Mary's hospital, Ospringe, where local support was considerable, Hubert de Burgh and Henry III were the only major benefactors; BL, Stowe MS. 850, f. 130. **31** Richard de Valbadoun gave land in Whitfield, William de Hannsard gave land in Selton, Manasseri de Pecham gave land in Pising (confirmed by Henry in 1227); Simon de Warden gave a mesuage and land in Warden, his tenants giving rents in cash and kind, Solomon de Hardes gave a mill in Hardes (confirmed by Henry in 1228); William, son of Richard de Wiggehall, gave land and houses in Sheppey, Christine de Mandeville, countess of Essex, gave 100s. of rent from the manor of Dersingham, Turgis de Illeye gave rents from property in Dover, William de Say gave the manor of Colrede (confirmed by Henry in 1231); BL, Add. Ch. 16428. **32** Stephen Harengod quitclaimed land in the manor of Eastbridge to the hospital, receiving ten marks; Churchill, Griffin and Hardman, *Cal. Kent Feet of Fines*, p. 126. Hugh le Coit, Alice daughter of Robert the Bedel, Petronilla and Christina sisters of Hugh, Reinilda daughter of Thomas, Christina daughter of Knithwin quitclaimed a tenement for which they received one mark in 1257; Thomas son of Gabriel quitclaimed half an acre of land in the parish of River to the master and brothers in 1281; Henry le Gold and Isabella his wife exchanged land with the hospital; Statham, *Dover charters*, pp. 9, 13; EKA, DO/ZQ 04, 05, 06. Richard de Cretinges and Hawyse his wife in 1260 quitclaimed a messuage and an acre to the master, brothers and their successors, for which the master received the donors and their heirs 'into all the benefits and prayers which henceforth were to be made in that house'; Churchill, Griffin and Hardman, *Cal. Kent Feet of Fines*, p. 309.

grantors belonged to the lesser nobility or knightly class, who were drawn to the hospital through their knowledge of its patrons and reputation rather than their residential proximity to the hospital, the one possible exception being Turgis de Illeye who held property in Dover.[33] A characteristic of members of this group was their willingness to support a number of religious houses. Bertram de Crioil, a member of the lesser nobility, whose connections through office holding, marriage and landholding linked him to the crown and other regionally important families, sought burial in the abbey church. He had previously donated several pieces of land to St Radigund's for his soul and witnessed a number of charters of other benefactors to the abbey.[34] His gift to the Dover hospital was substantial, with the result that his obit (10s./year) was still celebrated by St Mary's hospital staff in the early sixteenth century.[35] His gift exchanges gave him the knowledge that he was fulfilling his duties to God through his alms to Christ's poor, including the voluntary poor of the monastery. This placed him among the select group of benefactors to whom the grateful institutions would be expected to offer counter-gifts for his soul, his relationship with the hospital and abbey demonstrated in legal terms within the formal framework of the spiritual economy.

As a consequence of such gift exchanges, the hospital received its income from a variety of sources, including its considerable landholdings in east Kent and further afield. Though valuable, such scattered assets were time consuming to manage, which may have had implications for the charitable activities of the hospital. These activities included burying the dead in its cemetery for the poor and staffing the nearby chapel. This chapel had been consecrated by Bishop Richard of Chichester, while he was staying at St Mary's in 1253.[36] He was seriously ill at the time, dying a few days later at the hospital from whence his body was carried to Chichester for burial, his entrails having been buried with due ceremony in the newly consecrated chapel.[37] Miracles were said to have occurred within a short time, and in 1261 his name was added to the catalogue of saints, his cause having been espoused by the king and magnates.[38] For the master and brothers, their new chapel had the potential to be a minor focus of St Richard's cult. The chapel, shrine and cemetery may be seen as representing sites of different types of gift exchange, which may have been more visible to the towns-

---

33 The other exception might be the countess of Essex who was related to Hubert de Burgh through marriage, Hubert having married Isabella, the widow of Geoffrey de Mandeville. The apparent lack of local interest may relate to Henry's patronage, the citizens being less favourably disposed towards the king after the failure of the military campaigns of 1230 and 1242, and his indictment of Hubert de Burgh; Clanchy, *England*, pp. 217, 231.   **34** Bodleian, Rawlinson MS. B.336, p. 3, ll. 19, 88–9, 93, 96; Statham, *Dover*, p. 335. His family held the right of advocacy in the late thirteenth century; Wood, *English monasteries*, p. 20.   **35** *Valor Eccl.*, vol. 1, p. 56.   **36** Bishop Richard had been on a preaching expedition on behalf of the forthcoming crusade; T. Tanner, *Saint Edmund's chapel, Dover, and its restoration* (Dover 1968), p. 2.   **37** Ibid. p. 8.   **38** *Cal. Pap. Let.*, 1198–1304, p. 332.

people compared to the work of the brothers in the hospital itself. The provision of Christian burial for the poor and strangers was one of the corporal acts of mercy, and the hospital was also aiding the town corporation by burying those who might otherwise have been the town's responsibility. Such a provision may date from the mid-thirteenth century, a response to the growing number of sick pilgrims who never reached Canterbury or who succumbed on their return, whose belongings were insufficient to cover their burial. One of the priest brothers celebrated divine service at the chapel, where he also acted as shrine keeper and performed the requiem masses for the poor. Thus, by giving 'the bowels of his body to the poor' St Richard facilitated the provision of counter-gifts: first, the shrine where the poor pilgrims might receive aid as a consequence of their prayers and offerings to him, and second, the offerings supplemented the hospital's income, allowing it to offer the charitable gift of hospitality to the poor.[39] This addition income may have been especially valuable during the civil war, when Henry, and then his son, stopped the annual payment of £32 10s., an earlier gift from the king to the hospital. The grant was not restored to St Mary's hospital until 1267.[40]

St Bartholomew's hospital

Established about sixty years before St Mary's, St Bartholomew's hospital was a much poorer institution. The hospital had been founded by two brothers, monks at Dover priory, from the goods of their parents.[41] It was sited to the north of the town at Buckland. As benefactor and patron, the priory provided the hospital with a degree of autonomy, the master holding the hospital's seal, but the subprior at St Martin's acted as warden of the house, and the prior undertook all the important business connected with the hospital. Initially St Bartholomew's catered for poor pilgrims and other travellers, but soon became a leper hospital, where the long-term inmates, the twenty brothers and sisters, were either poor or lepers, living separately.[42] These people donated their labour, their counter-gift, for the gift of board and lodging, the sisters primarily maintaining the house, while the brothers worked on the hospital's holdings and reared livestock for sale and consumption. All took an oath of obedience to the master, agreeing to abide by the rules of the house and to love their fellow brothers and sisters. When the hospi-

---

39 St Richard's gift was recorded by Ralph Bocking, the bishop's confessor, in his 'Life of St Richard', written c.1270; Tanner, *Saint Edmund's chapel*, p. 8.   **40** *CPR* 1258–1266, p. 541; *CPR* 1266–1272, p. 31.   **41** Haines considers that the brothers were probably from the original group of monks who came with Ascelin to Dover from Christchurch priory in 1139. They would, therefore, have known Lanfranc's two hospitals at Canterbury and possibly St Bartholomew's hospital at Chatham; C. Haines, *Dover priory* (1930), p. 184; Bodleian, Rawlinson MS. B.335, not numbered.   **42** Early grants to the hospital were for the sustenance of poor pilgrims, the possibly later ordinances providing information on the number and type of inmates; Bodleian, Rawlinson MS. B.335, ff. 2, 5v, 7v.

tal register was compiled in 1373, an entry fee of 100s., a fee of 6s. 8d. to the warden, and 3d. to each of their fellows was obligatory, but whether such fees were required a century earlier is unknown.[43] Similarly, the rule whereby each inmate promised to surrender half of his/her chattels at death for the good of the hospital may have been long standing. Such ordinances seem to indicate that the house was primarily housing lepers and poorer people, not the destitute, which may suggest that it conforms broadly to the early leper hospital model.[44]

For those seeking a semi-religious life, especially the leprous, St Bartholomew's may have offered a desirable alternative. The specified daily food allowance appears to have been adequate and the inmates were expected to attend chapel daily, wear the prescribed habit and remain within the hospital precincts unless given permission to leave.[45] As part of the reciprocal exchange between the inmates and the hospital's patron and benefactors, the brothers and sisters prayed daily for the prior and convent of St Martin's, the king and queen, and the burgesses of Dover on land and sea.[46] Unlike individual donors, these recipients were never classed as deceased, which meant that the cycle of gift exchange was unending provided the respective parties continued to honour their commitments, a position that may have become increasingly important following the martyrdom of Becket and the growth in pilgrim traffic through Dover. This traffic, though a great asset to the town's economy, presumably was also a considerable strain on Dover's resources, those of the priory, and its hospital, at least during the house's early history.

The hospital register provides evidence of a wide range of gift exchanges between the hospital and its benefactors. Following the priory's lead, many of the early donors were members of the regional nobility, who either included the hospital in their strategy of pious gift-giving or were local landholders for whom St Bartholomew's provided a reputable avenue for their good works.[47] From the

---

43 Ibid. ff. 1–2v. Compared to the entry fees recorded for the Sandwich hospitals in 1301, those at the Dover hospital were closer to its namesake at Sandwich rather than St John's. Similarly the level of nutrition at Dover was closer to St Bartholomew's hospital, Sandwich, especially when the produce from the home farm is taken into account; Boys, *Sandwich,* pp. 20, 127.   **44** Bodleian, Rawlinson MS. B.335, f. 2v. See chapter 2.   **45** The daily food allowance seems comparable to that quoted by Dyer for a retired woman; C. Dyer, *Standards of living in the later middle ages* (1989), p. 153. Those at the hospital were to receive a bushel of wheat per month to be baked into bread in the common oven, one and a half bushels of barley per month to be brewed in common, cereals and beans for pottage, fish, and at Christmas half a pig, as well as other food and cash allowances on certain feast days; ibid. ff. 2–2v.   **46** Although the role of the priory as benefactor and patron is known, it is not clear from the hospital's register whether St Bartholomew's had received royal grants, except possibly the fair to be held in the precincts on the feast day of St Bartholomew. The inclusion of the burgesses may have resulted from the tolls and tithes given by them to the priory, thereby possibly aiding the hospital indirectly; Bodleian, Rawlinson MS. B.335, f. 1v; Lyon, *Dover,* p. 56.   **47** One of the largest grants the hospital received was 100s. worth of land in the manor of River given by Stephen de Arcelles. His grant was confirmed by his overlord, Gilbert de Gant, earl

1250s, this group apparently lost interest in the hospital, being replaced by a small number of donors from among the townspeople who used a variety of gift exchanges with the hospital, including some grants provided at the instigation of the hospital as it attempted to consolidate its holdings.[48] This suggests that there was limited local interest in the well-being of the hospital, possibly because the burgesses generally believed the hospital was the priory's responsibility. Furthermore, they had aided, and continued to aid St Bartholomew's through the tolls and fish tithes they paid to the priory. The commonalty intended that the tithes should be used for victuals for the monks and towards the gift of hospitality for the poor, either through the almoner or at the hospital.[49] Such neighbourly considerations at Sandwich led the burgesses to found their own hospital, but the men of Dover believed the priory should undertake this charitable work at the almonry gate and at its daughter establishment.[50] Moreover, the hospital community was discharging its spiritual duty to the commonalty through its daily prayers, which meant those in a position to do so generally sought further spiritual counter-gifts elsewhere. Others, however, did support the hospital, like Cylwyn le Wodemonger and Cecily his wife, who granted two acres for the sustenance of a chaplain in the service of God at the hospital.[51] The notion that donors were special people who had certain rights in the spiritual life of the hospital was also understood by those who wished to be included in the hospital's mortuary list, or through their inclusion in terms of the liturgical services, possibly invoking similar ideas to the counter-gift of confraternity.[52] Nevertheless,

---

of Lincoln and was included in Pope Adrian IV's confirmation charter. The hospital also received an indulgence of twenty days, a gift from Archbishop Theobald; Bodleian, Rawlinson MS B.335, ff. 6v, 5v. **48** For example, Thomas Fisshman of Dover gave a piece of land in Dover to the hospital in pure and perpetual alms for his soul, those of his ancestors and successors; ibid. f. 23v. The charters referring to land the hospital acquired at Charlton suggest that the master was adopting a pro-active approach; ibid. ff. 38v–48v. **49** According to Henry II's charter, the burgesses had offered these gifts upon the altar (presumably St Martin's), which may imply they placed no restrictions on the priory's use of the gift; LPL, MS. 241, f. 2v; Sheppard, *Literae Cantuarienses*, vol. 3, p. 371. However, the priory register contains a number of letters, charters and statements about the fish tithes, which suggest that the gift was made on behalf of the souls of the fishermen involved. Moreover, under the confirmation grant of Archbishop Richard the burgesses were to receive the gift of confraternity from the priory; LPL, MS. 241, ff. 35, 36v, 37. **50** The importance of the almonry as an exchange partner to the priory's benefactors may be inferred from the devotion of one section of the priory register to grants to the almoner, with further grants regarding the almonry scattered among the Buckland and Guston charters; LPL, MS. 241, ff. 94–5v, 106v–8, 109–10v, 112, 113–14v, 123v–5v, 127–8. **51** Bodleian, Rawlinson MS B.335, f. 36v. **52** Two couples who donated land (in the tenure of Dover priory) to the hospital for their souls, for those of their children and parents, intended that they should be included in the liturgical services, though the second couple did not specify which services; ibid. ff. 43v, 46. Petronilla daughter of Solomon de Mari was more precise; she sought the benefits of masses, matins, vespers, prayers, alms and other good works in exchange for her gift to the hospital of thirty acres and two messuages in Tilmanstone; ibid. f. 90.

the poor were not totally neglected within the terms of the *in vitam* grants, because the master, brothers and sisters agreed to organize on behalf of Alice Ferrarie an annual distribution of ale to the poor forever, in honour of God, Our Lady and all the saints for her soul, those of her ancestors and the hospital's benefactors.[53] After the hardship of the civil war and its aftermath the poor were probably grateful for such gifts, repaying their benefactors through their prayers, but it seems likely the value of the gift was primarily in the remainder of the citation. This suggests that ideas about purgatory and the spiritual economy of the dead, as described by Burgess, were becoming increasingly important from the thirteenth century.[54] Some benefactors, however, sought more temporal counter-gifts from the hospital. The heirs of Herlewyn received the patronage of a bed near the door in the hall for a gift of eight marks (the master buying land with the money); it was to be used by a leprous member of the family or a person chosen by the donors.[55] At St Leonard's hospital, York, people employed similar methods to provide for old age, sickness or infirmity, though the idea of bed money may have severely restricted the access of the sick-poor to the hospital.[56] It seems the bed was held in perpetuity or for several lives, and such a form of leasing may have been more common than extant records suggest.[57]

During this period, the hospital was not only engaged in systems of exchange and reciprocity with lay people, but also with senior churchmen and local religious houses, including its parent institution. Though small in number, these exchanges illustrate the diversity and complexity of the actions of the participants. The priory sought to aid the poor at St Bartholomew's through a gift of land, receiving in return six marks from the hospital.[58] It also seems likely that the prior was involved in the procurement of a papal grant from Clement III, wherein the faithful were exhorted to give generously to St Bartholomew's.[59] In 1252 Bishop Richard of Chichester offered a twenty-day indulgence to all those who supported the poor at the hospital, a gift which aided the work of St Bartholomew's directly, as well as enhancing the house's reputation through its association with this saintly man.[60] Another benefactor was the abbot of Langdon,

53 Ibid. f. 37v.   **54** Burgess, 'Benefactions of mortality', p. 67.   **55** Bodleian, Rawlinson MS B.335, ff. 36v–7.   **56** Cullum, 'Hospitals in Yorkshire', p. 161. At St Bartholomew's hospital, Gloucester, in 1380 Simon the Cripple was charged 6s. 8d. for his bed money; Orme and Webster, *English hospital,* p. 101. This type of patronage was found by Cavallo in early modern Milan; S. Cavallo, *Charity and power in early modern Italy* (1995), p. 141.   **57** Yet, it is the only known reference to the acquisition of a bed in an English leper hospital. I should like to thank Max Satchell for this information.   **58** LPL, MS. 241, f. 118v.   **59** Without the active involvement of the prior, probably during discussions with John, bishop of Anagni and papal legate, while the bishop was staying at the priory in 1189, it seems unlikely that the pope would have shown any interest in this small and insignificant hospital among the plethora of such institutions founded in the twelfth and early thirteenth centuries; Haines, *Dover priory,* p. 200; Bodleian, Rawlinson MS B.335, f. 5.   **60** The indulgence was issued at Dover, which suggests that he was staying at the priory; Bodleian, Rawlinson MS B.335, f. 7v.

who aided the hospital through an exchange of property with his house.[61] This form of negotiation between religious institutions was a useful means of consolidating their capital assets, but for the smaller, poorer or subordinate establishment, success was dependent on the degree of reciprocity obtained. In this instance both partners appear to have been satisfied with the result.

Other religious institutions

The priory too engaged in systems of exchange and reciprocity with a range of partners, whose activities are examined here. Such exchanges might be extremely complex, creating multi-relationships, like the gift of an indulgence offered by Pope Honorius III in 1226 to all those who visited the altar of Our Lady Undercroft in the church of St Martin-le-Grand as pilgrims on the anniversary of its dedication.[62] In this case the pope, as donor, initiated exchanges with different groups of recipients: the named altar, its parent church, the pilgrims and the priory, and these, in turn, may have developed further exchange relationships among themselves over time. Hospitality was one of the main counter-gifts sought by the papacy from the priory, though the prior was, on occasion, also expected to conduct visitations on the papacy's behalf in the southern province.[63] For the priory, the papacy was an important exchange partner because, in addition to the gift of indulgences and the papal confirmation charter, Rome was involved in the long-running dispute between Dover priory and Christchurch. At times both the prior and sub-prior of Dover were required to enter into gift exchanges with the Vatican, and the resultant drain on the priory's resources was sufficiently serious that certain sacred objects were mortgaged in order to continue the litigation.[64] Such exchanges demonstrate a lack of regard among those involved and the problem of negotiating and renegotiating the rela-

---

61 The abbot and convent of Langdon quitclaimed to the brothers at St Bartholomew's an annual rent of 4s. and four hens from a property in Swingfield in exchange for an annual rent of 5s. from land in the parish of River; ibid. f. 72. **62** The indulgence was one of a growing number the priory had received since its refoundation; in this case the indulgence was for a quarter of all the recipient's mortal sins and half of all his venial sins truly confessed; LPL, MS. 241, ff. 56v, 94. St Martin's church and all its altars were under the jurisdiction of Dover priory, and the importance of this gift for the prior may be gauged by its inclusion in the priory register alongside indulgences given to the priory. Episcopal indulgences were also offered, though the only archbishop to give an indulgence during this period (in 1268) was Boniface (of twenty days); LPL, MS. 241, ff. 52v, 53v, 54v–55v. **63** However at times there were disagreements between the priory and the papacy over the value of the gift of hospitality during the thirteenth century. In an attempt to clarify the level of expectation acceptable to both parties Pope Gregory IX issued two statements and wrote to the prior at Christchurch; *Cal. Pap. Let.,* 1198–1304, p. 139; Sheppard, *Literae. Cantuarienses,* vol. 3, p. 374. Gregory IX also decided to initiate visitations to certain religious houses in the southern province because there had been rumours of malpractice. His visitation team sent to Waltham included the prior of Dover, Haines, *Dover priory,* p. 212. **64** The sub-prior mortgaged to the sub-prior of Winchester an ordinal and a reliquary of silver and gold containing saints' relics for 15s.; Haines, *Dover priory,* p. 226.

tionship through the provision of gifts and counter-gifts. Yet this was an extreme case, and most of the relationships involving the priory and other religious institutions were mutually beneficial, or at least not acrimonious. Nevertheless, occasionally the gifts two religious houses had received from a third party led to problems because the exchanges were mutually incompatible, requiring a compromise between them involving the need for further exchanges.[65]

A particularly complex set of relationships resting on reciprocity involved the priory, Christchurch, the see at Canterbury, the Maison Dieu, the local parish churches and the Dover burgesses. At the centre of this structure based on hierarchy and patronage was the church of St Martin-le-Grand to which at times all Dover's parish churches had been subordinate, and which itself was subordinate to St Martin's priory.[66] The relationships among the different parties were displayed in a variety of different forms. These included in monetary terms the payment of pensions to the priory by the parish churches; by acts of deference both with respect to time and space, where the parish priests were not to begin the chant of Vespers until it had begun at St Martin's; and in the provision of sacred objects because the altars of St John's and St Nicholas were provided with holy oil and chrism annually by St Martin's.[67] In addition, the priory controlled the appointment of the parish clergy, except at St Mary's, and the priory monopolized the provision of schooling in the town. Many of these reciprocal exchange processes were extremely visible to the townspeople, who may have resented the apparent appropriation of their parish churches, and in particular the ancient minster church of the town's saint who appears on the reverse of the town's seal. Possibly as a result, these exchange processes were strongly contested on various occasions, requiring the participants, including the civic authorities and the prior, to engage in negotiation and renegotiation.[68] Those involving St Mary's hospital and the priory centred on which institution held the advowson of St Mary's church, the size of the pension and certain assets held by the rectory. Following a series of gift exchanges, the last in 1279, the priory had strengthened its position with respect to the hospital.[69]

65 This appears to have occurred in 1249 when the prior had attempted to distrain the abbot of Bec and his men in his claim for the customs of the passage, Dover priory's gift from the crown. The abbot refused to accept this demand, saying that he had royal charters giving his house immunity from such charges. The resultant agreement was produced by the priory's gift of its acknowledgment of the privileges enjoyed by Bec on this issue, for which the abbot gave Dover the counter-gift of fifteen marks to seal the relationship; Churchill, Griffin and Hardman, *Cal. Kent Feet of Fines*, p. 229. **66** Details are recorded in a copy of a document relating to the jurisdiction claimed by the archdeacon of Canterbury; Corpus Christi College, Cambridge, MS. 59, f. 27. **67** The pensions are also listed in the priory register; LPL, MS. 241, ff. 4, 48. **68** On a number of occasions the burgesses contested the priory's demand that they should offer specific gifts annually to the priory on the altar of St Martin. The relationship between the town and the ecclesiastical authorities was further complicated by the stipulation that the appointment of the archipresbyter to St Martin-le-Grand rested with the priory and the commonalty. **69** LPL, MS. 241, ff. 43–3v, 46,

For the townspeople, the comprehensive nature of this clerical deference to the priory might have been considered detrimental to the parish clergy and their parishioners, which may explain the lack of voluntary support given to the priory, individually and collectively. There are only fifteen charters from Henry III's reign in the priory register covering gift exchanges with people from Dover. Of these few donors, most indicated the grant was made for the good of their souls and those they named, though they were rarely more specific in terms of the counter-gift sought. One of these charters, dated 1301, was the gift of a messuage for which the priory was to maintain a lamp burning before St Katherine's altar in its church forever.[70] This apparent indifference to the priory was consequent on a number of factors, including, perhaps, its extensive assets compared to some other religious houses locally, its position *vis-a-vis* Christchurch, the infrequency of the use of the gift of confraternity, and the heavy financial demands placed on the burgesses by the crown and the church.[71] There is little to suggest the townspeople in the thirteenth century were generous benefactors to any of the local religious establishments, but this cannot be ascertained for the parish churches because only St Mary's survived after the late sixteenth century. Since then a great deal of restoration work has taken place.

However, even if the priory did not develop strong links with the Dover townsfolk generally, individual priors were apparently concerned about certain priory servants and their families. As a result they very occasionally instigated corrodies, either in terms of an annual allowance in food and money, or in one instance as a tenant in priory property.[72] Such charitable acts were probably acknowledged by the grateful recipient in his prayers, and enhanced the reputation of the priory through public knowledge. The latter type of corrody is particularly interesting because it bears a striking resemblance to the later maisondieu-type almshouse. The recipient lived in the property of the donor

---

47–8. The place of the priory in the spiritual life of the region was also one of negotiation at this period because it held the advowsons of several parish churches around Dover. The priory register records a number of disputes, grants, agreements and appropriations concerning these livings, involving the incumbents, those holding local lordship, local religious houses, the archbishop and the priory. This suggests that matters like tithes and church property were frequently at the centre of the negotiated process of reciprocal exchange. The parishes involved were Colrede, Appledore, Brookland, Kenardington, Snargate and Buckland; LPL, MS. 241, ff. 49v, 106, 184v–5v, 191, 225v–6v, 228v–30v. **70** Ibid. f. 63. An example of what Thompson called a contractual type of grant, which he believed benefactors favoured from the late thirteenth century; Thompson, 'Monasteries', ' p. 108. **71** Though slight, there is evidence that St Radigund's abbey provided the gift of confraternity to some of its benefactors; Churchill, Griffin and Hardman, *Cal. Kent Feet of Fines*, pp. 171, 296, 346. Archbishop Edmund in 1236 issued a warning that non-payment of tithes would be punished by excommunication; LPL, MS. 241, f. 38. **72** According to an undated charter, William the son of Jordan, late seneschal of the priory, was so impoverished that the prior took pity on him. In exchange for relinquishing his rights to land and a messuage outside the priory walls, which his father had held of the priory, William was to receive two silver marks and become a priory tenant for life, living in the same messuage; LPL, MS. 241, f. 70v.

where he was known locally as the living embodiment of the benefactor's charity; the agreement between them left the spiritual counter-gifts unspecified since both parties believed this to be unnecessary.

In consideration of its capital assets, the priory also sought relationships with neighbouring religious houses, and to a far lesser extent other ecclesiastical establishments in east Kent, probably because distance was a limiting factor.[73] Apart from its daughter house, St Bartholomew's hospital, the priory was engaged in negotiating a series of exchanges with the Maison Dieu. Some of these were concerned with matters of patronage and privilege associated with St Mary's parish church, as noted above, but also involved various landholdings, rents and tithes in Dover and at River to the north of the priory.[74] These issues were important enough for the prior to record the various charters in the priory register, along with a copy of an agreement between the hospital and the priory dating from 1246.[75]

The priory seems to have been less successful in securing a strong relationship with the crown through gift exchange. Henry III apparently showed little interest in the house, possibly a consequence of his patronage of the Maison Dieu on the other side of the road. One of his few recorded charitable acts was to recompense the priory for its losses sustained during the siege of Dover by the French, though he did confirm his father and his grandfather's gifts to the priory.[76] Yet he was present in Dover on numerous occasions and was presumably aware of the priory's ambitious construction plans, which might have prompted him to provide the occasional gift of alms for the new work.[77] He was, however, sufficiently concerned about the state of the priory in the 1270s to take custody of the house because of its dispute with Christchurch and the resultant discord within the priory itself.[78] This offer of royal protection was not emulated by his son, who with his official, the constable of Dover castle, appear to have used their exchanges with the priory to their own advantage.[79] They sought to place their own nominee in charge, and though unsuccessful, it does indicate the problems

---

73 Examples of institutional exchange partners included the Knights Templar and two Canterbury hospitals (St James' and St John's); ibid. ff. 95, 171v; Duncombe and Battely, *Three archiepiscopal hospitals*, p. 264. **74** LPL, MS. 241, ff. 41–3v, 47, 48. **75** Ibid. ff. 43v–4. **76** Henry's grant was more explicit than his grandfather's in terms of the spiritual services desired; he granted in frankalmoin La Menesse marsh, near Sandwich to the priory; *CChR* 1226–1257, p. 50. In contrast, Henry II gave land to the priory for the good of his soul, the souls of his parents, that of his grandmother, and all his kin; his gift of a fair was for the good of his soul, the welfare of his children and the stability of his realm; ibid. ff. 57v, 59v. Yet Henry III did provide the priory with three protection grants, as well as providing confirmation charters; *CPR* 1225–1232, p. 169, *CPR* 1266–1272, pp. 504, 665; *CChR* 1226–1257, pp. 227, 228. **77** Dugdale, *Monasticon*, vol. 4, p. 536; Haines, *Dover priory*, p. 211. **78** Wood, *English monasteries*, pp. 96–7. **79** *CPR* 1266–1272, pp. 613, 631, 694, 700, 712. The prince seems to have tried to use the appointment of a custodian to the priory, even though the prior was still in office, as a counter-gift to a monk from Reading who had given him £100 towards his forthcoming crusade; ibid. pp. 66–7.

of discontinuity when the relationship between the exchange partners was sev-
ered or under strain following changed circumstances. Thus, due to its problems
with Christchurch, the priory's fragile position in Dover society was further
eroded by this change in its relationship with the crown.

In addition to the parish churches (see above), there were at least three more
partners available to the Dover townspeople with regard to the spiritual economy: the parish church of St Mary de Castro, the chapel of St Mary of Pity (or
'Our Lady of the Rock'), and an anchoress who lived at the castle. The castle
church served the garrison and permanent staff, but local townspeople may have
visited the place, especially on Fridays when the relics were displayed.[80] These
might similarly attract pilgrims and their offerings, and the church also received
a number of gifts from the king, suggesting a wide range of potential exchange
partners.[81] In contrast, the Lady Chapel on the shore to the west may have been
dependent on small cash offerings from those pilgrims who had safely crossed
the Channel and those about to embark.[82] The anchoress at the castle may have
received a few offerings from those who wished to consult her about spiritual
matters, though she was fortunate to receive a penny halfpenny per day from
the king.[83]

The mid-fourteenth century

From the surviving records, it is difficult to gauge the economic and demographic fortunes of the town, but with regard to this study of the hospitals it is
possible to discuss two important characteristics of Dover: its continuing depen-
dence on the carrying trade and the fluid nature of its population. The formation of the guild of ferrymen in 1348 highlights the importance of the cross-
Channel passenger trade to Dover. In addition to the ferrymen, those providing
hospitality and allied services also gained from this lucrative trade.[84] Moreover,

---

80 From 'The Statutes of Dover Castle' c.1267; Statham, *Dover*, p. 275.   81 Ibid. p.235. *CLibR*
1240–1245, pp. 197, 212; *CLibR* 1245–1251, pp. 27, 54, 112, 123.   82 It was reputed to have been
founded by a nobleman from northern England who, having been saved from shipwreck, wished
to provide a chapel as a mark of thanksgiving; C. Buckingham, *Catholic Dover* (1968), p. 19.   83
CPR 1258–1266, p. 63. *CLibR* 1251–1260, pp. 323, 324, 446.   84 Probably the first official occu-
pational organization in the town was the 'Fership', which appears to have consisted of twenty-
three members (though Jones says eleven) who carried passengers between Dover and Witsand,
and Calais after its capture in 1348. The ordinances for this group included the tariff to be charged,
the organization of the membership, and the surcharge to be paid to the town government; Statham,
Dover, pp. 66–7, Jones, *Dover*, p. 11. Even with this surcharge, the ferrymen were seen to be making
considerable profits, and other townsmen attempted to gain some of the trade. Consequently, in
1346 the town received a royal charter allowing any man from the port to take his turn within the
cycle, on the understanding that his ship was seaworthy and that he paid the surcharge; Jones, *Dover*,
p. 11. To provide some idea of the importance of Becket's cult, in 1320 offerings received at the
shrine amounted to £670 13s. 4d., considerably more than at the previous jubilee (£207 2s. 10d.);
C. Woodruff, 'Financial aspects of the cult of St Thomas of Canterbury', *Arch. Cant.*, 44 (1932),

board and lodging were similarly required by construction workers and others employed at the castle, and by troops waiting to embark, but at times the provisioning and policing of these itinerant groups caused severe problems for the civic authorities.[85]

The Black Death and subsequent plague outbreaks, and the onset of hostilities with France had a detrimental effect on the passenger trade, but the provisioning of Calais and the supplying of the English forces did alleviate this loss.[86] However, the chamberlains' accounts from the period do suggest that the town was experiencing economic difficulties, which continued to worsen over the later medieval period. In part, this was a consequence of the town's heavy reliance on the carrying and allied trades and the lack of manufacturing industry beyond a small number of craftsmen; which seemingly also contributed to the high turnover of families in the town. Interestingly, it was not only the poorer and middling families who disappeared within or after one generation; the evidence similarly indicates a high turnover of surnames among the leading families.[87] Yet a small nucleus of families had survived in Dover for several generations, like members of the Hurtyn family who were present for over fifty years and the Monyn family who had been resident there for about 150 years. The considerable contrast between the two groups, the large number of short-term residents and the few long-term families from across the social spectrum, may help to explain the attitudes of the townsfolk towards Dover's religious and charitable institutions.

18–19. **85** For example, in 1354 and 1357 workmen were required by royal mandate to repair the castle, and in 1355 the mayor and bailiff drafted into the port carpenters and other workmen from across the county to build and repair ships ordered by the king; *CPR* 1354–1358, pp. 79, 212, 512. Furthermore, the town government was employing a large number of masons in the 1370s, especially in 1377, in the construction and repair of the town walls; BL, Add. MS. 29615, ff. 49–50. Another factor that caused problems nationally as well as locally was the entry of debased or counterfeit coinage to the kingdom. The problem was considered so important that in 1355 the king set up a table of exchange at Dover, the official being directly answerable to the exchequer; *CPR* 1334–1338, p. 153. Prior to the establishment of the Fership, some of the ferrymen had been charging the poorer travellers too much, who then gathered in the town where 'debates, contentions and riots have often taken place ... to the great peril and loss of the whole commonalty of the town', Statham, *Dover*, p. 66. Moreover, bad weather, hostile forces in the Channel (in 1338 the French attacked Dover and several other south coast ports), and disputes with the men of Witsand could confine the Dover men to the port; *CPR* 1334–1338, p. 295; Statham, *Dover*, p. 71. **86** Though there were certain disadvantages, the king might commandeer ships, and the crown purveyors took food stocks from across the region, which they often failed to pay for at all; J. Bolton, *The medieval English economy, 1150–1500* (1980), p. 181. According to Michael, a monk at Dover priory, the plague visited the town in 1349, 1362, 1369, 1375, and in 1355 'many persons went mad on seeing demons'; Haines, *Dover priory*, p. 361. **87** An illustration of this discontinuity is provided by Froissart's comment on his return to Dover in 1395 after an absence of twenty-seven years 'but when I reached Dover, I found no one with whom I had been acquainted in the days when I lived in England. The hostelries and houses were all repopulated with strange people and the little children had grown into men and women who did not know me, as I did not know them'; Brereton, *Froissart's Chronicles*, p. 403.

St Mary's hospital or the Maison Dieu

This section will assess the systems of exchange and reciprocity involving the two hospitals and, very briefly, the priory in terms of income and outgo to see how they sought to adjust to the difficult conditions of the fourteenth century. For St Mary's hospital, its capital assets – farmland, property including mills, rents and advowsons – provided the majority of its income, especially when Anglo-French hostilities in the Channel severely reduced the revenue the hospital received from the passenger trade.[88] As a major landholder in the Romney Marsh region, it may have employed direct-farming methods on at least some of its holdings, a strategy adopted by other ecclesiastical houses which held land in the same area.[89] For these institutions, such policies were profitable and, though it is risky to generalize from the experiences of others, it suggests that the hospital may have been spared some of the financial problems found at many hospitals by the mid-fourteenth century.[90]

Other forms of income, however, appear to have been extremely limited, and there is little to indicate St Mary's hospital was the beneficiary of either *in vitam* grants or testamentary bequests from the Dover townspeople.[91] Though many late-twelfth- and early-thirteenth-century hospitals generally received few *in vitam* grants a century after their foundation, the apparently continuing absence of support by the Dover townspeople may be significant with regard to the hospital's place in Dover society. Contact between the hospital and the townspeople may have been restricted to St Mary's parish church, the house's role as a minor landlord in the town (though conversely a major landlord regionally), the payment of rent for town property, and the few gifts it received from the civic authorities.[92] Local people also may have believed it was sufficiently well endowed under its royal patron. Thus, even though it was caring for pilgrims, a trade that was seen as vital to Dover, there was probably a degree of ambivalence to the presence of such people, especially the poor ones, who might cause

---

88 *CChR* 1327–1341, p. 456. Statham, *Dover charters*, pp. 45, 47. In 1306 the hospital apparently had problems collecting its share of the profits of the port, a gift assigned to them by Henry III. Such difficulties with the constable may not have been isolated events; *CPR* 1302–1307, p. 381. **89** In 1395 the hospital held 681 acres in Romney Marsh; A.F. Butcher, personal communication. Other religious houses, like Christchurch priory, continued to direct-farm their demesne lands until the beginning of the fifteenth century. This policy may only have been possible or feasible as a consequence of its large size and extensive resources; A. Gross and A.F. Butcher, 'Adaptation and investment in the age of the great storms' (1995), pp. 115–16. **90** M. Mate, 'Kent and Sussex' (1991), pp. 119–20. **91** The only known *in vitam* grant was one given by John the son of Alexander Venesoun of 40*d*. of free and perpetual rent from a tenement in Dover to Brother John, the master of the hospital and the brothers. The gift was made in pure and perpetual alms for his soul, and for those of his parents, his sons and relatives, a form which was rare by this date and may imply that there was some kind of personal connection between John and Brother John; Statham, *Dover charters*, p. 39; EKA, Do/ZQ 07. **92** For example, the mayor and jurats gave four gallons of mass wine to the hospital in 1369; BL, Add. MS. 29615, f. 12v.

problems for the corporation. Furthermore, recent migrants to the town presumably had little emotional attachment to the Maison Dieu, instead they probably looked to the parish church as a focus for their spiritual gift-giving.

Turning to the other side of the exchange process for the hospital, the outgo, there are two main areas: provision for the living and provision for the dead. The former comprised out-relief for the poor and pilgrims daily and larger numbers on specific days, care for the poor and pilgrims as temporary residents, provision for corrodians, the supplying of an education and a clerical title for novices, accommodation and hospitality for royal visitors and officials, activities for the benefit of the crown, and the use of the hospital by the civic authorities.[93] All these demands were a drain on the hospital's financial and other resources. Even though certain donors had provided assets for the services they had requested, the problems of inflation and higher prices at times meant the gift was no longer adequate, and the master had few means to ease such discrepancies.[94]

Even if the hospital was apparently able to sustain its primary function, caring for Christ's poor, other demands placed on it by its royal patron were particularly crippling.[95] Henry III and his successors claimed the gift of hospitality for themselves and others, and these later kings also sought corrodies for their aged retainers. The first royal corrodian, Henry le Blessid, resided at the hospital until his death in 1315, and thereafter the place was almost continually filled by a royal nominee.[96] Such an imposition, though seen as part of the patronage exchange

---

[93] It seems likely that the provisions for the living recorded in 1535 were very similar to those employed in the mid-fourteenth century, like the feeding of fifteen paupers using 2s. 6d. annually at the obit of John Mawlyng; *L and P Henry VIII*, vol. 9, p. 379; *Valor Eccl.*, vol. 1, pp. 56–7. *CPR* 1367–1370, p. 247, BL, Add. MS. 29615, f. 50v. [94] Presumably, the benefactors had intended that the especially elaborate and costly distributions of food and drink to the poor on the days of commemoration would be funded from their general gifts to the hospital, but times of dearth and high prices may have caused considerable problems for the master. An idea of the scale of this distribution of alms can be gained from the 1535 figures. Almsgiving on St Edmund's day for the soul of Henry III required the distribution of two quarters of wheat for bread, two oxen or four barrels of herring costing in total 53s. 4d., and enough ale to sustain those receiving the dole. In addition, the hospital was providing two pittances daily of bread, meat and drink for two honest paupers, costing annually £9 2s. 6d., while the care of the resident poor and pilgrims cost the hospital £40 per year; *L and P Henry VIII*, vol. 9, p. 379; *Valor Eccl.*, vol. 1, pp. 56–7. [95] Wood, *English monasteries*, pp. 101–12. [96] After the death of Henry le Blessid, the place was taken by Henry de Oldington, one of the king's yeomen; *CCR* 1313–1318, pp. 220, 319. Other corrodians included Richard Waytewell, granted his place for good service to Queen Isabella and the king in 1327, and John Monyn, who gained his place following the death of the previous corrodian, John Lambe, in 1330; *CCR* 1327–1330, pp. 233, 594. Whether James le Palmere of London, clerk, was particularly favoured is not known, but the provisions he was to receive in 1360 indicate a good standard of living. He was to 'sit at the master's table at breakfast and dinner every day of his life and shall be served meat and drink as others at the table either in the refectory or in the master's chamber or elsewhere in the hospital, wherever the master shall feed or dine and if he be ill or the master absent he shall take daily from the hospital two white loaves, two gallons of ale and two messes of fish or meat as shall be served to two of the brothers in the refectory; and granting to him also a robe of the master's suit yearly on the feast of the

process, was a long-term drain on the house's resources, both in terms of the cost of board and lodging and the problem that this non-paying guest never died. Consequently, the master was unable to offer the place to another person, who, at least, would have paid an entry fee.[97]

Similarly, the provision of hospitality for members of the royal family and the chancellor and his clerks was a great expense, and in some years may have been extremely detrimental. Moreover, the offer of hospitality, the hospital's counter-gift to its patron, had been appropriated by the crown, and it was in the king's gift to offer hospitality at the Maison Dieu to the chancellor. By the early fourteenth century, therefore, the master at St Mary's had lost all control over the gift of hospitality at his house, taking away his ability to demonstrate his willingness to provide the reciprocal act.[98] In contrast, the dominant position of the king gave him total mastery over the reciprocal process, which allowed him to begin new exchanges in his usurped role as the supplier of hospitality, thus demonstrating the importance of hierarchy between benefactor and beneficiary. The inequality between the exchange partners was also apparent in the king's employment of the master to fulfil certain commissions on the crown's behalf.[99] This use of the master's time was presumably a drain on the house's resources, but might also indicate that St Mary's was seen as a royal institution which might be similarly appropriated by the secular authorities as necessary, a precedent exploited on a far greater scale during the later history of the hospital.

The hospital's provisions for the dead were interlinked with those for the living, whether it was the maintenance of lamps before specific altars or the giving of doles to the poor as part of the services of intercession and commemoration for the deceased.[1] By so doing, the master was fulfilling the expectations of the donors with regard to the three-fold obligations as well as undertaking the tasks for which the hospital had been established. Such services for the dead were occasionally initiated by others, like Henry III's establishment of a chantry priest funded by the port dues for the soul of Raymund de Burgh, and for his own after his death.[2] Under the agreement, the hospital was expected to provide a

Nativity of St Mary or two marks at his choice, and the new chamber in the hospital over the larder and upon the water flowing there opposite the prior of Dover's watermill for life'; *CPR* 1358–1361, p. 512.   **97** Or alternatively the corrodian might offer his labour in exchange for his place, like Thomas de Wodelond in 1359; Sheppard *Literae Cantuarienses*, vol. 2, pp. 384–5.   **98** In 1325, for example, as an act of courtesy, the chancellor allowed Prince Edward and his household to stay at the hospital as his guests; the king stayed at Langdon abbey; *CCR* 1323–1327, p. 503.   **99** The master was responsible for the delivery and care of the king's stores at Dover castle in 1369, and in the following year he and the abbot of St Radigund's abbey inspected the repairs to the castle; *CPR* 1367–1370, p. 247; *CPR* 1370–1374, p. 1.   **1** Both Philip Columber and Alice Wynter had initiated the provision of lights at the hospital chapel at some date before 1535; *Valor Eccl.*, vol. 1, p. 56. Special doles for the poor were part of the acts of commemoration for the souls of Henry III, Hubert de Burgh, his daughter Margaret, John Mawlyng and Beatrice Salkyn; *CPR* 1391–1396, p. 147; *L and P Henry VIII*, vol. 9, p. 379.   **2** *CChR* 1226–1257, p. 191.

mass priest or allocate the task to one of the priest brothers, thereby providing for the living as well as the dead. For St Mary's hospital, the financial implications of its role as an intermediary within the processes of multiple reciprocal exchanges became apparent when it failed to receive its share of the port dues following disruption to the cross-Channel trade. As a consequence, it was forced to continue supporting the daily mass from its own resources.[3] This meant that the Maison Dieu was caught in a relationship with a dead king, the patron and benefactor of a chantry for a third party whose needs were as great, perhaps, as they had been at its inception, and to which had been added the obligation to pray for the king's soul. Thus the hospital was morally bound to continue celebrating mass for Raymund's soul, and since his death Henry III's, even though at times this was difficult and impinged on other activities there.

Consequently the hospital's plea for tax exemption on the grounds of poverty in 1325 may reflect its financial position.[4] The heavy taxation of Edward I, a compulsory loan to his son in 1310, the agricultural disasters of the times, and the continuing burdens on the hospital already described may have caused the house certain financial difficulties.[5] It seems likely that income from produce and rents had declined if the hospital's experience was similar to other religious institutions in the county, and it appears such problems were not offset by new grants or testamentary bequests.[6] The evidence suggests that the king's initial close relationship with the Maison Dieu was a decisive and detrimental factor concerning the likelihood of its taking part in future processes of gift exchange with local benefactors (except members of the regional nobility during its early history). In addition, this relationship with the crown seems to have influenced the hospital's place in Dover society throughout its later history.

St Bartholomew's hospital

Like many modest leper hospitals in England, St Bartholomew's received very few *in vitam* grants during this period. Of the three grants recorded in the hospital register from the early fourteenth century all concerned property close to its other holdings in Buckland and, though not always explicit, it seems all three took the form of Thompson's free-alms tenure.[7] However, as at St Mary's, it is

---

3 Although not explicitly stated as affecting the daily mass for Raymund's soul in 1306, the problem of not receiving the port dues was causing the hospital serious difficulties; *CCR* 1302–1307, p. 381. The situation became more serious in 1338 as a result of war with France and the attack on Dover; the king acknowledged this and offered some relief; *CCR* 1337–1339, p. 352. **4** *CCR* 1323–1327, p. 421. The hospital also claimed poverty in 1328, 1333, 1337, 1338 (due to war with France it was unable to receive its share of the issues of the passage), 1340, 1341, 1345, 1347; *CCR* 1327–1330, p. 255; *CCR* 1333–1337, p. 13, 198; *CCR* 1337–1339, p. 352; *CCR* 1339–1341, p. 499; *CCR* 1341–1343, p. 185; *CCR* 1343–1346, p. 437; *CChR* 1341–1417, p. 64. **5** *CCR* 1307–1313, p. 266. **6** Mate, 'The impact of war', 771–8. **7** Of the donors two were Dover men, John Joseph (1323), a leading citizen, had been mayor in 1332 and 1333, and Adam ate Children (1337) was a

the house's apparently continuing lack of local support which is interesting, and may similarly highlight the detrimental effect of the hospital's close relationship with outside authority, in this instance Dover priory.[8] Unlike their counterparts at Sandwich, who held the patronage of two of the town's hospitals, a factor that seemingly was important in the construction of civic identity there in the thirteenth century, the Dover burgesses had no jurisdiction over either hospital, and may as a result have had little interest in these institutions.

Consequently, St Bartholomew's needed to manage its small estate in order to maintain its charitable function of caring for the resident poor inmates and a few short-term sick-poor. Although lepers were said to be in the Dover area as late as 1511, the evidence suggests that St Bartholomew's was no longer housing many/any lepers by the mid-fourteenth century.[9] Yet whatever its clientele, it needed an income, the master achieving this through a number of strategies, including leasing the hospital's property, firstly for life and, from the 1360s, for a fixed term.[10] In addition to revenue from its capital assets, the master looked for income from the exchanges with the house's resident inmates – the provision of entry fees and the further counter-gift of the inmates' labour on behalf of the house. Those outside supplied income to the house through fees from the annual fair, casual alms and other gifts given by those seeking explicit acts of reciprocity. Such reciprocal processes leave few records, but the priory register does include a reference to the hospital bed which the heirs of Herlewyn had purchased in the thirteenth century. Their descendant, Beatrice, the daughter of John atte See, now wished to sell the bed to the prior, presumably having no further use for it.[11] It is not clear whether St Bartholomew's gained anything from the transaction, but the bed's changed status may have entailed some income for the hospital.

This income was needed to fulfil the hospital's increasing commitments to the living and to the dead. Its more limited resources compared to the Maison Dieu

cheese maker there. The other benefactors were John de Hwetacre and Juliane his wife (1336) who were from the neighbouring rural parish of Charlton; Bodleian, Rawlinson MS. B.335, ff. 46–7, 54v–5. **8** Nothing in the register indicates that other grants covering gifts or acquisitions were for some reason not recorded there. Even though several folios are now missing from the end of the book, the simple index at the front does not suggest that these included copies of any charters. **9** During the visitation of 1511 it was reported that at the nearby parish of St Margaret at Cliffe a leper was maintained contrary to the law; Wood-Legh, *Kentish visitations*, p. 115. The hospital register entry dated 1346 reported that the resident inmates were of the poor, with a few sick persons nursed there; Bodleian, Rawlinson MS. B.335, f. 97v. **10** Because there are only a few leases and no rentals it is difficult to know how badly the hospital's income was affected by the Black Death and other factors. Comparing the leases of two properties in Wolves ward for 1295, 1332 and 1356, the annual rent remained the same for one of the properties following a new agreement in 1332, but when a new lease was drawn up for the second property in 1356 the rent had dropped from 2s. 8d. per year to 2s. per year; Bodleian, Rawlinson MS. B.335, ff. 26–8v. **11** LPL, MS. 241, ff. 102–2v.

may explain the apparent absence of doles to the poor at its gates, but it did provide some care for the sick-poor, like its namesake at Chatham, in addition to catering for the welfare of the permanent community. For the authorities, the provision of spiritual aid was more important than caring for the bodily needs of those at the hospital, a responsibility they discharged through the maintenance of a chapel and chaplain at the hospital.[12] Besides being part of the reciprocal process with those inside the house, the presence of a chaplain provided opportunities to conduct gift exchanges with those outside through the counter-gifts of confraternity and the furnishing of other spiritual services.[13] Yet the lack of local interest in such services may have had severe financial implications for the hospital. Various masters responded by sending out proctors to gather alms from further afield, and securing the offer of an indulgence at the hospital, thus widening the house's catchment area.[14] This seems to have been relatively successful in the short term but did not overcome the important problems of the imbalance between income and outgo, and the apparent indifference of the local population.

Other religious institutions
Like the hospitals, Dover priory was involved in the spiritual economy, but its interests were far more extensive. As well as trying to secure income from sources like its share of the Dover tolls, fish tithes, other tithes and clerical dues from the town's parish churches, various rents and other rights from its agricultural, urban and clerical holdings, the prior sought further funds from *in vitam* grants, indulgences, testamentary bequests and casual alms.[15] Such sources have been dis-

---

12 Bodleian, Rawlinson MS. B.335, ff. 4–4v. **13** One of the few concerned the parents of John Joseph, who gave an acre of land to the hospital in free and perpetual alms for the souls of their sons, daughters, parents and all the departed faithful. They sought the counter-gifts received by other benefactors: masses, matins, vespers, prayers, vigils, alms and other good deeds which constituted the gift of confraternity; ibid. f. 45v. **14** In 1330 a proctor named Andrew Durant de Swettone collected alms for one year, and in 1346 John de Chellesfelde was collecting for two years. The latter could offer an indulgence of 240 days; ibid. ff. 97v–98v. **15** Like the hospitals, the priory at times experienced considerable problems collecting dues. In 1338 the prior testified before the barons of the exchequer that the French had raided the priory and taken the royal charters detailing its rights to a share in the port dues, a situation made more difficult by the barons wishing to make further enquiries; *CPR 1338–1340*, p. 17. In the same year the priory petitioned for tax exemption because the war with France had meant there was no profit from the customary dues (St Mary's hospital was highlighting the same problem), and in 1347 the priory cited its heavy losses on account of the war with France, which was reducing the profits from passenger traffic; *CCR 1337–1339*, p. 303; *CPR 1345–1348*, p. 347. Tithe disputes with various parish clergy, like the priest at Appledore in 1317, caused problems in collecting the money and in the time needed to attend the church courts; LPL, MS. 241, f. 227v. The priory was also in dispute with the town over certain ancient dues: the fish tithes dispute in the 1340s appears to have revolved around who should receive them; LPL, MS. 241, ff. 38–9v. The quarrel over the position of the archipresbyter was finally resolved by the archbishop in 1389, the townspeople agreeing to enter into a reciprocal exchange with the priory. They would give offerings at the high altar of St Martin's on the four

cussed with regard to the Dover hospitals, and though there were differences of emphasis, timing and expectations among the different institutions, only the formation of the cult of the priory's own martyr is considered here.

Thomas de la Hale, an elderly monk, was murdered by the French during their raid on the priory in 1295.[16] His tomb became a centre of pilgrimage, following the offer of certain indulgences, a number of miracles and the production of a life of the saintly monk.[17] It is unclear whether the new cult had a detrimental effect on the Maison Dieu's shrine of St Richard, but the monks at Christchurch were sufficiently concerned about this potential rival to block the proposal to canonize the martyred monk.[18] Their hostility may have stemmed from the decline in the level of alms offered at Becket's shrine by the mid-fourteenth century, but may also reflect the acrimonious dispute between the two houses.[19] Yet for the monks at Dover, their saint may have been seen as a gift from God at a time when the house was suffering severe financial problems.

These problems were partly due to the priory's dispute with Christchurch, but an imbalance between the house's income and outgo was also important.[20]

principal feast days on the understanding that the priory would provide a secular priest to serve them there; Haines, *Dover priory*, pp. 128–9; LPL, MS. 241, f. 34v. In a petition dated 1363 the prior spoke of the house needing extra income 'propter sterilitatem terarum olim frugiferarum', suggesting it was experiencing agricultural problems; Haines, *Dover priory*, p. 272; CCAL, DCc/Reg. H, f. 6. **16** Thomas' martyrdom occurred when the priory was invaded by a group of men from Calais who broke down the gates, slew the servants and ransacked the buildings in their search for booty. All the monks fled except Thomas de la Hale, an old and infirm monk, who confronted the raiders about their acts of sacrilege and, on refusing to divulge the whereabouts of any treasure, was cut down as his namesake had been at Canterbury. He was found by the returning monks who reproached themselves for their conduct. They buried him the next day before the altar of Our Lady and St Katherine, where he had spent his days in prayer; Haines, *Dover priory*, pp. 244–7. **17** In 1296, while visiting Dover, John of Pontoise, bishop of Winchester, offered an indulgence of forty days to all who prayed for the soul of the dead monk, and six years later he offered a similar indulgence; LPL, MS. 241, ff. 52, 53v–4. For example, he was credited with restoring a withered hand, making four blind men see, returning the wits of a madman, making limbs whole and bringing four men back to life; whereas at Canterbury the miracle in 1395 was so rare that Richard II wrote to the prior congratulating him on the event; Zeiger, 'Survival of the cult' p. 25; Haines, *Dover priory*, p. 476; LPL, MS. 241, f. 54. According to Haines, the *Vita* was the work of John of Tynemouth, the manuscript having been written in 1377 at Bury St Edmunds. Other accounts apparently were derived from different sources; Haines, *Dover priory*, pp. 169–76. **18** The little wax boats offered by grateful sailors at Thomas' shrine may have encroached upon the offerings made at Our Lady of Pity chapel on the foreshore, and the presence of another potential saint may have reduced the gifts made at St Richard of Chichester's shrine in St Edmund's chapel, especially as the main centre of that cult was at Chichester; Haines, *Dover priory*, p. 247. Among the commissioners who inquired into Thomas' case for canonization were the priors of Christchurch and St Gregory's, Canterbury; Haines, *Dover priory*, pp. 248, 477–8. **19** Although the figures are difficult to interpret, in broad terms the cult was far less lucrative for the Canterbury monks by the early fifteenth century; Woodruff, 'Cult of St Thomas', 20–1, 23. **20** It is impossible to assess how much the priory spent on the struggle to retain control over its own affairs, but it might be valuable to look at Christchurch's litigation costs. In the thirty-seven years preceding 1322, it spent

The priory's concerns for the living included the sustenance of the monks, the furnishing of corrodies, the counter-gift of confraternity, the provision of hospitality, the giving of alms, and the supplying of labour on behalf of the king and the town. Some of these counter-gifts had implications for the two hospitals because, for example, the crown expected the priory to provide places for aged royal servants, as at St Mary's hospital.[21] Whether such corrodies reduced the pressure for places on other local institutions is unclear. But for the priory the spectre of an unending stream of royal corrodians was made worse by the expectations of others that the house would provide places when required, sometimes at the priory's expense as part of an earlier gift exchange.[22]

Similarly, the prior was expected to provide hospitality for royal visitors, papal officials and other churchmen as part of the privileges of patronage.[23] Such guests must have been a considerable strain on the priory's resources, but may have been a boon to the master of the Maison Dieu, whose own commitments regarding hospitality for various groups has already been noted. The king had his own chamber at the priory, suggesting another act of appropriation, which allowed him to welcome his guests into the priory without recourse to the prior.[24] Moreover, the 'economy of regard' between the priory and some of its guests seems to have been severely limited, leading to the need for frequent refurbishment of the house by the prior.[25] This seems to highlight the debasement of the

£3,624 on lawsuits in Rome and England concerning its dispute with Dover priory, and its desire to maintain the prior's spiritual authority during vacancies of the see in the southern provinces; Dobson, 'Canterbury', p. 97. **21** These included John Pyk, yeoman of the king's buttery, who entered in 1331 following the death of Richard de Dover, who himself had replaced William de Kent, a corrodian from Edward I's reign. In 1333 it was stated that John Pyk's grant was not setting a precedent, but after his death his place was taken by William Gardrobier, yeoman of the wardrobe, who survived there until 1382 when his room was taken by Oliver Martyn; *CPR* 1330–1334, p. 398; Haines, *Dover priory*, pp. 263–4. There appear to have been two royal nominees in the priory during the 1350s and 1360s, because in 1360 William Beaufilz, the king's watchman, for his good service took the place of John le Graunt, deceased; and in the following year William Gardrobier replaced John Pyk, deceased; *CCR* 1360–1364, pp. 139, 258. **22** Queen Isabella may not have specifically intended her earlier actions on the priory's behalf would have been reciprocated by the prior through the giving of a corrody to her son's servant, but this is what appears to have occurred; Haines, *Dover priory*, p. 263, n. 3. Archbishop Reynolds seems to have considered he too had rights of placement at the priory, and in 1325 the abbot of Faversham was forced upon the house. The prior appears to have protested strongly but his objections were overruled, his only consolation being that the abbot was paying for his place; Haines, *Dover priory*, p. 261. Possibly much more agreeable to the prior was the relationship with Nicholas de Beere, a Dover citizen, who had inherited the right to a corrody from his father, the late seneschal there (in 1314 Nicholas wished to give up this privilege); LPL, MS. 241, f. 27v. **23** Haines, *Dover priory*, pp. 344–5. **24** In 1308, for example, while the king was staying in the king's chamber at the priory, he handed the great seal to the chancellor because he was about to leave the country. Also present at the meeting were a knight, two clerks, and the bishop of Chichester; *CCR* 1307–1313, p. 18. **25** Although the reasons for the priory's need for tax exemption were not stated in 1332, it seems likely that its reduced income formed only part of the problem; *CCR* 1330–1333, p. 552. By 1363

reciprocal exchange process, where the king's guests did not see themselves as exchange partners with the priory, which meant they felt they owed it nothing.

For the priory, the distribution of alms may have been less of a drain on its resources. Such charitable acts were part of its gift exchange with the local burgesses, but a few individuals also sought to initiate almsgiving at the priory, whereby they received other spiritual services on their behalf.[26] As at the hospitals, these benefactors were not local townsfolk, but included certain English kings and senior churchmen and a small number of wealthy men who held land in east Kent.[27] This apparent lack of local support for the priory in terms of its exchanges for the living was mirrored in its exchanges for the dead. Few from the town or from the local knightly families sought intercessory and commemorative services, including chantries, and of those who did their choices seem to reflect either personal connections or the priory's place in their complex and wide-ranging spiritual strategy.[28] Instead, the leading townspeople probably directed their pious giving towards the parish churches (though this cannot be tested because of the lack of evidence), and towards the town's gift to St Thomas of Canterbury.

Dover's votive offering may have begun in the thirteenth century, presumably after 1220, because the triennial gift was taken to Canterbury cathedral on the eve of the feast of the translation of St Thomas. But the first record of its existence is in the early extant chamberlains' accounts from the late fourteenth century.[29] The town's offering comprised a long candle, the length of the circumference of the town of Dover, which was wound round a great reel and car-

---

this had been recognized, because it was said that so many kings and other nobles claimed hospitality there that it was in great need; Haines, *Dover priory*, p. 272. **26** The only person known to have sought the counter-gift of confraternity was Nicholas de Beere; LPL, MS. 241, f. 28. **27** Of the few laymen involved in this type of gift-giving, Nicholas de Beere (see above) intended that as part of his agreement with the priory the almoner should, at his obit, furnish 100 paupers with a penny each at the priory's expense; ibid. The only other evidence for the priory's almsgiving is an account of 1530–1, where the sum of £3 8s. 2d. is listed under the heading 'Alms given according to ancient custom of the House'; and from the *Valor* where it was recorded that alms were given on twenty-seven occasions annually, giving a total yearly expenditure of £13 19s. 2d.; Haines, *Dover priory*, pp. 451–5; *Valor Eccl.*, vol. 1, p. 54. The poor, were rarely explicitly mentioned, the obit of Michael le Roche being one of the rare exceptions; he intended that 4s. 8d. would be spent on bread for 'poor folks'; Haines, *Dover priory*, p. 421. **28** The case of Nicholas de Beere has been noted already. The only person known to have endowed a chantry at the priory was Ralph Basset, who appears to have devoted several years to organizing his donation and agreement with the priory; LPL, MS. 241, ff. 60, 166. The priory register notes one further gift exchange of this kind, for the sustenance of lights before the altars of holy cross and St Mary Magdalene in the priory church; LPL, MS. 241, f. 83v. **29** 'Item illa longa candela contenta in quadam rota baronum uille Douorie omni tercio anno contra Festum Translacionis Sancti Thome sub forma que sequitur renouatur'. From the fifteenth century customary of St Thomas Becket, the transcription kindly supplied by Mark Bateson and the translation provided by Peter Rowe from his dissertation, 'The customary of the shrine of St Thomas Becket' (1990), p. 91.

ried to the shrine at Canterbury by the town's four porters.[30] Such a gift probably represents an act of thanksgiving relating to a particular event; presumably
St Thomas was believed to have saved Dover, but the continuing performance
of the gift-giving seems to imply an ongoing relationship with England's premier saint, where the mayor and commonalty sought his continuing protection.
Even though this spiritual protection might have been seen in terms of aid against
natural disasters or foreign attack, the at times uneasy relationship between the
civic authorities and the crown may have been a contributing factor.[31] The view
of St Thomas as the champion of righteousness against Henry II may have
remained significant in the reciprocal gift exchange between the town and the
saint. Furthermore, the idea of outsiders, those outside the town's jurisdiction
and so outside its protection, may have been important with regard to the two
hospitals and the priory. All of these were outside the line of the town wall (there
seems to have been a wall of sorts from at least the early thirteenth century) and
none were under the patronage of the civic authorities. The saint's, and thus the
town's protection, might be said to include the ancient minster church of St
Martin (and possibly Dover's other parish churches), which was within the topographical boundary of the town.[32] Even though the relationship between the
civic and ecclesiastical authorities was extremely complex with respect to Dover
and St Martin's church (see page 141), it is likely that through these acts of inclusion the mayor and jurats were attempting to link symbolically the town and
this locally, and previously regionally, important church. Such a relationship,
founded on patronage and reciprocity and articulated through ritual and symbolism, was an important factor in the fashioning of corporate identity, and in
the spiritual life of the town.[33]

THE LATE MIDDLE AGES (C.1470–C.1530)

The two major topics for this period relevant to the history of the hospitals are
the problems of the harbour and their impact upon the town. Like the other

---

30 'Inde in tercio anno cum premissa candela pene uel totaliter consumpta fuerit uel perusta fere-
trarii tempore oportuno ante festum Translacionis Sancti Thome predictam rotam nudam trans-
mittent per aliquem: conductam pro vid ad donum seu habitacionem maioris uille Douorie qui
suis aliorum que baronum sumptibus ibidem nouam candelam fieri faciet cuius longitudo con-
tivubit ambitum siue circuitum dicte uille ...' supplied by M. Bateson from BL, Add. MS. 59616,
f. 9. Four porters were recorded taking the great candle to Canterbury in 1429, for example; BL,
Add. MS. 29615, f. 153v. **31** In France and the southern Netherlands, where the offering of such
civic candles was customary from the late twelfth century, most were given during time of siege
or when the town was suffering a plague epidemic; H. van der Velden, *The donor's image: Gerard
Leyet and the votive portraits of Charles the Bold* (2000), pp. 240–1. **32** S. Sweetinburgh, 'Wax, stone
and iron: Dover's town defenses in the late middle ages', *Arch. Cant.* (forthcoming). **33**
Sweetinburgh, 'Hospital in Kent', pp. 213–7.

Cinque Ports, Dover's livelihood from the sea was threatened by the effects of silting, though the town had also experienced severe storm damage during the fifteenth century.[34] Funding the repair of the town's sea defences had proved extremely difficult and, during the early decades of the sixteenth century, the authorities appear to have given up the struggle to keep the whole of the sea wall intact. In part, this was a consequence of the need for extensive work on the harbour if Dover was to regain its status as a port, the work beginning during the early years of Henry VIII's reign. However, any advantage from the new initiative was short-lived, and during the 1520s civic revenue was insufficient to continue the new construction.[35] Having failed to find outside sources of funding, the town authorities appealed to the king on the grounds that the work was of national strategic importance, which Dover was unable to fund due to its extreme poverty.[36] Henry sanctioned the expenditure and work began in 1535 under the master of the Maison Dieu and John Whalley, the king's paymaster. For almost a decade, vast sums were spent on the project, but its limited success saw the king lose interest, and the venture was not revived until Elizabeth's reign.

The scale of the operation and the need for manpower and materials stimulated Dover's ailing economy, especially in regard to the service industries, but the long-term economic trend was still one of decline. Moreover, the seasonal flood of migrant workers each year into the town caused severe problems in accommodating, feeding and paying this army of craftsmen and labourers.[37] Thus the short-term economic advantage merely masked the long-term problems and at the same time brought additional difficulties, like an increasing pool of poor workers and others to the town and the threat of civil unrest.

During the first part of the period, the mayoralty was still dominated by a few families whose commercial interests extended beyond Dover into the local countryside.[38] The 1520s witnessed a broadening of this ruling group, as the lead-

---

34 The mayor and jurats petitioned the crown on a number of occasions in the fifteenth century about the problems of storm damage and their inability to repair the sea wall; *CPR* 1429–1436, p. 496, 1467–1477, p. 393, 1476–1485, p. 462. 35 For an assessment of the difficulties of the harbour and the new works; M. Dixon, 'Economy and society in Dover, 1509–1640' (1992), pp. 19–20. 36 The civic authorities had previously petitioned the Merchant Adventurers for aid, the letter delivered by Sir John Clerke, master of the Maison Dieu; BL, Egerton MS. 2093, ff. 44–5. 37 Nor, presumably, was a lack of victuals the only problem, because the need to maintain law and order over both the resident and itinerant work force and their neighbours had to be addressed by the town authorities through the system of the town constables and the wardmen. As a result, men were brought before the town court, like Adrian Cooper, a Fleming, who in 1522 was fined 20*d*. for walking abroad after 10 p.m. and using unfitting language against the watch and the mayor; BL, Egerton MS. 2092, f. 248v. 38 A few men appear to have controlled the mayoralty, though only the Hexstall family produced men beyond one generation: between 1462 and 1499 Thomas and Edward Hexstall held the mayoralty for eleven years, and Edward was again mayor in 1506. These leading townsmen were frequently active in business outside Dover, many holding land in the local rural parishes; while William Warren (mayor in 1493), in addition to his Dover prop-

ing citizens allowed in certain migrants and others of rising expectation, who were drawn from the town's middling sort.[39] These 'new men', drawn from the victualling trades, with their commercial interests centred on Dover, joined the sons of the 'old men' in the town government in the late 1520s and 1530s. Such men had different priorities concerning Dover's future, and their presence may partly explain the events that led to the destruction of the priory, the two ancient hospitals and three of the town's parish churches. For men like John Bowle, the opportunity to acquire property and other assets seems to have been more important than the religious controversies of the times. And even though anticlericalism was a factor in Dover society, there is little to suggest the presence of those holding strong reformist convictions.[40]

To investigate these issues, this section examines the spiritual economy in late medieval Dover to see what types of relationship the hospitals, the two town almshouses (founded in the late fifteenth century), the priory and parish churches were able to develop with particular individuals and various groups.[41] By looking at the counter-gifts such institutions might offer and the willingness of donors to furnish gifts in the expectation of receiving these benefits, it is possible to gain some perception of the value placed on the hospital by local people and those from east Kent. Although certain counter-gifts were more applicable at particular institutions, there were nine main types linked to the Dover hospitals: patronage of a place or bed, the labour of the hospital staff (including the provision of hospitality), confraternity, burial, intercessory prayers of the priest brothers, prayers of the almsfolk or the poor who stayed overnight, prayers of named hospital personnel, an obit or similar periodic act of of intercession and commemoration, and a chantry (temporary or permanent). Though such reciprocal acts were sought by different people, the available evidence (testamentary materials, Dover chamberlains' accounts, a few *in vitam* grants) suggests that they can

---

erty, held land in the lordships around Calais (this was inherited by his son, John, who was mayor in 1525); CKS, PRC 32/9, f. 104. **39** Dixon has discussed the town's ruling group and the changes that appear to have occurred during the 1520s; Dixon, 'Economy', pp. 424–8. **40** Even though the changes in the personnel of the civic government appear to show several parallels with those for Sandwich, at Dover this does not seem to have produced men of strong reformist religious convictions, or at least not until later in the century. At Sandwich Thomas Holye, William Norres and Richard Butler (only William was not a town officer in the 1530s) were proto-Protestant activists in the town and surrounding countryside, but there is no record of anyone from Dover; *L and P Henry VIII*, vol. 18, pt 2, pp. 299, 311. Anticlericalism seems to have had a long history among the Dover citizens, but it does not appear to have developed into doctrinal radicalism at this time. Instead it may have been fuelled in the 1530s by fears of a French invasion and the desires of land-hungry townsmen; Clark, *English provincial society*, pp. 29, 37. However, Dixon believes that the smooth and swift transition from Catholicism to Protestantism over the Reformation period might indicate that at least a minority of the town's citizens held reformist views; Dixon, 'Economy', pp. 497–8, 500, 502, 505. **41** There were at least two almshouses; the first 'at Wall gate' was in existence by 1488, and the second, 'at Butchery gate', was operating before 1498; BL, Egerton MS. 2107, ff. 14v, 58v.

be divided into four groups: local townspeople, those from the town's hinterland, Dover corporation, and those from Canterbury and the other Cinque Ports.

Looking first at counter-gifts for the living, the desirability of seeking a place,
either for oneself or for another, varied considerably among the four hospitals. As
patron of the Maison Dieu, the king retained the right to send his aged retainers
there, but he did not appear to have exercised his prerogative during this period.
However, John Whalley, Henry VIII's paymaster of the new harbour works,
apparently used a chamber at the priory, presumably residing there at that house's
expense. Nevertheless, the hospital did have at least one guest chamber, which
might imply that accommodation was available.[42] Whether this chamber was in
frequent use is difficult to ascertain, but the sources suggest that though the poor
and pilgrims may have stayed overnight, there was little interest among the laity
in becoming resident inmates at St Mary's. For those seeking to enter the priesthood, St Mary's may have been a more attractive proposition.[43] Yet, even though
there were a few priest brothers from locally prosperous families, it is not clear
whether the small total number of brothers indicates poor recruitment or the
inability or unwillingness of the house to support a larger community.[44] For the
Maison Dieu, in addition to entry fees, these local recruits provided links with
Dover and its hinterland, but interestingly, in terms of testamentary gifts at least,
family connections apparently produced very little income.[45]

For the other Dover hospitals there is no evidence of this type of connection at all and, though it might be expected that the majority of the inmates at
St Bartholomew's and the almshouses would have come from the locality, there
is nothing in the testamentary sources to support this. Unlike the position with
regard to Canterbury and its hospitals, none of Dover's testators sought a place
at these houses for either their servants or kin. Instead, the only interest was in
St Bartholomew's hospital at Sandwich.[46] This seems to imply that the Dover

42 The naming of Richard Elam's chamber and the room assigned to John Whalley at the priory
in the inventory of 1535 may imply these were used, on occasion, for lodging outsiders; Walcott,
'Inventories of St Mary's hospital', 278; *L and P Henry VIII*, vol. 9, p. 241. 43 From the only
surviving rental for the hospital, it appears that those in holy orders each received 26s. 8d. per
year and the lay brothers 20s.; BL, Add. MS. 62710, f. 2v. Furthermore, the hospital had an extensive library of 117 books; BL, Stowe MS. 850, f. 130. 44 Of the local men who became priest
brothers, members of John Hebbynge's family were prominent citizens in the neighbouring town
of Folkestone, and Simon Tempilman came from a leading Dover family. 45 One of the few
exceptions concerned John Hebbynge, whose kinsman and namesake, a prosperous draper in
Folkestone, made his will in the same year that John was ordained a priest at the hospital. In his
will he bequeathed his messuage, stable and two lodges to the Maison Dieu to hold forever on
the death of his wife, the hospital in return providing specific acts of intercession; C. Harper-Bill
(ed.), *Register of John Morton*, vol. 1 (1987), no. 433; CKS, PRC 17/5, f. 90. 46 For example in
1464 John Baker of Folkestone intended that his wife should have one of the best sort of corrody at St Bartholomew's hospital, Sandwich, for the rest of her life after his death; CKS, PRC
17/1, f. 164. Preference was still being shown for the Sandwich hospital in the sixteenth century

hospitals were not seen as attractive alternatives by the moderately prosperous who were seeking a semi-religious life or a place in an almshouse, either for themselves or for their dependents, rather the resident inmates were poor or poorer people from Dover, and probably to a lesser extent its hinterland.[47] Those entering the civic almshouses, in particular, may have been heavily dependent on the largesse of their family and friends or the receipt of casual alms, because there is nothing in the chamberlains' accounts regarding their welfare other than certain monies spent on repairs to the two houses.[48] As members of the deserving poor, these possibly elderly or infirm almsfolk were a living reminder of civic beneficence, a part of the mayor and jurats' gift exchange with the town, whereby they enacted their role as good governors.

Apart from seeking places at other hospitals in east Kent, a more local alternative was the priory, which did house a few corrodians, including one woman, during the late middle ages.[49] This charitable act might have been expected to enhance the house's reputation, especially as she was said to be of good character, but there is nothing in the testamentary sources to indicate that such acts extended the priory's place in the spiritual economy, and in 1538–9 the corrodians were swept away with priory. These people may have provided other more immediate benefits, at least in the short term, but the payment of entry fees was not sufficient compensation when the corrodian outlived the value of the corrody, unless it was open to renegotiation.

The second type of counter-gift for the living, the provision of hospitality and other work undertaken by the hospital staff, was especially important with respect to St Mary's hospital and its relationship with the town. In part, this may have resulted from a lessening of the house's public connections with the crown, at least until the mastership of Sir John Tompson, the last master. During his predecessor's long mastership, neither the king nor his officers appear to have stayed at the hospital, and Sir John Clerke rarely seems to have undertaken crown business. Instead, he was often active on the town's behalf, especially in the late 1510s and 1520s when he became one of the wardens of the harbour works.[50] His activities apparently enhanced the hospital's reputation as well as his own, making the hospital a less marginal institution in Dover and triggered a series of

---

when William Gybbe of Hythe sought a corrody there for his daughter in his will of 1527; CKS, PRC 32/14, f. 210. **47** George, from St Bartholomew's hospital, was probably poor (he was paid by the civic authorities to clean the market place), but whether he was local is unknown; BL, Egerton MS. 2107, f. 88. **48** It is known that at certain hospitals the inmates were sustained from the food and clothing brought in by family and friends; P. Tucker, 'The medieval hospital of St Mary Bethlehem' (1996). **49** She had given £20 to the priory, which seems to have provided her with some form of lodgings within the precincts, presumably secluded from the monks; Haines, *Dover priory*, p. 332. **50** The accounts' book for the harbour works was better kept following the appointment of Sir John Clerke and Richard Fyneux as wardens in March 1518; BL, Egerton MS. 2108, f. 25.

testamentary bequests to the house and Sir John.[51] The testators often sought prayers from the hospital's priest brothers, though few were named except for Sir John, who was called upon to act as executor or overseer on at least nine occasions.[52] Through these activities he was in contact with a wide circle of people in Dover and the surrounding parishes, which might in turn have generated further gift exchanges, so enhancing the institution's reputation, a situation that seems to have ended with the death of Sir John and Tompson's appointment. In contrast, there is nothing to suggest that the other hospitals were involved in similar relationships with either individual townsfolk or the corporation.[53] The only reference to anyone from St Bartholomew's working for the town was to 'poor George' and his unnamed successors, who were paid for cleaning the market place.

The third counter-gift that might be provided for the living was the gift of confraternity. Although there are no known references to those seeking this provision, two testators did seek something similar in terms of being remembered within the hospital community at St Mary's. Giles Love, with regard to his obit, stipulated that the brothers should buy annually 2s. worth of cakes to remember him, while Isabel Wyke wished her name to be recorded in the 'mortelage among the brothers and sisters'.[54] Both bequests imply the importance of per-

---

51 The first year the prior and master were listed in the chamberlains' accounts as receiving wine at the four principal feasts was in the 1510s, a reflection of the master's integration into the civic ceremonial life of the town (the inclusion of the prior possibly linked to the master's rather than the prior's perceived worthiness); BL, Egerton MS. 2092, f. 146v. Even though few remembered the hospital, the number of these testators doubled between the first and second halves of the period, and the bequests were clustered in the late 1510s and early 1520s. Sir John was to receive gifts from the wills of William Warren, Giles Love, Richard Fyneux, Robert Ruttier, Robert Dyer; CKS, PRC 32/9, f. 104, 32/12, f. 172, 32/13, f. 23, 32/14, f. 1, 32/15, f. 158, 32/15, f. 371. **52** Such pastoral care was not only sought from Sir John by testators from Dover, because William Mowbrey of Colrede placed his sons in Sir John's care. He was to act as the custodian of William's lands on their behalf and also see that William's obit was celebrated at Colrede church; CKS, PRC 17/13, f. 56. Of the priest brothers: Henry Wood , John Burnell and William Noole were each named three times as recipients; Thomas Fuller, John Soly were each twice named; and William Baker and John Knight were each named once. Interestingly, neither John Hebbynge nor Simon Tempilman was named as beneficiaries in any of the wills. It is possible in Simon's case, this was connected to his dispute with the master and brothers at St Mary's, a situation investigated at the 1511 visitation; Wood-Legh, *Kentish visitations*, p. 25. **53** St Bartholomew's was left 3s. 4d. towards repairs there by Robert Ruttier in 1518; CKS, PRC 32/14, f. 1. It is possible that as one of the county's lazar houses the hospital received a small gift from Edward Mynot of Canterbury's executors, and it may have been among the four lazar houses which were to receive bequests in Richard Lambisfelde of Hythe's will, dated 1488; CKS, 17/5, f. 67, 32/3, f. 185. **54** Isabel was a married woman which makes her will especially interesting. Her connection with the hospital was probably through Simon Tempilman, a brother there, who was one of the witnesses of her husband's will. She made two bequests to the hospital: 40s. for this privilege, the sum being divided among the brothers, and a further ten marks to the master and

sonal contacts between the donor and members of the hospital staff, as well as the idea that by securing a place among the company of the hospital they were joining a special community of the living and the dead.

Dover's townsfolk and those from the neighbouring parishes, including members of the gentry, were apparently equally uninterested in seeking confraternity or similar relationships with the town's other religious houses.[55] This may reflect a lack of concern for these institutions, but also appears to mirror an absence of interest in fraternities more generally. Unlike most towns where parish fraternities were an integral part of the spiritual life of the community, the testamentary evidence for Dover fails to provide a single bequest relating to such a fraternity. The only evidence of a parish fraternity concerns St Mary's church, where there was a fraternity of St John the Baptist, but whether this was the same as the fraternity of St John's Bothe which met in Bygon Street is unknown.[56] The situation in Dover's hinterland was not dissimilar, though a few testators did remember their parish fraternities.[57] It is not clear why the townspeople and those in the neighbouring countryside acted like this, especially in an area where migrant workers and other itinerants frequently outnumbered the native population, who might as a result have looked to the parish church and its fraternities as substitutes for family and friends.[58]

Very few Dover testators wished to be buried at the Maison Dieu or the priory; over 90% of the townspeople and their rural counterparts sought burial in their parish church or churchyard.[59] Though the choice of their own parish

brothers so that they should pray for her soul, and for her father's and mother's souls and those of the departed faithful; CKS, PRC 32/4, f. 109. Giles Love provided further symbolic gifts in the form of six silver spoons and twenty bushels of bay salt to the hospital; CKS, PRC 32/12, f. 172, see introduction. **55** For example, Thomas and Jane Frognall, a gentry couple from the neighbouring parish of Buckland, engaged in gift exchanges with the parishes of Lynstead, Graveney and Westminster Abbey or the Savoy in London; CKS, PRC 32/8, f. 97, 17/13, f. 89. **56** BL, Egerton MS. 1912, f. 13. For the fraternity of St John's bothe; EKA, Do/ZZ 02/01 15. **57** From the testamentary evidence there were fraternities at East Langdon (St Augustine, Allhallows), at Ewell (Our Lady, St Peter, Holy Cross, St James), at Folkestone (St Euswithe, Our Lady, the palm cross, Corpus Christi). **58** Nor, apart from the 'Fership', do there appear to have been any craft fraternities in the town before at least the late sixteenth century. **59** Burial at the Maison Dieu: Thomas Petytt (1501), Giles Love (1514), Sir Robert Long of Eastbridge, Romney Marsh (1529); at Dover priory: Robert Lucas (1484), John Otway (1497), Sir Thomas Ryche of Buckland (1499), Henry Fravell (1514), Roger Coost of West Langdon (1525); CKS, PRC 32/7, f. 29, 32/12, f. 172, 32/15, f. 371, 32/2, f. 613, 32/4, f. 180, 32/5, f. 54, 32/11, f. 114, 17/17, f. 56. Those seeking burial away from their parish church: Joane Sherman (1464) wished to join her late husband at St Mary's church; Robert Fooche (1491) did not specify his burial place; William Lovell (1492) sought burial outside the town; William Horn (1498) wanted to be buried in the castle church; John Warmyngton of Poulton (1500) requested burial at St Radigund's abbey; Simon Tenderby of Hougham (1504) at Dover castle church; John a Bygge (1509) in the churchyard of St Martin-le-Grand; CKS, PRC 32/2, f. 454, 32/3, f. 304, 32/3, f. 340, 32/4, f. 191, 17/8, f. 235, 17/9, f. 46, 32/10, f. 8. [All dates relate to the making of the will unless otherwise stated.]

church for their internment and funeral service might be expected to be the norm, the disinterest in the town's religious houses mirrors the attitude of the majority of Dover's leading citizens towards the offer of other spiritual counter-gifts from these establishments. Of those who did seek burial at the hospital, personal and/or family connections were apparently important in most cases. Sir Robert Long, the nephew of Sir John Clerke, had presumably received the living of Eastbridge church through his uncle, and his choice of burial place, the hospital church, was a way of honouring the family connection.[60] However, he was prepared to be guided by his uncle, and if Sir John refused his request, he sought burial at St Mary's church, Dover. Like the church at Eastbridge, St Mary's was under the patronage of the hospital, and the priest brother who served at St Mary's was a friend of Sir Robert's, which suggests that mutual regard between the two men was a significant factor here.[61] For certain individuals, the reputation and longevity of the house might have been more important. Thomas Petytt, an apparently childless parishioner at St John's, may have felt the Maison Dieu offered a more prestigious and secure place of commemoration, especially as his parish church had for some decades suffered serious physical neglect due to its subordinate position with respect to St Martin-le-Grand.[62]

What prompted individuals to seek burial at the priory is more difficult to establish, but the prior may have adopted a policy of promoting the worthiness of the place in the late fifteenth century at a time when the house was acutely short of funds to undertake major repairs. If this was a deliberate strategy, its success was severely limited among the local population, the prior complaining in 1511 that the Dover citizens were withholding their mortuary gifts, though it was slightly more successful further afield in terms of testamentary gifts from wealthy Canterbury citizens and certain kings.[63] As at the hospital, patronage and

---

60 Sir Robert made his will in 1529, but the probate date of 1537 post-dates his uncle's death by two and a half years; CKS, PRC 32/15, f. 371. 61 In his will Sir Robert Long bequeathed to Sir Robert the books his friend had borrowed from him; ibid. 62 Thomas did not mention the master or any of the brothers by name, which may suggest he was more concerned about the hospital's reputation, and possibly its longevity; CKS, PRC 32/7, f. 29. Problems relating to the structure of St Nicholas' church were recorded in 1467, and in the archiepiscopal visitation of 1511 the church was again under threat from neglect (St Martin-le-Grand's damaged steeple was harming St Nicholas' church); Haines, *Dover priory*, p. 289; Wood-Legh, *Kentish visitations*, p. 134. 63 Wood-Legh, *Kentish visitations*, p. 22. Only one local testator, Robert Lucas, seems to have aided the priory in this way. He sought burial there in 1484, and bequeathed 33s. 4d. towards the making of the cloister at the priory; CKS, PRC 32/2, f. 613. Henry Trewonwall of Canterbury (1483) may have been a migrant from Cornwall who had been successful in business and was able to make a number of bequests to religious houses in Canterbury, and also St Radigund's abbey and Dover priory; CKS, PRC 32/2, f. 583. Edward Mynot (1487), a wealthy Canterbury citizen, made a large number of bequests to religious houses, including Dover priory, a choice that seems to have been influenced by his wife, who had connections with the Fuller family of Dover; CKS, PRC 17/5, f. 67. Both Richard III and Henry VII supported the priory; Haines, *Dover priory*, pp. 294–5.

personal links seem to have prompted a few to request burial at the priory, but Henry Fravell's choice was probably the result of his desire to be near his mother rather than regard for the priory *per se*.[64] Yet even if the priory gained little financially from Henry's will, his desire to be buried in the priory church may have been seen as a prestigious event because he was an important Dover citizen.

The testamentary sources indicate that after 1500 Dover testators were far more likely to specify the spiritual services they wished performed at their three funeral days.[65] This more regulated system of intercession and its concentration on the parish church might have been expected to lessen such gift exchanges with the local religious houses. In broad terms this appears to have occurred with respect to the priory (St Bartholomew's only received one testamentary bequest throughout the whole period), but does not reflect the situation in terms of the Maison Dieu, especially from the late 1510s. As noted earlier, this was apparently linked to the charitable work of the master on behalf of the town, who was actively involved in the maintenance of the harbour and was prepared to subsidize the town from his own funds.[66] Such work raised the reputation and status of the master and the hospital among the townspeople, possibly aided by the public recognition of their value to Dover through the inclusion of the master and the prior in the civic ritual year. As a result, the hospital and Sir John received testamentary gifts from an increasing number of Dover citizens and those from its hinterland, a recognition of their worthiness as exchange partners in the spiritual economy. For some, like Robert Dyer who had served in town government in the 1520s, their choice of the hospital as a reputable institution was reinforced by personal connections with the master.[67] Others in the town's hinterland

---

64 Proximity to his mother may have been the most important factor for Henry. The site of their burials, before St John's altar, may reflect her choice, not his, because there is nothing in his will to indicate a particular devotion to St John. Furthermore, he intended that his three funeral days should be celebrated at his parish church of St Peter, as well as at the priory. Thus, for this prosperous jurat and friend of many in the town government, the corporation church of St Peter was a vital part of his strategy to be remembered and commemorated in the town through a series of pious and charitable bequests; CKS, PRC 32/11, f. 114. In contrast, Sir Thomas Ryche, vicar at Buckland and a faithful servant of the priory, may have been influenced by personal connections and matters of patronage when he sought burial next to the late prior in the priory church. Through his testamentary giving, he also displayed his devotion to three altars in the priory church, including the altar to the blessed Thomas de la Halys; CKS, PRC 32/5, f. 54. **65** In the late fifteenth century, 13 out of 76 Dover testators specified their funeral services, and in the early sixteenth century the figures were 53 out of 87. **66** For example, in 1523 Sir John paid for some of the harbour work out of his own purse; BL, Egerton MS. 2108, f. 61. **67** Like Sir John, Robert Dyer as a civic officer had been prepared to support the town from his own resources, a situation which may, in part, explain his bequests to the master and brothers in his will of 1527; CKS, PRC 32/15, f. 158. He may also have influenced others of the justice of aiding the hospital at a time when its resources were being diverted for the town's advantage, like John Browne and John Halyday, fellow town officers, whose wills he witnessed; CKS, PRC 32/13, f. 191, 32/13, f. 127.

may have known him through the hospital's position as a major landlord in the region, but the hospital's reputation may have been more significant here.[68] In addition, some like Thomas Howgym, a leading citizen at Hythe, may have been drawn to the hospital through their devotion to Our Lady, the most important fraternity at his parish church.[69] Such reciprocal exchanges with those from Dover and the surrounding region were probably seen as mutually beneficial in spiritual, social and financial terms. Yet, for the small staff at the Maison Dieu their liturgical and intercessory duties may have reduced their activities on behalf of the poor and pilgrims, who may have been left to the care of two women, under the control of the one or two lay brothers present.

Testamentary sources indicate that in the sixteenth century the growing desire to formalize the funeral coincided with a wish to initiate provisions for the celebration of the testator's obit.[70] For those seeking such services, wealth may not have been the primary factor; age and longevity of residence in the town may have been more significant in terms of the choices made.[71] As well as a rising number of testators seeking obits, the early sixteenth century witnessed a growing concentration of these services at St Mary's church, and to a lesser extent at the Maison Dieu church.[72] In part, this was a consequence of the predominance

---

68 Personal links between Sir John and Thomas Hempstede, and later his daughter, are strongly indicated by their wills. Sir John witnessed Thomas's will in which he bequeathed two acres to the master and brothers of the Maison Dieu, and in 1500 Elizabeth Yoklett of Ewell confirmed her father's bequest in her own will, naming Sir John as overseer; CKS, PRC 17/6/237, 17/7/214. Other factors may account for William Poyshe's bequest of forty wethers to the master of St Mary's hospital in 1521. William was a landholder in Colrede, a parish where the hospital held land, and he may, as a tenant or through his neighbours, have known the master and hospital; CKS, PRC 32/14, f. 26. **69** He bequeathed 20s. to the hospital. In addition, his bequest to the master may signify his personal connection and/or knowledge of Sir John, while friendship with the family of Sir John Knyght (one of the priest brothers) may account for Thomas' gift to him (there were members of the Knyght family in Hythe, including William, for whom Thomas was a feoffee); CKS, PRC 32/10, f. 51. **70** There is little to suggest Thomas Feasy was a prosperous Dover citizen when he made he will in 1521. In it he bequeathed the small sum of 4d. to the high altar of St Peter's church, and made very few bequests to either his parish church or his wife. She was to ensure six masses were performed at each of his three funeral days, and then annually two masses on the day of his obit for the remainder of her life; CKS, PRC 32/13, f. 55. **71** Because of the incidence of remarriage and the presence of children from more than one marriage, it is difficult to determine the testators' ages from the sources. However, most of those who mentioned their obits did not appear to have young children, possibly implying a high proportion of older men. This age group may have had stronger links to the local parish based on long-term residence or business links, with the possibility of other family members residing nearby. Yet, with regard to choice, this was probably almost as diverse as the number of testators, being dependent on a wide range of factors. **72** Interestingly, even Sir Robert Long appears to have preferred St Mary's church to the hospital chapel for his obit, and only Giles Love intended his obit should be performed at the hospital from the start, others preferring to use the Maison Dieu chapel if their original arrangements failed through the death of the heir or the neglect of the organizer; CKS, PRC 32/15, f. 371, 32/12, f. 172.

of parishioners from St Mary's choosing these spiritual services to be performed close to their burial place, but other factors may have contributed to this development. For some, the personal links they had forged with the hospital probably aided their decision, but local knowledge was also important, a perception that the Maison Dieu as an ancient, prosperous, charitable institution would honour its spiritual commitments for all time.[73] As the other exchange partner, the master and his staff may have welcomed such bequests, particularly those for a prescribed number of years, thereby saving the hospital from being committed to a never-ending cycle of prayers where the value of the initial gift may have been insufficient to meet the costs incurred. These observations would also seem to reflect the situation with regard to the provision of obits sought by testators from Dover's hinterland. Again the parish church was the favoured venue and, where the Maison Dieu was involved, personal links and the reputation of the house appear to have influenced testators.[74] Reputation, rather than personal connections, seems to have been more significant for the priory's benefactors who wished the monks to remember their obit. Of those few known to have sought such intercessory services, none were from Dover itself, and though some intended their obit would be celebrated at the priory, others expected the monks to attend their place of burial, resulting in additional expense.[75]

Similarly, chantries might involve considerable financial implications for the religious institution, a situation which apparently occurred at St Mary's church where the master of the Maison Dieu was taken to task for not providing a chantry priest there in 1511.[76] It is not known for whom the chantry had been established, but the priest might have been expected to undertake other duties on behalf of the hospital, like the provision of intercessory masses for a few Dover

---

73 For example, William Warren of St Peter's parish intended that initially his obit should take place at his parish church under his widow's and then his son's instructions. After his son's death, certain lands (revenue for the obit) were to pass to his cousin, who was then responsible for the transfer and subsequent enactment of the obit at the Maison Dieu; CKS, PRC 32/9, f. 104. Personal connections were probably more important for John Fuller, who appears to have had a brother at the hospital. He intended that after his wife's death the Maison Dieu should receive a messuage and in exchange the priest brothers were to celebrate at St Mary's church annually in July forever for his soul; CKS, PRC 32/2, f. 547.   **74** For Thomas Walton of Hythe, his personal knowledge of the hospital and its staff may have been significant. He was a leading citizen and livestock farmer with interests in several parishes, and in his will he left his wife the profits of his tenement in Cheriton, a parish where the hospital held land. Thomas' daughter was to inherit the tenement after his wife's death, but if she died without issue the property and accompanying land were to pass to the hospital on condition an obit was celebrated on behalf of his soul, with a similar provision in regard to the nunnery at Canterbury; CKS, PRC 32/9, f. 135.   **75** For example, Edward Mynot, a wealthy Canterbury citizen, expected his gift of 20s. to the prior should ensure that the monks attended his month's mind. There they were to celebrate a requiem mass for his soul, presumably at Bishopsbourne church at the site of his elaborate tomb, which was to be constructed next to his mother's grave; CKS, PRC 17/5, f. 67.   **76** Wood-Legh, *Kentish visitations*, p. 132.

citizens and other local people who sought temporary chantries from the hospital staff. The master's unwillingness to supply a chantry priest may have deterred others from choosing the Maison Dieu in this way, but this is difficult to judge from the surviving evidence.[77] During the late middle ages, only one man is known to have wished to establish a perpetual chantry at the hospital church, and in this instance his kinsman's presence at the hospital may have been the deciding factor.[78] The priory seems to have experienced a similar lack of interest in its own church, though one testator from Dover, Henry Fravell, intended his temporary chantry should be there, one element in his complex strategy for the care of his soul.[79] His other provisions included a chantry priest celebrating in St Peter's church for a year, and a second, being a 'quireman', to celebrate the morrow mass daily there during the same period, a final charitable gift to his fellow townsmen and a meritorious act in the eyes of the Almighty.[80]

Although the town was home to a considerable number of religious, they were very rarely remembered in the wills of the Dover citizens. Instead, most testators favoured their parish priest, or more occasionally a local chaplain, the one exception being St Mary's church where the priest was also a brother at the Maison Dieu.[81] Presumably as a consequence of his role in the spiritual life of

---

77 Only Robert Ruttier involved the master in his chantry provision, which may reflect the strength of the relationship between the two men, though he was to act in conjunction with the mayor and town clerk in the sale of Robert's lands and tenements in the event of his son dying without heirs. Under these circumstances part of the cash received was to be used to provide a priest for a year at St Mary's church; CKS, PRC 32/14, f. 1. **78** According to John Hebbynge's will dated 1489, the priest brothers were to receive two lodges in Folkestone following the death of his wife, which they let to local fishermen, the proceeds being used to fund a perpetual chantry at the hospital church for John's soul, his wife's soul and the souls of the departed faithful, CKS, PRC 17/5, f. 90. **79** Henry sought the intercessory services of a monk for a year there. The monk was to receive ten marks and licensed by the prior to perform the temporary chantry services; CKS, PRC 32/11, f. 114. Henry Trewonwall of Canterbury is the only other known testator who sought this form of intercessory service at the priory. He did not seek the service on his own behalf, but bequeathed five marks for the monks to pray for the soul of John Hender, a priest, which may represent a daily mass for six months; CKS, PRC 32/2, f. 350. **80** Temporary chantries of a year were the favoured option among those who employed this form of intercession and commemoration. For example, Johanna Aldaye (1532) stipulated that her executors were to hire a good priest immediately after her death for £10 to celebrate for her soul for a year at St Mary's church; CKS, PRC 32/15, f. 257. Such funding may have been welcomed by the Dover citizens because at times there were considerable problems regarding the provision of masses in the town due to inadequate organization or funding. It was reported at the visitation in 1511 that the only mass celebrated daily at St Martin-le-Grand was the passenger mass, and at St Mary's church the master, as patron, was ordered to insist that his parish priest celebrated the mass on two days a week at least; Wood-Legh, *Kentish visitations*, pp. 132, 134. **81** During this period about one in five of the Dover testators included a specific bequest to a priest, usually their own parish priest, though only Edward Hexstall favoured the archipresbyter at St Martin-le-Grand; CKS, PRC 32/9, f. 160. In part this may reflect the poverty of the Dover parish clergy as a consequence of their subordination to the priory. At the 1511 visitation it was reported that the parson of St Nicholas' paid the prior 11s. a year, though the benefice was only worth five marks; Wood-Legh, *Kentish visitations*, p. 133. **82** Sir Robert Long

St Mary's parish Sir John Soly, in the late fifteenth century, was named by a few testators, and one of his successors in the early sixteenth century, Sir Robert Yong, received seven bequests. Kinship and, occasionally, friendship, as in the case of Sir Robert Long, seem to have been important in the choices testators made. But the presence of these two priests as witnesses and/or executor in the wills of most of the hospital's benefactors at this time suggests the selection of the professional who would care for one's soul was dependent upon matters of reputation, personal connections and influence.[82]

Yet, even if the master and priest brothers at the Maison Dieu were considered worthy recipients in the spiritual economy, the poor accommodated at their house or supplied with alms at the gate were not seen in this light.[83] Nor, apparently, were the boys housed at the hospital, who only once were the recipients of a Dover testator.[84] This lack of interest in the charitable work of St Mary's hospital, at least in terms of the testamentary evidence, may imply it was thought to have sufficient resources. However, the almost total absence of bequests towards aiding the poor at St Bartholomew's hospital (assuming it was housing such people) and the two almshouses suggests a more general disinterest in the institutional poor by the leading citizens.[85] Instead, these men may have believed the establishment and maintenance of the corporation's almshouses was sufficient recompense for those living there, giving them other opportunities to demonstrate their charitable concerns for the poor.[86] Nonetheless, during the late fifteenth century few appear to have made testamentary bequests to the poor, but the proportion did rise to one in six in the early sixteenth century.[87] The

witnessed Robert Dyer's will, was executor and witness for Richard Inglott, and executor for John Halyday; Sir Robert Yong was executor and witness for Robert Dyer.   **83** Of the Dover testators, 14% made a bequest of some kind to the master and brothers, but none of the hospital's benefactors mentioned the institutional poor in their will. According to the *Valor*, the hospital continued to fulfil its charitable role to the poor; *Valor Eccl.*, vol. 1, pp. 56–7.   **84** The only testamentary record concerning boys was Richard Inglott's bequest of 4*d.* to each of the boys of the church in the Maison Dieu; CKS, PRC 32/13, f. 196.   **85** The only bequest to St Bartholomew's was directed towards repairing the house, not care for the poor directly; CKS, PRC 32/14, f. 1. The three Dover testators who left various types of bedding to the almshouse did not specify which one, nor did John Halyday in 1545 when he bequeathed 20*s.* for the maintenance of the house; CKS, PRC 32/3, f. 316, 32/4, f. 77, 32/21, f. 15, 32/22, f. 58.   **86** Dover corporation appears to have repaired the almshouses as necessary; for example, work was done on both houses in 1498 and 1499; BL, Egerton MS. 2107, ff. 58v, 61. The authorities were also prepared to exchange one of them with Oliver Lythgo's house to provide better facilities for the almsfolk; BL, Egerton MS. 2107, f. 117v. **87** Comparing Dover with Sandwich, for Dover 1470–1499: three testators in 75 wills (4%) specifically mentioned the poor, though there were another seven who gave to charitable deeds, which might be considered to have included the poor; the Sandwich figure for the same period was 17 bequests (10% of testators). For Dover 1500–1529: 14 bequests in 81 wills (over 17%); the Sandwich figure was slightly lower 23 in 167 wills (over 13%). However, the Sandwich testators, unlike their counterparts at Dover, appear to have aided the poor through the town's hospitals, especially pre-1500 when St John's and St Anthony's were well supported.   **88** With regard to the poor outside these institutions, the civic authorities neither implemented a harsh policy of control, as at

number of poor people in the town was also rising, which may in part account for the greater almsgiving, the civic authorities apparently unwilling or unable to formulate a strategy regarding the poor, unlike their counterparts, for example, at Lydd and Sandwich.[88] Possibly as part of their response to the increasing numbers of poor people, particularly migrants, the Dover testators sought to limit their largesse by stating the total amount which was to be spent or by targeting certain groups, like aid for poor maidens at marriage.[89] Few specified that the poor were to pray for them, but this may represent common knowledge and that by staging the distribution at a particular place and time, often to a symbolic number of people, the poor would have responded appropriately.[90] Yet it is possible the use of such events as the funeral feast by testators as a time for one's neighbours, rather than specifically for the poor, may highlight ideas about community, neighbourliness and good standing, as well as the more spiritual concerns of commemoration and intercession.[91]

This concentration on the Maison Dieu, and to a lesser extent the other hospitals and priory, should not disguise the fact that all these institutions remained peripheral for the vast majority of the townspeople. Though Sir John Clerke's activities on behalf of the town raised public awareness of the hospital, leading

Sandwich, nor a policy of regular aid (grain was distributed at Christmas and at Easter), as at Lydd; S. Sweetinburgh, 'Care in the community: local responses to the poor in late medieval Sandwich' (1996); A. Finn (ed.), *Records of Lydd* (Ashford 1911), pp. 49, 71, 72, 74, 75, *passim*. Instead the mayor and jurats responded on an ad hoc basis, though this rarely involved the giving of alms, and then in individual instances; BL, Add. MS. 29616, f. 85v; Egerton MS. 2092, ff. 97, 146v, 202, 260v. **89** Thomas Toky (1484), for example, stipulated that at his burial and twelve month's mind a total of six quarters of wheat were to be distributed as bread; William Horn (1498) bequeathed part of the cash received from the sale of his lands to be given to the poor; Johanna Toky (1509) intended that at each of the three funeral days a seme of wheat should be distributed as bread to the poor by her executors; and John Symon (1518) expected that after the death of his wife £6 13s. 4d. would be distributed among poor maids for their marriage; CKS, PRC 32/2, f. 614, 32/4, f. 191, 32/10, f. 17, 32/12, f. 124. An interesting variant was used by Richard Fyneaux. In his will dated 1518, he bequeathed to each of thirty poor churches a vestment worth 13s. 4d.; CKS, PRC 32/13, f. 23. **90** The staging of the events seems implicit within the details of Richard Fyneaux's will: on the day of his death each poor man was to receive a penny dole, on each Friday between then and his month's mind thirteen poor people were to receive a penny each, at his month's mind each poor person was to be given a penny and each poor child a loaf of bread, and at his twelve month's mind each poor person to get a penny loaf of bread and each poor child a halfpenny loaf; CKS, PRC 32/13, f. 23. Henry Fravell too saw the importance of the event; he stipulated that each poor maid who was to receive 6s. 8d. at marriage should receive the sum at 'the gospel time of the mass or masses at the time of their marriage'; CKS, PRC 32/11, f. 114. **91** Like Thomas Curtyer's intention in his will of 1528 that he wished his executors to provide at each of his funeral days four dozen breads and a vessel of beer for 'the company rich and poor'; CKS, PRC 17/18, f. 98. Similarly, this sense of charity and conviviality may have been in John Upton's mind when he made his bequest for the annual 'yevale' on the feast of the nativity of St John the Baptist in his home parish of Westcliffe. The holder of his lands providing a quarter of wheat for bread and a quarter of malt as ale for those of the parish; CKS PRC 17/19, f. 36.

to a cluster of testamentary bequests, the interest was confined to a small minority of the leading citizens. During the same period, the town's parish churches were relatively well supported compared to other towns in east Kent, a considerable change compared to the late fifteenth century when little except named votive lights received bequests.[92] This trend is interesting, though it needs qualifying because the testators comprised only a small proportion of the town's population, and were biased towards the most prosperous, and possibly long-term residents. The majority of these testators came from St Mary's, St James' and St Peter's parishes, the three which would survive the 1530s and 1540s at the expense of the church of St Martin-le-Grand and its constituent parishes. It is not clear why the Dover citizens were prepared to support their parish churches during the early sixteenth century, but appears to mirror their continued funding of the great candle or 'trendyll' until the destruction of Becket's shrine in 1538.[93] As a symbol of civic identity articulated through the town's special relationship with the saint, the trendyll remained an important political and religious statement about Dover's relationship with outside lordship. Even though there may have been a slight move to include the Maison Dieu and to a lesser extent the priory in the life of the town, the leading townsmen, individually and collectively, continued to show little interest in these institutions, a sentiment that appears to have been keenly embraced by many among the corporation in the 1530s. Thus, when the opportunity came to destroy these 'outside' religious institutions there was little local opposition.

THE HISTORY OF DOVER'S TWO HOSPITALS

Having examined the spiritual economy in terms of the choices people and institutions made at various points in the town's history, this section uses these 'stills'

92 Using a crude comparison between the testators of Dover, the neighbouring towns of Hythe, New Romney, Folkestone, and the rural parishes of Dover's hinterland for the period 1470–1500. Bequests to: own church fabric: Dover 23.5%, near Dover 26%, Folkestone 36%, Hythe 63%, New Romney 30%; own special church fabric: Dover 18%, near Dover 29%, Folkestone 28%, Hythe 21.5%, New Romney 24%; own named lights: Dover 67%, near Dover 57%, Folkestone 71.5%, Hythe 32%, New Romney 51%; own unnamed lights: Dover 23.5%, near Dover 15%, Folkestone 8%, Hythe 1.5%, New Romney 3.5%; fraternities: Dover 1%, near Dover 0%, Folkestone 7%, Hythe 20%, New Romney 25% (these include reversionary bequests). Using the same method, about half of Dover's testators made bequests to their parish church's works/fabric for the 1510s and 1520s, over a third giving something specific or to a specific piece of the church fabric. Even though the percentage giving to named lights dropped in the 1510s, in the decade either side over two-thirds of testators made this type of gift. The small number of extant testaments from the 1530s makes any comparison meaningless. 93 In 1534 gifts given 'of the peoples devotion' amounted to 13s. 4d. and three years later, the last time before the shrine's destruction, 'Mastres Mayeres' collected almost the full amount required (15s. 8d. for thirty-two pounds of new wax); BL, Add. MS. 29618, ff. 294, 304v.

to construct a 'moving picture' of the social history of the hospitals, placing the house at the forefront rather than being one of the many actors on the set. To achieve this, each hospital is considered under the following headings: foundation, readjustment, later history, and destruction. The resulting assessment demonstrates the hospital's ability to respond to the changing conditions, both inside and outside the institution, especially to the long history of anticlericalism in Dover and the town's ambivalent attitude towards royal authority.

St Bartholomew's hospital

1	foundation	1141
2	founder	two brothers, monks at Dover priory, by the authority of Archbishop Theobald and consent of Dover priory
3	foundation gift	the parents' goods of the two monk brothers
4	size	initially twenty, had fallen to sixteen by late 14th century
5	inmates	lay brothers and sisters (first pilgrims and poor, then lepers and poor, later poor or poorer people); priest
6	patronage	Dover priory
7	own chapel	yes
8	*in vitam* grants	some, mainly first 100 years, laity (nobles or knights with east Kent connections, east Kent townspeople, a few from Dover); range of grant types
9	diversification from 14th century	unclear, non-lepers, sick-poor, poor and poorer people (entry fee – start date unknown)
10	casual alms	probably important – proctors (locally and nationally), at hospital gate and chapel, indulgences
11	testamentary benefactors	almost none

In 1141, at a time when civil war was still episodic, St Bartholomew's hospital was probably founded in response to local conditions of hardship. The two brothers' charitable initiative may have been intended to emulate the episcopal foundations of Canterbury and Chatham, providing Dover with comparable provisions for the town's poor, and possibly within a short time the local lepers. Its site, a piece of land in Buckland to the north of the town, close to the main road from Canterbury and with its own water supply, was ideal for a leper hospital. The hospital appears to have been under the patronage of Dover priory throughout its existence, in part a result of its initial gift to the hospital, which demonstrated the priory's ability to respond charitably to the needs of the town and surrounding countryside.

In addition to this grant of *totam tegham*, all the thatching straw, before St Bartholomew's to the hospital community, the prior may have sought to aid his hospital by petitioning certain senior churchman to try to gain papal and archiepiscopal aid, including an indulgence of twenty days.[94] For the hospital such gifts were important in themselves, and as a way of promoting the house, which might result in the donation of casual alms and *in vitam* grants. Its early benefactors were primarily crown officers with local connections or nobles who held land in east Kent. One of these men was Gilbert de Gant who gave 100s. in rent from land in the parish of River.[95] For such men, like William de Say in the late twelfth and Hamo de Crevequer in the early thirteenth centuries, St Bartholomew's served as an additional and complementary institution within the complex charitable strategies they developed for the welfare of their souls. The donor received, in addition to the merit of the deed given in pure and perpetual alms, the prayers of the grateful lepers and the poor, as well as those of the professional intercessor, the hospital's chaplain. Although the presence of several religious houses in the area might have been expected to reduce the gift exchanges with St Bartholomew's, in Dover this may have been less important than the apparently limited interest generally in the town's religious institutions. Other possibilities may have been the relative poverty of Dover townsmen compared to their counterparts in Canterbury, who did provide the city's hospitals with considerable local property; or that the burgesses believed their corporate act of benefaction was sufficient. For whatever reason, in the century after its foundation relatively few Dover citizens aided St Bartholomew's, with the result that it gained little property in the town beyond a small number of plots. Although some of these donors provided gifts in free-alms tenure, others used Thompson's contractual form of grant, where the benefactor stipulated what he expected in return. In part this may reflect generally changing perceptions of charity in the thirteenth century, but for St Bartholomew's it may denote a local awareness of the hospital's subordinate position relative to the priory, and of the priory to Christchurch in Canterbury. As a consequence, the benefactors may have believed St Bartholomew's was primary the responsibility of these outside institutions which were answerable for the hospital's charitable commitments and the donor's expectations within the spiritual economy. Thus, at a time of heightened awareness of the power exercised over the religious life of the town by outside institutions, when the civic authorities were also beginning to engage in a struggle with the town's other outside authority, the crown, the townspeople may have felt it was more appropriate to seek a tangible reward for their

94 Max Satchall noted this gift to the hospital in his doctoral thesis; Satchall, 'Leper-houses in medieval England', p. 117; Bodleian, Rawlinson MS. B.335, no folio number, ff.5–6. According to the Rev. Lyon, Dover priory gave a piece of land called 'Thega', which bordered the road to Canterbury, to the hospital, and there is a record of land held by the hospital called 'la thegha' in the register; Lyon, *History of Dover*, p. 51; Bodleian, Rawlinson MS. B.335, f. 3. **95** Ibid. f. 6v.

benevolence. Assuming the income was greater than the outgo, such reciprocal exchanges were not disadvantageous for the hospital, though such grants placed a greater public duty on the master to see that the counter-gift was provided. Failure to do so might adversely affect the reputation of the house, reducing the likelihood of further gift exchanges.

Unfortunately, it is not clear when the entry fee was introduced for the resident brothers and sisters, but it may date from early in the hospital's history. If so, this suggests that absolute poverty was not one of the selection criteria employed, instead the destitute were relegated to the dole queue at the priory, or possibly to seek overnight shelter at St Mary's. The size of the entry fee was relatively modest, which may indicate that for those of moderate means, it was not a barrier to admittance. For the lepers, this opportunity to join a semi-monastic community may have been seen as advantageous, particularly over the longer term when the effects of the disease became more debilitating. Moreover, having entered the hospital they joined a community that was not totally isolated from the world. The value of the inmates was recognized in terms of their labour for the house, their prayers for the Christian world, and, finally, half their goods to the hospital at death. For St Bartholomew's, these provisions may have been important with regard to income and as a means of being as self-sufficient as possible within the limitations of the house's charitable obligations. The ordinances, recorded in the fourteenth century, stress this commitment to farming its local holdings, but the lands outside Buckland were presumably rented out from the beginning, possibly managed by the warden, the priory's sub-prior, a part of the ongoing reciprocal relationship between the two institutions.

During the late thirteenth and fourteenth centuries, St Bartholomew's was apparently able to maintain its income at a higher level than its outgo, though it may have experienced some short-term difficulties in the 1290s, a consequence of high royal tax demands and its continually fragile financial position.[96] These difficulties may have persuaded the master to lease three pieces of property in the town, each for sixty years, and to continue this more flexible management strategy after the Black Death, thereby reducing property maintenance expenses.[97] The priory had adopted a similar policy and, even though the master held the hospital's seal, such changes to the hospital's assets presumably required the agreement of the prior. Such a move away from direct management of the house's property might be assumed to have enhanced the financial position; otherwise why do it, but the lack of evidence regarding rent levels, dilapidations and vacant holdings means that it is difficult to know whether the master acted from a position of strength or weakness. The latter seems more likely because the hospital received few *in vitam* grants after the Statute of Mortmain, and there is little to

96 Mate, 'The impact of war', 761–2.   97 Bodleian, Rawlinson MS. B.335, ff. 16, 26, 27v.

suggest it benefited from post-mortem gift-giving, the house remaining reliant on its small plots of land scattered over a number of local parishes.

In terms of its role within the spiritual economy, St Bartholomew's was able to offer a number of counter-gifts, like acts of commemoration, chantry facilities, and the provision of intercessory prayers from both the chaplain and the lay community at the hospital. Such facilities were not cost-free, and though the house had received grants from the various donors as part of the exchange process, the discrepancy between income and outgo may have become increasingly detrimental in terms of the charitable work of the hospital. By the late fourteenth century, if not before, the number of resident inmates had been reduced to sixteen from twenty, due it was said to the poverty of the place, not that it had lost its inmates to the plague. This may imply that its financial difficulties pre-dated the Black Death, plague worsening an already deteriorating situation.[98] The likely reduction in its charitable work for the sick-poor, due in part to declining income after the agricultural disasters of the early fourteenth century and the reduction in the number of sisters, seems to have coincided with a reduction in the charitable work undertaken by both the priory and the Maison Dieu. Consequently, this was probably a very difficult period for the increasing number of poor people from Dover and its hinterland, many of whom sought aid at the various institutions. Yet it is difficult to know whether such charity ever made much impression on the level of poverty, though presumably for certain individuals it meant the difference between life and death. Moreover, the assumption that the poor will always be on earth was a pertinent reminder of their role in the reciprocal arrangement with the rich. The teaching of the church fathers highlighted the need for both groups in society, permitting the hospital to function as a mediator between the rich and the poor, a role it also exercised concerning the living and the dead.

Probably, like many other small hospitals, particularly leper houses, St Bartholomew's was heavily reliant on casual alms, either at the hospital itself or to the house's proctors who solicited alms from those outside its walls. The provision of two proctors for the hospital was recorded in the ordinances, one proctor collecting from Dover and its environs, the other seeking gifts throughout the country.[99] The sending out of such men may have been a regular occurrence, but on occasion the hospital sought royal protection grants for the collection of alms, and the hospital register records the names of two proctors, one for 1330 and another for 1346. For the second occasion, it was noted that he could offer indulgences worth 240 days, these having been given to St Bartholomew's by various archbishops and bishops.[1] These expeditions were presumably particularly important from the early fourteenth century for the reasons noted above, and the continued survival of the hospital may rest, in part, on the master's ability to gather funds compared to his counterparts at the other Cinque Ports, espe-

98 Ibid. f. 2. **99** Ibid. f. 4. **1** Ibid. ff. 97v–8v.

cially at Hythe and New Romney.[2] Thus the hospital's readjustment to the changing circumstances of the fourteenth century, the shift to care for the poor and
sick-poor and the provision of chantry facilities, enabled it to survive as a hospital even though support from local townspeople remained muted.

Yet even this level of local support was not sustainable, or not in terms of
post-mortem gift-giving, a situation that did occur at St Anthony's leper hospital and St John's hospital for the poor, Sandwich, during the second half of the
fifteenth century. Such differences in the degree of local support are often difficult to explain because they rest on a complex range of factors like reputation,
patronage, function, status and fashion, which in turn relate to personal connections, and a general willingness to aid the poor. During the later middle ages, it
is not clear whether the sick-poor were still accommodated at St Bartholomew's
under the care of the few lay brothers and sisters, but the community did include
men like poor George. The founding of the civic almshouses in the late fifteenth
century may not discount this idea, because there were more than enough poor
local people to fill all the institutions, especially once the number began to rise,
a product of Dover's economic difficulties. Furthermore, if St Bartholomew's
was catering for poor migrants or members of the itinerant poor or sick-poor,
like those accommodated in the harbinge at St John's hospital, Sandwich, it may
have been seen as serving the town, because such people would not have been
welcomed at the civic almshouses. It seems more likely, however, that there was
a greater overlap in the personnel of the different houses when comparing the
brothers and sisters at St Bartholomew's with the civic almsfolk. Under these circumstances it is possibly surprising that Dover's leading citizens did not support
St Bartholomew's in its worthy charitable labour. This seems to suggest that other
factors were involved in the very low level of aid the hospital appears to have
received. One of these factors might have been its subordinate position with
regard to the priory, the hospital's welfare seen as part of the priory's responsibility, not that of the local townsmen. Such considerations may have been particularly significant in terms of the last will and testament, a public document that
displayed the maker's ideas, aspirations and prejudices, in contrast to the potentially anonymous giving of casual alms. Thus the hospital's long history in the
shadow of the priory, a factor reinforced by the occasional presence in the town
of the brothers and sisters clothed in the hospital's uniform, may have confirmed
to the testators their right-thinking in ignoring St Bartholomew's, especially as
they, individually or collectively, appear to have shown little interest in the poor
generally. A similar disinterest in the poor characterizes the testamentary mate-

2 The leper hospital at Hythe seems to have been refounded as a house for the poor by Hamo of
Hythe, bishop of Rochester; *CPR* 1340–1348, p. 427. The hospital of St Stephen and St Thomas,
New Romney, became little more than a chantry chapel for the Fraunceys family; Butcher, 'St
Stephen and St Thomas', 20–1; Sheppard, *Literae Cantuarienses*, vol. 2, p. 436.

rials from early-sixteenth-century Dover, though these testators were apparently slightly more generous than their counterparts in Sandwich. This low level of interest in the poor, whether inside or outside an institution was, according to McIntosh, characteristic of the early sixteenth century.[3] Yet the increasing number of poor people might have been expected to result in harsh civic policies, whereas the mayor and jurats of Dover were apparently remarkably tolerant, or disinterested, primarily concerning themselves with watching for vagabonds and occasionally giving small sums to certain destitute individuals.

For hospitals like St Bartholomew's, the early sixteenth century may mark an important change in attitudes regarding the treatment of the poor, especially in consideration of the type of institutional care provided and a desire to aid poor householders. Instead of supporting the ancient leper hospitals and bedehouse-type almshouses, like Milett's house at Dartford, there seems to have been a preference for small almshouses based on the concept of neighbourhood and town. In Elizabethan England this form would become increasingly popular (though some, like Manwood's almshouse at Canterbury might be thought to hark back to Milett's ideas but applying a Protestant ethos), a consequence, perhaps, of a growing appreciation of humanist ideas. Moreover, at ports like Dover, the citizens may have been aware of the changes that had taken place regarding the form and function of some hospitals in the cities of the Low Countries, Paris, and Italy.[4] How far, if at all, this was linked to anti-clerical attitudes said to be prevalent in certain areas of Kent is difficult to establish, and may be too broad a term for the attitudes displayed by Dover's leading citizens. Even though the citizens had a long history of obstructing the priory's collection of parish dues from Dover, and only provided the house with limited support throughout its existence, they were not as belligerent as their counterparts at Canterbury.[5] But at the same time, their testamentary support for the town's secular clergy, and possibly increasingly the fabric of the local parish churches outside St Martin-le-Grand, in the 1510s and 1520s, might imply their spiritual and charitable interest was focused on the parish. The civic almshouses provided complementary institutions, which authorized the leading citizens to see themselves as moral guardians of the community through their individual and collective charitable actions using the twin institutions of parish (clergy and churchwardens) and town (mayor and jurats). Such a partnership, based on responsibility for their fellow townsfolk, might be considered to be offering a similar service to that provided initially by the priory and hospital:

3 McIntosh, 'Responses to the poor', 212. **4** Paris seems to have seen the founding of specialized hospitals from the fourteenth century that were intended to provide medical care; Geremek, *Margins of society*, pp. 170–1. The rise of the bedehouse-type almshouse for this period has been charted for eight counties in south-east England and the midlands; McIntosh, 'Responses to the poor', 220–1. For the European perspective; Slack, *Poverty and policy*, pp. 8–9; J. Henderson (ed.), 'Charity and the poor in medieval and Renaissance Europe' (1988), 145–8. **5** Dobson, 'Canterbury', p. 148.

alms to those outside and sustenance for those inside, but there were significant differences. First, the gift-giving was now primarily in the hands of the laity, who selected the recipients and controlled what they should receive; and second, the emphasis within the exchange process had changed. There was a greater concern for the body instead of a total focus on the soul, leading to a less explicit desire for the counter-gift of prayers for the donor. This is not to deny that most bene-factors would expect the grateful poor to pray for them, but that they seem to have relied far more on the intercessory services of professional priests.

Thus by the 1530s some in Dover's town government apparently felt they were better able to care for the commonalty than these outside institutions and, of greater concern to St Bartholomew's, that they could make better use of the hospital's assets for the greater good of the town. However, altruism was not the only motive, nor for some, were the interests of the town of primary concern. John Bowle may have coveted the hospital's lands, and at the first opportunity he demolished the place and presumably carried off everything of value.[6] He was an innkeeper, one of Dixon's 'new men', whose prosperity brought him into contact with various leading citizens and officers at the castle. He was first elected as a jurat in 1531, becoming mayor in 1539–40, the year St Bartholomew's was dissolved.[7] The destruction of a large part of the priory and St Martin-le-Grand was the work of other leading townsmen, but Bowle also appears to have prospered from the demolition (he used St John's churchyard to keep his pigs). At his death in 1557 he still held part of the hospital's prop-erty: a fulling mill with seven acres and one yard, and a meadow of nine acres in the parish of Buckland.[8] It is not known what happened to the last inmates when their hospital was closed, and though the civic authorities may have aided them, there is nothing to indicate this in the chamberlains' accounts.[9]

St Mary's hospital

1	foundation	*c.* 1203
2	founders	Hubert de Burgh, Henry III
3	foundation gift	extensive lands in Dover's hinterland
4	size	unclear, probably twelve to sixteen staff
5	inmates	priest brothers (under rule), lay brothers and sisters
6	patronage	crown

6 Haines, *Dover priory*, pp. 50–1. **7** M. Dixon, 'Dover in the early sixteenth century' (1982), p. 39. **8** In his will he bequeathed nothing to the poor and nothing except 12*d.* to the high altar of his parish church of St Mary, though he wished to be buried in St Katherine's chancel in the church. His widow was to organize a trentall of masses in connection with each of his funeral days. He bequeathed the majority of his extensive estate to members of his family; CKS, PRC 32/26, f. 145. **9** The only reference in the accounts occurs for the year after the hospital's dissolution. John Honywode, the last master, had apparently entered a tenement previously leased by the hospital, possibly intending to live there; BL, Egerton MS. 2093, f. 212.

7 own chapel	yes
8 *in vitam* grants	relatively few – noble, knightly families, towns-people
9 diversification from 14th century	chantry, probably few fee-paying corrodians
10 casual alms	probably important (shrine of St Richard of Chichester, hospital gate and chapel)
11 testamentary benefactors	clusters linked to penultimate master (especially 1510s and 1520s), majority local (town and environs), explicit reciprocity (burial, intercessory services, care of testator's estate for heirs)

Hubert de Burgh is traditionally said to be the founder of St Mary's hospital. The house was built on the eastern side of the main road from Canterbury, opposite the priory, and just outside the town's northern boundary. It was probably founded during the first decade of the thirteenth century, as a response to the growing number of pilgrims and as a replacement for St Bartholomew's (this hospital may have solely accommodated lepers by then). Hubert's gifts to his hospital may indicate his charitable concern for this vulnerable group and for Dover; he seems to have been well liked and respected by the townsfolk. Consequently, the endowment would have enhanced his status as a worthy and generous nobleman, though, interestingly, there is nothing in the wording of his grants to suggest he was seeking specific intercessory services at his institution. The provision of a chapel by his lord, Henry III, might have been a welcome addition to Hubert's hospital, but also signaled the transfer of patronage to the crown, which may explain his choice of Westminster rather than Dover as the primary location for the intercessory services for his soul. Henry's confirmation of Hubert's gifts to St Mary's and his own provided the hospital with large landholdings to the north of Dover and on Romney Marsh, the patronage of several churches, and certain valuable rights and privileges, including a tithe of the issues from the port of Dover. For the master such a diversity of assets may have been extremely valuable, allowing him to adopt a flexible management strategy which produced sufficient funds for the work of the hospital: caring for the poor pilgrims, maintaining divine service in the chapel, including prayers for the house's patron and benefactors, and providing for the resident community.

The community comprised the lay brothers who worked on the hospital's holdings, leaving the sisters to care for the poor pilgrims, and the priest brothers, who from the 1230s became more numerous because of the increasing liturgical demands placed on the house. Henry appears to have been responsible for the change in emphasis, either directly through his patronage or because the hospital was now required to undertake a number of intercessory services, the counter-gifts in the reciprocal exchange between the king and St Mary's. However, he presumably intended that care for the pilgrims would remain an integral part of the hospital's function, explaining the retention of the sisters. For Henry, his relationship with the hospital produced considerable advantages in the form of spiritual provisions for himself and those he named, as well as enhancing his reputation as the guardian of his people and the nation's premier saint. He also gained more tangible rewards, like hospitality for his chancery clerks, and at times other members of his household similarly stayed there. Over the next two centuries, the need to provide the counter-gift of hospitality became increasing significant for the hospital. In part, this reflected contemporary perceptions about hospitality and the function of the household (or institution) where wealth, reputation and status were signalled through consumption, including that of guests. Thus at St Mary's, the master was obliged to entertain his guests well with limited regard to cost. By so doing, he was demonstrating the place of the hospital, but he also might recoup at least some of his expenses through further gift exchanges, either with the king, members of the royal family, or other benefactors who wished to be associated with this prestigious charitable institution.

Even at this early stage in the history of the hospital, the dominance of the king within the relationship may have been obvious to the master. He was presumably grateful to his royal patron, yet he may have welcomed the chance to supplement the hospital's income from offerings collected at the shrine of St Richard of Chichester. The arrival of this saintly man a few days before his death, his consecration of the hospital's new chapel, and his desire that his entrails should be buried there for the sustenance of the poor through the mediation of St Mary's, aided the house financially, but equally enhanced its status and reputation. This heightened profile of the hospital locally and regionally probably increased the demands placed upon it regarding the number of pilgrims seeking shelter, but may mark the start of limited local interest. Earlier benefactors had been members of the minor nobility, whose charitable strategy had included St Mary's, the hospital's worthiness as a recipient resting on reputation rather than any personal acquaintance of the institution or its staff. For them gifts given in free alms were apparently seen as the most appropriate form for the relationship they wished to develop with the hospital. In contrast, the new local donors sought explicit counter-gifts from the Maison Dieu, including the first known request for some form of confraternity. Such a provision was probably especially valuable when the recipient institution was a local charitable house, the donor and his descendants able to monitor its implementation over several generations.

Local interest in St Mary's was not sustained, however, at least in terms of *in vitam* grants, which may reflect that it, like St Bartholomew's, was under the control of outside authority, in this case the crown. During the thirteenth century, the town's leading citizens were seeking greater autonomy, and in their protracted struggle with the crown, the mayor and his colleagues may have considered the place of St Mary's hospital. Dover's association with and reliance on the pilgrim trade might have meant the civic authorities would have wished to claim the patronage of this premier pilgrim hospital on the borders of their town, thereby emulating their cobarons (freemen) in Sandwich concerning that town's hospitals. Yet the crown's continuing control of St Mary's hospital provided no opportunities for civic appropriation, leading the civic officers to seek other means of establishing their collective identity. Thus, in some senses the absence of support for the Maison Dieu by the leading citizens might be thought of as an active decision, especially when seen in conjunction with the creation of the civic ritual regarding Dover's triennial gift exchange with St Thomas of Canterbury. This suggests that by the end of the thirteenth century, if not before, the leading townsmen envisaged the hospital as being legally and symbolically outside the jurisdiction and protection of the town, a belief that remained important, and may in part explain the house's ultimate dissolution.

In the shorter term, however, St Mary's apparently suffered from poverty. The situation was officially recognized in 1325 when the house sought tax exemption from the crown, and such problems continued until at least the mid-century. Having received a royal licence to acquire property worth 100s. a year in 1320, St Mary's might have been expected to implement it in the short-term, but it did not do so and the licence was not surrendered until 1410.[10] The desire to acquire further assets may have been prompted by heavy royal demands on the house, the boarding of royal corrodians, but especially the provision of hospitality for various members of the royal household as well as the king as 'guests' of the chancery.[11] For the master, the apparent appropriation of his position as host by the king, and secondly the chancellor, may have cost the hospital far more than it could afford because the chancellor would have expected to entertain his 'guests' lavishly.[12] Thus at a time when it was proving extremely difficult for the hospital to collect its income, due to the likelihood of renewed Anglo-French hostilities in 1323 and the agricultural disasters of the previous decade, its outgo continued to rise.

In spite of these difficulties during the last years of Edward II's reign and that of his son, the Maison Dieu appears to have been a wealthy and locally important charitable institution in the late fourteenth century.[13] The appointment of Valentine de Bere as master in 1378 was advantageous because he was a member of the locally prominent and long resident de Bere family, and it may have been

10 *CPR* 1317–1321, p. 492; 1377–1381, p. 370; 1391–1396, p. 164.   11 Edward II's eldest son was lodged there in 1325; *CPR* 1323–1327, p. 503. King John II of France, on his return to his homeland, stayed at the Maison Dieu; D. Webb, *Pilgrimage in medieval England* (London and New York 2000), p. 224.   12 Even though he would have expected to provide hospitality as a measure of largesse, and as part of the economics of consumption; Dyer, *Standards,* pp. 53–5.   13 For the local townspeople its patronage of St Mary's church may have been the most significant point of contact. A number of benefactors from Edward II's reign were noted in the royal records in 1410; *CPR* 1408–1413, p. 212.

through his influence that the hospital acquired several grants in mortmain.[14] These extended the house's holdings in Romney Marsh and provided it with rents from fifteen shops and two messuages in Dover.[15] One such donor of town rents was Beatrice Salkyn and the value of these new assets is reflected in her inclusion in the *Valor* as one who was annually commemorated by the hospital. St Mary's received very few further grants in the early fifteenth century and none of the donors appear to have been local townspeople, though fortunately for the financial well-being of St Mary's, these new benefactors did not seek expensive or complex counter-gifts, like chantries.[16] Moreover, the apparent decline in royal demands for hospitality may have allowed the master to allocate a larger proportion of the house's revenue towards its charitable work, its income enhanced by the provision of two further opportunities. In 1448 the hospital received a licence to acquire in mortmain lands and rents worth £40 per year for the sustenance of the poor and pilgrims, and thirty-five years later St Mary's was given a royal grant in frankalmoin of lands in Thanet.[17] These acquisitions reinforced the perception of the hospital as a regionally important institution, and its continuing association with the crown may have deterred the leading townspeople from supporting it through their testamentary bequests, regardless of its charitable activities.[18]

This locally marginal place of a regionally important establishment appears to have changed in the 1510s, especially after the appointment in 1518 of Sir John Clerke as one of two wardens in charge of the harbour works.[19] He seems to have viewed his work as an act of charity on the town's behalf because the town owed him money from the first year of his appointment and he also appears to have used part of the premises of the Maison Dieu for storing materials for the town.[20] His personal generosity included paying for certain work to be done and

---

14 *CPR* 1377–1381, p. 177. His namesake had been bailiff of the town in the last years of Edward I and during his son's early reign; LPL, MS. 241, ff. 73, 80. The previous master appears to have been a pluralist, serving simultaneously as a canon at Wingham and as a king's clerk; *CPR* 1367–1370, pp. 168, 171. **15** *CPR* 1377–1381, p. 370; *CPR* 1391–1396, pp. 147, 164. **16** One such early fifteenth-century donor was Nicholas Haute, knight, who wanted a lamp to burn daily before the high altar in the hospital chapel; *CPR* 1408–1413, p. 212. **17** The latter was George Browne's estate, his lands forfeit to the crown as a defeated rebel; *CPR* 1446–1452, p. 131; *CPR* 1476–1485, p. 406. **18** For example in 1472, John Barbour, the master, leased two mills to Robert Salter, a miller at River. He was only to take one of the mills after the completion of a previous agreement between the master and John le By of Ewell; Statham, *Dover charters*, pp. 251–2; EKA, Do/ZQ 11. It is possible that by the late fifteenth century, if not before, the master was adopting a leasing policy for its financial advantages. And it may also have been advantageous because of the hospital's staffing problems: in 1457–8 the master sought papal permission to present brothers under age for holy orders due to the heavy death rates from plague the house had recently suffered; Seymour, 'Hospital in the later middle ages', p. 258. Forty years later the master was again seeking papal assistance, this time in the form of an indulgence to facilitate the continued provision of hospitality for pilgrims. This had been endangered by the damage the hospital had sustained 'because it is close to the seashore'; *Cal. Pap. Let.* 1495–1503, p. 4. **19** BL, Egerton MS. 2108, f. 25. **20** Ibid. ff. 26v, 28, 44v, 55, 70, 75.

he may have persuaded others to do the same.[21] Through his work, he became well known locally and his contacts with the civic authorities presumably generated feelings of regard, both for him and his hospital. Even though it did not lead to grants or testamentary bequests for the hospital's work for the poor, it did produce a few gift exchanges in terms of the hospital's other work: intercession and commemoration. Sir John was not the only member of the hospital's staff remembered in this way, but he did receive the greatest attention, yet few from the town were as intimate with the master as Giles Love, who seems to have developed a strong relationship with him before his greater local renown after 1518.[22] However, there were a number of prominent Dover testators, others from the town's hinterland and even men from Hythe, New Romney and Canterbury who wished the master to organize services of intercession, act as guardian of their children and manage their estates for designated heirs. Others provided Sir John with gifts, which might have been intended to symbolize feelings of personal esteem and friendship.[23] Though most testators saw the hospital as providing additional or complementary intercessory acts for their souls, this growth in the demand for spiritual and other services was a considerable extension of the hospital's activities. St Mary's was consequently engaged in a greater number of gift exchanges with local people than possibly ever before, which may suggest a change in the status of the hospital from a royal to a Dover institution.

Yet its higher local profile may not have been entirely advantageous. This was recognized by Sir John in 1533 when, as a sick man, he commented that it was unlikely any of the brothers would receive the mastership because the crown coveted the appointment 'for it [the hospital] is named very rich'.[24] He was right, and after his death in 1535 Cromwell chose the new master and had a detailed inventory taken of the hospital's assets.[25] The new master, Sir John Tompson, had courted Cromwell's favour by attacking the behaviour of his fellow priests in Dover and by producing a plan for the harbour works, a project he wished to direct.[26] For the hospital, Tompson was a disaster because he was involved in Dover's factional disputes, and seems to have spent most of his time on the harbour works, where he spent well over budget; that brought him into conflict with the royal paymaster.[27] Moreover, his apparently limited interest in the fate

---

21 In 1523, for example, Sir John gave the use of his horse and cart and the labour of three men to the town; ibid. f. 61. **22** Among his bequests to the hospital, he gave Sir John a silver goblet; CKS, PRC 32/12, f. 172. See introduction. **23** In 1521 John Williamson of Canterbury bequeathed to Sir John a standing cup of silver with a cover; CKS, PRC 17/15, f. 101. **24** *L and P Henry VIII*, vol. 6, p. 413. **25** Cromwell had been alerted to Tompson's character by Christopher Hales who called him 'the worst priest I have ever known'; ibid., vol. 6, no. 1148. John Anthony, Cromwell's servant, seems to have weighed all the silver as well as counted all the hospital's livestock and deadstock; ibid., vol. 8, no. 96. **26** Ibid., vol. 6, no. 65; vol. 7, no. 1170. **27** Ibid., vol. 9, no. 734; vol. 10, nos 146, 214, 347, 614, 640, 985; vol. 11, nos. 275, 289, 745, 1254, 1321; vol. 12(2), nos. 982, 1108, 1229, 1230. He was only once recorded in the Dover wills when he witnessed Robert

of Dover priory when looters broke in probably reflects his abdication of responsibility for the well-being of his own house.[28] The three priest brothers and two
lay brothers (those who signed the oath of acknowledgement of royal supremacy
in 1534) were apparently attempting to continue the work of the hospital. The
priest brothers celebrated for the souls of the house's benefactors and the lay
brothers, and the wife of one of them, cared for the poor in the infirmary and
organized the hospital farm when time allowed.[29] There were even fewer in
1544 at the surrender of the hospital, just the master and the priest brothers,
which might imply that the house had almost ceased to function.[30] This situation had been recognized by at least one of the brothers, and Sir William Noole
was already working among the townsfolk, possibly in particular for the parishioners of St James'.[31]

Consequently, its change in function to a victualling yard may not have been
very different from its last years as a hospital because Tompson's obsession with
the harbour had apparently turned the hospital premises into a builder's yard.
Furthermore, even before the surrender the house was labelled as 'the king's',
which suggests that the crown had re-appropriated it and was using the buildings for its own use under Tompson.[32] He may have readily agreed to the
changes, especially as he was engaged in a gift exchange of his own with the
crown in 1543 in which he received the rectory of Edberton, Sussex, and became
one of the king's chaplains, thereby sealing the fate of the Maison Dieu.[33] In
1545 he also received a considerable pension of £53 6s. 8d., whereas his fellow
priests were allocated £4 or £6 13s. 4d., and had to wait until the following year
to receive it.[34] Initially at least two of the priest brothers remained in the town.
Sir William maintained his connections with St James', while Sir John Wood
helped at St Mary's church until 1551, their efforts sustaining the spirit of the
old hospital through their liturgical and pastoral activities for the benefit of
Dover's townspeople.[35]

Stilman's will in 1537; CKS, PRC 32/19, f. 30.   **28** *L and P Henry VIII*, vol. 10, no. 146.   **29** Ibid.,
vol. 7, no. 769. Walcott, 'Inventories of St Mary's hospital', 278–9.   **30** *L and P Henry VIII*, vol.
19(2), no. 728.   **31** Raynold Alye (1540) and John Taverner (1543) said he was their confessor in
their wills; CKS, PRC 32/18, f. 10, 32/19, f. 43.   **32** *L and P Henry VIII*, vol. 19(1), no. 724.   **33**
Ibid., vol. 18(1), no. 346.   **34** Ibid., vol. 20(1), p. 678; vol. 21(1), ff. 139v, 144v, 191v.   **35** Sir
William was named as his 'gostly father' by Thomas Bannester in October 1544, he was named as
William Lewes' executor in May 1545 and witnessed Richard Creke's will in August 1545; CKS,
PRC 32/19, f. 33, 32/19, f. 64, 32/20, f. 15. Sir Henry was paid 16d. for helping in St Mary's church
at Christmas in 1547, and in 1551 he was paid for riding to Canterbury on behalf of the church;
BL, Egerton MS. 1912, ff. 34v, 50v. He was also the 'gostly father' of William Envyer, yeoman in
1548, and this William may have been one of the lay brothers named in 1535; CKS, PRC 32/22,
f. 14.

CHAPTER 4

The hospitals of Sandwich

This chapter develops the analysis of the significance of local context in town and hinterland by close consideration of the functions and fortunes of the four hospitals of Sandwich. These provide examples of the leper hospital, houses for the poor and infirm, and the almshouse. The houses for the poor, moreover, have the added interest of having been under the patronage of the civic authorities throughout their histories. As a small provincial town, Sandwich, like Dover, is a valuable contrast to the recent work on the hospitals of London, York, Norwich and Cambridge because it provides a more representative picture of the place of the hospital in English urban society, where the majority of provincial towns in the later middle ages had populations of under 3,000.[1]

Over the medieval period, it is apparent that the relationships between the hospital and its partners in the spiritual economy became more complex. Furthermore, this build-up of a picture of the increasingly diverse choices available to and used by individuals, groups and institutions in terms of their charitable and pious giving highlights the changing role of the hospital in the spiritual economy locally, and at times regionally. In the first part of the chapter, the chronological sections chosen to illustrate developments in Sandwich incorporate this growth in diversity: 1 and 2) relate to the foundation dates of two of the town's hospitals in the late thirteenth and late fourteenth centuries, 3) c.1470–1530, coincides with the development of new cults and fraternities in the town, as well as apparently more sophisticated and discriminatory attitudes towards the poor by the local citizens.

In order to demonstrate the significance of the changing role of the hospital, the second part of the chapter outlines the social histories of two of the town's hospitals, St Bartholomew's and St John's, from their foundation to the late Tudor period. The hospital narratives highlight the significance of civic patronage in the long-term development and survival of both institutions. Through their action as governors and benefactors, the mayor and jurats sought to demon-

---

1 Using Dyer's population figures for 1377 (based on the poll tax returns with a multiplier of 1.9): York was 13,771, Norwich was 7,509, Cambridge was 3,614; thirty-four out of the fifty-seven largest provincial towns had a population under 3,000; A. Dyer, *Decline and growth in English towns, 1400–1640* (1991), pp. 72–4.

183

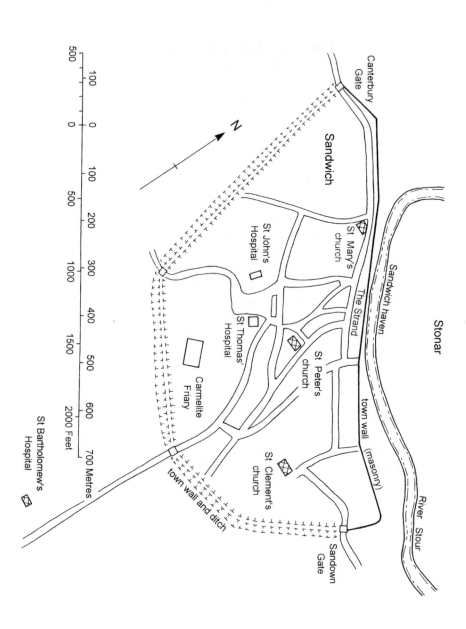

Figure 6 Map of Sandwich

strate their social and religious responsibility for their hospital inmates, the poorer and weaker members of the town. However, the relationship between the town authorities and the hospitals was far more complex, and in the case of St Bartholomew's hospital provided the patrons with certain political advantages, whereas St John's was used by the civic authorities as a central part of their strategy on vagrancy in the early sixteenth century. Thus the study of Sandwich provides important evidence for the role of the local hospital with regard to such topics as patronage, power, the maintenance of order, social control, and the value placed on almsgiving by both donors and recipients.

THE PLACE OF THE HOSPITAL IN SANDWICH

The late thirteenth century

For at least 600 years the port of Sandwich had been an important entry point into mainland Britain, and its defensive role appears to have been recognized pre-Conquest.[2] Its privileged status as one of the head ports in the Cinque Ports Federation seems to have fuelled a desire among the leading citizens to seek further autonomy from Christchurch priory and the crown, the town's two over-lords.[3] Like other coastal ports, the town's trading economy grew rapidly in the early thirteenth century, a consequence of rising population, the growing demands of urban merchants and the expanding network of markets and fairs.[4] After the mid-century, however, the growth in trade passing through Sandwich had apparently slowed, which may imply a fall in the town's prosperity, possibly at a time of increasing population.[5] Wine and wool were perhaps the most

---

2 The first reference to the town's importance in the defence of the eastern coast occurs in the Anglo-Saxon Chronicle for AD 850/1, subsequently its role as a provider of ship service may have been initiated by Edward the Confessor, further developed by William I and his sons, and culminating for this period in the first general charter for the Cinque Ports of 1260; G.N. Garmonsway (trans. and ed.), *The Anglo-Saxon Chronicle* (1953), pp. 64–5; Murray, *Constitutional history*, pp. 12, 14–5, 28–9. **3** According to the Domesday entry for Sandwich, the town was a manor of Christchurch priory returning £70 and 40,000 herrings to the priory, and to the crown sea-services as at Dover; Morgan, *Domesday, Kent*, 2,2; D. Gardiner, *Historic haven: the story of Sandwich* (1954), p. 6. During the exile of the Christchurch monks from 1207 to 1213 the king was increasingly employing Sandwich as an embarkation port for his French campaigns. Consequently, even though the monks managed to retain their nominee, Sir Henry de Sandwich, as the portreeve, control of the town had effectively passed to the king, who instructed the freemen (barons) of Sandwich to take control of the town's ship service under his authority; Gardiner, *Sandwich*, p. 14. **4** Bolton considers the importance of transport in the thirteenth century, while Britnell assesses the significance of markets and the rise in consumer demand; Bolton, *Medieval economy*, pp. 150–2; R. Britnell, 'The proliferation of markets in England, 1200–1349' (1981), 86–8, 102–4, 125–6. **5** Butcher has argued that the growth in revenue up to the 1250s received by Christchurch from sources in Sandwich may reflect an increase in the economic life of the town, though it should be remembered that these sources primarily reflect trading activity. Moreover, the priory's abil-

important commodities passing through the town, and both trades were subject to disruption, and wool to increasing taxation, over the period.[6] Thus the last quarter of the thirteenth century in Sandwich may have seen the expectations and ambitions of the leading merchant families checked by such matters as the rise in royal taxation.[7] For those further down the social scale, the combination of royal taxes and high grain and livestock prices were probably even more detrimental, leading to an increasing differentiation between the leading citizens and the poorer social groups in the town.[8]

This apparent decline in the town's prosperity by the end of the century was influenced by and informed the continuing three-way dispute over jurisdiction between the mayor, the priory and the crown. As supporters of Simon de Montfort, the townsmen suffered royal retribution in 1266 when Roger de Leyburne forcibly restored the royal mandate at Sandwich.[9] Further disagreements followed, the most serious incidents taking place in 1274, 1281 and 1300,

ity to collect customs dues may have been restricted by royal officials, which suggests that the overall level of trade may have been higher than the priory accounts indicate; A.F. Butcher, 'Sandwich in the thirteenth century' (1977), 28–31.   **6** The wine trade with Gascony was adversely affected by the increasing shipment of supplies to London, and by 1292 there were fifty-four foreign wineships paying royal customs in London compared to eleven ships in Sandwich; Gardiner, *Sandwich*, pp. 81, 85. The figures, however, may not reflect the true level of trade involving the Sandwich freemen because such men were exempt from prisage (the custom due on wine), like certain foreign merchants who had been enfranchised by the town, and so their trading activities were not recorded in the customs accounts; Gardiner, *Sandwich*, pp. 81, 84–5. Though the town's merchants were competing with their counterparts from London for the Flanders trade, wool shipments from Sandwich increased considerably over the century, and for some local families, like the Penys and Wyberts, the trade was their primary source of income; Gardiner, *Sandwich*, p. 86. The rise in Italian involvement in the trade following the end of the Flemish ascendancy in *c.*1270 did not curtail the activities of certain Sandwich merchants, and between 1271 and 1274 nine townsman obtained royal licences to export wool. It is notable that during the same period ninety-six Londoners similarly obtained licences; T. Lloyd, *The English wool trade in the middle ages* (1977), pp. 50–1, 55. Yet, even during the latter part of the century when the trade was particularly affected by political issues, like the suspension of the trade in 1274, the subsequent rise in royal financial demands and the greater involvement of foreign merchants as tax collectors on the king's behalf, the wool trade probably remained important for the town's economy (merchants from Florence also used the port), and at least one Sandwich merchant was additionally exporting from a Sussex port; Gardiner, *Sandwich*, p. 87; Lloyd, *Wool trade*, pp. 70–1, 78, 80.   **7** Both Bolton and Britnell consider that household consumption (and expectations) of the crown, the nobility, senior churchmen and some merchants rose over the thirteenth century, a situation Bolton feels was adversely affected by the ambitious military policies of Edward I, while Britnell points to the likelihood that agricultural expansion through technology and colonization of land had reached its limits; J. Bolton; 'Inflation, economics and politics in thirteenth-century England' (1992), pp. 9–12; Britnell, *Commercialisation of society*, pp. 113, 126–8.   **8** Bolton believes that this period was characterized by 'very great extremes of wealth within the towns'; Bolton, *Medieval economy*, p. 143. In Sandwich, for example, the wealthy merchant, Thomas Shelfing, sought to monopolize the wool trade through his home port in the late 1280s; Lloyd, *Wool trade*, p. 71.   **9** Gardiner, *Sandwich*, pp. 31–2.

when leading members of the town attempted to obstruct the execution of the king's writ.[10] The priory's part in these disputes continued to centre on its rights within the town. In particular the appointment of its official, the portreeve, became a major source of contention.[11] Possibly as a consequence of such difficulties and the decline in the priory's revenue from the port, Henry de Eastry, the new prior, was prepared to relinquish his house's rights and privileges there to the king in exchange for sixty librates of land in 1290.[12] This left the leading citizens in dispute with the king again as they tried to curb the expansion of royal authority over the town.[13] Thus at a time of continuing political conflict and reduced prosperity in Sandwich, the townspeople apparently welcomed the arrival of a group of Carmelite friars and founded a hospital for the poor, the town's third hospital.

St Anthony's hospital or the 'Maldry'

This leper hospital was sited about a mile and a quarter west of Sandwich at Eche End, at the end of the causeway that formed the initial part of the road to Ash and Canterbury.[14] Although the hospital's dedication to St Anthony is only found in the late medieval documents, it is feasible the hospital had a chapel and burial ground by the early thirteenth century.[15] Nothing is known about its early history, the most likely founder being a member of a local knightly family, or one or a number of prominent townsmen.[16] Its position away from the town suggests an early foundation, late twelfth or early thirteenth century, though the foundation of St Bartholomew's hospital, c.1180, for the old and infirm, might imply that there was already provision for the leprous in Sandwich.[17] For the lepers the proximity of the causeway may have provided opportunities to beg

10 Ibid., pp. 34–5; J. Croft, 'The custumals of the Cinque Ports c.1290–c.1500' (1997), pp. 96–9. 11 Gardiner, *Sandwich*, pp. 36–7. 12 Butcher, 'Sandwich', 30. 13 Croft has argued that the *Quo Warranto* campaign of 1278 and the subsequent inquisitions into town liberties were important developments in the struggle between the men of Sandwich and the crown over autonomy. The writing of the custumal in 1301 was an integral part of the process; Croft, 'Custumals', p. 100. 14 In 1474 George Langrege referred to the lazars at Eche; CKS, PRC 17/2, f. 304. During the Roman period there was a ferry from Stonar to Eche End on the mainland; Gardiner, *Sandwich*, p. 2. 15 In Christchurch priory's gift of bread in 1315 to commemorate Archbishop Lanfranc 'the lepers of Sandwich' received twenty-five breads; CCAL, DCc/DE 26; Orme and Webster, *English hospital*, p. 39; Satchall, 'Leper-houses in medieval England', pp. 33–4, 365. 16 From the Yorkshire evidence, Cullum considers that where the founder is known, noble foundations were the most important. Monastic foundations were significant, but there was some evidence of collective action by the local community with respect to the leper hospitals at Guisborough and Scarborough; Cullum, 'Leperhouses and borough status', pp. 40–2. Satchall disagrees with Cullum concerning the likelihood of civic foundations; Satchall, 'Leper-houses in medieval England', pp. 127–31. 17 According to Cullum, in Yorkshire there appears to be a close correlation between the presence of a prosperous urban community pre-1200 and a leper hospital. If this finding is applied to Sandwich, its urban status in Domesday may indicate an early foundation date for the local leper hospital; Cullum, 'Leperhouses and borough status', p. 46.

for alms from passing travellers, but there was a later tradition at least of begging for alms in St Mary's churchyard, the nearest of the town's parish churches.[18] This relationship may reflect St Mary's initial foundation as a Saxon convent in the seventh century, though interestingly it was also the only parish church where there were no civic meetings, which may have increased the marginalization of the lepers in the life of the town.[19] Whether the parish clergy at St Mary's had jurisdiction over the selection of the lepers is unknown, but there is nothing in the surviving town archives to suggest the direct involvement of the civic authorities with the lepers at all.[20]

St Bartholomew's hospital

In contrast, the history of St Bartholomew's hospital was strongly interlinked with the history of the town, the hospital playing an important part in the construction of civic ideology at Sandwich.[21] The town's appropriation and construction of the events surrounding the refoundation of the hospital in 1217 (the first founders or early benefactors were Thomas de Crauthorne and his wife, William Bucharde and his wife, and Sir Henry de Sandwich) probably occurred at a time of crisis for the leading citizens, the town's dispute with the king.[22] To understand the role of the hospital in the ideological struggle between the crown and the town, it is important to examine the references to its foundation made

---

18 Thomas Pynnok's will (1494) refers to the place where the lepers beg; CKS, PRC 17/6, f. 70. Rawcliffe considers the Norwich *leprosaria* were heavily dependent on alms in cash and kind from family and friends, doles from the almoner at Norwich priory, and possibly when these were insufficient, they begged in the market place; Rawcliffe, *Hospitals of Norwich*, p. 52. Geremek has evidence that beggars in Paris believed the areas around churches provided lucrative sites; Geremek, *Margins of society*, pp. 187–9.   **19** R. Tricker, *St Mary's church, Sandwich, Kent* (1985), p. 1. St Mary's was not the only pre-Conquest church; M.McC. Gatch, 'Miracles in architectural settings: Christ Church, Canterbury and St Clement's Sandwich in the Old English *Vision of Leofric*', *Anglo-Saxon England*, 22 (1993), 243.   **20** Cullum has found evidence from York of the civic authorities giving confiscated victuals to the local lepers, and she cites other examples, Chester and Carlisle, where tolls or other dues were given by the authorities to the local lazar houses; Cullum, 'Leperhouses and borough status', pp. 43–4. Elsewhere, as Rawcliffe noted, urban authorities produced bye-laws in an attempt to keep lepers off their streets and out of their towns; Rawcliffe, *Hospitals of Norwich*, pp. 40, 52. During this period the diagnosis of leprosy was primarily in the hands of the clergy; Demaitre, 'Diagnosis of leprosy', 343; Richards, *Medieval leper*, pp. 41, 43; Rawcliffe, *Hospitals of Norwich*, pp. 39–40.   **21** Sturken and Cartwight's discussion of the ideas of Roland Barthes concerning myth, which may be thought of as 'the hidden set of rules and conventions through which meanings, which are in reality specific to certain groups, are made to seem universal and given for a whole society' seems applicable here; M. Sturken and L. Cartwright, *Practices of looking* (2001), p. 19.   **22** The hospital is thought to have been first founded *c.*1190; Boys, *Sandwich*, p. 1. Martin in his essay on the English borough suggests that 'a substantial practical problem – as with defence – was often the catalyst for the formation of urban government' and it seems likely this might apply equally to the creating of a civic ideology; G. Martin, 'The English borough in the thirteenth century' (1990), p. 29.

by people outside the town, and then by the men of Sandwich. The first contemporary reference is in the poem *L'Histoire de Guillaume le Marechal*, which states that after the decisive battle of Sandwich on 24 August 1217, William Marshal, the king's commander, ordered that part of the extensive booty from the French ships should be divided among the sailors and portsmen. A further portion was to be used to found a hospital in honour of St Bartholomew, who had given them the victory, for the care of God's poor, a directive that was carried out.[23] The narrative fails to provide a role for the men of Sandwich beyond their involvement in the battle, but in the subsequent reworking of the narrative, at some point in the thirteenth century, a new myth became the locally accepted version.[24] In the *Polistorie de Jean de Canterbury*, written *c.*1315, the role of the townsfolk is highlighted through the reporting of the day's events – the significance of the commonalty as founders of the hospital and chapel, following the battle their construction and maintenance of the establishment for the benefit of the town by housing the aged poor, and the desire to commemorate the town's deliverance on an annual basis.[25]

When the hospital's custumal as part of the town's custumal was written up in 1301, the civic authorities were far less concerned about the events of 1217.[26]

---

23 H. Cannon, 'The battle of Sandwich and Eustace the monk' (1912), 667 n.144, citing the editor's paraphrase *L'Histoire de Guillaume le Marechal*, ed. P. Meyer (1901), for the text, ii, lines 17501–68. **24** The narrative did, however, highlight certain points regarding national security and English kingship. For example, the emphasis on William as initiator of the hospital reflected his role as overall commander of the English forces, providing him with the opportunity to fulfil his promise to recompense the portsmen for their previous hardship on behalf of the crown and, in addition, to stress the rightness of the Englsh cause through the counter-gift to the Almighty of a hospital for the poor; ibid., 656–8. Moreover, through this charitable act William sought to stress God's favour towards the English, and their humility and his own in seeking divine approval for their actions. The arrogance of the French king's son was a marked contrast; he was seeking to invade England against the expressed wishes of the papacy, and so by association, the Almighty, and his wrongdoing was further compounded by his alliance with Eustace the monk, a man considered to have traitorously defected to the French in 1212. Eustace was so reviled by the English that after his death at Sandwich his head was displayed on a lance throughout the country; ibid., 655 citing Roger of Wendover's *Chronica sive Flores Historiarum*, ed. H. Coxe, iii, 363–7; 662–5. Burgess noted that as well as the Latin chronicles of Roger of Wendover and Matthew Paris which recount the activities of Eustace and the battle of Sandwich, there is the chronicle of Walter of Guisborough, probably early fourteenth century, but possibly as early as 1270; this too makes no mention of the hospital; G. Burgess, *Two medieval outlaws* (1997), pp. 5, 32–9. Matthew Paris is particularly interesting because his illustrated account of the battle has a bishop absolving all those who are about 'to die for the liberation of England'; T. Turville-Petre, *England the nation* (1996), p. 3 and n. 10; Corpus Christi College, Cambridge, MS. 16, f. 56. **25** BL, Harley MS. 636, ff. 201v–2v. **26** According to the custumal, the three priest brothers at the hospital were to pray daily for the souls of Bertine de Crauthorne, William Bucharde and Sir Henry de Sandwich; EKA, Sa/LC 1, f. 19v. With regard to the dating of the earliest surviving copy of the custumal, Croft has successfully argued that the late fourteenth-century edition was predominantly copied from Adam Champney's custumal of 1301; Croft, 'Custumals', p. 348.

Instead, the first article was the annual procession on St Bartholomew's day, which suggests that they wished to emphasize their role as guardians of the community.[27] The detailed description of the procession providing a public statement concerning the place of the hospital as one of the town's institutions, thereby highlighting the continuing moral and spiritual relationship between the civic authorities, their ancestors and successors, and the town's saint in his hospital. For the mayor and jurats the annual event, as a ritual associated with the myth narrative, was a means of producing a heightened awareness of ideas about patronage, authority, responsibility and power, all elements in their construction of a civic ideology, made more accessible through the use of symbols. One of the most powerful themes for the town officers, for example, was the linking of church, civic governance and charity by starting the procession at St Peter's church and ending at St Bartholomew's hospital. St Peter's church was near the town centre, certain civic officials were elected there, it was the site of the town court and the town held jointly the advowson.[28] Consequently, the mayor, jurats, and freemen of Sandwich, with the clergy from St Peter's, set out from a special, sacred space, under ecclesiastical jurisdiction but one where the civic officials had dispensed justice on the town's behalf as moral guardians of Sandwich. The procession then passed through the town and out to the hospital. By so doing the procession could be seen as a bridge, a symbolic link between the central church and St Bartholomew's hospital on the margins, which emphasized the hospital's subordinate role in the exchange process. Its role as a grateful receiver of civic largesse was reinforced still further by a number of other elements in the annual procession.[29] Through the construction of the myth and ritual, therefore, the civic authorities were able to signify the town's continuing concern for its members, a concern they had usurped from the crown.

St John's hospital

Like St Bartholomew's hospital, St John's was under the jurisdiction of the mayor and jurats, but the relationship between the hospital and the civic authorities was

---

27 EKA, Sa/LC 1, f. 15v.   **28** Boys, *Sandwich*, pp. 309, 431; G.J. Turner and H.E. Salter (eds), *The register of St Augustine's abbey, Canterbury*, vol. 2 (1924), p. 543.   **29** For example, the provision of wax lights, presumably carried by the senior town officers who presented their gift to St Bartholomew on behalf of the commonalty at the high altar of the hospital chapel. Their gift, an offering of thanksgiving for the past, was also a submission of hope for the future from the mayor and commonalty to their saint in his hospital who, as a consequence of their humble demeanour, would continue to guard the town. The leading citizens, therefore, may have perceived their actions as symbolizing good government on behalf of the town and the hospital. In their role of moral governors of the hospital, the mayor and jurats were also receiving the offering, the act of guardianship emphasized by their control over the storing of the tapers. The duality of their duties as supplicants and recipients is interesting, apparently underlining the power and control of the civic authorities in the town. Also this was a special situation, possibly unique, being divinely sanctioned through the intercession of the town's saint.

even more unbalanced, since the hospital's initial endowment was far smaller, and the circumstances of its foundation far less prestigious. Although the foundation charter does not survive, the earliest known benefactors were local leading townsmen, whose small grants suggest the house was from the beginning heavily dependent upon other sources of income.[30] The charging of an entry fee may imply the brothers and sisters were poorer people rather than the poor, but people from this group, especially the sick, may have found temporary shelter in separate rooms at the back of the hospital in an area called the 'harbinge'.[31] It is possible, therefore, that the foundation of St John's was in part a response to the charging of high entry fees at St Bartholomew's and the consequent loss of a haven for the town's poor. Yet it seems more likely that the motives of its individual benefactors and the senior town officials were more complex concerning their spiritual and temporal duties and desires.[32]

The mayor and jurats wished to display locally and more widely their credentials as moral guardians of the town; one way of achieving this was to found and maintain a small hospital. Through various processes of reciprocity, the town officers demonstrated their guardianship of the hospital and its inmates, such measures being enshrined in the custumal recorded in the town book in 1301.[33] The custumal set out the roles of the town and the hospital, the two exchange partners, indicating the balance of power between them. The town (mayor and jurats) provided a number of gifts: good governance of the house and its inmates, board and lodging for the hospital community, income from the use of the standard bushel, permission to collect alms each Sunday at the town's parish churches, permission to beg fish from boats in the haven and bread from the leading townsfolk at Christmas, permission to allow a brother to travel abroad gathering alms, and the use of officially impounded livestock, as well as confiscated fish, meat and some bread which had been illegally presented for sale.[34] In return, the master was to keep proper accounts, maintain the hospital buildings and furnishings, and allocate fairly any alms the house received. His responsibility to the mayor also covered the good governance of the hospital community, though this gift might, in addition, be seen as his gift to the brothers and sisters alongside his gift to them of his good management of the house's resources. In response, the broth-

---

30 Three charters are extant dated pre-1300: in 1287/8 Thomas de Shelvinge, wool merchant, granted a release of payment in frankalmoin to the brothers, sisters and their successors at St John's of an annual rent of 2s. 10d. previously paid by them; in 1293/4 John de Ho granted in frankalmoin to the hospital an annual rent of 3d.; and in 1296 John Long similarly granted a quitrent of two marks; EKA, Sa/Ch 10J T1. **31** According to the custumal, the resident inmate entry fee was two marks or 40s.; EKA, Sa/LC 1, f. 21v. Presumably the sick had free entry, including those due to give birth; EKA, Sa/Ch 10J A1. **32** The entry fee at St Bartholomew's hospital was set at ten or twelve marks or £10, with some allowance for those of good character or who were freemen of the town by birthright; ibid., f. 18. **33** The first entry in the hospital's custumal states that the governance of St John's was the responsibility of the mayor and jurats; ibid., f. 20. **34** Ibid., ff. 20–1v.

ers and sisters were obliged to offer a series of counter-gifts, thereby establishing and sustaining the bonds between the exchange partners. The first gift was the entry fee. Thereafter, the inmate freely gave labour and obedience as decreed by the ordinances, until death or departure from St John's. These gifts were also part of the exchange system between the master and the brothers and sisters, and between individuals and the rest of the hospital community, a process initiated at admission when the new inmate took an oath of obedience, and gave a penny to each of the assembled brothers and sisters.

In contrast to these public, corporate processes of gift exchange, individual benefactors to St John's, as to St Bartholomew's, sought more precise spiritual benefits. Most gave grants in frankalmoin, and though the gift might be directed towards the welfare of the brothers and sisters, this clause implies that the donors' concerns were also directed toward their own spiritual needs. In this instance the use of Thompson's contractual form of gift exchange with the hospital was particularly complex because the charitable act was directed at members of the town's poor, those in Sandwich for whom the town officers had assumed responsibility. It was these same men who, as individuals, were seeking intercessory services from the hospital.[35] Collectively, as governors of St John's, it was they who had the power to provide such services through the provision of a chapel and priest. Moreover, as the dominant partners in their own gift exchange with the hospital community, the leading citizens were well placed to solicit such services from the inmates who, as members of the respectable poor of the town, were under their patronage and care, and so might expect civic protection.[36] These relationships between the hospital and the civic authorities, collectively and individually, may in part explain the apparently relatively limited interest in personal gifts to the hospital. Instead, the more prosperous townsfolk probably directed their activities in the spiritual economy towards the town's parish churches.

Other religious institutions
There were three parish churches, and St James' chapel in St Mary's parish, which meant the principal process of reciprocity for the townspeople was the tithe system. The customary nature of the system resulted in local variation. At St Clement's parish, for instance, this included fish tithes.[37] Variation also occurred with regard to who collected the great and small tithes. For St Mary's, the rec-

---

35 The idea behind the Statute of Provisors may be worth considering here; Thompson, 'Monasteries', 108, 111–2. **36** Certain donors also directed their grant towards the poor of the house for a precise purpose. Thomas de Shelvinge's grant of the rent to provide straw for the poor resorting there and for the use of the brothers and sisters, demonstrates the complexity of the relationship between this group of donors and the hospital, where the apparent needs of the hospital were not being met by their (collective, civic) gift exchange with St John's; EKA, Sa/Ch 10J T1. **37** Swanson, *Church and society*, pp. 210–2. The vicar at St Clement's appears to have collected fish tithes from the haven; Boys, *Sandwich*, p. 279.

tory was held by the archdeacon of Canterbury, who received the great tithes, the vicar collecting the small tithes, his stipend.[38] As well as his gift exchange with his parishioners, the vicar was also involved in an exchange with the archdeacon as patron of the benefice, which had necessitated an initial gift to secure the post.[39]

The position at St Peter's was different because the rector was the incumbent, the advowson held jointly by the mayor and St Augustine's abbey, Canterbury. This greater control for the town's leading citizens and parishioners may have resulted in a good relationship between the priest and parish at a time when the implementation of papal reforms was placing greater emphasis on the role of the parish priest as the provider 'of pastoral care and sacramental mediation, through which (and through which alone) folk could enjoy the promise of salvation, good health, good crops, neighbourly peace and justice'.[40] The theological centrality of the Eucharist provided the church, through the action of the priest, with a vital counter-gift, a necessary requirement for all Christians at least once a year, and just before death. For this ultimate gift, the laity were expected to fulfil their duty through the provision of involuntary and voluntary offerings, furnishing the priest and his church with the correct accoutrements for 'the recurrent miracle of resummoning of the incarnate historical body of Christ'.[41] Evidence for the local success of this exchange process might be inferred from church building or refurbishment, donation of ornaments or other items, and the declaration that all was well in the visitation records. Though severely limited, the structural evidence from the surviving churches appears to indicate that, either collectively or as individual donors, some of the townspeople had honoured their commitments in terms of the spiritual economy.[42]

The last extra-parochial exchange partner in this economy was the Carmelite friary, founded on a piece of marshland to the south-west of the town *c.*1268.[43] The order had established two other houses in Kent and there were Carmelite friaries in France, but patronage may have been the most important factor with regard to Sandwich. The foundation charter has not survived, but three of the earliest known benefactors had connections with the town; only the fourth, Henry Cowfield, an 'Almain', is more difficult to link with Sandwich.[44] Yet he

---

38 Boys, *Sandwich*, p. 312. **39** As part of these relationships the vicar was expected to be a priest at his appointment and to reside in the parish, as well to provide pastoral care, including aid to the poor of his parish; Swanson, *Church and society*, pp. 44–5. **40** Rubin, 'Eucharist', p. 49. **41** Ibid., p. 50; F.D. Logan, *A history of the church in the middle ages* (2002), p. 146. **42** R. Tricker, *St Peter's church, Sandwich, Kent* (1984), pp. 1, 4, 9. For example, at St Mary's church the provision of a recess for a banner stave might indicate the probability of processions and the possibility of parish guild(s), which seems to imply the active participation of at least some parishioners in the voluntary sector of the spiritual economy; Tricker, *St Mary's church*, p. 1. **43** Boys, *Sandwich*, p. 175. **44** *VCH Kent*, vol. 2, p. 204; E. Deighton, 'The Carmelite friary at Sandwich' (1994), 317. A few German merchants were involved in the wool trade, and it is possible Henry had frequently traded at Sandwich; Lloyd, *Wool trade*, p. 49.

may have been one of a growing number of foreign merchants who saw the town as a useful entry point into the English market. And as a consequence of his contacts with the local townspeople and clergy, the civic authorities and his fellow merchants, such a man might wish to be associated with the provision of a religious house which, through its preaching and charitable ministry, would aid the spiritual well-being of Sandwich.

Of the other three, Lord Clinton was a member of the nobility, whose position as an officer of the crown presumably brought him to the Cinque Port towns of Sandwich and Dover in particular.[45] If he was instrumental in the choice of Sandwich as a home for the friars, his decision may have rested in part on his knowledge of the other religious houses in the area. At Sandwich, unlike Dover, there were no monastic establishments. Under such circumstances, the townspeople might be more willing to support a local religious house, especially one of the new orders of friars. For men like Lord Clinton, the friars' mendicant lifestyle and changing attitudes to the religious meant that the establishing of a friary was a more attractive proposition compared to a house for one of the old monastic orders, an idea that was likely to be endorsed by the local citizens.[46] His gift to the friary formed part of his pious strategy in the pursuit of salvation. He does not appear to have sought more tangible benefits, like burial there, but he may have enjoyed the counter-gift of hospitality, a provision the friars later extended to the king and his officials.[47]

Sir John de Sandwich's gift to the friars might be seen as a typical response of those from local knightly families. Like his father he supported various types of religious institution in east Kent, though the form of his gift-giving seems to have related to the proximity of the house to Sandwich, a reflection presumably of the 'economy of regard', and to changing attitudes among benefactors over the thirteenth century.[48] Because of his beneficence, his local connections and his place in Sandwich society, the townspeople may have been encouraged to follow his example, and also the example of Thomas Crauthorne, the other known early local benefactor. Though less involved in the town's trading community than his kinsman, Thomas appears to have been a leading Sandwich citizen, whose family, like Sir John's, had strong links with St Bartholomew's hos-

---

45 According to Page (ed.), the benefactor may have been John de Clinton, not William; *VCH Kent*, vol. 2, p. 204 n. 2.   **46** Golding, 'Burials and benefactions', p. 73; C. Holdsworth, 'Royal Cistercians' (1992), p. 139.   **47** According to Boys, Lord Clinton was buried in St Mary's church, Sandwich, which seems to support Page's view [above n. 44]; Boys, *Sandwich*, p. 184. With regard to the friary's relationship with the crown, it may in part have rested upon Edward I's gift to them of 5s. for a day's food in 1300; *VCH Kent*, vol. 2, p. 204; *CCR 1413–1419*, p. 368.   **48** Offer, 'Economy of regard', 450–7. Thompson, 'Monasteries', 107–9. Sir John's gift to the Carmelites seems to have been made without recourse to specific demands for his soul, while his grant to St Radigund's abbey, near Dover (his father and father-in-law had both supported the abbey), did not include the phrase in pure and perpetual alms, which may indicate differences in perception; *CPR 1272–1281*, p. 404; Bodleian: Rawlinson B.336, p. 174.

pital, linking him and his family to the town's past, present and future.[49] His own gift exchange with the friary was a public statement of his pious duty to God, to his neighbours, and to himself. The friars responding by fulfilling his wish to be buried in their church, and presumably by providing the appropriate intercessory services for a benefactor of his status. This might suggest that the friary church was the central space in which the reciprocal exchange process between local benefactors and the recipient friars was articulated. The donors, members of local knightly families but probably increasingly leading Sandwich citizens, providing gifts to beautify the church and to aid the work of the friary; the friars reciprocated through the counter-gifts of burial, intercession, commemoration, and confraternity, the act of preaching, and the provision of hospitality to poor pilgrims and others who sought aid at their gate.[50]

Evidence of individual and civic gift-giving from the early fourteenth century appears to follow the same pattern.[51] Although altruism might have been a significant factor for the leading citizens who supported the friars, their gift-giving may have allowed them to develop the idea that they had certain proprietary rights over the friary. Such an idea was given particular expression in terms of themselves as town officers, who, through the gift of a share of the underweight loaves confiscated by the 'common weigher' on market days, had created a bond between the town and the friary, a bond which had become enshrined in the town's custumal of 1301.[52] However unlike the bond that had been created between the civic authorities and the town's own hospitals of St John and St Bartholomew (the other recipients of the underweight bread), institutions of the poor, the relationship between the leading citizens and the friars was more equal, possibly in part a product of the economy of regard between the exchange partners.[53]

The late fourteenth century

The tensions within Sandwich society at this time appear to have their roots in the successive demographic crises from 1348, as well as the town's variable economic circumstances, dependent on the changing fortunes of war, and the uncer-

---

49 The ancestors of both men were named in the St Bartholomew's hospital custumal; EKA, Sa/LC 1, f. 19v. **50** Confraternity was a common feature of such houses, yet there appears to be nothing in the little surviving documentation to suggest that this counter-gift was available at Sandwich; G. Rosser, 'Communities of parish and guild in the late middle ages' (1988), pp. 41–2. **51** In 1306 Thomas de Shelvinge, wool merchant, gave the friars a small piece of land in neighbouring Woodnesborough, which contained a spring, and gave them permission to make a conduit from his lands to their house; *CPR 1301–1307*, p. 440. John de Welles, Raymond de Sparre, John de Thaxstede, Thomas Gilet, John Botoun and William de Mounty, together, gave them two acres of land in 1336; *CPR 1334–1338*, p. 230. **52** Boys, *Sandwich*, p. 544. **53** Comparing the friary to St Bartholomew's hospital, the friary was within the town, the hospital outside; the friary had a large number of professional intercessors (fifteen friars rather than three priest brothers); the friary church was far larger (the church was 150 feet long and nearly forty feet wide, making it longer than the parish church of St Peter) than the small hospital chapel. It had several altars, and the friary had more burial space; Deighton, 'Carmelite friary', 318.

tain trading conditions experienced during the second half of the century.[54] The town's international trade was particularly vulnerable, but many of the leading merchant families were able to maintain their position by adopting a flexible trading strategy.[55] It is not clear whether the town suffered a serious decline in terms of falling rents, but if the Canterbury evidence is comparable, it suggests that Sandwich was continuing to attract migrants, at least in the short-term, from the town's hinterland.[56] A few of these migrants adapted successfully to urban conditions, and by the 1380s these new men had joined men from the surviving middling Sandwich families in the town government. The newcomers, in particular, appear to have espoused new ideas as they sought to adapt to the changing social, economic and political circumstances of the period, compared to those whose families had been in power in the town during the early part of the century.[57] And even though it would be simplistic to consider that these groups among the leading citizens of Sandwich could be characterized by two examples, the founders of two local chantries appear to provide different approaches to this act of reciprocity. The men concerned were the Condys, John and William his son, whose family had been active in the town throughout the fourteenth century, either as civic officers or in the king's service; and Thomas

54 Although the town's complaint to the king that 'the town is so much weakened by divers plagues and other losses and grievous calamities that the inhabitants are not sufficient to defend it against assaults of the enemy' may be employing common rhetorical ideas, it seems likely that it presents a fairly accurate picture; *CCR* 1381–1385, p. 519.   **55** The port's international trade involved various foreign nationals from the Italian city states, the Hanse towns, merchants from the Low Countries, several French provinces and the Iberian peninsula; and the London merchants; Gardiner, *Sandwich*, pp. 124–32. Wool and wine were the staple commodities. Sandwich was the wool port for Kent (Canterbury being the staple town) until 1368 when both were relocated to Queenborough. This hit wool exports considerably, but in 1377 the staple was moved to Sandwich, whereupon the trade began to recover. During the same period cloth exports were also rising; whereas ninety-eight cloths had been exported annually in the 1350s this had risen to 279 per year in the 1400s; Lloyd, *Wool trade*, pp. 213, 255–6; Gardiner, *Sandwich*, pp. 94–7; Croft, 'Custumals', p. 136; J. Wallace, 'The overseas trade of Sandwich, 1400–1520' (1974), p. 56. Other commodities traded through Sandwich included fish from Flanders and agricultural produce from the town's hinterland and beyond, which was exported to the English army in France and the garrison at Calais, though the trade with Flanders, in particular was intermittently disrupted by changes in forign policy; Gardiner, *Sandwich*, pp. 116–24.   **56** Using the treasurer's accounts from Christchurch priory, which include rents of property in a large number of Canterbury parishes, Butcher has shown that the figures 'of the 1370s and early 1380s give no sign of post-plague stagnation', suggesting that Canterbury's experience 'seems to have been one of resilience and even buoyancy' due to 'rapid immigration, a redistribution of wealth and changed patterns of consumption', even though mortality rates in the town had been high; A.F. Butcher, 'Rent and the urban economy' (1979), 38–9, 42.   **57** Butcher's analysis of the situation in Canterbury at this time in terms of its changing social structure and the problems faced by the civic authorities may have interesting parallels with Sandwich, though the men of Sandwich do not appear to have taken part in the 1381 revolt; A.F. Butcher, 'English urban society and the revolt of 1381' (1984), pp. 86–7, 95–101, 110; Croft, 'Custumals', p. 135.

Elys, whose family was from Otham, though he was a prosperous draper and Sandwich merchant.[58]

Details concerning the Condy chantry are to be found in two documents: the first a licence of mortmain dated 1344/5 covering the provisions of the chantry, and the second a note in the town custumal written in 1368 soon after the death of William Condy. Taken together they seem to provide interesting insights about the complexities of belief for those living at this difficult time. As a town and later crown officer, John Condy was a leading figure in Sandwich when he established a chantry in St Mary's church.[59] His use of a grant *in vitam* instead of a post-mortem will and testament may imply that he was seeking to establish a more personal relationship within the spiritual economy.[60] Moreover, by refraining from employing conditional clauses or stipulating details covering the masses, he was demonstrating his faith in his priest to provide for his soul, as well as allowing his son the opportunity to develop his own gift exchange, thus extending the family's relationship with St Mary's church.

Though the family may have dwelt in St Mary's parish, John's choice may relate to his vision of the family and its place in the history of the town. As well as personal links with the parish clergy, John apparently had connections with leading families like the Loveriks who also supported St Mary's church.[61] The church was a suitable site for his chantry, having recently been refurbished, and its location on the Strand was a fitting place of remembrance and commemoration for the man whose naval exploits had been recognized by the town and the crown. St Mary's may have also seemed appropriate because, unlike the other two parish churches, there were no civic links with the church, a situation that may have appealed to John, whose major official role in Sandwich was as a crown rather than a town officer. William appears to have endorsed his father's decision regarding St Mary's, selecting the church for his own burial.[62] Consequently,

58 Hussey, *Kent chantries*, p. 263. **59** John had been mayor of Sandwich in 1326 and 1338, before receiving royal favour following his naval exploits at the battle of Sluys in 1340. Thereupon he was elevated to the bailiwick of Sandwich, which he held as a hereditary office until his death in 1345; *CPR* 1341–1343, p. 69; Croft 'Custumals', p. 122; Gardiner, *Sandwich*, pp. 103–6. **60** He wished for a chaplain to celebrate mass there daily for his good estate, for his soul post-mortem, and for the souls of the departed faithful, this was to be funded from an annual rent of £4 from property in Sandwich; *CPR* 1343–1345, p. 378. **61** Thomas Loverik, a prosperous Sandwich merchant, built a chapel adjacent to St Mary's church called 'the chapel of St Mary at the East Head' in the late fourteenth century. This would have provided a worthy site for his own commemoration and for his fellow townsman, William Condy. The chantry and the chapel were the first entries in the bede-roll for St Mary's, dated *c.*1447, which implies that there was a strong link between them; CCAL, U3/11/6/5. **62** Having inherited the bailiwick from his father, he remained in office for nine years before resigning in 1355 on very favourable terms. In 1363 he was appointed as controller of customs and seems to have remained active in the economic and political life of the town until his death in 1368; *CPR* 1361–1364, p. 410. He and his wife were buried in the south aisle of St Mary's church.

the family's apparent alignment in death with the most ancient Christian site in the town, but not the site of civic administration, may suggest that John and William wished to be seen as honorific descendants of the early portsmen who had served the crown against invaders before the question of self government became a contentious issue. Their close association with the town in death, as in life, was intended through the medium of the chantry to ensure intercession and commemoration, and to act as a bridge between the crown and the town, as they done during their working lives.

Possibly as a means of furthering this relationship, William entrusted the management of the chantry to the civic authorities, though the circumstances of the post-Black Death period may also have meant he had lost faith in the survival of his family in the town. In turning to his peers to oversee the maintenance of his family chantry, William may have believed that they too would see it as part of their (the town government's) strategy to present an image of continuity at a time of discontinuity.[63] In addition to trying to create an idea of constancy, of which he and his family were a part, William may have intended that the chantry would be considered the responsibility of the town, as in the past the Condys had discharged their responsibility to the townspeople of Sandwich.[64] These ideas may have appealed to the mayor and jurats, but they appear to have extended the exchange process beyond themselves, the Condys and the chantry priest to include others in the town.[65] The stipulation that the chantry priest should say the morrow mass daily provided an opportunity for the working townsmen, especially the poorer workers at the port, to hear mass.[66] For the mayor, this gift of the sacrament to the lower social orders in the town might be seen as discharging his civic responsibility, an act of charity benefiting those outside the freedom who were frequently publicly excluded (at civic elections and rituals like the St Bartholomew's day procession). Such an act in the late 1360s might be perceived as a measure intended to deflect the tensions among the various social groups in Sandwich relating to matters like employment and taxation, whereby those in power sought to legitimize their position at a time when this might have been under threat.[67]

63 Croft has argued that the inclusion in the second writing up of the town's custumal of named personnel from earlier in the century, whose descendants were present among the civic officers in the 1360s and 1370s, was the work of 'an insecure oligarchy' who wished to highlight ideas of continuity and stability; Croft, 'Custumals', p. 135.   **64** An interesting slant on this three-way relationship between the Condys, the chantry priest and the town authorities was that the town rented the courthall from the chantry priest. Consequently, the civic authorities and the chantry remained bound together until the Reformation, the town paying 10*s*. in rent annually; EKA, Sa/FAt 2–38. **65** The note in the town custumal, probably written soon after 1368, the year William Condy son of John died, describes the chantry thus: 'Habent maior et communitas cantariam Johannis Coundy et Willielmi filii eiusdem Johannis in ecclesia beate Marie dicte ville; in qua cantaria si quis capellanus eiusdem cantarie fuerit missam matutinalem celebrabit'; Boys, *Sandwich*, p. 184; EKA, Sa/LC 1, f. 115.   **66** Duffy, *Stripping of the altars*, pp. 99, 140.   **67** Butcher, 'Urban society', pp. 104–5.

In contrast, the chantry and associated hospital founded by Thomas Elys appears to demonstrate feelings of confidence in his and his peers' ability to govern the town and to ensure their survival as honoured men to future generations. Where William Condy had looked to the past, his father and men of the pre-1350 generation, Thomas placed his faith in his contemporaries and younger men, new men who had successfully adapted to late fourteenth-century conditions, and who would be active in town government after his death. His apparent confidence in the future may reflect his position as a prosperous draper and merchant, whose fortune had brought him royal recognition, a leading role in the affairs of Sandwich, the opportunity to buy substantial landholdings locally and to marry his daughters into local knightly families.[68] Unfortunately, little is known about his family except that he appears to have had numerous offspring, though few may have reached adulthood, and the direct male line may have died with Thomas. As a consequence, he apparently sought permanent memorials in the form of his tomb, his chantry and his hospital as a way of seeking his and his family's salvation; and for his commemoration by his fellow citizens and their successors in Sandwich.

Though nothing today survives to identify conclusively his tomb, the most likely in St Peter's church is the central tomb recess in the north aisle, an altar tomb with an elaborate stone-carved tracery and six shields, including the arms of the Septvans family, the arms of the Chirch family and the arms of the town of Sandwich.[69] Assuming this is Elys' tomb, it provided a number of symbols that might have been intended to maintain him and his family in the social memory of the local townspeople. For example, the absence of any effigies might suggest a lack of personal ostentation, while the extensive decoration of the stonework signalled his wealth and status. Its position, moreover, in the recently rebuilt and extended north aisle was probably close to where the town officers were elected and the town court held, a point of contact with the town government which was reinforced by the Sandwich town arms above the tomb recess. His tomb similarly acted as a bridge between his persona (prosperous, leading citizen of Sandwich and senior town officer) and that of Thomas whose wealth, good standing and marriage policies had placed his family within the ranks of the local gentry. The shields around his tomb, including those of two of his sons-in-law, apparently implying that he wished his ambitions for his family and its name to be preserved in stone for all time in his parish church: he and his daughters would remain there while his and their descendants would become part of the aspiring local gentry.[70]

---

68 From the 1380s, in particular, the export of cloths through Sandwich grew considerably; Wallace, 'Overseas trade', p. 56. Thomas was mayor in 1370 and 1382, and was a Member of Parliament in 1369 and 1377–8, when he lent £40 to the new king. His daughter, Constance, married John de Septvans of Ash, whose family was connected by marriage to the de Sandwich family; Boys, *Sandwich*, p. 165. **69** Tricker, *St Peter's church*, pp. 10, 13; Boys, *Sandwich*, p. 307. **70** The Septvans family were well established in the neighbouring parish of Ash, the local church gaining consider-

The second device, his chantry of three priests, was also located in St Peter's church, under the control of his feoffees, who had been instructed to endow it with considerable land and property.[71] In his will he provided detailed proposals regarding the duties of the priests and the management of the chantry: the chantry chaplains were permitted a very limited role in the liturgical life of the parish because such activities were not to impair their ability to fulfil their obligations to Thomas Elys and those he had named.[72] Consequently they were only to attend divine service for the parish on Sundays and festivals, and then solely during the chants and singing of psalms. However, a possibly later provision (it does not occur in the copy of the chantry agreement preserved in the Sandwich Year Book), the instruction that one of the chaplains should give basic schooling to boys from the town, might be said to characterize Thomas' acts of remembrance because such a charitable act would benefit individual townsmen and the town, so producing living memorials of his benevolence.[73]

St Thomas' hospital

It is possible that his hospital dedicated to St Thomas of Canterbury for the maintenance of twelve poor people should be seen similarly. This institution, also founded post-mortem, was to be governed by the same feoffees who organized the chantry, and was almost as well endowed.[74] The lack of surviving ordinances for the house means that any assessment of the hospital rests on sixteenth-century testamentary materials, an early engraving of the hospital, and the surviving porch/gateway.[75] There is nothing to suggest from this evidence that the hospital inmates were regularly involved in providing intercessory services for Thomas Elys, nor that there was a link between the activities of the chantry priests and the hospital inmates. In addition, the engraving appears to suggest the presence of a common hall at the hospital, not a chapel, and the only ornamentation on the hospital porch was the Sandwich town arms. Together these seem to imply that Thomas saw his two institutions as separate, but complementing each other, his hospital foundation principally providing a means of ful-

ably from their patronage, including a fine alabaster effigy of John de Septvans, who died in 1458. **71** He named four feoffees: Thomas Rollyng, vicar of St Mary's church; William Swan, clerk; John Godard, and Richard Benge. John Godard was mayor in 1379, 1383, 1384–6, 1392, 1403–6, and a Member of Parliament in 10, 18, 20 Richard II and in 1 and 3 Henry IV; Richard Benge was mayor in 1407–8 and a Member of Parliament in 20 Richard II; Boys, *Sandwich*, p. 166; Croft, 'Custumals', p. 135. They were to endow his chantry from two messuage, 216 acres of land and rents worth £4 from land in several local parishes. Most of this land was part of the manor of Eastry held by Christchurch priory; Hussey, *Kent chantries*, p. 264; CCAL, DCc/Chartae Antiquae E. 159.   **72** EKA, Sa/AC 2, ff. 166v–7.   **73** Boys, *Sandwich*, p. 186.   **74** The hospital endowment comprised a messuage and 132 acres of land in neighbouring Woodnesborough; *CPR 1391–1396*, p. 109.   **75** The hospital records were apparently written up in 1450 following the loss of some of the documents, but the authorities seem to have lost all trace of these by 1725 when they had to create new regulations; EKA, Sa/LC 9; *VCH Kent*, vol. 2, p. 227.

filling his obligation to God and his neighbours. There is nothing to indicate he expected the inmates to act as his bedesmen and women in association with the three chantry priests. Rather, they appear to have been seen and saw themselves as members of St Peter's parish, the parish where the hospital was situated.[76] This suggests that Thomas was not primarily concerned for his, or their, spiritual welfare through their devotional activities, but that his charitable act in aiding God's poor, the poor of Sandwich, was important for its symbolism, which was signalled through the provision of twelve places. As a leading townsman who had held the highest office the town could bestow, he was apparently expressing ideas about civic responsibility and good governance, including care for the poor and maintenance of order, through the institutionalization of the poor. His choice of leaving the governance of his hospital to his feoffees, not the mayor, seems strange under these circumstances, especially as the town's coat of arms on the porch might suggest that it was a civic institution, but may imply instead that he intended his hospital should be envisaged symbolically as an institution of the town, while remaining under the control of those he had personally selected. This patronage from beyond the grave was further reinforced by Thomas' use of conditional clauses for the nomination of other guardians if his feoffees failed in their duties, his final choice being the archdeacon of Canterbury.[77] By so doing, he was looking to a wide set of potential exchange partners who would provide him and his descendants with fitting memorials through a range of complex systems of reciprocal exchange.

St Bartholomew's hospital
The hospital received few gifts in the form of *in vitam* grants during the fourteenth century, though there was a small cluster of grants in the early 1390s. These grants, often given by local, joint donors, concerned tiny pieces of land in fee.[78] It is not known whether these were direct farmed or rented, but the hospital community may have been badly affected by the plague.[79] Decimation of the hospital population might explain John Gybon's petition to Edward III to grant the profits of the ferry between Sandwich and Stonar (the town on the other side of the estuary) to St Bartholomew's as a means of providing muchneeded revenue to compensate for the brothers' inability to either work their

---

76 Unfortunately, there are few surviving wills, but John Newman in 1540 intended that he should be buried in St Peter's churchyard beside his late wife, who may have been a sister there. He expected that his three funeral days would be celebrated in the same church; CKS, PRC 17/23 f. 56. **77** Boys, *Sandwich*, pp. 185–6. **78** For example, Stephen Reyner and John Cardon in 1391 granted in fee to the master, brothers and sisters half an acre of land in Worthelle field and a further half acre in Hambreggebroke field; ibid., p. 48. **79** Elsewhere hospital populations had suffered considerably from the plague. At Clyst Gabriel hospital near Exeter, of the two chantry priests and eleven infirm brothers, nine died between the beginning of January and the end of March, 1349; N. Orme, 'Mortality in fourteenth-century Exeter' (1988), 201.

own land or collect casual alms.[80] It may also have been seen as a symbolic gift. The hospital was a charitable institution traditionally associated with the provision of hospitality for travellers, though in most cases such gifts were linked to bridges, not ferries. For St Bartholomew's the gift may have been extremely valuable, the lease of the ferry to various ferrymen during this period providing the house with much-needed income.[81] For the civic authorities, as patrons of the hospital, it may have had the double benefit that it provided for the town's hospital at no cost to themselves and transferred a further privilege from the crown to the town.

St John's hospital

It is hard to assess the fortunes of St John's hospital because of the limited documentary sources, but it like the leper hospital did survive this difficult period. It seems likely the inmates at St John's were heavily dependent on casual alms, their few pieces of land in the town providing relatively little in the form of rent, and the produce from their gardens supplying only a part of the house's daily requirements. However, the hospital did receive a few further *in vitam* grants from local townspeople, folk from the middling sort as well as men like Thomas Elys.[82] These gifts of rents or property predominantly concerned holdings in St Peter's parish, especially property in the fish market. Such commercial assets were useful additions, providing the hospital with larger rents. Yet it seems to have had some problems finding tenants in the early 1370s, though the use of indenture agreements forever in the 1380s and in the early fifteenth century might suggest that the rented sector was relatively stable during this period.[83] Thus the hospital, as the recipient of various gift exchanges with individuals, married couples and collectively (under the corporation), had received sufficient gifts to survive. The twelve brothers and sisters were able to repay the donors through various counter-gifts: the saying of prayers in the hospital chapel for the souls of their benefactors, the care of the sick in the harbinge at the back of the hospital, and their activities in the hospital and in the town where they fulfilled their role as the humble poor, who were the living embodiment of civic charity and social responsibility.[84]

---

80 *CPR* 1348–1350, p. 341.   81 In 1383 Robert Grymysby, ferryman, agreed to pay the hospital twenty marks a year when he took a seven-year lease of the ferry; EKA, SA/Ch 10B A1; Boys, *Sandwich*, p. 45.   82 There are some discrepancies between Boys and the surviving deeds. The hospital received the following grants: one in 1347, one in 1349, two (three) in 1366 and two or three in 1384; EKA, Sa/Ch 10J T1; Boys, *Sandwich*, pp. 132–3.   83 In 1385 the brothers and sisters granted forever to Walter Taylour and his heirs and assigns a tenement in the fish market at a yearly rent of 26s. 8d.; in the first two decades of the fifteenth century they made a number of similar grants of which the annual rents ranged between 3s. and 7s.; EKA, Sa/Ch 10J T1; Boys, *Sandwich*, p. 133. Wallace, 'Overseas trade', pp. 61–2.   84 Gardiner stated that the hospital initially accommodated fifteen inmates, but she does not cite the reference and the custumal does not give a figure; Gardiner,

Other religious institutions

The friary may also have encountered difficulties during the period, but because of its regional and national importance was not dependent on local benefactors, unlike the hospitals.[85] Though it probably received some *in vitam* grants, the two documented forms of reciprocal exchange are an indulgence and wills. In 1370 Thomas Brantingham, bishop of Exeter, offered an indulgence of forty days to those of his diocese who should devoutly visit the Carmelite church there 'in which, as we have heard, a fair image of the blessed virgin and martyr Katherine is held in great veneration.'[86] Such a gift may not have produced a large return for the friary, but does imply that the house was well visited by pilgrims seeking to venerate Our Lady and St Katherine, two cults which were becoming increasingly important in the later middle ages.

In addition to casual alms, there is some evidence to show that the friary received testamentary bequests from a broad spectrum of society.[87] As well as hosting the Provincial Chapter of the Carmelite order in 1398, the friary also provided hospitality for the king, and such links may in part explain John of Gaunt's bequest of 40*s.*, to the friars.[88] Personal connections might also result in testamentary giving by those from east Kent, but William Vaus of Maidstone gave to a large number of religious houses in the region, which may imply that reputation was of greater concern for him.[89] Due to the bias of the surviving wills, the main known supporters of the friary were members of the local gentry, men like John de Septvans of Ash who sought commemoration at the Carmelite friary and two friaries in Canterbury.[90] Each house received cash and malt, but only the Carmelites received a special gift, which may indicate that he was personally acquainted with the religious there, and considered it was an especially fitting place in his search for salvation.

For most of the townspeople, however, their predominant exchange partner in the spiritual economy was their parish church. This is discussed in the next section, but it may be worthwhile to mention the fraternity of St Katherine at the chapel of St James in St Mary's parish. Women were often drawn to the saint because of her association with childbirth and her perceived ability to pro-

Sandwich, p. 169. However, twelve (or thirteen) was more common and the first surviving entry in the St John's register records four brothers and three sisters for 1397 and seven brothers and five sisters in 1399, while a now lost entry for 1391 listed six brothers and six sisters; EKA, Sa/Ch 10J A1; Hussey, *Kent chantries*, p. 275. **85** There were twenty-four friars in 1331, but it is not known how many there were later in the century; Deighton, 'Carmelite friary', 321. **86** *VCH Kent*, vol. 2, p. 204, citing *Exeter Epis. Reg. Brantyngham*, vol. 1, p. 223. **87** Unfortunately, however, the only wills surviving from this period relating to people in Sandwich and its hinterland are the *Sede Vacante* wills, most of which are in the Christchurch priory registers; CCAL, DCc/Register G. **88** Deighton, 'Carmelite friary', 324. **89** In 1368 William Vaus bequeathed 13*s.* 4*d.* to the Carmelites of Sandwich, 20*s.* to the same order at Aylesford and 6*s.* 8*d.* to those at Lossenham; A.C. Wood (trans. and ed.), *Registrum Simonis Langham* (1956), p. 352. **90** CCAL, DCc/Register G, f. 270.

vide good marriages for young women. She was also seen as exemplar in terms of her sexual purity and devout piety.[91] It is difficult to establish the strength of the fraternity or its place in the life of the parish and town, but there is a later reference to the sisterhood of St Katherine and from this period there is a surviving *in vitam* grant suggesting that St Katherine was seen as a particularly strong advocate for women.[92] John Wynchelse senior appears to have made the grant primarily on behalf of Matilda, his late wife, for whom the members were expected to pray, though he may have hoped that at a later date he too would be commemorated.[93]

THE LATE MEDIEVAL PERIOD (c.1470–1530)

The most important feature of the town's history during this period was the decline in the economy, which affected the social and political life of Sandwich, and had significant implications for the local spiritual economy. The town's problems were linked to national and regional factors, like royal foreign policy and its vulnerability to the French, but local conditions were also important.[94] Silting of the haven and the consequent inability of large vessels to enter the port resulted in a restructuring of the economy, the cross-Channel carrying trade replacing the international mercantile trade.[95] To try to combat the town's difficulties, the civic authorities introduced a series of measures, but by the early sixteenth century Sandwich was experiencing further problems, which led to some local resistance among the inhabitants.[96]

---

91 K.J. Lewis, *The cult of Saint Katherine of Alexandria* (2000); Duffy, *Stripping of the altars*, pp. 171–9, 182. **92** EKA, Sa/AC 3, f. 79. **93** The grant was of a garden given in pure and perpetual alms for the emendation and sustenance of the fraternity; Boys, *Sandwich*, p. 187. **94** In 1457 the town was sacked, and the mayor and several other senior officials were killed. As a result of the devastation, the corporation embarked on a considerable rebuilding programme, and large sums were spent on the town defences; Gardiner, *Sandwich*, pp. 195–9; C. Coulson, 'Battlements and the bourgeoisie' (1995), p. 126, n. 30; H.L. Turner, *Town defences in England and Wales* (1970), pp. 163–5. **95** Wallace, 'Overseas trade', pp. 73–6, 441–5; Gardiner, *Sandwich*, pp. 195–9. By c.1485 the town had lost the Mediterranean trade to Southampton and London, a situation reflected in the lower total tonnage entering the port and the fall in the value of the goods carried during this period compared to the figures for the reigns of Henry VI and Edward IV. The position continued to deteriorate, and in 1548 the town sent a petition to Somerset in which the corporation stressed the inability of 'middle-sized' ships to enter the haven. Rather they were forced to anchor in the Downs where they transhipped their cargoes to small lighters operating out of the port, thereby defrauding the crown of its rightful customs; Wallace, 'Overseas trade', pp. 97–9, 446–7. Another consequence of the town's dwindling international trade was the disappearance of the Geneose colony, which had flourished in the 1440s. A group of Netherlanders seems to have left Sandwich about the same time, though some individuals from the Low Countries and France continued to reside and trade in the town; ibid., pp. 352–65. **96** For example, the mayor introduced a policy of collective responsibility towards the maintenance of the haven through the imposition of a series of

Although it might be an exaggeration to imply there was a flight from office in Sandwich, the problem of finding enough office holders became an annual event in the civic calendar from the beginning of Henry VIII's reign.[97] Yet, even though the financial obligations and the time required to conduct town business continued to be a cause for concern among the leading citizens, the power afforded such men and the opportunities for such matters as patronage may have provided sufficient recompense for some.[98] Factionalism was a feature of Sandwich politics, and though only a small proportion of the adult male population were directly involved in town government at any level, disputes occurred concerning issues like fiscal policy, the maintenance of order and the introduction of restrictive policies. Furthermore, the influx of new men and new ideas into the town and its government in the 1520s and 1530s was perceived by some to be a threat to the established order.[99] Against this background of changing national, regional and local conditions and the resultant tensions the processes of reciprocal exchange in Sandwich are explored. This assessment rests primarily on the testamentary evidence, but it should be remembered that other forms of gift exchange, *in vitam* grants and casual alms, were also available to prospective benefactors.

St Anthony's hospital or the Maldry

This is particularly true with regard to the leper hospital because it seems likely casual alms did provide a significant proportion of its income.[1] However, the only evidence of the gift exchanges involving the Maldry is to be found in the testamentary materials. Yet these records do appear to show that the townsmen

---

local taxes and the requirement that the town wards should provide labourers to work on the haven and the town defences. This policy met with some success, though some individuals and groups, like the master and brothers at St Bartholomew's, initially refused to pay their contribution towards repairing the wharf at Davygate in 1528, and work on the haven was impeded by the marsh drainage policies of the major monastic houses in the neighbourhood; EKA, Sa/AC 3, f. 10v; Gardiner, *Sandwich*, pp. 195–201. **97** The treasurership was seen as particularly irksome. In 1500 both candidates sought exemption, William Morgan because he was intending to go on pilgrimage to St James of Compostela and Thomas Bigge because he was impotent and aged; EKA, Sa/AC 2, f. 75. In 1511 Thomas Aldy, Robert Nasby, John Somer and John Worme sought to avoid being elected as jurats by missing the election. As a result, all lost their privileges as freemen, but only John Somer appears to have yielded to official pressure and agreed to serve; EKA, Sa/AC 2, ff. 192–2v. **98** In the dispute during the 1520s between Sir Edward Ringley, bailiff, and certain members of the town government, Henry Bolle, leader of the town party, was actively supported by Vincent Engham, who owed his advancement as a jurat to Bolle's patronage; Gardiner, *Sandwich*, p. 153. **99** For example, Thomas Holy, an advocate of Protestant ideas by the 1540s and probably from a much earlier date, was in dispute with the vicar of St Mary's over the paying of tithes on the farm of the town crane. He refused to attend the town court and swore 'evil words' against the mayor and jurats, which resulted in his imprisonment in the town stocks till he acknowledged his fault; EKA, Sa/AC 2, ff. 371–1v. **1** Thomas Pynnok in 1494 wished to be buried in St Mary's churchyard 'where the lepers beg'; CKS, PRC 17/6 f. 70.

of Sandwich were more generous towards the local leper hospital than their counterparts in the other Cinque Ports, but far less generous than the townsmen of certain northern towns.[2] Although donors may have seen their gifts in symbolic terms, for the hospital there appears to have been a relationship between gifts received and viability. Thus, while benefactors, *in vitam* and post-mortem, gave gifts to St Anthony's it survived, but once this flow began to dry up, the hospital's position weakened, further reducing the likelihood of support. The decline became terminal, a situation that occurred towards the end of the first decade of the sixteenth century.[3]

During the late fifteenth century, testamentary benefactors generally favoured the lepers over the poor inmates living at St Anthony's, possibly because they considered aiding the lepers particularly meritorious. Though few donors specifically sought prayers from the recipients for their small cash gifts (frequently the symbolic sum of 12*d*.), most may have believed that, in addition to the merits of the deed, they were providing a role for this marginal group of the hospital inmates, thereby symbolically reintegrating them into Sandwich society.[4] Such ideas, the clustering of gifts in the periods 1473–5 and 1483–5, and the apparent links between several of the benefactors may underline the important influence of certain prominent citizens and the clergy on local social and religious attitudes.[5]

---

2 Between 1470 and 1500 almost a quarter of the Sandwich testators (thirty-seven bequests in 167 wills) supported the Maldry. In contrast, St Bartholomew's at Dover received one testamentary bequest during the period. The leper hospital at Hythe appears to have disappeared by this time and the hospital of St Stephen and St Thomas at Romney was barely surviving as a chantry, before being incorporated into Magdalen College, Oxford in 1481. However, there may have been a leper colony or hospital at Lydd until the 1480s; Butcher, 'St Stephen and St Thomas', 23–4; *Royal Commission on Historic Manuscripts*, 5th report and appendix, p. 527. Trying to find comparable data for other towns outside Kent, especially for small towns, is difficult, but it appears 40% of the testators of fifteenth-century Scarborough gave to the lepers; Cullum, 'Hospitals in Yorkshire', p. 293. The figure for Norwich was slightly lower; just over a third of testators between 1440 and 1489 gave to at least one of the sick-houses at the gates, the old leper hospitals; Tanner, *Norwich*, p. 223.   **3** In 1506 William Brok of Sandwich bequeathed 10*s*. to be given to the Maldry following the death of his wife, though whether the hospital survived long enough to collect it is unknown; CKS, PRC 17/9, f. 311. The last known bequest to the hospital was made in 1508; CKS, PRC 32/9, f. 80. It is difficult to suggest why the wealthier citizens were apparently prepared to ignore the leper hospital at a time when there were still lepers in the region. However, the likely decay of the hospital may have meant that the inmates preferred to take their chances outside the hospital, especially as the isolation of the leprous may have been less rigorously enforced by this time; Wood-Legh, *Kentish visitations*, p. 115; Richards, *Medieval leper*, pp. 40–1; Rawcliffe, *Hospitals of Norwich*, pp. 52–3.   **4** Thomas Janyn and George Langrege sought the prayers of the leprous, Johanna Rushton the prayers of the poor and Nicholas Haryngton hoped for prayers from all the inmates: CKS, PRC 17/2, f. 112; 17/2, f. 304; 17/2, f. 194; 17/6, f. 43.   **5** For example, John Lynch made a single bequest of 2*s*. to the lazars in his will dated 1487, but he had been active in at least two other gift exchanges with the hospital. As Thomas Mundy's executor, he presumably paid the 3*s*. 4*d*. bequeathed by Thomas to the leper hospital two years earlier; and in the same year was overseer for his friend, Lawrence Condy, who left 12*d*. to the lepers at Eche; CKS, PRC 32/3, f. 137; 32/3, f. 59; 17/4, f. 46.

Local connections and knowledge and the influence of friends and others may similarly have been significant with respect to testamentary benefactors from the town's hinterland and from other east Kent towns. For example, for the early sixteenth century it is possible to trace links among the group of donors from Deal, but it is not clear why they supported the ailing hospital, though they, like Edward Mynot of Canterbury, may have continued to recognize the special merits of aiding these unfortunates as part of the their post-mortem charitable strategy.[6]

St John's hospital

Unlike the leper hospital, it is possible to investigate reciprocal exchanges between St John's and four groups: the inmates, the civic authorities as patrons, various individual benefactors, and other local institutions. Regarding the exchanges between inmates and the hospital, these occurred at entry, during residence and at departure (predominantly at death). Such exchanges were examined in the late thirteenth century section, but certain changes had taken place by this period. The entry fee varied considerably, though the underlying trend was downwards, and in some cases the inmates paid in installments.[7] Compared to other hospitals the fees were low, possibly in part a reflection of the next stage in the relationship, the giving of the inmate's labour in return for a place in the hospital community; that is, board and lodging, and a share of the alms collected *in pixide*.[8] In addition to working in the hospital's gardens and caring for the sick-poor in the harbinge, the devotional duties of the brothers and sisters were (re)stated during this period, possibly in response to increasing laxity and an attempt by the hospital authorities to enhance the spiritual reputation of the house.[9] For most inmates at St John's

---

6 The four benefactors from Deal were John Bodar, Alice his wife, Richard Mois and Thomas Baker. One of Thomas Baker's executors was a man of moderate wealth from Sandwich. One of John Bodar's two executors was John Baker, possibly Thomas's brother and a witness to Thomas' will seven years later. Both John and Thomas Baker agreed to act for Richard Mois, as executor and overseer respectively. Between them, John and Alice supported three establishments in Sandwich: the leper hospital, St John's hospital and the friary; and the other two men similarly gave bequests to the lazar house and to the Carmelites; CKS, PRC 32/5, f. 70; 32/6, f. 5; 32/6, f. 25; 32/9, f. 80. **7** During the late medieval period the fee ranged between 53s. 4d. and 3s. 4d., the majority of entrants paying 6s. 8d. and the so called 'brother and sister pence'. However, occasionally the hospital authorities sought other types of entry fee. In 1464 John Grey was expected to provide for the 'dawbyng and latthyng' of the new building on behalf of his wife's corrody and for his own place he was to donate six weeks work on its construction; EKA, Sa/Ch 10J A1. For those who wished to pay cash in installments, four seems to have been the most common, like Thomas Hatche who in October 1512 agreed to pay 20d. at each of the next four feast days of Christmas, the annunciation of Our Lady, the nativity of St John the Baptist and Michaelmas; ibid. Although rarely used (the hospital register suggests three were given during the early fifteenth century and none later), the mayor might at his discretion provide a free corrody to those who had given good service to the town or who were of good standing, like John Sacry alias Pipar in 1429, who was admiited on these terms for his good services; ibid. **8** In addition to alms gathered in the town and across the region, there were probably almsboxes or other containers at the hospital gate and in the chapel; ibid. **9** The ordinance

the last stage in the their relationship with the hospital was at death. At some hospitals the inmates were expected to leave part or all of their possessions to the house, and though there is nothing to suggest this occurred regularly at St John's, some may have donated certain items, at least, to the hospital.[10]

During the early sixteenth century, however, the relationship between the inmates and the hospital came under increasing strain. The hospital appears to have suffered financial difficulties, in part a cause and a result of the increasing unwillingness or inability of particular inmates to pay the entry fee, and to reside at the place (so withdrawing their labour).[11] For the majority of the inmates, such difficulties were apparently resolved following a renegotiation of the exchange process, suggesting that even if not all the problems had been addressed, hospital life was a better alternative than living outside St John's.[12]

The relationship between the hospital and the civic authorities demonstrates a similar pattern. The mayor and jurats apparently conducted their reciprocal exchange with St John's as described for the late thirteenth century, but from the 1520s they saw the hospital fulfilling another role in their strategy for the poor. Beggars given permission to beg in the town by the civic authorities had to stay at the harbinge during their time in Sandwich, presumably taking the place of the voluntary sick-poor.[13] This shift from the provision of aid to one of containment and, to a certain extent, confinement seems to parallel the town government's policy with regard to prostitutes.[14] In both cases, they were seek-

---

stated that all should attend the hospital chapel daily and say two psalters of Our Lady, one before dinner and one after, presumably in conjunction with prayers for the hospital's benefactors. Those failing to attend risked losing their place at the hospital. Unfortunately, the dating is not clear because the rule is recorded in the town custumal book out of sequence and is said to have been made when John Westclyve was mayor (the first known mayor with that name was mayor in 1465). The more likely candidate was his son or nephew who was mayor there in the early sixteenth century on a number of occasions; EKA, Sa/LC 2, f.70v; Boys, *Sandwich*, p. 574. **10** Only the wills of three inmates are known. Of these, Geoffrey Berde and John Mekyn left the residue of their goods to their respective executors to use for the good of their souls, their lands passing to family members or sold for the provision of commemorative services at their home parish and St Peter's, Sandwich; CKS, PRC 13/3, f. 407; 32/3, f. 89. In 1516 Sir John Wylkens, chaplain at St John's, sought burial in the hospital chapel and the provision of services for his soul there from the sale of his lands; PRO, Prob 11/18, q. 26. **11** Certain inmates resigned or were dismissed from the hospital. They were John Bell in 1520, John Carnabe in 1524, John Daniell in 1523, Alexander Tropham in 1524, William Brade in 1529, John Jasper in 1532 and Petronilla Boys in 1523. She had been absent at the election of a new sister in 1514 and as a result her 6*d*. from the 'sister pence' had been confiscated for repairs to the hospital and her allowance had been stopped until she agreed 'to do as the others do'; EKA, Sa/Ch 10J A1. **12** In 1511, for example, the hospital auhorities were unable to pay the allowances and after discussion it was agreed that all who still owed for their place should be discharged the debt. In the following year two pairs of sheets were missing, whereupon it was agreed that the brothers and sisters should replace one pair and brother Overey the other; ibid. **13** The ordinance of 1524 was partly in response to national legislation with which the town authorities seem to have been in total agreement; EKA, Sa/AC 2, f. 326. **14** The town brothel called the 'Galye' had been set up in 1473; EKA, Sa/AC 1, f. 217v.

ing to discharge their primary duty to the commonalty by maintaining order in the town. For the resident inmates such changes in the policies of the authorities were probably seen as detrimental in all respects, but for the town officers it meant they had created a more relevant role for the town's hospital in the early sixteenth century.[15]

Such changes may also have adversely influenced benefactors, though this is difficult to access except in terms of testamentary giving. *In vitam* grants were extremely rare by this period, and even though the hospital received casual alms, the amount is impossible to quantify. Regarding the testamentary giving, St John's was better supported by the local townspeople during the late fifteenth century, twenty-eight bequests to the hospital in 167 wills (one in six testators) compared to the later period when it was the named recipient in 1506, and twice in the 1520s.[16] The limited interest shown by the Sandwich citizens in the hospital as a member of the spiritual economy, even during the earlier period, was mirrored by those from the town's hinterland.[17] This may suggest that testators considered the civic authorities primarily responsible for the sustenance of the hospital, and, if they did support St John's, their bequest was part of their charitable strategy. Such gifts might predominantly be seen in symbolic terms, signalling the donor's regard for St John's as a worthy charitable institution, a part of the civic scheme for the welfare of the poorer members of the commonalty, the grateful recipients responding appropriately to his act of mercy on their behalf.[18] For potential benefactors, choice was an important issue, and one which was only open to those of sufficient means who might be influenced by those

---

15 It is difficult to assess the reaction of the resident inmates, but Robert Cok's vocal disagreements with various masters and several mayors were probably related to such issues. The authorities viewed his opposition with sufficient seriousness that they warned him about his attitude and conduct within a year of his entering the hospital. Five years later he was again in trouble when he was fined in the town court for calling the mayor a traitor and maintainer of thieves, and in 1532 he was finally dismissed for his many infringements against the hospital and its mayoral governors; EKA, Sa/Ch 10J A1; Sa/AC 2, f. 360. **16** In 1506 John Botler bequeathed 12*d.* to the hospital and William Brok intended that after the death of his wife, St John's should received sheets worth 10*s.*; CKS, PRC 17/10, f. 227; 17/9, f. 311. John Sympson gave 3*s.* 4*d.* to the house in his will dated 1525 and three years later William Baldock left the same sum to the brothers and sisters; EKA, PRC 17/16, f. 257; PRO, Prob 11/24, q.3. **17** The only known testamentary support came from John Swan the elder of Canterbury, a former Sandwich resident, and Alice Bodar of Deal; CKS, PRC 17/7, f. 148; 32/6, f.5. This apparent lack of support is interesting, especially as some of the brothers and sisters are known to have come from the area around Sandwich: John Cowper was from Staple, Avice Gyles was from Harbledown near Canterbury, and Peter Tyme and his wife were from St Nicholas in Thanet; EKA, Sa/Ch 10J A1. **18** Like the doles distributed at funerals, the symbolism of numbers seems to have been important. At St John's 12*d.* was the most common gift, while others bequeathed standard amounts ranging between 4*d.* and 20*s.*, though 3*s.* 4*d.* and 6*s.* 8*d.* were fairly common at a time when the number of inmates varied between eleven and fifteen. Interestingly, only John Kenet (1466) and Thomas Colman (1494) specifically requested the prayers of the brothers and sisters for their souls; CKS, PRC 17/1, f. 341; 17/6, f. 90.

from among their friends, neighbours and business associates, or the local clergy. The clustering of gifts to the hospital may mark the importance of influence, and there seems to have been a group of benefactors who were apparently linked through John Botelere.[19] Alternatively, a few leading citizens, like Nicholas Burton, may have used their testamentary good works to demonstrate their personal commitment to the long-term well-being of the town's charitable institution, a duty they had previously discharged as members of the town government.[20] The giving of gifts to a collective recipient (the hospital, the brothers and sisters, for use in the harbinge) rather than to a named inmate might similarly reflect the importance of symbolism in the gift exchange, though the apparent total absence of such bequests to individuals is difficult to explain.

St John's hospital also conducted gift exchanges with two parish churches in Sandwich. The sick-poor who died in the harbinge were buried in St Peter's churchyard, the hospital paying the necessary fees to provide a Christian burial unless the pauper concerned had sufficient possessions to cover the cost.[21] At St Mary's church one of the hospital brothers was hired to carry the processional cross.[22] Labour was the currency in the exchange with St Bartholomew's hospital in 1525, while William Baldock, a brother there, bequeathed 3*s.* 4*d.* to the brothers and sisters at St John's hospital.[23]

The poor

Before turning to the other two hospitals, it is worthwhile to consider the exchanges involving the poor who lived outside St John's and the leper hospital.[24] Even though the poor were not a homogeneous group, a factor recognized by contemporaries who targeted different sub-groups and discriminated against others, for the purposes of this overview it is necessary to retain the term.[25] For

---

19 John Botelere bequeathed 20*s.* for repairs to the hospital in 1453. His executor was Simon Ruddock who similarly aided the hospital; CKS, PRC 32/1, f. 61. John Botelere's feoffees, Robert Mayhewe and Simon Leycester, had already granted an annual rent to the hospital in 1451, and another Robert Mayhewe (possibly a son or nephew) remembered St John's in his own will of 1487; EKA, Sa/Ch 10J T1; Boys, *Sandwich*, p. 134; CKS, PRC 32/3, f. 164. **20** Nicholas Burton, a merchant and frequent town officer, bequeathed two gifts to St John's: a number of pieces of bedding, probably for use in the harbinge, and a perpetual annual rent of 2*s.* from his tenement in the High Street, suggesting a concern to demonstrate his continuing ability to discharge his civic responsibility to the town and commonalty from beyond the grave; CKS, PRC 32/3, f. 368. **21** Boys, *Sandwish*, p. 131. The second entry in the St Peter's parish register records the burial of two poor men from St John's hospital; CCAL, U3/12/1/1. **22** During most of his residency at the hospital, Thomas Hatche annually received 4*d.* for bearing the cross when required, the exchange continuing until at least 1547; CCAL, U3/11/5/1. **23** A brother from St John's undertook bridge repairs on behalf of St Bartholomew's hospital; EKA, Sa/Ch 10B F1. PRO, Prob 11/24, q. 3. **24** The almost complete tax list of 1513 noted fourteen paupers in the town (the names of four others had been crossed out), as well as 248 persons assessed at the lowest level of 4*d.*, who perhaps were, had been or would be among the epidemic and episodic poor during their residence in Sandwich; BL, Add. MS. 33511; Henderson, *Piety and charity*, p. 246. **25** Henderson, in his work on Florence,

the poor, probably the most important exchange partner was the civic author-ities, their policy apparently resting on two ideas: aid for the poor who were from Sandwich, primarily by regulating the prices of essential commodities, and the removal of the foreign poor when they posed a threat to the town.[26] In broad terms this approach was employed by the town government throughout the period though, as noted above with regard to the town brothel and St John's hospital, there was a change in emphasis from aid to discrimination over time.[27]

In consideration of their post-mortem strategy towards the poor, many of the leading citizens apparently adopted a similar policy to the one they had employed collectively as town officers.[28] From the testamentary materials it would appear that the unnamed poor were a low priority group among the testators of Sandwich.[29] During the period 1470–1500 there were seventeen bequests to the poor (10% of testators), and for the first three decades of the sixteenth century there were twenty-three such bequests, representing a marginally higher per-centage of testators (14%).[30] Indiscriminate gift-giving to the poor, with a max-

noted three forms of poverty: endemic (the elderly and chronically sick), epidemic (those suddenly forced below the subsistence level by severe dearth or epidemic disease), episodic (life-cycle poverty); Henderson, *Piety and charity*, p. 246.   **26** The commodities concerned were wheat, malt, meat and tallow for candles; EKA, Sa/AC 1, f. 230; AC 2, ff. 123, 141, 153, 165v, 278v, 342v. It is not clear whether Thomas Fode, common bedesman, was the special recipient of civic charity; EKA, Sa/AC 1, f. 185. However, there may be a parallel at Bury St Edmunds, where several leading members of the town each bequeathed a russet cloak to a named pauper, John Barrie, in the early sixteenth century. I should like to thank Mary Merry for the reference to John Barrie.   **27** The four pros-titutes housed at the Galye received a food allowance and the town's protection, as well as their accommodation; in return they were expected to offer their compliance within the system and at least part of their earnings; EKA, Sa/AC 1, f. 217v; Sa/AC 2, ff. 35–5v. The incidence of trouble-makers in the town books, including women indicted as whores, was first recorded in 1465 and the first recorded vagabond in 1483; EKA, Sa/AC 1, ff. 130, 292v. The civic authorities introduced two ordinances in 1523 in an attempt to control, and where possible, rid the town of beggars and vagabonds, a policy that remained in force throughout the period, and in 1535–6 nine people were banished from the town for various petty offences, including vagrancy; EKA, Sa/AC 2, ff. 326, 328; Sa/AC 3, f. 74. For the position nationally; Slack, *Poverty and policy*, pp. 54, 114, 118; McIntosh, 'Responses to the poor', 211–12, 224.   **28** There are certain analytical problems associated with working with testamentary materials, they were generally produced by a small minority of the more prosperous citizens. Women are very poorly represented, and particular customary practices may distort the findings, as may the failure to identify some poor people among the named beneficia-ries.   **29** It is possible, for example, that testators may not have considered it necessary to specify funeral doles for the poor because it was part of the customary practice in east Kent. A testament from a man from Selling included the provision that at his month's mind he wished to have three masses, plus bread, ale and pasteys 'as custom of the parish hathe been in times past'; CKS, PRC 17/14, f. 282.   **30** The figures from a study of the Wealden parish of Tenterden suggest a similar level of post-mortem gift-giving to the poor: between 1449 and 1535 36 testators from a total of 261 (14%) made specific bequests (not including reversionary gifts) to the poor; Lutton, 'Heterodox and Orthodox', p. 175. A study of the Rochester diocese revealed a similar lack of interest in the poor; Lee, 'Monastic and secular religion', pp. 179–84. Studies from outside the county indicate a wide range of levels of charitable giving. Figures for Bury St Edmunds appear to resemble those

imum cash figure, seems to have been the favoured option, in part a reflection of the increasing emphasis on the three funeral days and the testator's desire to leave written instructions for his executors on such matters.[31] Standard sums were often bequeathed, but some benefactors employed symbolism in the post-mortem gift exchange process with regard to the number and type of recipients, the time and place of distribution, and the gifts themselves, in their desire for immediate aid for their soul and in the longer term through the accumulation of prayers by the poor on their behalf.[32] Though the use of such measures might indicate some local knowledge about the poor, very few bequests suggest a degree of intimacy between benefactor and beneficiary. One of the exceptions was Nicholas Haryngton's gift of a bed and bedding for the exclusive use of poor women from Sandwich in childbirth, under the care of his wife as midwife, and after her death by her successors.[33]

However, even if personal connections were rarely significant between donor and recipient, they may have been important between benefactors. Mutual ideas regarding charity and the poor, and the likelihood of influence among family, friends, neighbours and local clerics appear to have led to clusters of bequests to a particular institution or category of recipient.[34] Though the evidence examined here was confined primarily to the testamentary materials, elsewhere the better survival of a wide range of sources has shown the value of record linkage

for Sandwich and have been provided by Mark Merry from his doctoral work on the Suffolk town. In contrast, giving to the poor was apparently much more common among the testators of York and Hull, but the analysis seems to have included the residue, which presumably alters the figures considerably; Cullum, 'Hir name was charite', pp. 184–7; Heath, 'Urban piety', p. 224. **31** Assuming that penny doles were the standard unit of charity to the poor, Nicholas Burton was expecting or hoping for 480 paupers at each of his three funeral days. Their prayers, large number of masses on the same days, further intercessory services at his chantry in St Clement's church and the prayers of the grateful recipients at St John's and the leper hospital were presumably deemed sufficient to safeguard his soul from the perils of purgatory; CKS, PRC 32/3, f. 368. **32** An item which combined practical usage and symbolism was the lamb, and John Baxtre donated thirty to be distributed by his executors among thirty poor children. This valuable resource for the recipient was also a reminder of Christ's gift to mankind through the symbol of the Agnus Dei; CKS, PRC 17/9, f. 34. **33** CKS, PRC 17/6, f. 43. The special nature of his gift may be emphasized by an example from Canterbury. Dorothy Laurence made a bequest of three sheets and two pillows with coats for the use of women in childbirth, the items remaining in the custody of the churchwardens of St Andrew's church when not in use. By so doing she was keeping the recipients at a distance from her own family, the churchwardens and local midwife acting as intermediaries, though presumably such measures would not have impeded the grateful recipients from offering prayers on her behalf; Cotton, 'Churchwardens' accounts of St Andrew', 7. The possible differentiation between the poor and poor or poorer people who were known locally by name may have some validity with respect to attitudes towards benefaction in Sandwich; M. Mollat, *The poor in the middle ages: an essay in social history* (1986), pp. 1–11, 295–300. The poor were very rarely named in the Sandwich wills. Elizabeth Engeham was extremely unusual because she named some of the poor women who were to receive a contribution towards their dowry; CKS, PRC 17/21, f. 21. **34** R.G. Davies, 'Religious sensibility' (1996), p. 120.

in the analysis of personal networks and the probability of shared values and ideas, as well as the importance of influence.[35] Testators in the town's hinterland appear to demonstrate similar patterns with regard to post-mortem gift-giving to the unnamed poor. Interestingly, they were generally equally reticent about specifically aiding the unnamed poor, the major exception being the Thanet parishes. This possibly indicated the importance of local conditions and attitudes, in addition to the influence of certain families and, sometimes, particular clerics.[36]

There is little evidence of the poor as recipients on a parochial, sub-parochial or extra-parochial level in Sandwich. In the churchwardens' accounts for St Mary's (the only parish church for which they survive) the poor are very occasionally listed as recipients at particular obits.[37] None of the accounts survive from any of the town's parish fraternities, a possible source of aid for poor guild members (like the provisions available from the few craft guilds in the town), especially in relation to the brotherhood of the poor at St Peter's church which was in existence in the 1540s.[38] Evidence is similarly scarce with respect to the Carmelites, and the hospitals of St Bartholomew and St Thomas, though certain inmates at both hospitals did leave testamentary bequests to the poor of Sandwich and/or the poor from their natal parish.[39]

---

35 There seems to have been a network of influence involving at least three parishioners at St Mary's, which was centred on Sir John Harre, a chaplain there; Sweetinburgh, 'Hospital in Kent', pp. 138–9. **36** In the late fifteenth century almost one in four testators from Thanet gave specific alms to the poor (84 benefactors from 364 testators), which compares very favourably with no such bequests from the 40 testators of Eastry and one in 66 at the nearby parish of Ash. For the early sixteenth century the people of Eastry apparently continued to ignore the poor in this way (one bequest in 32 wills), though a contrary influence was apparently seen in certain parishes: nine of the 28 testators of St Nicholas at Wade gave bequests to the poor, of whom a third were members of the locally prominent Everard family. **37** For example, John Archer intended in 1490 that 4s. should be spent annually on his obit. He appears to have left the details to his executors and the vicar who seem to have distributed between 2.5d. and nothing to the poor each year; CKS, PRC 32/3, f. 268; CCAL, U3/11/5/1. The chantry certificates of 1548 indicate that the poor were not aided at the chantries in the various parish churches; the only reference to the relief of the poor was linked to an obit at St Peter's church; Hussey, *Kent chantries*, pp. 249–70; A. Hussey (ed.), *Kent obit and lamp rents* (1936), p. 103. **38** The ordinances of the few craft guilds (barber-surgeons and wax-chandlers in 1482, tailors in 1492) in the town included those relating to the care of poorer members of the profession and the implementation of protectionist policies; EKA, Sa/AC 1, ff. 280, 284v; Sa/AC 2, f. 34v. Interestingly the brotherhood of the poor was apparently supported by men who favoured the new religious ideas; Thomas Dikdall (1545), CKS, PRC 17/25, f. 76; William Norres (1546), CKS, PRC 17/24, f. 241. **39** Of the twenty-five brothers and sisters at St Bartholomew's who made wills pre-1540, four (possibly three more within 'gifts of alms'), are known to have made bequests to the poor. Unfortunately, the scanty testamentary records from St Thomas' makes any assessment difficult, but both surviving testaments include provisions for the poor, though in John Newman's case only to the 'good' poor as defined by his executors; John Harrison (1538), CKS, PRC 17/21, f. 205; John Newman (1540), CKS, PRC 17/23, f. 56.

St Bartholomew's hospital

Like their counterparts at St John's, the brothers and sisters at St Bartholomew's were prepared to negotiate their gift exchanges with the hospital. Entry fees were generally between £10 and £19. Free places might be awarded to those who had given good service to the town; and the number of installments was similarly negotiable.[40] These relatively high fees may indicate heavy local demand for places, possibly because it was seen as a desirable alternative for those of moderate means, thereby attracting applicants from across the region.[41] Though providing the house with useful cash, the second part of the reciprocal exchange process was more important for the welfare of St Bartholomew's because the hospital relied on the inmates to maintain a high level of self-sufficiency. They were expected to work on the home farm and at the house's other holdings, and inmates with a particular expertise may have been especially welcome at the hospital.[42] In addition, the hospital authorities seem to have placed a greater emphasis on the spiritual duties of the inmates, possibly in response to the need to reduce the number of priest brothers from three to two for financial reasons.[43] However, for some of the inmates at least, their work commitments on the hospital's behalf were not too arduous to stop them engaging in business and other activities on their own account.[44] Only rarely did this appear to result in conflict, but William Baldock's case does highlight the danger of allowing the interests of the individual to override those of the hospital community.[45]

40 Walter Payntour, town clerk, was one of the few recipients of a free place when he entered the hospital in 1490; EKA, Sa/AC 2, f. 8v. 41 William Gybbe in 1527 bequeathed £10 to his daughter, probably seen as equivalent to her dowry, to enter St Bartholomew's or some other honest hospital, a possible alternative to marriage, assuming she could find a suitable place for that entry fee; CKS, PRC 32/14, f. 210. Also from the south coast, John Baker of Folkestone intended his wife should be admitted to the hospital after his death. In 1464 he stipulated that his executors should provide her with adequate goods for the best sort of corrody; CKS, PRC 17/1, f. 164. 42 The hospital authorities were prepared to pay the inmates for their work. For example, in 1525 brother Bukke was paid 4d. for his food and drink when he went ploughing, and sister Carles was paid 3s. for maintaining William Old for sixteen days while he was working at the hospital; EKA, Sa/Ch 10B F1. 43 The ordinance requiring the brothers and sisters to attend the daily service in the hospital's chapel, the saying of two psalters of Our Lady at set times, and the saying of prayers for the benefactors and patrons of the house seems to have been introduced at a time when the oath taken by the entrant was also changed to incorporate this obligation to pray for the founder and to attend divine service; EKA, Sa/LC2, f. 70v; Clay, *Hospitals of England*, p. 160. 44 Evidence for this diversity of employment and engagement in communal drinking at the 'Pelican' on special occasions or in the inmates' own rooms comes primarily from the early sixteenth century masters' accounts; EKA, Sa/Ch 10B F1. For the sisters, the farming of a single cow appears to have been the extent of their business activities, whereas some of the brothers were engaged in trading and money lending. For example, Thomas Rigton traded in cereals and livestock, lent money and rented out farm implements and livestock; CKS, PRC 17/26, f. 314. 45 William Baldock made complaints against the hospital at a commission in 1526 which brought him into dispute with the master and several of the brothers. He had previously been before the town courts with regard to his own trading activities; EKA, Sa/AC 2, ff. 279v, 363.

Death was the time of the third reciprocal exchange. Although the inmates were expected to give all their goods to the hospital at death according to the ordinances, the testamentary evidence shows that this too had been renegotiated in a variety of ways. For some burial in the hospital chapel or graveyard provided a means of remaining part of the hospital community, a position reinforced through the giving of bequests for services of intercession and commemoration.[46] Such provisions were a powerful reminder of the fellowship of the dead with the living, and that the living should aid the dead as the dead were aiding them, thereby producing chains of gift-giving and reciprocity to form a continuum forever.[47] The focal point of this relationship was to a large extent the hospital chapel, but a few inmates left gifts to their fellows which would either be enacted in other communal spaces and times, the eating of dinner in the hospital hall, or were not time and space specific, like Jane Aschowe's gift of seven kerchiefs to seven women at the hospital.[48] Thus for the brothers and sisters the ongoing process of exchange with their fellows, the master, and the mayor and jurats (patrons) was central to their existence at the hospital, a situation which was exemplified every Sunday night at the communal drinking in the hall.[49]

The annual St Bartholomew's day procession continued to provide the civic authorities with a public display of their power and authority over St Bartholomew's, underlining the role of the hospital in the life of the town.[50] As the recipient in a number of gift exchanges with the mayor, the hospital provided in return a feast at the annual procession for the participants; entry fees from new inmates which might be used for the good of the town; contributions towards civic works, like the town defences; on special occasions the assets of one of the deceased inmates; and due deference and respect through the daily prayers of the priest brothers and lay inmates for the house's patrons and bene-

---

46 William Paytwtyn in 1532 intended that 6s. 8d. should be spent on a dirge, masses and alms at his burial in the chapel, with a further 5s. spent at each of his other two funeral days; CKS, PRC 32/15, f. 185.   **47** Like the three bequests for the gilding of the image of St Bartholomew, including Robert Marten's gift of 5s. 8d.; and donations of wax for the various lights there; CKS, PRC 17/16, f. 1.   **48** Jane Aschowe; CKS, PRC 32/14, f. 119. Such bequests included William Gyblott's gift of 5s. to be used on bread, pottage and other victuals on behalf of the hospital's community, William Wodechurch's donation of 10s. to worship in his memory, and Robert Ferrar's intention that his executor might orgainize the copying of two books of surgery, if he so wished, for the hospital's benefit; CKS, PRC 32/2, f. 326; 32/4, f. 117; 17/21, f. 106.   **49** S. Sweetinburgh, 'Joining the sisters: female inmates of the late medieval hospitals in east Kent', *Arch. Cant.*, 123 (2003), 29. A mazer with a silver medallion showing the donor, which was given by Christine Pikefish to St John's hospital, may have been used at that hospital for similar communal drinking events. See figure 7.   **50** In 1489–90, in addition to the customary civic expenditure on seven and a half pounds of wax for the tapers given to the hospital, the treasurers paid 10d. for the painting of 'Stace monkes hedde', presumably an item associated with the procession. They also arranged the transport of the organs to the hospital's chapel from the friary; EKA, Sa/FAt 9.

Figure 7 Mazer belonging to St John's hospital, Sandwich, the gift of Christine
          Pikefish, a sister there. Courtesy of Sandwich Town Council.

factors.[51] Because of this ongoing relationship between the hospital and the civic
authorities, and the considerable assets held by the hospital, local people and
those from the region may have felt their charitable giving would be better
directed elsewhere.[52] Of the few known testamentary benefactors from outside
the hospital, most appear to have had some kind of personal link with one of
the resident inmates.[53]

---

51 EKA, Sa/AC 1, ff. 184v, 287. William Baldock's case seems to have been unusual, which may
explain why the town officers were concerned to establish their legal position before using his assets
after his death towards buying the bailiwick from the crown; EKA, Sa/FAt 29; Sa/AC 3, f. 98v.
52 John Coly in 1475 bequeathed 6s. 8d. to St Bartholomew's, the only testator known to have
supported all four hospitals post-mortem; CKS, PRC 17/2, f. 428. Of those from outside Sandwich,
William Kendall of Canterbury was the sole benefactor. He gave St Bartholomew's two painted
cloths for its high altar, one illustrating the crucifix, Mary and John and the second showing St John
the Baptist, St Bartholomew and St Peter. The bequest possibly linked to his son's presence as a
friar in the town; CKS, PRC 17/10, f. 90. **53** Katherine Best's desire to be buried beside her husband, a former brother, may suggest that she hoped to join the hospital community in death even
if she had not done so during life; CKS, PRC 17/16, f. 38.

Connections were also important with regard to the reciprocal exchanges with local religious institutions. For example, within the spiritual economy, the hospital paid tithes to the vicar of St Clement's church and to the vicar of Worth parish church, as well as entertaining 'the procession of Worth' when it annually beat the bounds.[54] And at St Bartholomew's itself, the two priest brothers continued to provide the liturgical and intercessory services, their labour recognized through the receipt of Easter and other special offerings and a few testamentary bequests from others at the hospital.[55] Yet, interestingly, some of the inmates apparently preferred the local Carmelite friars as intercessors on their behalf, either at the friary or at a designated church.[56]

St Thomas' hospital
It is difficult to investigate St Thomas' because of the dearth of hospital records, but the inmates probably engaged in similar gift exchanges to their counterparts at the other town hospitals. There is little to indicate the size of the entry fee or how it was paid and, with regard to their life at the hospital, the brothers and sisters may have had a much less regulated existence, though they were apparently continuing to dine communally in the hall in the mid-sixteenth century.[57] Even though the evidence is extremely limited, it appears some of the inmates at least, bequeathed a proportion of their goods to the hospital. In his will, John Newman gave 40s. to St Thomas' for repairs, while his fellow brothers and sisters were to receive all his unpaid allowances from the hospital, half a load of wood and 7s., which they were to use to make merry, presumably as an act of remembrance and as a way of stressing his honoured place in their company, a way of linking the fellowship of the dead with that of the living through the memory of his peers.[58]

As at the other hospitals, the relationship between the inmates and patrons, the wardens or feoffees, was based on a series of gift exchanges, beginning with the selection of potential inmates.[59] Several criteria were probably employed, though patronage may have been particularly important. As a prosperous citizen, senior town officer and probable member of the prestigious St George's

54 EKA, Sa/Ch 10B F1. Though, on occasion, the hospital was involved in tithe disputes with the vicar at Eastry, as in 1549; CCAL, X.10.3, ff. 97–102. I am grateful to Paula Simpson for information regarding this dispute. **55** In 1525 Sir Harry was paid 2s. 1d. for the bread and wine, 4d. for watching the sepulchre and 8d. was paid for the St James taper; EKA, Sa/Ch 10B F1. **56** Jane Aschowe intended that the prior at the Carmelites should celebrate for her soul at the parish church of Eastry, where she wished to be buried, and during the second year post-mortem he was to celebrate at the friary church, her executors giving 20s. and her large brass pot to him; CKS, PRC 32/4, f. 116. **57** Although Agnes Bolton was to receive 53s. 4d. from the estate of Nicholas Orpathe in 1533 to become a sister at St Thomas', there is nothing to indicate whether this comprised the whole fee or only a percentage; CKS, PRC 17/20, f. 3. **58** CKS, PRC 17/23, f. 56. **59** In exceptional circumstances the mayor seems to have chosen the entrant, like John Somer's selection of John Gryshingham in 1513; EKA, Sa/AC 2, f. 207.

gild, Nicholas Orpath's patronage of the daughter of his friend in his will may have been extremely valuable in the gaining of a place at St Thomas'.[60] Agnes Bolton was a widow of moderate means, and for the feoffees this and her personal connections presumably made her a very suitable candidate.[61] These men, through the giving of places to such candidates, were fulfilling their own exchanges with the hospital, and by inference were commemorating the memory of Thomas Elys, their venerable patron.[62]

St Thomas' received few gifts, either *in vitam* or post-mortem during this period, possibly because the local townspeople felt that the house had been well endowed by its founder, but also that it was primarily the responsibility of the feoffees (as St Bartholomew's was the responsibility of the mayor and corporation).[63] For those few testators who did support the hospital, St Thomas' was one recipient within their charitable strategy, most apparently preferring to place the welfare of their soul in the hands of the friars or the local clergy.[64] However, Lady Alice Septvans' familial links with the house may have meant she saw the inmates as her bedesmen and women because she stipulated in her will that each was to receive 6*d.* at her burial and month's mind, presumably at the funeral services which were to take place at the family church of Ash.[65]

Other religious institutions
The Carmelite friars appear to have developed a symbiotic relationship with the civic authorities. For their part they preached in the town, offered hospitality

---

60 He was a wealthy citizen who had previously held senior office in the town. When he made his will in 1533 his other charitable gift-giving included redeeming the church plate belonging to St Clement's church, where he was a parishioner and probably a member of the prestigious St George guild; CKS, PRC 17/20, f. 3. **61** Agnes, William Wattes' eldest daughter, had inherited a tenement and seven acres of land from her father three years earlier; CKS, PRC 17/19, f. 3. **62** John Swan was the only feoffee known to have engaged in a personal gift exchange with the hospital; that is other than in his official capacity, and his actions seem to reflect Thomas Elys' relationship with the hospital and its sister institution, the chantry at St Peter's church. He gave the lands of the old castle in perpetuity to the chantry priests, and in exchange they were to celebrate for his soul and the soul of John Grene (one of his fellow wardens for the hospital in 1464). They were also to record his bequest to them in their mass book. In contrast, his gift of 6*s.* 8*d.* to St Thomas' hospital might be seen to imply more neighbourly considerations, though he may have expected the inmates to remember him in their prayers; CKS, PRC 17/7, f. 148. **63** The only *in vitam* grant the hospital is known to have received at this time was twelve acres of land in Woodnesborough in 1481 from Henry Greneshild, a staunch Lancastrian and former mayor of Sandwich; Boys, *Sandwich*, p. 149. **64** Margaret Graunt, for example, intended St Thomas' hospital would receive each New Years Eve 100 billets of wood from her executor post-mortem for twenty years, the Carmelites receiving a slightly larger allocation under the same conditions. Her strong connection with St Peter's church may have influenced her choice of beneficiaries, especially as she wished annual masses and a dirge should be celebrated for her soul a few days after Epiphany each year during the same period. The timing appears to imply a connection between the billets and the acts of commemoration, possibly suggesting that some from the friary and hospital would have been expected to attend; CKS, PRC 17/7, f. 181. **65** CKS, PRC 31/1, f. 89.

for crown officials and others dignitaries, produced men of learning, provided an additional reservoir of confessors and mass priests and a place of commemoration at their church. In exchange, they received gifts from the town authorities and from individual citizens, many of whom had been civic officers.[66] The scale and grandeur of the friary buildings would imply that the friars continued to be well supported, but most of the surviving evidence relates to testamentary sources.[67] These sources show that in comparison with other religious houses in east Kent, the friars were relatively well supported by the local citizens. Throughout the period, some benefactors seem to have seen their charitable bequests to the friary in terms of the deed's intrinsic merit. Others, however, sought more precise counter-gifts in the form of burial or specific intercessory services.[68] Yet, for most testators, the friars were apparently seen as providers of a second tier of intercession, the parish remaining the predominant place and provider of burial, intercession and commemoration.[69] Possibly one consequence of this attitude was the absence of bequests to named friars, most benefactors apparently preferring to see their relationship with the friars in terms of a salaried priest from a worthy, local religious institution.[70]

Testators from the Cinque Ports and Canterbury showed almost no enthusiasm for the Carmelites at Sandwich, and in geographical terms the greatest interest was from Folkestone where three testators included the friars among

66 For example, in 1482 at the last meeting of the Provincial Chapter at Sandwich, the mayor and jurats gave to the Carmelites a gift of five marks for their expenses; EKA, Sa/AC 1, f. 273v. Eight years later one of the friars received 3s. 4d. to preach on the first Sunday in Lent, and afterwards he appears to have received a further 6s. 8d.; EKA, Sa/FAt 9. Such gift exchanges were still taking place in the early 1530s when, for example, in 1531, the civic authorities gave the friary a considerable number of fatstock for the visit of the king, in which the town officers wished to be involved; Deighton, 'Carmelite friary', 325.   67 Between 1450 and 1510 about a third of the Sandwich testators made bequests to the friary, the proportion remaining relatively constant per decade; for the next twenty years the likelihood fell to about one in five, though there was a cluster of gift-giving *c.*1526.   68 Although Helen Bigge, in 1496, did not seek burial at the friary, she did intend that her obit would be celebrated there for twenty years after her death, the longest act of intercession and commemoration she requested; CKS, PRC 17/6, f. 302.   69 Even though only ten testators in 334 wills sought burial at the friary, this may reflect a positive endorsement of the parish church rather than a negative reaction to the friary. Ralph Richer's pious and charitable gift-giving strategy would appear to exemplify this idea. In his will dated 1494 he wished for intercessory services to be conducted at St Clement's church, his proposed place of burial. His other bequests included the provision of a lifetime almshouse for an old man and his wife from one of his tenements, the property passing to the friars once the couple had died, a gift for which he presumably expected counter-gifts of intercession forever; CKS, PRC 17/6, f. 155. Although a few testators made bequests to the light of St Cosmos and St Damian and to the light of St Crispin and St Crispianus, none appeared to support the guild of St Katherine in this way. Yet it might have have been expected that the cult would have continued to act as an important focus of lay piety in the town, a spiritual bridge between the townsfolk and the friars.   70 Jane Aschowe was one of the few exceptions, and it seems familial connections may explain her personal gift to the prior there; CKS, PRC 32/14, f. 119.

their beneficiaries.[71] A few from the town's hinterland, however, did support the friary post-mortem, and it was the house most frequently aided.[72] Thus, in Sandwich and its hinterland the Carmelite friars were apparently the most favoured extra-parochial exchange partners by the local inhabitants.[73] Yet even they were not chosen by a majority of testators, who were primarily drawn from the prosperous leading citizenry. Instead, the parish and sub-parish were the most active areas of the spiritual economy.

Taking the parish first, the physical evidence of the town's three parish churches indicates that this was a time of continuing aggrandizement of the buildings and their contents. The primacy of the parish for the most prosperous townspeople was demonstrated by their frequent desire to be buried next to a favoured image, altar or place in the parish church; and through their inclusion in the parish bede-roll.[74] Looking more broadly at the testamentary sources for

---

71 However, these three men were among the more prosperous members of the town, so providing them with the opportunity to support a number of religious houses in the region: Matthew Warren (1458), Thomas Newsole (1465), Arnold Hebbynge (1490); CKS, PRC 17/1, f. 23; 17/1, f. 235; 17/10, f. 150. Support for religious houses generally was extremely limited with respect to testators from the other Cinque Ports. The friars were no exception, though when gifts were given they were far more likely to be directed towards the Canterbury friaries. **72** Of the testators from the town's hinterland, about 5% made bequests to the friary. With regard to the desire for counter-gifts, only the vicar at Ham, who had been a member of the friary, sought burial at the house; CKS, PRC 17/4, f. 90. Instead, testators favoured intercessory services, like a trentall of masses, though the majority rarely specified their requirements, apparently leaving such details to be negotiated by their executors and the friars. **73** Other extra-parochial exchange partners in the town included hermits living in the corner of the churchyard of St James' chapel in St Mary's parish, whose presumably meagre needs were covered by casual alms-giving. The anchoress there and Richard the hermit each received a single testamentary gift: William Baldock in 1529, CKS, PRC 17/20, f. 87; Richard Overaye in 1522, CKS, PRC 17/15, f. 188. The hermit at Stonar chapel, John Style, may also have been poor. His only known bequest concerned the chapel goods, which he left to the mayor and jurats at Sandwich in 1469; CKS, Sa/AC 1, f. 248v. His successor there was the recipient of a ewe in 1498 from the will of John Hamon of Minster in Thanet; CKS, PRC 17/7, f. 142. Of the extra-parochial exchange partners outside the town, there was a single bequest to St Anthony's college in London, a few bequests to the Trinitarian friars at Mottenden; and two chaplains in Sandwich, Sir Thomas Norman and Sir Thomas Clerke, supported St Mary's hospital in Dover; CKS, PRC 17/3, f. 475; 17/4, f. 123. **74** Such aggrandizement included the foundation of two chantries at St Clement's church by John Grene and Nicholas Burton; Hussey, *Kent chantries*, pp. 249–56. The success of local chaplains rather than the parish priest in promoting the needs of their local church has been noted by Swanson elsewhere. He considered this was because they often became engaged in pastoral work, including acting as executors, feoffees, witnesses and scribes for the wealthier members of the town, a situation that appears to have occurred in Sandwich; Swanson, *Church and society*, p. 50. For example, Sir Thomas Norman, a chaplain at St Mary's church, was involved in a number of wills belonging to parishioners from St Mary's, including that of John Quykman where he was one of three feoffees instructed to sell John's principal tenement. The money from the sale was to be used in a series of reciprocal exchanges with the church: the purchase of a new testament, the repairing of the main window at the altar of St John the Baptist there, the construction of John's tomb, and the provision of a priest to celebrate

Sandwich and the other Cinque Ports, it would appear that a large minority of the Sandwich testators were able and willing to leave bequests to their parish church, while the number of gifts to special items and named lights may suggest that for certain testators sub-parish institutions were equally significant.[75] Changing recording practices may partly explain the apparent decline in support for the parish church in the early sixteenth century, but possibly more significant was the widening of the economic status of testators, the less wealthy primarily concerned with the welfare of their families.

Another means of measuring the place of the parish in the spiritual economy and its financial well-being, is to use Kumin's method of comparing the church's revenue gained *in vitam* and post-mortem recorded in the churchwardens' accounts.[76] The churchwardens' accounts for St Mary's (the only surviving accounts) show that in 1451–2 the percentage of income from the living was 43% and from the dead 57%.[77] Over the next 50 years the annual income from the living remained relatively stable, whereas that from the dead fluctuated considerably.[78] At the end of the century, therefore, the financial position was more

for his soul; CKS, PRC 17/3, f. 237. It is possible that each of the three parish churches had a bede-roll, but only the one from St Mary's survives. The churchwardens' accounts for the same parish show that the vicar was paid 4*d.* in 1462–3 for writing the bede-roll that year and 12*d.* for reading it on Sundays; CCAL, U3/11/5/1, pp. 150–1. The donors and their families forming a continuum of believers and benefactors who would expect to receive commemoration and intercession from their neighbours and friends on earth and from the saints in heaven. **75** These figures are given to provide an indication of the relative support for aspects of the parish church at the four Kentish head ports of the Cinque Ports Federation. For the period 1470–1500, bequests to: own church fabric: Sandwich 42%, Dover 23.5%, Hythe 63%, New Romney 30%; own special church fabric: Sandwich 24.5%, Dover 18%, Hythe 21.5%, New Romney 24%; own named lights: Sandwich 31%, Dover 67%, Hythe 32%, New Romney 51%; own unnamed lights: Sandwich 19%, Dover 23.5%, Hythe 1.5%, New Romney 3.5%. For the period 1500–1530, bequests to: own church fabric: Sandwich 19%, Dover 50%, Hythe 41.7%, New Romney 43.8%; own special church fabric: Sandwich 22%, Dover 27.6%, Hythe 14.4%, New Romney 26%; own named lights: Sandwich 27%, Dover 60%, Hythe 28.8%, New Romney 68.4%; own unnamed lights: Sandwich 10%, Dover 30%, Hythe 11.4%, New Romney 10.5%. **76** B. Kumin, 'The late medieval English parish *c.*1400–1560' (1992). **77** Using Kumin's categories with regard to the revenue components; that is, for the living: offerings, including an indulgence offered on Christmas day, Good Friday, Whit Sunday, the feast of Corpus Christi, the feast of the Salutation of Our Lady and the feast of the Assumption of Our Lady. For the dead the revenue came from rents and bequests, though this assumes that all St Mary's church property had been donated post-mortem; ibid., p. 88, appendix C: description of items and definitions used in graphs and tables, pie chart 2b. **78** Collections in 1451–2: £3 12*s.* 9*d. ob.*; in 1494–5: £4 7*s.* 8*d.*; CCAL, U3/11/5/1, pp. 101–2, A, B, 172. Throughout the period, but during the 1460s in particular, rent arrears were a considerable problem, but the parishioners were prepared to provide general gifts for the church (the weekly offerings and at the feast days, especially Easter), and in response to parish building projects, like the collection for the construction of the steeple in 1448, and a second special collection in 1531. For example, in 1462–3 the unpaid rents and bequests amounted to £20 10*s.*, and in the same year the churchwardens appear to have reclaimed a house in the churchyard due to

serious because the slightly higher annual *in vitam* income now represented 71%, while the income post-mortem was 29%, though the spiritual obligations imposed on the living by the dead had not fallen.[79] As a result, in certain years the church-wardens at St Mary's found themselves in debt to the church, a situation that this apparently prosperous and well-endowed church might not have been expected to face, and which may partly explain the absence of almsgiving to the poor from church funds.[80]

   The situation with regard to the sub-parish may be illustrated using the new feast of the Name of Jesus, established at St Mary's church before 1466, and the fraternity of St George at St Clement's church, because the former was pre-dominantly an inclusive parish-based institution, whereas the latter was an exclusive civic-based organization.[81] For its adherents, the doctrinal concerns of the Jesus mass with the humanity of Christ and the claim of the ordinary sinner on the rights of kinship with him as a loving brother might have been important in terms of intercession.[82] But it may also have been interpreted symbolically, the cult acting as a bridge between the more explicit pious and charitable aspects of the gift exchange. In these circumstances the charitable gift-giving by the donor was incorporated into the celebration of the humanity of Christ, rather than for the poor of Christ, the earlier recipients of such charity. Whether such ideas may have had a wide appeal is not clear, but the testamentary evidence shows that during the 1470s and 1490s (the two clusters of bequests to the mass), support for the Jesus mass among the middling sort of the parish was relatively strong.[83]

---

rent arrears and the non-completion of repairs; ibid., pp. 147, 154–5.   **79** In 1494–5 the income from the living was £4 7s. 8d. (offerings) and from the dead £1 15s. (bequests). The only reference to the church property was to two tenements standing empty; ibid., pp. A, B, 172.   **80** Although the church presumably suffered some damage in the French raid of 1457, its wealth during the late fifteenth century in terms of ornaments, books, vestments, hangings, relics and the provision of a clock and organs indicates that it had considerable assets, implying that it was vulnerable to a cash flow crisis rather than to a lack of capital; CCAL, U3/11/5/1, U3/11/6/1, U3/11/6/2, U3/11/6/5.   **81** The first reference to the Jesus mass occurs in Richard Bilton's will dated 1466; CKS, PRC 17/1, f. 256.   **82** According to Duffy, it may be seen as one of the most popular votive masses of the period, though its attachment to the duties of a chantry priest, as at St Mary's church, Sandwich, where it was celebrated weekly by the Condy chantry priest at the Jesus altar, was a common situation by the last decades of the fifteenth century; Hussey, *Kent chantries*, pp. 257–9; Wood-Legh, *Kentish visitations*, p. 112; S. Robertson, 'St Mary's church, Sandwich' (1885), lviii. This, he felt, was the reason why the mass often became the exclusive province of the local elite, even if less wealthy people continued to provide small sums towards its maintenance; Duffy, *Stripping of the altars*, pp. 115–6, 236. Pfaff considers that although it was widely known, this does not mean it was widely celebrated; R. Pfaff, *New liturgical feasts in later medieval England* (1970), p. 80.   **83** The group of testamentary benefactors of the mass from 1466 to 1477 comprised ten lay men, a woman and a chaplain, all parishioners of St Mary's who were of the middling sort (from the 1471 tax assessment those paying between 6d. and 13s. 4d.); EKA, Sa/AC 1, f. 199. Apart from their support of the Jesus mass, this group appears to have had little common ground with regard to charitable giving. Some supported the leper hospital, others St John's hospital and some the poor out-

During the 1490s the wealthier townsmen became interested in the cult, though they do not appear to have appropriated it until the 1510s when the mass came under the patronage of certain leading families in the parish.[84] This patronage apparently continued for a further decade but by the early 1530s the memory of the Webb family as benefactors seems to have faded, and the mass was again supported by a wider section of the parish.

In contrast, the fraternity of St George at St Clement's church was the province of the leading civic officials. Such men apparently saw their fraternity as an extension of civic authority and identity, thereby legitimizing their allocation each year of 6s. 8d. from the town revenue for the annual St George procession.[85] Moreover, St Clement's was the site of the yearly mayor-making ritual, and certain leading town officers copied this collective appropriation of sacred space by the mayor and jurats. In particular, Nicholas Burton, a former mayor, established his perpetual chantry at the altar of St George.[86] His lead was followed by Henry Pyham, another prosperous townsman and former neighbour of Nicholas, who intended that 5s., from the rent of a tenement he had given to the mass should be allocated to the parish clerk, so that he might teach the boys pricksong each week and keep the mass at the appointed time.[87] Such actions were an important reminder of the power and authority vested in a tiny minority of the town's citizens, who were able to engage in a series of reciprocal exchanges intended to enhance their prestige (collectively and

side the hospital. For the 1490s the less wealthy of St Mary's parish who supported the mass may be represented by Richard Kentwell whose assets seem to have been relatively small. He left 8d. to the high altar at St Mary's and 4d. to the Jesus mass in 1498; CKS, PRC 17/7, f. 87. **84** In the 1490s only the incumbent, John Lee, might be said to have sought to appropriate the mass through his will dated 1494. In it he bequeathed to the mass a few pieces of property to be administered by the wardens of the fraternity, including the tenement next to the vicarage. The wardens of the Jesus mass were to receive the tenement on condition they funded an obit of 5s. per year for the souls of his parents, benefactors and the departed faithful; PRO, Prob 11/10, q. 23. His intention to use the mass for the commemoration of himself and his family is suggestive of the methods adopted by certain townsmen elsewhere (see Duffy below) and may reflect John's background. He was the illegillimate son of Sir Richard Lee, Lord Mayor of London, and during his incumbency at Sandwich he was in receipt of several other appointments, including a canonry at Chichester cathedral and the mastership at Maidstone college; Emden, *Register of Oxford to 1500*, vol. 2, p. 1123. According to Duffy, the Martin family 'acquired' the Jesus mass at Long Melford; Duffy, *Stripping of the altars*, p. 116. At Sandwich, Benet Webb and his family may be considered the most successful in this way because, like Benet, his wife's first husband, William Salmon, a leading merchant of the town, was also buried in the Jesus chancel. In her will dated 1520, Katherine, Benet's widow intended to join them both there, and she, like her second husband, sought to establish a temporary chantry at the Jesus altar; CKS, PRC 32/9, f. 137; 17/14, f. 206. **85** The money was first granted in 1481; EKA, Sa/ACi f. 262v. **86** He intended that Sir Thomas Bland, a chaplain, should serve at the altar for the rest of his life, and after his death the chantry should continue from the property assigned for its upkeep, his executors hiring another priest. This would continue the intercession and commemoration for Nicholas' soul, his wife's soul and for the souls of their parents forever; CKS, PRC 32/3, f. 368. **87** CKS, PRC 17/6, f. 291.

individually), and might be expected to have significant implications beyond the grave.[88]

Thus, the Sandwich hospitals formed only one group of a large number of exchange partners actively engaged in the town's spiritual economy. For all those involved, and particularly the hospitals, flexibility was an essential element in their exchange strategies. This factor is one of those considered in the following assessments of two hospitals from their foundation to *c.*1560.

THE HISTORY OF TWO SANDWICH HOSPITALS

This section examines the history of the two town hospitals in terms of the relationships each developed over time and their ability to respond to changing circumstances. Assessment of each institution's flexibility and adaptability is important because it provides an indication of the place of the hospital in provincial society during the medieval period.

St Bartholomew's hospital

1	foundation	*c.*1190 (1217)
2	founders	Thomas and Bertine de Crauthorne (William Marshal and the town of Sandwich)
3	foundation gift	unknown (French booty captured at the battle of Sandwich)
4	size	sixteen inmates including three priests
5	inmates	priest brothers, lay brothers and sisters
6	patronage	mayor and commonalty
7	own chapel	yes
8	*in vitam* grants	few; local, long-term support (mainly leading townsmen, some knightly families)
9	diversification from 14th century	little change
10	casual alms	probably not significant
11	testamentary benefactors	rare; few local townspeople, few inmates (intercessory services, to hospital community)

Founded in the late twelfth century, St Bartholomew's hospital was part of the first period of rapid expansion in hospital foundations nationwide, and its prob-

---

88 In his will of 1533, Nicholas Orpathe, for example, was apparently demonstrating his responsibilities to his parish and town: he redeemed the church plate at St Clement's church and was a benefactor of the altar of St George, thereby gaining the gratitude and prayers of his fellow parishioners, gild members and civic officers; CKS, PRC 17/20, f. 3.

able site beside the road to Dover just outside the town walls was also charac-teristic of these early establishments.[89] Another common feature was the early support it received from certain leading townspeople and members of the local knightly families, but what is unusual is the way the hospital foundation was first appropriated by a leading aristocrat and then the civic authorities in the name of the town. For William Marshal and his royal master, the defeat of the French forces at the battle of Sandwich in 1217 was a fitting climax to the civil war, and his subsequent refoundation of St Bartholomew's hospital might be construed as a suitable memorial. Such a charitable act was a worthy gift exchange between the king (through his surrogate, William Marshal) and his people, and between the king and the Almighty. This meant it was a valuable example of good king-ship at a time when the young Henry remained vulnerable to outside forces and required the continuing support of men like the portsmen.

However, the leading men of Sandwich appear to have appreciated the value of the narrative regarding the hospital's foundation for their own purposes. This led them to usurp the story and construct a myth in which they became the prime actors in its refoundation on behalf of the town with the full authority of the commonalty for whom they were responsible. The main features of the myth were the intervention of St Bartholomew at a critical point in the battle on behalf of the portsmen, the desire to honour their saviour in a manner that might be considered worthy of this special relationship, the central role of the mayor and commonalty in the gift exchange at the foundation of the hospital, and the annual public manifestation of this act of good governance and civic responsibility: the St Bartholomew's day procession and the offering of the unlit tapers to the hospital. For the hospital, its initial endowment and the early gifts it received apparently provided the master and the poor inmates with a viable establishment for their care and maintenance, at which the main responsibility for providing the counter-gifts was undertaken by the three priest brothers in the hospital's own chapel. Most of these early benefactors did not specify the nature of the reciprocity except that the gift was for their soul and occasionally for others they named, thereby implying that the gift exchange was envisaged as being with the whole house. The poor inmates in their role as recipients rep-resented the donor's neighbourly concerns and his desire to perform good works, while more personal considerations relating to the ultimate welfare of his soul post-mortem might be addressed, in particular, by the intercessory services of the hospital's professionals. The custumal provides little indication of the involve-ment of the lay brothers and sisters in the spiritual life of the hospital; instead, it stresses their counter-gift of labour on behalf of the physical well-being of the community.[90]

89 Orme and Webster, *English hospital*, pp. 35, 45. It may also have been situated close to a heal-ing spring; Everitt, *Continuity*, p. 296. **90** Although it might be expected that the lay community

Apart from their own collective role in the initial endowment of the hospital, the civic authorities were concerned to stress the participation of individual townsmen in the process, and also the activities of the knightly de Sandwich family. The family was a considerable patron of ecclesiastical institutions in the area, and its valued support of the town's hospital added to the house's reputation and to that of the town. The hospital was, therefore, in a strong position because it had been supplied with ample resources. Its individual benefactors were local men who required few specific obligations of its personnel, while the implementation of these counter-gifts did allow the hospital to offer future donors similar intercessory services, which may have aided the hospital over time. Moreover, the civic authorities had a vested interest in the hospital's success as a town institution for which they had taken responsibility. Its assets and regime may have attracted corrodians from the beginning, which meant the hospital was engaged in a range of exchange processes that might be considered to have aided its long-term survival. In addition, it may have been able to exploit its position alongside the Dover road as a means of collecting alms from those who passed its gatehouse and who may have been drawn to its chapel.[91] Thus, local patronage and civic governance provided the hospital with an enviable combination that may be reflected in the identities of some of the earliest known inmates, townspeople like John and Alice le Jeune, members of one of the town's leading families in the 1270s; and William Sandwich and Sir Luke Sandwich, a priest from the same period, who may have been kinsmen of Sir Henry and Sir John de Sandwich, patrons of St Bartholomew's.[92]

The low incidence of *in vitam* gift-giving to the hospital during the late thirteenth century and the willingness of the chaplain to enter the land market on behalf of the hospital during this period may imply that the townspeople were aware of the hospital's financial position.[93] The hospital may have been seen by a few as a valued exchange partner because it was well able to offer long-term counter-gifts for donors and its reputation made it a worthy recipient; yet a large majority of the local population apparently ignored it (at least in terms of giving *in vitam* grants). Instead, most apparently focused their gift exchanges on the

at the hospital should remember the founders and benefactors in their daily prayers, the custumal instead lists working in the fields and brewing and baking, while the oath mentions that they were to be good and faithful to the hospital and commonalty; EKA, Sa/LC 2, f. 10v. **91** The use of entry fees seems an early innovation by the civic authorities who appear to have sought such fees from all entrants by 1300 (and possibly before) as part of the reciprocal exchange process, thereby implying that poorer townspeople, not the poor, were the recipients in this system; EKA, Sa/LC 1, f. 18. **92** Alice received her corrody for life, her allowances included 4*s.* at Easter for clothing and shoes for herself and two pigs at Christmas worth 6*s.*; Hussey, *Kent chantries*, p. 272. **93** Sir Luke Sandwich procured an annual rent of 6*d.* from Robert le Cuteller in 1292/3, which he then granted in pure and perpetual alms to the altars of St Philip and St James, and St Margaret in the hospital chapel; EKA, Sa/Ch 10B A1; Boys, *Sandwich*, pp. 32–3.

three parish churches and St James' chapel, the two late thirteenth-century foundations: St John's hospital and the friary and, to a lesser extent, the leper hospital. The situation in the early fourteenth century showed very little change,
which may imply that the hospital was able to consolidate its holdings, because
apart from land purchases it also exchanged areas of agricultural land with
Christchurch priory in 1317.[94] Whether this was a deliberate strategy is impossible to ascertain, but it does suggest that the period up to the Black Death was
favourable to the hospital. The willingness of a few of the townspeople of
Sandwich, usually leading citizens or craftsmen, to engage in a number of forms
of reciprocal exchange with the hospital at this time, including the use of grants
in frankalmoin, may indicate a changing emphasis on the process of reciprocity.
Benefactors sought a more explicit relationship with the recipients, a shift from
the neighbourly aspects of the exchange to a greater emphasis on the obligation
to oneself through intercessory services, the duty to God remaining throughout. This development may reflect the growing prominence of the doctrine of
purgatory, among other factors, which may have been strongly advocated by
the friars in their sermons because they too required exchange partners as a means
of maintaining their mendicant lifestyle. For the hospital, however, the arrival
of the friars in the late thirteenth century may have been detrimental. The friary
seen as a more suitable exchange partner for such services, while part of the friary
church might be appropriated as a burial space by the leading townspeople, as
had occurred at St Bartholomew's chapel by the de Sandwich family. Yet the
small number of grants involved suggests that the situation was unlikely to impact
significantly the viability of the hospital, but instead might be symbolic of changing local attitudes towards religious institutions in the town. Benefactors apparently showed an increasing concern for the welfare of their souls, rather than for
the well-being of the inmates (by this time the poor had probably disappeared
from the hospital community).

As governors of the hospital, the mayor and jurats selected the inmates.
Although the early fourteenth-century custumal still referred to them as the poor,
the imposition of an entry fee suggests that they were not poor townspeople.
The level of the fee, up to £10, was considerably higher than that sought by the
mayor from the inmates at the town's other hospital, St John's, which may imply
that the authorities were intending to attract different groups from within the
poorer sections of the commonalty, thereby producing the most advantageous
relationship for all the parties: the entrant, the hospital community, and the
house's patrons.[95] Imposition of an entry fee as part of the reciprocal exchange

---

94 EKA, Sa/Ch 10B A1; Boys, *Sandwich*, p. 34.   **95** As an indication of assets and wages for the
period *c.*1300, a craftsman at King's Lynn had goods worth £2 12s. 9d. and a building craftsman
might have earned between £4 and £5 a year, labourers were probably earning less than half this
amount; Dyer, *Standards*, pp. 206, 226.

between the entrant and the civic authorities had considerable implications for the hospital and the perception of the place of the hospital in their town by the local citizens. Even though the fee may have varied, it probably reflected an ability to pay within defined limits rather than the idea of different classes of corrody, because the ordinances stress the notion of equality with respect to such matters as the allowances.[96] Similarly, the workload of individual inmates seems to have been allocated in terms of their abilities, and all were expected to labour for the house because the provision of their place there was based on the notion of reciprocity. Thus, the corrodian was not a privileged member of the hospital community, who had either gained admittance through the paying of a large fee or as the client of the patron and, as a consequence, either expected to be paid for his labour or did not intend to work for the hospital at all, but was expected to be committed to its welfare.[97] This suggests that those who drew up the hospital's ordinances in the fourteenth century saw the institution as a valuable opportunity for the poorer members of the town and its hinterland to join a lay fraternity which they could sustain through their own labours. The commitment of these worthy recipients of the town's charity to their hospital and to their benefactors might be perceived through the well-being of the establishment, the care with which the priest brothers conducted the daily offices and the prayers for the hospital's founders, and presumably the willingness of the lay community there to follow the example of the priests in their devotional duties. Such an apparently beneficial relationship for both donors and recipients, as set out in the custumal, may have been successful during the hospital's early history. It is possible that the situation altered during the fourteenth century, but any assessment is hampered by the lack of evidence. Consequently, the history of the hospital during this period rests primarily on the actions of the house's benefactors and patron.

For the hospital, the value of the mayor as exchange partner was not confined to his governance and selection of the master and inmates. He was also involved on their behalf in the land market, though at times this may have been seen as interference because the hospital had its own seal, and some masters may have felt they were in a position to conduct the hospital's business.[98] The mayor's support of the hospital against outside authority, especially Christchurch priory,

---

96 This seems to suggest that the individual circumstances of the applicant were seen as more important, possibly implying an early form of means-testing.   97 A corrody at Eastbridge, Canterbury cost £75 in 1358 (providing the corrodian with a generous allowance, lodging and a site for a stable), while liveries (possibly a minor corrody for one person) at St Leonard's, York in the late fourteenth century cost between £20 and £40 (usually for a married couple, possibly with one or two servants); Sheppard, *Literae Cantuarienses*, vol. 2, pp. 372–3; Cullum, 'Hospitals in Yorkshire', p. 177.   98 In 1342 the mayor, jurats and commonalty in the name of the brothers and sisters demised in fee to Robert Rollyng a void piece of ground. Attached to the deed were the seals of the corporation and of the hospital; EKA, Sa/Ch 10B A1.

may have been viewed by the inmates as a more positive aspect of their relationship.[99] For the mayor, opportunities to thwart the town's old adversary may
have been welcome, a situation that apparently continued into the sixteenth century. In 1514 John Ambrose, the prior's bailiff, arrested Robert Johnson, one of
the brothers at St Bartholomew's, and took him to Canterbury by force. The
mayor and jurats requested John Westclyve, a senior jurat, to call on the prior;
as a consequence, the bailiff appeared before the mayor at Sandwich where he
acknowledged his fault of acting outside his jurisdiction because the hospital was
within the liberty of the town.[1]

In addition to a number of *in vitam* benefactors during the pre-Black Death
period, a few individuals in the town and its hinterland may have made testamentary bequests to the hospital. Unfortunately, the only surviving testaments
are to be found in the *Sede Vacante* records. These include the testament of
Agnes of Eastry (1278), who bequeathed a bushel of peas to both St
Bartholomew's and St John's, as well as similar amounts to all the hospitals in
Canterbury, except for the Poor Priests' which was to receive a quarter of
wheat.[2] Such gifts may have had little intrinsic value, but did acknowledge
publicly the charitable status and probably good reputation of the hospital at a
time when a growing number of religious establishments were seeking benefactors, and the crown was attempting to limit the incidence of open-handed
benevolence towards religious institutions generally.[3] Yet, St Bartholomew's
may have been more fortunate than many hospitals in Kent during the early
fourteenth century because it apparently had a sufficient workforce and farmland, though it too presumably suffered crop failure and cattle murrains on its
agricultural holdings at this time. How far the period may be seen as one of
survival or sufficiency for the hospital is difficult to gauge, but the absence of
visitation records chronicling mismanagement, found at other hospitals, or petitions to the crown detailing the poverty of the house, may imply that the combination of its substantial assets and the close management of the mayor and
senior jurats, who had a vested interest in the hospital (possibly individually as
well as collectively), were significant factors.[4] Yet the hospital's apparent omis-
sion from the gift of bread given to commemorate Archbishop Lanfranc in

99 In the late thirteenth century, the mayor supported the complaint against John de Crawthorne
at the prior's court of Eastry concerning the theft of two oxen from St Bartholomew's hospital;
CCAL, EC II/35. **1** EKA, Sa/AC 2, f. 230v. **2** CCAL, SVSB II/184/1. **3** For Edward I's ideas
on ecclesiastic patronage and the role of the crown; J. Denton, 'From the foundation of Vale Royal
abbey to the Statute of Carlisle' (1992), pp. 135–7. **4** Though the *Sede Vacante* visitation of 1327,
under the prior of Christchurch's jurisdiction to St Bartholomew's saw the gates of the hospital
closed against the commissary, which may imply the possibility of certain problems at the place.
The hospital was laid under an interdict, which was not lifted until the mayor intervened on behalf
of the house and the master and one of the brothers were dismissed; C. Woodruff, 'Some early
visitation rolls preserved at Canterbury' (1918), 81–2.

1315 is interesting, especially as both of the other hospitals in the town received these gifts.[5]

The hospital may have encountered difficulties from the mid-fourteenth century, but it was not reported as suffering from poverty until the beginning of the fifteenth century. In part, this may reflect the greater availability of the documentary sources. Also before this time any assessment rests on a few extant records, like the petition by John Gyboun of Sandwich to Edward III for him to grant in alms to the hospital the revenues of the ferry between Stonar and Sandwich.[6] Yet this grant, and the further gift exchange between the mayor and the hospital concerning the goods and chattels of deceased orphans under the town's wardship, may imply that the leading citizens remained deeply committed to the welfare of the hospital, as well as seeking to retain at least a part of these assets within the town.[7] High mortality among the inmates presumably occurred at various times, the aged being especially vulnerable, but a better diet may have aided the survivors, assuming they were still able to work part of the hospital's agricultural land, while gifts like the revenue from the ferry were probably particularly valuable. The cluster of land grants to the hospital from the 1390s and from the first two decades of the fifteenth century might have been considered useful additions to the hospital's farmland, especially as some of these were adjacent to land the hospital already held and were up to fourteen acres in area.[8] Most donors were leading townsmen or craftsmen, the surnames including Westclyve, Loverik and Cacherell, families who would be important in town government during the fifteenth century. Their support of St Bartholomew's suggests that they were aware of the hospital's historical importance to the town, as well as its current value as a charitable institution under civic control for the continuing benefit of the commonalty.

Yet these gift exchanges were apparently insufficient to save the hospital from pleading poverty in 1435, whereupon the mayor and jurats decided that the cash from the next corrody should be spent on maintenance of the hospital.[9] Possibly this implied that previous fees had not been spent on the hospital, or at least only part of the fee, and may partly explain why the house was apparently in penury. Assuming the mayor had been appropriating some of the fee, it would suggest that the relationship had broken down within the economy of regard, an idea substantiated by an ordinance in the town book. The regulation stated that the mayor was not to sell corrodies except in his role as patron, which seems to imply that certain senior townsmen had been organizing the sale of corrodies, possibly for their own financial gain, to the detriment

5 St John's hospital was to receive twelve breads and the lepers of Sandwich twenty-five breads; CCAL, DCc/DE 26. 6 CPR 1348–1350, p. 341; Gardiner, Sandwich, p. 48. 7 If an orphan died, part of his inheritance was to pass to St Bartholomew's hospital in alms; EKA, Sa/LC1, ff. 27v–8. 8 EKA, Sa/Ch 10B A1. 9 EKA, Sa/AC 1, f. 24. 10 Ibid., f. 26v; Sa/Ch 10B A1.

of the town and the hospital.[10] Thus, patronage in the preceding years may
have been in the hands of a small number of the leading citizens whose exploitation of the exchange system may have badly damaged the hospital, a situation
which was seen and continued to be seen as a serious breach of the relationship between the civic authorities and the hospital. The granting of a corrody
to John Serle, common clerk, may have been an attempt to set the house in
order because he copied up the hospital archive into a register. By so doing,
he provided an opportunity for those concerned about the good governance
of the hospital to consult the regulations and appeal to ancient custom in order
to stop potential abuses of the system.[11] A further attempt appears to have been
made to reduce the mayor's power in 1467 when the common assembly
decreed that from henceforth all entrants to St Bartholomew's would be chosen
by them alone. Moreover, other inmates from the hospital were not to be present at the election, possibly implying that the assembly members were wor-
ried about questions of influence.[12] By 1480, the situation may have deteriorated to the point where the hospital was no longer able to fulfil its intercessory
obligations to its benefactors because the common assembly granted a corrody
to John Hobyn, priest, in that year on the understanding that the following
corrody should also be given to a priest. They also agreed that from henceforth
the hospital should house two priests, eight brothers and five sisters.[13] Even
though the shortage of priests may have seriously damaged the hospital's worth
as a chantry, the apparent absence of donors desiring such services, most preferring instead to seek intercessory services at their parish churches or at the
friary, may imply that the lack of priest brothers was common knowledge or
that primarily the hospital was not perceived in these terms. Instead, the hospital was valued for its role in the history of the town and its function as a residence and lay fraternity for the middling sort from Sandwich and its hinterland, especially for aged artisans and craftsmen.

The asymmetrical nature of the exchange partners (the corrodian and the
common assembly) was presumably reinforced by the assembly's second ruling
on the hospital in 1480, when it was stated that all joint corrodies previously
issued for husbands and wives were now null and void, and that no such corrodies would be given in the future.[14] The reasoning behind the desire to split
married couples is not clear, especially as husbands seem to have entered the
hospital before their wives in most instances and the civic authorities were concerned at this time about women living alone.[15] One possible explanation may

11 The register included the custumal, seventy-two deeds, a rental and other notes including the
revised oaths to be taken by the inmates and master; EKA, Sa/Ch 10B A1. 12 EKA, Sa/AC 1, f.
170v. 13 Ibid., f. 257. 14 Ibid., f. 257. Two years later, in 1482, a further ordinance prohibited
the brothers at St Bartholomew's, St Thomas' or St John's hospitals from entering into or retain-
ing any town office; ibid., f. 280. 15 The idea of women living alone or in all-female households
was seen as unacceptable by some civic authorities, for example Coventry in the 1490s, and the

be that the apparently reduced emphasis on the chantry function of the house meant that the hospital by the sixteenth century resembled the recent bede-house-type almshouse foundations. At these institutions the inmates were frequently the prime intercessors, though the parish or local chantry priest might be involved; and under such circumstances married couples may have been considered less suitable exchange partners.[16] The masters' accounts for the sixteenth century, however, indicate that the inmates had developed strategies to combat some of the problems of the split household, the wives entering the hospital to work there, possibly daily, and then returning to their own houses at night.[17] Thus the inmates were engaging in an ongoing exchange process with the hospital and the mayor and senior jurats (who seem to have regained control of the patronage of St Bartholomew's in 1481) on relatively favourable terms. For example, even though the entry fee had increased (up to £19), it was still lower than those at other hospitals; the regime, including daily prayer and labour for the house, may have been less arduous than conditions outside; the house employed servants, and some inmates may have had their own; the inmates were apparently able to continue in business on their own behalf; the hospital provided opportunities for heirs to continue in the family business and property; and the inconvenience of the lack of joint corrodies may have been overcome to a large extent.[18]

However, two events in the 1530s suggest that the processes of exchange and reciprocity between the hospital and the town remained subject to negotiation. The first concerned the failure of the St Bartholomew's day procession to take place in 1532 following the refusal of the parish priest, Sir John Yonge, to take part because he feared his premier place as the priest at the High Mass in the hospital chapel would be taken by another.[19] This event disrupted the annual gift exchange between the town authorities and their hospital at a time when social, political, religious and economic ideas and conditions were in a state of flux nationally and locally. A situation which seems to have led to tensions within and across the social groups in the town and was apparently made worse by dif-

Sandwich authorities seem to have concurred with this; M.D. Harris (trans. and ed.), *The Coventry Leet Book or Mayor's Register*, vol. 1, part 2 (1907–8), pp. 545, 568; EKA, Sa/AC 1, f. 194v. **16** The ordinance requiring attendance at divine service, the saying of the two psalters daily and the saying of prayers for the founder, as well as the revised oath, do appear to have been applied from this period, which does seem to indicate that the civic authorities intended a greater emphasis on the role of the inmates as bedesmen and women; EKA, Sa/LC 2, f. 70v. The reasons for this appear complex, possibly linked to the foundation of bedehouse-type almshouses elsewhere (the influence of London and continental Europe), the problems of a lack of suitable priest brothers, and/or a concern to introduce a more regimented regime as part of the civic policy concerning the moral standards of the poorer townspeople. **17** EKA, Sa/Ch 10B F3. **18** Brother Paytwyn's wife was pregnant with their fifth child when he made his will in 1532; CKS, PRC 32/15, f. 185. **19** EKA, Sa/AC 3, f. 36v.

ferences in age and outlook among the mayor and jurats. For many of the senior jurats in 1532 it seems likely that their strong orthodox piety might be displayed through the procession and corporate gift-giving because of the symbolism with which it had been invested by their forebears concerning ideas about civic identity, civic responsibility and good governance. These characteristics of the Sandwich administration had been achieved in part as a result of their struggle for autonomy from Christchurch priory and the crown, and the last battle was still being waged against the king during the early 1530s. Consequently, the inability of the mayor to enact this ritual, through the non-compliance of a priest who should have recognized the power of the town judiciary, was an apparent threat to good order that the mayor and senior jurats were not prepared to tolerate, and they acted accordingly. But even though the procession recommenced the following year and the priests involved at St Peter's were removed within a couple of years, the tensions within the town remained, which may explain the procession's disappearance at the beginning of Edward's reign. Moreover, it was not revived under Mary, presumably because conditions had changed still further and it was no longer valued by the town officers, who used other symbols and rituals to illustrate their civic identity.[20]

The second event was an ordinance issued by the common assembly in 1538, where it was decreed that corrodies at St Bartholomew's should only be given to 'decayed' inhabitants, that the inmates must not alienate or sell their corrody and that any mayor acting against this would be fined £10.[21] Although this suggests that the common assembly wished the hospital would once more care for the town's poor, for the inmates currently resident there it presumably implied that St Bartholomew's was seen as a less prestigious establishment. The apparent down-grading of the relationship between the town and its hospital was manifest in the emphasis placed on the 'decayed' residents rather than on the intercessory services for the benefactors and, like the town's saint, the place of the hospital in the town was almost consigned to history. Yet it survived the purge on colleges and chantries, possibly because its exchange value as a chantry was barely in evidence and its place within the town was now primarily that of an almshouse. The high level of self-sufficiency enjoyed by the house seems to have allowed the master a degree of control over the hospital's affairs, though remaining under the jurisdiction of the mayor, which meant that the relationship between them continued to be based on the concept of reciprocal exchange. Furthermore, the master and brothers were required, when necessary, to negotiate with other authorities/institutions as a means of establishing the status and

20 Like Canterbury, but probably unlike Dover, there was a small minority in the town who held what might be considered proto-Protestant ideas and a second group who were extremely orthodox in their religiosity; S. Sweetinburgh, 'Discord in the public arena' (2002). 21 EKA, Sa/AC 3, f. 98v.

position of the hospital within the town and its hinterland.[22] Archbishop Parker's visitation of 1562 showed St Bartholomew's was continuing to engage in gift exchanges with the townspeople with regard to housing the poor and, although the report of 1587 was critical of the abuses linked to the provision of corrodies there, little seems to have been done. St Bartholomew's continued to house the poor and the not so poor throughout the rest of the Tudor period, its place within the town secured if not secure.[23]

St John's hospital

1	foundation	pre 1287
2	founders	unknown, probably leading townsmen
3	foundation gift	unknown, probably small
4	size	average twelve resident inmates, range seven to fifteen
5	inmates	a priest?; twelve lay brothers and sisters; short-stay sick-poor
6	patronage	mayor and corporation
7	own chapel	yes
8	*in vitam* grants	very few; local, long-term support from leading townsmen
9	diversification	little change, possibly entry fee from foundation from 14th century
10	casual alms	vital, though probably variable
11	testamentary benefactors	local townspeople; numbers higher 15th century, almost none early 16th century; mainly directed towards hospital, explicit reciprocity rarely sought

St John's was the first of the Sandwich hospitals to be built within the town walls and its site near the centre of the town ought to have enhanced its visibility, providing it with opportunities to engage in a range of exchange processes with the townspeople and others from the locality. The two earliest references to the hospital might be seen to represent these two groups of benefactors, and their gifts to the hospital were apparently connected to its two functions: care for the poor and the provision of intercessory services.[24] Yet none of the extant grants were apparently specifically intended for the

---

22 In 1549 the master and several brothers were before the church court concerning a tithe dispute with the vicar at Eastry; CCAL, X.10.3, ff. 97–102. **23** *VCH Kent*, vol. 2, p. 226. **24** Agnes of Eastry (1278) bequeathed a bushel of peas to the Domus Die (St John's) of Sandwich; CCAL, SVSB II/184/1. Thomas de Shelvinge of Sandwich, wool merchant and jurat, granted in frankalmoin to the brothers and sisters an annual rent of 2s. 10d. to provide them and the poor resorting there with straw; EKA, Sa/Ch 10J T1.

maintenance of the chapel and its furnishings, a situation which might have been expected because the care of souls (those inside the hospital and their benefactors outside), should have generated gift exchanges for this purpose. In addition, alms to the hospital chapel might have been considered especially meritorious. For the master and inmates, this may have led to the channelling of scarce resources away from them and the sick-poor in the harbinge, the hospital's revenue instead used to maintain the chapel and clerk who served it, though whether the hospital provided a stipend is not known. It is possible that the unknown founder of the hospital endowed the chapel within the hospital building, which meant there was little need to provide further gifts for it, and the level of religious furnishings in the various inventories from the late fifteenth century indicates that the hospital had a sufficient collection of these accoutrements.[25] However, chapels were rarely thought to have too many ornaments and furnishings. At St John's this might imply that benefactors were less concerned about the appearance of the hospital chapel than in its ability to function, and under these circumstances felt it could be funded from general grants to the hospital. Nothing in the extant hospital archive suggests that there was a bede-roll kept in the chapel, though presumably there was some form of account of the benefactors which might be available for the inmates' use in daily prayers. Such acts of intercession within the system of exchange and reciprocity might also be undertaken on behalf of the collective, as well as the individual. Consequently, it is possible that the civic authorities, the mayor and senior jurats in particular, initially may have supplied the chapel, their successors providing replacements and/or additional items. However, evidence for such municipal gift-giving remains circumstantial, but the ordinances within the custumal seem to indicate that the monitoring of the goods in the chapel and at the harbinge were important aspects of the mayoral visitations. This might suggest that part of their claim to proprietorial rights over the hospital and its assets rested on their own gift exchanges with the place.

The level of endowment St John's received during its early history was not substantial, a small collection of rents and property in the town which were insufficient for the sustenance of the house. As a result, the brothers had to collect alms in the town and its hinterland on a frequent and regular basis and, probably similarly, at the gate and chapel of the hospital itself. Such casual alms-giving may have remained a vital source of revenue throughout the history of the hospital, presumably in monetary terms, but also as a means of publicly establishing the house as a charitable institution of and in the town. The importance of this public affirmation of the worth of the place and the need to support it may be inferred from the mazer donated by Christine Pikefish, one of

25 EKA, Sa/Ch 10J A1; EKA, Sa/AC 3, ff. 106–6v.

the inmates there in the early fifteenth century.[26] It is not known whether it was used as a communal drinking cup or as an almsbowl, but either use would signify the attributes of both community and charity. The hospital did have three silver crosses, listed in the 1494 inventory, which were employed at the town's three parishes to solicit alms. Competition for these alms may have meant that the brothers at St John's adopted a fairly aggressive policy, and even though the provisions laid out in the custumal were advantageous to the brothers, the foundation of the Carmelites during the same period may have affected the level of almsgiving to the hospital. Yet the friars, in their sermons, may have stressed the importance of giving alms to a number of different groups within the poor, including themselves as the voluntary poor, and the very limited evidence of charitable giving in the late thirteenth and early fourteenth centuries implies that there was a degree of overlap in the individuals who aided both houses. Thus, for the benefactors, gift-giving to these institutions may have formed parts of their own charitable strategy within the context of the three-fold Christian duties.

The majority of the townspeople, however, appear to have been unwilling or unable to engage in gift exchanges with St John's, except possibly small gifts of alms for which there are no extant records beyond the survival of the hospital itself. Presumably the civic authorities were concerned for its viability under their governance, which may have meant that individually and collectively they were prepared to aid it when necessary throughout the fourteenth century. For example, the ordinance concerning the donation to the hospital of part of the goods of deceased orphans, which was under the mayor's control, may represent a public statement of their corporate benevolence. Though difficult to investigate because of the lack of documentary sources, it seems likely that the house was less able to offer the counter-gift of intercession. Many of the brothers and sisters may have been victims of the plague and other epidemics, in part a consequence of their poor diet and the likelihood of infection from the sick-poor in the harbinge.[27] They were apparently able to maintain their charitable work in the harbinge, however, such work supported through continuing gifts of casual alms.[28]

During the early fifteenth century, the hospital was a viable institution, probably remaining heavily reliant on casual alms and, possibly, testamentary bequests, because its extremely limited capital assets were insufficient to sustain the hospital residents and the house's own charitable exchanges with the poor. The desire

---

26 Orme and Webster, *English hospital*, p. 57. See figure 7.   **27** The length of residence at hospitals was presumably extremely variable, being dependent on a wide range of factors, though activities like nursing the sick may have meant the sisters in particular were vulnerable.   **28** The late fourteenth- and early fifteenth-century inventories recorded in the hospital register were primarily concerned with the bedding in the harbinge, not the chapel furniture, which may indicate the priorities of the mayor and jurats; EKA, Sa/Ch 10J A1.

to create a more stable financial position in the first decade of the century meant that the inmates, probably under the guidance of the mayor, considered it advisable to lease for long periods most of the hospital's properties in the town. This strategy was presumably intended to generate a reliable form of income, but may not have been sufficient for the needs of the house. Consequently the mayor, as custodian of the hospital, apparently perceived the relative importance of the entry fee, especially as it was higher in the early fifteenth century than later in the century. Yet the sums were far smaller than those given to St Bartholomew's and appear similar to the higher level quoted in the custumal, which had been produced in 1301.[29] The highest fee appears to have been 53s. 4d., though there is no indication that the entrant also gave his goods post-mortem to the hospital. Rather, the extant testament of John Mekyn, a brother there, suggests that any customary rules of this kind were not generally applied; he left his goods and lands to be sold by his executors for his soul.[30] This implies that the reciprocal exchange between the entrant and the hospital was a complex arrangement. The entry fee was only a small part of the exchange, whereas the inmate's labour during his residence at the hospital was a far more important component, having the potential to generate a greater value in alms than the fee itself. The value of this labour was dependent on a number of factors, including length of stay at the hospital, the skills of the inmate, the health of the inmate, and his willingness to act on the hospital's behalf. This may have meant some fit long-stay inmates were a great asset to the place, providing a positive balance between income and outgo for St John's.[31] Thus the decline in the amount paid during the fifteenth century might have been less detrimental to the house than it first appears in purely financial terms, but it may signify that the socioeconomic status of the inmates had fallen because they could not afford the higher sums. Though alternatively, it may imply that the value of the hospital place had declined, making it less attractive than formerly. The evidence is not clear on these points, but some corrodians were behind in their payments during the late fifteenth century, and the position had deteriorated further in the early sixteenth century.[32] These defaulters,

---

29 The first extant copy of the custumal records the fees as two marks or 40s.; EKA, Sa/LC 1, f. 21v. **30** CKS, PRC 32/3, f. 89. **31** Only 12% of inmates, for whom the length of stay is known at St John's, died within a year, 44% survived for over five years, women especially lived longer in the hospital as over 50% of the sisters resided there for over five years, including 30% who were in the place for a minimum of ten years. Figures from other studies: at St Leonard's, York, for the period 1392–1409, the average stay of male corrodians was 8.1 years and for women 10.7 years, Durham hospital inmates averaged five years; Cullum, 'Hospitals in Yorkshire', pp. 188–9. At Clyst Gabriel, Exeter, almost a third of the priests were dead within a year of entry and less than 30% survived for over five years; Orme, 'Mortality', 200. **32** Even though the authorities operated a credit system so that inmates paid in instalments, some appear to have been unable to meet their commitments in the 1490s. The hospital register lists the inmates and the outstanding amounts; EKA, Sa/Ch 10J A1.

however, were still valuable exchange partners for the hospital, provided they worked for the community, which meant the master and mayor continued to tolerate them. In contrast, the hospital could not afford to tolerate those who failed to reside and labour on its behalf, which was a problem by the 1520s, and a situation that continued to trouble successive mayors in the following decade. As well as these problems of non- or late-payers, the mayor may have considered that the lower fees had adversely affected the worthiness of the applicants, which may explain the ordinance against unruly behaviour instigated in 1479 and the increase in the time the inmates were to spend in the hospital chapel, which was also apparently devised during this period.[33]

Such problems appear to pre-date the change of function of the hospital from a refuge for the sick-poor to a place of containment of those considered undesirable by the civic authorities, but it seems likely that the alteration was seen as adversely affecting the house and its work by the current inmates. As the dominant partner in the relationship with the inmates, the corporation was able to control the use of the harbinge, and the mayor and jurats may have considered that the change in the type (lower wealth and status) of resident inmates by the 1520s might justify their modification of the hospital's function. Consequently, as part of their ongoing policy against the itinerant poor, the mayor and jurats in 1523 decreed that from henceforth the townspeople were not to harbour beggars in their houses. Instead, such persons were to stay at St John's, the authorities punishing anyone who disobeyed the order.[34] Further rules were enacted in the following February, when it was decreed that only those of good and honest conversation might sell ale or beer at their houses. In addition, these people had to provide accommodation for at least two honest travellers, while vagabonds and those who lived evilly were to be examined by the mayor and then banished from Sandwich.[35] By consigning the beggars to the harbinge before ejecting them from the town, the mayor was presumably placing a great deal of stress on the hospital, both in terms of numbers and the types of persons to be accommodated. Such people were not interested in the hospital, possibly viewing it as a restriction on their ability to beg in the town, and, even though it did at least provide shelter, the food may have been extremely limited.[36] The number of beggars accommodated in this way is

33 Such measures may form part of the civic authority's ordinances about moral standards in the town, which in the case of the town's hospitals (St John's and St Bartholomew's) might be achieved through a more regimented and austere lifestyle; EKA, Sa/Ch 10J A1; Sa/LC 2, f. 70v. **34** EKA, Sa/AC 2, f. 326. **35** Ibid., f. 328. **36** If it had been seen as a desirable alternative by beggars presumably the civic authorities would not have introduced the idea of compulsion. Elsewhere, it would appear, certain hospitals were seen as advantageous if Copland is to believed; A.V. Judges, *The Elizabethan underworld* (1930), pp. 1–25; A.W. Pollard and G.R. Redgrave (eds), *A short title catalogue of books printed in England, 1475–1640*, vol. 1 (1986), no. 5732.

unknown but the bequests of bedding, during the 1530s in particular, may imply that testators saw a need for such items, as well as signifying their support for the hospital's work for the poor.

But this change of function, and so the worth of St John's to the civic authorities in the 1520s, does not explain the apparent loss of testamentary support in the previous twenty years compared to the late fifteenth century, when almost one in five testators left bequests to the hospital. It is possible that the events and changing circumstances of the decades either side of 1500 were significant: the high mortality of the 1490s, the apparent disappearance of the leper hospital *c.*1510, the decline in trade and its associated effects on local prosperity, and the likely increase in the number of the poor (indigenous and itinerant), may all have influenced the leading citizens with regard to their ideas about charity and reciprocal exchange.[37] For some of the leading townsmen it may have been convenient to set the poor inmates of St John's with the poor in the town, who were possibly less worthy of being classed as Christ's poor, thereby allowing them in good conscience to engage in gift-giving only with charitable institutions like the friars, and their own parish church. Though difficult to substantiate, the increasing incidence of petty criminal cases heard before the town court over this period, may signify the growth in civic and individual discrimination against the poor, especially by the leading citizens. Such attitudes probably adversely affected the relationship between St John's and the town, especially if those outside considered that there had been significant changes in the type of person who became an inmate.[38] Yet the hospital's new role from the 1520s provided a fresh impetus to the processes of reciprocal exchange for the will-makers, who were prepared to aid the work of the harbinge, if not the poor residents. The intercessory role of the brothers and sisters was presumably considered to be of little importance. There were more suitable alternatives, like the professionals at the friary and the parish churches. Others, for example hermits, were also available, and some testators may have preferred to have their 'own poor' at their burial and subsequent days of commemoration. This apparent concentration on the harbinge as the recipient in the systems of exchange and reciprocity enacted with the hospital may have increased the tension between the inmates and their patrons, who may have identified the principal benefactors with the mayor and senior jurats as belonging to the same social group. This might have led to disputes between certain brothers and particular mayors, while the whole hospital community may have been dissatisfied with the financial position of the house resulting from the uneven distribution of resources among its constituent parts. Thus, for the brothers and sisters, their subordinate position within the processes of reciprocal exchange, primarily with

37 St John's was also having difficulties collecting rents from its tenants; EKA, Sa/Ch 10J A1. 38 Sweetinburgh, 'Care in the community'.

the civic authorities but also with this group as individuals, seems to have meant that they had become a part of the corporation's strategy for law and order from the third decade of the sixteenth century. The duration of this imposition on the hospital is unknown, but the visitation of 1562 only mentions the twelve poor people, not the harbinge, which might imply that St John's too now functioned as an almshouse.[39]

---

39 In 1558 the hospital was still receiving bequests of sheets, though not specifically for the harbinge, but William Browne, merchant, did provide 5s. to repair the harbinge in that year; CKS, PRC 17/30, f. 122; 17/32, f. 104, 17/32, f. 235. *VCH Kent*, vol. 2, p. 226.

Conclusion

The history of the English medieval hospital is commonly seen to be one of a humble, ubiquitous charitable institution, whose survival was often largely dependent on the alms it received. As an active participant in the spiritual economy, the hospital needed to respond to the aspirations and demands of those inside and outside its gates, the fate of some that failed to achieve this being their disappearance from the landscape. Others, however, were more successful, becoming relatively prosperous establishments, where a larger staff of priest brothers and lay brothers and sisters ministered to the needs of the house's donors and recipients. Yet this national picture of individual institutions dedicated to the provision of medicine for the soul, rather than primarily for the body, hides a considerable degree of variation in terms of the form, function and wealth of English hospitals. Even though the reasons why individual hospitals developed in a particular way may be considered the result of a unique combination of factors, there would seem to be a number of observable trends in hospital development. For instance the type of patron affected its history: patrons whose hospitals were close to their sphere of interest frequently showed greater concern, though some monastic houses were known to abuse their position; whereas the crown often displayed much less regard, especially in the fourteenth century, preferring to exploit its rights to the detriment of the institution.

It would be naïve to see such trends as regionally distinct, but geography was one of the determinants with respect to the history of the hospital. As noted in chapter 1, the distribution pattern varied nationally and on a county basis. Broadly, these houses were more plentiful in more densely populated areas. They were also concentrated in and around towns, though there were considerable differences among towns, and along important pilgrimage roads or other routes, often close to bridges, gates and wells. Such factors also had implications in terms of the propensity for particular types of hospital to be found in certain areas. As Brown noted for the diocese of Salisbury, there was a contrast in the incidence of almshouses across the diocese; the greater number in Berkshire, a product of the more numerous small market towns compared to rural Dorset.[1]

---

1 Brown, *Piety in the diocese of Salisbury*, p. 201.

The presence of monasteries in a region, especially Benedictine houses, also seems to have been a contributing factor to a higher density of hospital provision, and many of these were urban or suburban institutions in the vicinity of the mother house. Ancient borough status similarly produced the likelihood of the foundation of neighbouring leper houses, the townsmen believing that their corporate duty should include places for the local lepers. Certain members of the nobility, some linked by marriage and/or friendship, were also heavily involved in the founding and supporting of early leper and non-leper houses. This group of founders was similarly instrumental in the establishment of monasteries, especially Augustinian houses, in the late eleventh and twelfth centuries; the houses, like the hospitals, were often sited near to the family's patrimony or other landholding. Consequently, patterns of seigniorial landholding and political influence affected the distribution of hospital building during the early phase, but were less significant for the late medieval almshouses whose founders were rarely men of noble rank.

Many of the almshouse founders were townspeople, either working individually or less commonly as part of guilds, whose houses frequently added to the places already available in the town. Other houses were established in towns where there had been no known hospital, a topographical widening of charitable provision for poor and poorer people. Yet some of these later houses employed strict discriminatory policies regarding those admitted, a practice that seems to have become more common at the surviving ancient hospitals by the late fifteenth century, though many of these, too, may always have employed a degree of selectivity. Thus, over the medieval period the availability of such charitable opportunities varied nationally, regionally and locally for those seeking institutional aid. However, as Harvey pointed out, this was not a simple shift from non-discriminatory to discriminatory almsgiving between the twelfth and fifteenth centuries; rather at certain places during particular times the types of recipient aided were subject to change.[2] Such changes were not incompatible with the charitable ideal because it was perceived to be an inclusive construct within which a wide range of gift-exchange processes might be employed. Benefactors and patrons might use the language of charity in the thirteenth century, for example, for a number of different exchange forms with the hospital, and their successors in the fifteenth century were similarly prepared to deploy a shared vocabulary whereby they too saw themselves as charitable donors. In some instances, as at God's House, Ewelme, this might involve more complex arrangements and the inclusion of conditional clauses which were intended to maintain the right working of these prayerful institutions, but elsewhere this responsibility was apparently placed on executors, feoffees or those in authority at the hospital.[3] Nonetheless, even though it was possible to pick out national

2 Harvey, *Living*, pp. 7–9.   3 Richmond, 'Victorian values', pp. 224–41.

trends towards an increasing complexity of the processes of gift exchange involving founders/patrons/benefactors and their hospital and the apparent rise in the number of such exchanges over the later middle ages, it was far more difficult to ascertain why this occurred except in broad terms.

One way of overcoming the difficulty and thereby understanding more fully the changing place of the hospital in medieval society was the employment of a regional approach. The assessment of the medieval hospitals of Warwickshire and Wiltshire provided a contrast between a county where most hospitals were in the two largest towns of Warwick and Coventry and one where six towns each had at least two hospitals. The importance of aristocratic patronage and later the founding activities of wealthy townsmen in the former were echoed in Wiltshire, though crown and episcopal patronage were also significant and the almshouse founders were drawn from more diverse social groups. The involvement of citizens in the founding and supporting of almshouses had interesting parallels in parts of Kent, suggesting the value, in terms of civic pride and duty, placed on such institutions, by townspeople from the middling sort, as well as members of the corporation.

Turning to the Kent evidence, the regions studied were characterized by their closeness to London and continental Europe and their high degree of urbanization. These factors had a considerable impact on such matters as the topographical distribution of foundations, types of founder, patronage, the variability of hospital function, sources of benefaction, the popularity of the hospital, both for donors and recipients, and how these changed over time. The aristocracy generally showed little interest in either founding or supporting hospitals in Kent, though there were a few remarkable exceptions, their indifference probably due to most having their main landholdings outside the county. Instead, senior churchmen and prosperous townsmen were the principal founders and benefactors, the former including several members of the episcopy at Canterbury and Rochester and abbots from many of Kent's Benedictine houses. Following the example of Archbishop Lanfranc, these churchmen saw their hospitals as literally and symbolically aiding the poor man at their gate, a charitable gift exchange with mankind which would enhance the prestige of their own foundation.

For the townsmen, too, the provision and support of houses for the leprous and the poor in or near their town was a symbolically rich act of charity. The predominance from the late twelfth century of this group of founders was a reflection of the considerable number of small, ancient urban settlements close to the old Roman road between London and Canterbury and the pre-Conquest towns of the Cinque Ports Federation. These town hospitals characteristically offered few places, most had a priest serving at the hospital chapel, the brothers and sisters living as a secular community. During the high middle ages such houses were sometimes supported by members of local knightly families, but throughout the medieval period most benefactors were local townspeople who wished to provide for poorer and infirm members of the local community, and occasionally those from further afield who probably already had connections with the town. For these people, their gift exchanges with the hospital encompassed many of the seven corporal acts of mercy, necessary prerequisites if they were to claim their place among Christ's sheep, but also demonstrated their concern for the well-being of the house as part of the secular and religious fabric of the town. By so doing they were fulfilling their social duty to their fellow townspeople, motives understood by some founders, like Simon Potyn of Rochester, who chose feoffees from among the citizenry and a local priest to act as patrons of his hospital.[4] Elsewhere, particularly in the Cinque Ports, the civic authorities were entrusted with the patronage of such hospitals and, like the feoffees, they were under a moral as well as a legal obligation to maintain and monitor the house and its inmates. This apparent confidence in the collective responsibility of the leading citizens and the desire to keep the hospital outside ecclesiastical governance seems to have been a feature of the Cinque Ports, but less so at the cathedral cities of Canterbury and Rochester. Here, lay foundations were more likely to fall under ecclesiastical patronage, which meant most of these hospitals were subordinate to a local Benedictine monastery or to the archbishop. As a result some of the hospitals were under a Rule, like those founded by the monasteries, a factor which seems to have had implications for their survival during the Reformation period. Unlike their counterparts in the Cinque Ports, which were under lay control and were part of the town's provision for its more unfortunate citizens, these hospitals were perceived to be outside the city, symbolically as well as often physically. Consequently, interest in their survival was minimal, even when some of the inmates had local connections. Yet a number of the Canterbury hospitals, in particular, did survive. The most important were Lanfranc's great hospitals and Maynard's far more modest establishment, while the third archiepiscopal hospital of St Thomas exchanged its pilgrims for soldiers returning from the French wars and the Poor Priests' hospital became the city's bridewell in Elizabeth's reign.

Other hospitals deeply affected by matters of patronage were those few under the jurisdiction of the crown. As discussed in chapter 2, the royal hospitals at Ospringe and Dover were pleading poverty in the fourteenth century. This was due primarily to the considerable demands of the king regarding short-term hospitality and the provision of places for aged and infirm servants, royal corrodians who, from the hospital's standpoint were immortal, because on the death of one, another took his place. The apparent lack of regard shown by successive kings and problems of maladministration, which absent patrons failed to correct, were significant factors in the loss of the Ospringe hospital in the late fifteenth century. Although it was one of a number of casualties in Kent in the late middle

4 Thorpe, *Registrum Roffense*, p. 546.

ages, its demise was characterized by a process of gift exchange that might be said to have 'gone wrong'.

The process also went wrong at the royal Dover hospital, but there its greater wealth apparently saved it until the same wealth became a liability, and St Mary's perished at the hands of Cromwell's treasure seekers. Its origins had been far more auspicious. It had been well endowed by first Hubert de Burgh and then his royal master for the sustenance of pilgrims, a traffic perceived to be the mainstay of the town's economy for most of the remainder of the medieval period. As such it might have been expected that the Dover townspeople would have supported the hospital, but its place outside the town in all senses was detrimental to its relationship with the local community. Although the townsfolk probably recognized its regional and national importance, the Maison Dieu remained a potent symbol of royal overlordship, alongside the castle and the warden of the Cinque Ports' court at St James' church, and consequently few of the known benefactors were from Dover. Instead, the citizens saw their spiritual affiliations in terms of the ancient minster church of St Martin-le-Grand, the town's parish churches and the great candle, the town's votive offering to St Thomas of Canterbury.

This did appear to change during the later part of Sir John Clerke's mastership of St Mary's hospital, once he had become active on the town's behalf with respect to the harbour works. Sir John's involvement included his time and money, and his commitment to Dover's welfare seems to have resulted in an increase in the testamentary bequests made to the house. Many of these were directed towards Sir John for the provision of intercessory services on behalf of the donor, though other priests there were also remembered, but not the poor who apparently continued to find sustenance at the hospital until its dissolution. The failure of the local townsfolk to support this aspect of St Mary's charitable activities, at least through post-mortem gifts, may be linked to the foundation of a number of civic almshouses in the late fifteenth century and the increasing employment of dole payments to the poor at funerals and other services during the early sixteenth century. Yet the poor people targeted by the Dover testators were probably frequently local persons, often known to the executors who saw their duty as the means of providing respectability, like the giving of dowries to poor maidens. Consequently, these beneficiaries, like the priest brothers, were expected to 'repay' their benefactors through the giving of counter-gifts, which meant that they, too, were seen as belonging to the community of Dover. In the case of the Maison Dieu, however, it was not enough to save the house and some of the townspeople viewed its demise as advantageous, personally and communally.

St Bartholomew's hospital also seems to have remained an outside institution conceptually for most of its existence, except possibly during its early years when it is known to have received a number of *in vitam* grants from local people. Thus, even though its leper and later poor and infirm brothers and sisters were expected to pray daily for the Dover citizenry on land and at sea, there is little to suggest that this counter-gift generated further gift exchanges, either on an individual or group basis. Moreover, as a daughter house of Dover priory, it was associated with a religious establishment that had acquired the assets of the minster church and had taken the place of that church at the apex of the ecclesiastical structure in Dover. Like St Mary's hospital, therefore, St Bartholomew's connections with an institution which exercised jurisdiction over the town did nothing to strengthen its own links with Dover but, unlike that hospital, none of its personnel are known to have aided the town as Sir John Clerke sought to do. Instead, its main point of contact may have been as a collector of rents for its town properties, an activity that presumably did not enhanced its reputation, nor make it attractive to testators seeking charitable recipients, either in the form of professional intercessors or poor persons. The almost total absence of testamentary bequests to St Bartholomew's hospital during the fifteenth and early sixteenth centuries seems to support this view and, when the hospital was destroyed, shortly after the sacking of the priory, there were men like John Bowle ready to prosper from its demolition.

This is in marked contrast to the attitude of the leading townsmen of Sandwich who, through their patronage of at least two of the town's hospitals, recognized them to be significant local and regional institutions, a perception further acknowledged in the extent of the area of recruitment of the hospitals' inmates. Even the less prestigious St John's hospital housed those from other Cinque Ports and from several east Kent villages, while St Bartholomew's more extensive catchment area underlined the town's role in the provision of renowned charitable accommodation. Moreover, the survival of both hospitals and St Thomas' into the seventeenth century, even though there were some problems over the type of inmate selected, may have influenced one of the town's leading Elizabethan citizens, Sir Roger Manwood, to found a school in Sandwich but his almshouses at Canterbury.

The importance of the town hospitals to the local community was not confined to their charitable role. The myth concerning the foundation of St Bartholomew's hospital was part of the civic ideology, an ideology perpetuated through the annual civic pilgrimage to St Bartholomew's and the gift exchange of Sandwich's votive offering to its saint in his and the town's hospital. Like any ritual, the annual procession was open to a range of interpretations over time by participants, bystanders and others, and for the senior members of the corporation its continuing relevance was its value as a symbol of their and their ancestors' and successors' good governance of the town. This symbol was especially potent at times of crisis, like the 1260s, the 1290s, the 1360s and 1370s, and the 1520s and 1530s. Consequently, when the ritual was under attack in 1532 by members of the clergy and those outside the leading citizenry, the senior civic officials took swift and drastic action to reclaim the procession. It is interesting that like their counterparts at Dover, who continued to send the giant candle until the destruction of Becket's shrine in 1538, the leading men of Sandwich sanctified their role as guardians of the town through the rich symbolism of Catholicism until the last years of Henry VIII's reign, but made no attempt to revive it under Mary, and thereafter developed other civic practices.

The roles undertaken by St John's hospital were similarly wide ranging, and its adaptability meant that it, too, remained an integral part of local society from the late thirteenth century. During its early history the civic authorities, as patrons, viewed it as a corporate charitable establishment for the benefit of Sandwich, its chaplain and lay brothers and sisters, the poorer middling sort who may have been old or infirm, administering to the needs of a few sick-poor people. However, by the early sixteenth century Sandwich's needs had changed, according to the leading citizens, and St John's was envisaged as an important part of the town's strategy against vagrancy and the containment and control of the poor. This departure from the traditional notion of voluntary entry to the hospital and the problem of keeping undesirables out seemed to mark an early attempt at what Pullan called the 'redemptive' role of charity, and its use in Sandwich may indicate the influence of continental ideas regarding the treatment of the poor.[5] Yet, as at St Bartholomew's, the introduction of change brought a degree of tension to the life of the hospital, leading to disagreements and a widening of the social divide between the resident inmates and their patrons. For the mayor and jurats this may have been seen as unfortunate but necessary, because their prime objective was the good of the commonalty through the maintenance of order.

The foundation of St Thomas' hospital in the late fourteenth century seems to mark earlier changes regarding the nature of institutional aid for the poor in Sandwich. Unlike certain almshouse founders in England during the late fourteenth and fifteenth centuries, Thomas Elys apparently envisaged his chantry and hospital as separate but complementary, a strategy that meant his almshouse was closer in conception to the maisondieu than to the bedehouse. Although the paucity of the extant testamentary sources in Kent for this period may explain why his house appears to be a new development in the county, Cullum's Yorkshire evidence indicates that elsewhere such houses were in existence by 1400.[6] Furthermore, maisondieu-type almshouses were founded in Kent from at least the mid-fifteenth century. Many were ephemeral, some surviving only for the lifetime of the first recipient, but the concept that aid for one's neighbour might be sufficient in the eyes of God without placing the beneficiary in the role of bedesman continued to inspire the thinking of some founders throughout the sixteenth century.

This use of detailed town studies to inform the findings of the regional study of Kent and vice versa with regard to an assessment of the role of the hospital

5 B. Pullan, 'Support and redeem' (1988), 181–2.   6 Cullum, 'Pore people harberles', pp. 43–4.

in the provincial town is successful because of the quality of the documentary sources. Those for Sandwich are especially rich, offering rare insights into the relationships particular hospitals developed with different individuals and groups, fellow partners in the spiritual economy. As a consequence, it has been possible to gain a better understanding of the importance of the hospital as one partici-pant among many, but one which might be significant on a number of levels, its place at times unstable, a product of complex systems and processes of gift-giving and reciprocity. Moreover, such insights were not confined to the hos-pital's religious roles; rather, the sources allowed the assessment to be extended to encompass the social and political. Thus, through the employment of a com-plementary strategy which examined the hospital across a wide range of differ-ent levels, the resulting analysis enhances our understanding of the social and religious history of medieval England.

Bibliography

MANUSCRIPT SOURCES

Bodleian Library, Oxford
Rawlinson MS. B.335, Register of St Bartholomew's hospital at Buckland by Dover
Rawlinson MS. B.336, Cartulary of St Radigund's abbey at Bradsole near Dover

British Library, London
Add. Ch. 16176, 16180, 16181, 16428, 16429, 16434, 16439, Maison Dieu Charters, Dover
Add. MS. 6166, ff. 213–217v., Charters of the Maison Dieu, Dover
Add. MS. 25108, Maison Dieu Deeds, Dover
Add. MS. 29615, Dover Chamberlains' Accounts 1365–1453
Add. MS. 29616, Dover Chamberlains' Accounts 1462–1485
Add. MS. 29618, Dover Chamberlains' Accounts 1509–1546
Add. MS. 29810, Dover Chamberlains' Accounts 1434–1458
Add. MS. 32098, Cartulary St James' hospital, Canterbury
Add. MS. 33511, includes Sandwich Treasurers' Accounts for 1462–3
Add. MS. 62710, ff. 1v–6, Rental of the Maison Dieu, Dover
Egerton MS. 1912, Churchwardens' Accounts of St Mary's church, Dover
Egerton MS. 2090, Dover Chamberlains' Accounts 1465–1479; Record of pleas before the mayor, bailiff and jurats 1466–1476
Egerton MS. 2091, Dover Chamberlains' Accounts 1382–1424; Record of pleas before the mayor, bailiff and jurats 1383–1386
Egerton MS. 2092, Dover Chamberlains' Accounts 1439, 1509–1545
Egerton MS. 2093, Records of Hornblowings, Common Assemblies etc. 1520–1547
Egerton MS. 2094, Records of Hornblowings, Common Assemblies etc. 1506–1511, 1550–1577
Egerton MS. 2107, Dover Chamberlains' Accounts 1485–1511
Egerton MS. 2108, Dover Harbour Accounts 1510–1564
Harley MS. 636, *Polistorie de Jean de Canterbury*
Stowe MS. 850, Inventory of evidences, charters, writings belonging to the Maison Dieu, Dover; Dover Custumal

Canterbury Cathedral Archives and Library
CC/FA 2, 4, 5, Canterbury City Accounts 15th century
CC/Woodruff Bundle LIV/2

DCc/Almoner 60, Christchurch priory almoner's accounts 1437–8
DCc/Chartae Antiquae E.159
DCc/Chartae Antiquae W.237
DCc/DE 26
DCc/EC II/35
DCc/EC IV/74
DCc/EC V/7
DCc/FX 7, Account roll of Eastbridge hospital, Canterbury 1327–8
DCc/Lit. MS. C11, Accounts of monk keeper of Martyrdom
DCc/Lit. MS. C20, Register of St Lawrence's hospital, Canterbury
DCc/Reg. E, Christchurch priory register
DCc/Reg. G, Christchurch priory register
DCc/Reg. H, Christchurch priory register
DCc/U13/1, Pittance Book of St John's hospital, Canterbury 1538–49
DCc/U13/2, Admissions register St John's hospital, Canterbury 1538–57
DCc/U14/2, Account roll St Augustine's abbey, Canterbury 1510x1530
DCc/U24 A–H, J–N, Deeds of Eastbridge hospital, Canterbury
SVSB II/184/1
SVSB II/186/1
SVSB II/190/1
U3/11/5/1, Churchwardens' Accounts of St Mary's church, Sandwich 1444–1582
U3/11/6/5, Bede-roll of St Mary's church, Sandwich c. 1447
U3/12/1/1, Composite register of St Peter's church, Sandwich from 1538
U39/2/K
X.10.3.
Y.4.4. AC

Centre for Kentish Studies, Maidstone
PRC 16/1 – 3, Original wills
PRC 17/1 – 35, Wills registered in the Archdeaconry Court of Canterbury 1448–1558
PRC 32/1 – 27, Wills registered in the Consistory Court of Canterbury 1396–1558
PRC 33/1, Wills registered in the peculiar of Wingham
Wills examined for the following parishes:
   Alkham, Ash, Buckland, Canterbury (All Saints, Holy Cross, St Alphage, St Andrew,
   St Dunstan, St George, St Mary Bredin, St Mary Bredman, St Mary de Castro, St
   Mary Northgate, St Mildred, St Paul, St Peter, St Sepulchre, Christchurch & not spec-
   ified), Capel le Ferne, Charlton, Chislet, Coldred, Deal, Dover (St James, St John, St
   Mary, St Mary de Castro, St Nicholas, St Peter), East Langdon, Eastry, Folkestone,
   Fordwich, Goodnestone, Great Mongeham, Guston, Hakington, Ham, Harbledown,
   Hawkinge, Hougham, Hythe, Little Mongeham, Lydd, Minster in Thanet, Monkton,
   New Romney (St Laurence, St Martin, St Nicholas), Nonington, Northbourne, Old
   Romney, Poulton, Preston by Wingham, Ringwold, River, Sandwich (St Clement,
   St Mary, St Peter), Saltwood, Sholden, Staple, Stourmouth, St John in Thanet, St
   Lawrence in Thanet, St Margaret at Cliffe, St Nicholas at Wade, St Peter in Thanet,
   Sutton, Swinfield, Thanington, Tilmanstone, Waldershare, Walmer, Westbere,
   Westcliffe, West Hythe, West Langdon, Wingham, Woodnesborough, Worth.

Corpus Christi College, Cambridge
MS. 16
MS. 59

East Kent Archives
Do/ZQ 01–11, Maison Dieu deeds 1227x1472
Do/ZZ 02/01 15
hbarth 5, 8, 21, 22d, 24–26, 26a, 26b, 26c, 27, 29–71, Deeds of St Bartholomew's hospital at Hythe (transcription supplied by A.F. Butcher)
Hythe: 1178a, Churchwardens' Account 1480–1
NR/FAe 3, New Romney Chamberlains' Accounts 1448–1527
NR/JB 1A, New Romney Court Book 1446
Sa/AC 1, Sandwich Year Book (The Old Black Book) 1431–1487
Sa/AC 2, Sandwich Year Book (The White Book) 1488–1527
Sa/AC 3, Sandwich Year Book (The Old Red Book) 1527–1551
Sa/Ch 10B A1, Register of St Bartholomew's hospital, Sandwich
Sa/Ch 10B F1, Account roll of St Bartholomew's hospital, Sandwich c. 1525
SaCh 10B F2, Account roll of St Bartholomew's hospital, Sandwich 1534 or 5
Sa/Ch 10B F3/1–17, Account books of St Bartholomew's hospital, Sandwich 1543–
Sa/Ch 10B T1, Deeds of St Bartholomew's hospital, Sandwich
Sa/Ch 10J A1, Admissions Register of St John's hospital, Sandwich 1397–
Sa/Ch 10J T1, Deeds of St John's hospital, Sandwich
Sa/FAt 2–30, Sandwich Treasurers' Accounts 1454–1534
Sa/LC 1, Sandwich Custumal late 14th century
Sa/LC 2, Sandwich Custumal early 15th century
Sa/LC 9, includes list of mayors from 1415
Sa/LZ 2, Tithe dispute involving St Bartholomew's hospital 1549
Sa/TB 1, Sandwich Deeds 1311–1421
Sa/TB 2, Sandwich Deeds 1430–1484
Sa/TB 3, Sandwich Deeds 1484–
U2246/1/Q1, Maison Dieu lease 1387

Lambeth Palace Library, London
MS. 241, Register of Dover Priory
MS. 1131 & 1132, Charters, deeds, regulations for Northgate and Harbledown hospitals, Canterbury

Medway Archives, Strood
DRc/T573 – 611A, Deeds of St Mary's hospital, Strood
DRc/F44 Master's Account, St Mary's hospital, Strood 1347–8
DRc/F45 – 47 Warden's Accounts, St Bartholomew's hospital, Chatham 15th century

Public Record Office, London
C 143/394/35
C 143/421/9
C 143/441/2

C 143/441/8

E36/154

E179/230/200b

Wills proved in the Prerogative Court of Canterbury [Prob] for Sandwich, Dover, Ash
    1415–1558

St John's College, Cambridge

D8.33–5; D8.170; D8.225

D9.16; D9.220

D10.10,

D12.1–4

D2/1/3b

PRINTED SOURCES

An entry followed by a ★ indicates a primary source

J. Adair, *The pilgrims way: shrines and saints in Britain and Ireland* (London 1978).

D. Aers, *Community, gender, and individual identity: English writing, 1360–1430* (London and
    New York 1988).

A. Appadurai, 'Introduction: commodities and the politics of value' in A. Appadurai
    (ed.), *The social life of things* (Cambridge 1986), pp. 3–63.

Y. Arai, 'Sir William Stonor and the God's House at Ewelme' in *What do 'medieval doc-
    uments' reflect?*, summarized proceedings of the sessions of 107 and 207 of the
    International Medieval Congress, Leeds University (2002), pp. 103–7.

M. Aston, '"Caim's Castles": poverty, politics, and disendowment' in R. Dobson (ed.),
    The church, politics and patronage in the fifteenth century (Gloucester 1984), pp. 45–81.

— 'Death' in R. Horrox (ed.), *Fifteenth-century attitudes: perceptions of society in late medieval
    England* (Cambridge and New York 1994), pp. 202–28.

B. Bailey, *Almshouses* (London 1988).

A.T. Bannister, 'The hospital of St Katherine at Ledbury', *Transactions of the Woolhope
    Naturalists Field Club*, 25 (1918–20), 63–70.

C.M. Barron, 'The parish fraternities of medieval London' in C.M. Barron and C.
    Harper-Bill (eds), *The church in pre-Reformation society: essays in honour of F.R.H. du
    Boulay* (Woodbridge 1985), pp. 13–37.

— 'London 1300–1540' in D.M. Palliser (ed.), *The Cambridge urban history of Britain*, vol.
    1 (Cambridge 2000), pp. 395–440.

J. Barrow, 'Churches, education and literacy in towns 600–1300' in D.M. Palliser (ed.),
    The Cambridge urban history of Britain, vol. 1 (Cambridge 2000), pp. 127–52.

S. Bartlett, 'The leper hospitals of St Margaret and St Mary Magdalen, by Gloucester',
    Transactions of the Bristol and Gloucester Archaeological Society, 20 (1895–6), 127–37.

G. Baumann, 'Ritual implicates 'Others': rereading Durkheim in a plural society' in D.
    de Coppet (ed.), *Understanding rituals*, European Association of Social Anthropologists
    (London 1992), pp. 97–116.

G. Belfield, 'Cardinal Beaufort's almshouse of Noble Poverty at St Cross, Winchester',
    Proceedings of the Hampshire Field Club Archaeological Society, 38 (1982), 103–11.

J. Bennett, 'Conviviality and charity in medieval and early modern England', *Past & Present*, 134 (1992), 19–41.

— 'Debate', *Past & Present*, 154 (1997), 223–42.

P. Bennett, 'The Poor Priests' hospital – the chapel', *Archaeologia Cantiana*, 98 (1982), 216–20.

— 'St John's hospital and St John's nursery', *Archaeologia Cantiana*, 108 (1990), 226–31.

H. Bentwich, *History of Sandwich* (Sandwich 1971).

C. Berridge, *Almshouses of London* (Leatherhead 1987).

W.H. Bird, 'Bond's and Ford's hospital Coventry', *Transactions of the Birmingham and Midland Institute*, 38 (1912), 1–7.

J. Bolton, *The medieval English economy, 1150–1500* (London 1980).

— 'Inflation, economics and politics in thirteenth-century England' in P.R. Coss and S.D. Lloyd (eds), *Thirteenth-century England*, proceedings of the Newcastle upon Tyne conference 1991, vol. 4 (Woodbridge 1992), pp. 1–14.

G. Bosanquet (trans.), *Eadmer's History of recent events in England* (London 1964).★

P. Bourdieu, *Outline of a theory of practice* (Cambridge 1977).

W. Boys, *Collections for an history of Sandwich in Kent, with notices of the other Cinque Ports and members and of Richborough* (Canterbury 1792).

G. Brereton (trans.), *Froissart's Chronicles* (London 1968, reprinted 1985).★

J. Brewer et al. (eds), *Letters and papers, foreign and domestic, of the reign of Henry VIII*, 21 vols and Addenda (London 1862–1932).★

A. Bridbury, *England and the salt trade in the later middle ages* (Oxford 1955).

R. Britnell, 'The proliferation of markets in England, 1200–1349', *Economic History Review*, 2nd series, 24 (1981), 209–21.

— *The commercialisation of English society, 1000–1500* (Cambridge 1993)

J.W. Brodman, *Charity and welfare: hospitals and the poor in medieval Catalonia* (Philadelphia 1998).

N. Brooks, 'Rochester bridge, AD 43–1381' in N. Yates and J. Gibson (eds), *Traffic and politics: the construction and management of Rochester Bridge, AD 43–1993* (Woodbridge 1994), pp. 1–40.

A.D. Brown, *Popular piety in late medieval England: the diocese of Salisbury, 1250–1550* (Oxford 1995).

R.A. Brown, H.M. Colvin and A.J. Taylor, *The History of the King's Works: the middle ages*, vol. 2 (London 1963).

C. Buckingham, *Catholic Dover* (Dover 1968).

V. Bullough, 'A note on medical care in medieval English hospitals', *Bulletin of the History of Medicine*, 35 (1961), 74–77.

C. Burgess, '"By quick and by dead": wills and pious provision in late medieval Bristol' *English Historical Review*, 405 (1987), 837–58.

— '"A fond thing vainly invented": an essay on Purgatory and pious motive in later medieval England' in S. Wright (ed.), *Parish, church and people* (London 1988), pp. 56–84.

— 'Late medieval wills and pious convention: testamentary evidence reconsidered' in M. Hicks (ed.), *Profit, piety and the professions in later medieval England* (Gloucester 1990) pp. 14–33.

— 'The benefactions of mortality: the lay response in the late medieval urban parish' in D. Smith (ed.), *Studies in clergy and ministry in medieval England*, Borthwick Studies in History, vol. 1 (York 1991), pp. 65–86.

G. Burgess, *Two medieval outlaws: the romances of Eustace the Monk and Fouke Fitz Waryn* (Cambridge 1997).

A.F. Butcher, 'The origins of Romney freemen, 1433 –1523', *Economic History Review*, 2nd series, 27 (1974), 16–27.

— 'Sandwich in the thirteenth century', *Archaeologia Cantiana*, 93 (1977), 25–31.

— 'Rent and the urban economy: Oxford and Canterbury in the later middle ages', *Southern History*, 1 (1979), 11–44.

— 'The hospital of St Stephen and St Thomas, New Romney: the documentary evidence', *Archaeologia Cantiana*, 96 (1980), 17–26.

— 'English urban society and the revolt of 1381' in R. Hilton and T. Aston (eds.), *The English rising of 1381* (Cambridge 1984), pp. 84–111.

— See also A. Gross and A.F. Butcher.

Calendar of Charter Rolls (London 1903–).★

Calendar of Close Rolls (London 1892–).★

Calendar of entries in the Papal Registers relating to Great Britain and Ireland: Papal Letters (London 1893–).★

Calendar of entries in the Papal Registers relating to Great Britain and Ireland: Papal Petitions (London 1896–).★

Calendar of Inquisitions Miscellaneous (London 1916–).★

Calendar of Inquisitions Post Mortem (London 1904–).★

Calendar of Liberate Rolls (London 1916–).★

Calendar of Patent Rolls (London 1891–).★

J. Caley and J. Hunter (eds), *Valor Ecclesiasticus temp. Henrici VIII, auctoritate Regia Institutus*, Records Commission, 6 vols (London 1810–34).★

H. Cannon, 'The battle of Sandwich and Eustace the Monk', *English Historical Review*, 108 (1912), 649–70.

M. Carlin, 'Medieval English hospitals' in L. Granshaw and R. Porter (eds), *The hospital in history* (London and New York 1989), pp. 21–39.

B.T. Carpenter, 'St John's hospital and the commonalty of Winchester in the middle ages', *Proceedings of the Hampshire Field Club and Archaeological Society*, 19 (1957), 20–34.

S. Cavallo, *Charity and power in early modern Italy* (Cambridge 1995).

C. Cheney, *Handbook of dates for students of English history* (London 1991).

I. Churchill, R. Griffin and F. Hardman (eds), *Calendar of Kent Feet of Fines*, Kent Records, vol. 15 (1956).★

M. Clanchy, *England and its rulers, 1066–1272* (Glasgow 1993).

P. Clark, *English provincial society from the Reformation to the Revolution: religion, politics and society in Kent, 1500–1640* (Hassocks 1977).

— and L. Murfin, *History of Maidstone: the making of a modern county town* (Stroud 1995).

R. Clarke, *The medieval hospital of St John the Baptist, Sevenoaks* (Sevenoaks 1971).

R.M. Clay, *The medieval hospitals of England* (1909, reprinted London 1966).

A. Cohen, *The symbolic construction of community* (London 1985).

— *Self consciousness: an alternative anthropology of identity* (London and New York 1994).

— and N. Rapport, 'Introduction: consciousness in anthropology' in A. Cohen and N. Rapport (eds), *Questions of consciousness* (London 1995), pp. 1–18.

S.K. Cohn Jr, *The cult of remembrance and the Black Death: six Renaissance cities in central Italy* (Baltimore and London 1992).

P. Collinson, 'The Protestant cathedral, 1541–1660' in P. Collinson, N. Ramsey and M. Sparks (eds), *A history of Canterbury cathedral* (Oxford 1995), pp. 154–203.

D. de Coppet, 'Introduction' in D. de Coppet (ed.), *Understanding ritual,* European Association of Social Anthropologists (London 1992), pp. 1–10.

C. Cotton (ed.), 'Churchwardens' accounts of the parish of St Andrew, Canterbury AD 1485–1509', *Archaeologia Cantiana,* 32 (1917), 181–246.*

C. Cotton (ed.), 'Churchwardens' accounts of the parish of St Andrew, Canterbury AD 1509–1523', *Archaeologia Cantiana,* 33 (1918), 1–62.*

C. Cotton (ed.), 'Churchwardens' accounts of the parish of St Andrew, Canterbury AD 1524–1557', *Archaeologia Cantiana,* 34 (1920), 1–46.*

C. Cotton, *The Grey Friars of Canterbury, 1224–1538* (Manchester 1924).

C. Coulson, 'Battlements and the bourgeoisie: municipal status and the apparatus of urban defence in late-medieval England', *Medieval knighthood,* papers from the sixth Strawberry Hill conference 1994, vol. 5 (Woodbridge 1995), pp. 119–95.

J. Cowper (trans.), 'Churchwardens' accounts of the parish of St Dunstan, Canterbury AD 1484–1514', *Archaeologia Cantiana,* 16 (1886), 289–321.*

P.H. Cullum, 'Leperhouses and borough status in the thirteenth century' in P.R. Coss and S.D. Lloyd (eds), *Thirteenth-century England,* proceedings of the Newcastle upon Tyne conference 1989, vol. 3 (Woodbridge, 1991), pp. 37–46.

— '"And hir name was charite": charitable giving by and for women in late medieval Yorkshire' in P.J.P. Goldberg (ed.), *Women is a worthy wight: women in English society c. 1200–1500* (Stroud 1992), pp. 182–211.

— and P.J.P. Goldberg, 'Charitable provision in late medieval York: "to the praise of God and the use of the poor"', *Northern History,* 29 (1993), 24–39.

— '"For pore people harberles": what was the function of the maisonsdieu?' in D.J. Clayton, R.G. Davies and P. McNiven (eds), *Trade, devotion and governance: papers in later medieval history* (Stroud 1994, pp. 36–54.

Curia Regis Rolls of the reign of Henry III: preserved in the Public Record Office, 16 vols (London 1922–1979).*

C. Daniell, *Death and burial in medieval England, 1066–1550* (London 1997).

F. Davies et al. and D. Douie (eds), *Register of John Pecham archbishop of Canterbury AD 1279–1292,* Canterbury and York Society, 2 vols (Torquay 1968, 1969).*

R.G. Davies, 'Lollardy and locality', *Transactions of the Royal Historical Society,* 6th series, 1 (1991), 191–212.

— 'Religious sensibility' in C. Given-Wilson (ed.), *An illustrated history of late medieval England* (Manchester 1996), pp. 103–26.

A. Davis (trans.), *William Thorne's Chronicle of St Augustine's abbey* (Oxford 1934).*

J. Davis, *Heresy and Reformation in the south-east of England, 1520–1559* (London and New Jersey, 1983).

J. Davis, *Exchange* (Buckingham 1992).

N.Z. Davis, *The gift in sixteenth-century France* (Oxford 2000).

E. Deighton, 'The Carmelite friary in Sandwich, *Archeaologia Cantiana,* 114 (1994), 317–27.

L. Demaitre, 'The description and diagnosis of leprosy by fourteenth century physicians', *Bulletin of the History of Medicine,* 59 (1985), 327–44.

J. Denton, 'From the foundation of Vale Royal abbey to the statute of Carlisle: Edward I and ecclesiastical patronage' in P.R. Cox and S.D. Lloyd (eds), *Thirteenth century*

England, proceedings of the Newcastle-upon-Tyne conference 1991, vol. 4 (Woodbridge 1992), pp. 123–38.

R. Dinn, 'Death and rebirth in late medieval Bury St Edmunds' in S. Bassett (ed.), *Urban responses to the dying and the dead, 100–1600* (Leicester 1992), pp.151–69.

B. Dobson, 'The monks of Canterbury in the later middle ages, 1220–1540' in P. Collinson, N. Ramsey and M. Sparks (eds), *A history of Canterbury cathedral* (Oxford 1995), pp. 69–153.

M. Douglas, 'Forward' in M. Mauss, *The gift: the form and reason for exchange in archaic societies,* translator W. Halls (1915, republished London 1990), pp. vii–xviii.

C. Drake, 'The hospital of St Mary of Ospringe commonly called Maison Dieu', *Archaeologia Cantiana,* 30 (1914), 35–78.

F. Du Boulay (trans. and ed.), *Registrum Thome Bourgchier, Cantuariensis Archiepiscopi AD 1454–1486,* Canterbury and York Society (Oxford 1957).★

E. Duffy, *The stripping of the altars: traditional religion in England, c.1400–c.1580* (New Haven and London 1992).

W. Dugdale, *The antiquities of Warwickshire,* 2 vols, 2nd edn (London 1730, republished).

W. Dugdale, *Monasticon Anglicanum,* eds, J. Caley, H. Ellis and B. Bandinel, 6 vols in 8 (London 1817–1830).★

J. Duncombe, and N. Battely, *The history and antiquities of the three archiepiscopal hospitals at or near Canterbury viz. St Nicholas at Harbledown, St John, Northgate and St Thomas of Eastbridge, with some account of the priory of St Gregory, the nunnery of St Sepulcre, the hospitals of St James and St Lawrence and Maynard's spittle* (London 1785), pp. 175–452. Part of *Bibliotheca Topograhica Brittanica,* eds. J. Duncombe & N. Battely.★

A. Dyer, *Decline and growth in English towns, 1400–1640* (Basingstoke 1991).

C. Dyer, *Standards of living in the later middle ages* (Cambridge 1989).

C. Ellis, *Hubert de Burgh* (London 1952).

M. Ellis, 'The bridges of Gloucester and the hospital between the bridges', *Transactions of the Bristol and Gloucester Archaeological Society,* 51 (1929), 169–210.

F. Elliston-Erwood, 'Plans of, and brief architectural notes on, Kent churches', *Archaeologia Cantiana,* 60 (1947), 15–23.

A. Emden, *A biographical register of the University of Oxford to AD 1500,* 3 vols (Oxford 1957–9).

— *A biographical register of the University of Oxford, AD 1501–1540* (Oxford 1974).

K. Evans, 'The Maison Dieu, Arundel', *Sussex Archaeological Collections,* 107 (1969), 65–77.

A. Everitt, *Continuity and colonization: the evolution of Kentish settlement* (Leicester 1986).

N. Farriss, 'Forward' in A. Appadurai (ed.), *The social life of things* (Cambridge 1986), pp. ix–xiv.

A. Finn (ed.), *Records of Lydd* (Ashford 1911).★

P.W. Fleming, 'Charity, faith and the gentry of Kent 1422–1529' in A. Pollard (ed.), *Property and politics: essays in later medieval English history* (Gloucester 1984), pp. 36–58.

K. Flynn, 'Romanesque wall-paintings in the cathedral church of Christ Church, Canterbury', *Archaeologia Cantiana,* 95 (1979), 185–95.

J. Ford 'Marginality and the assimilation of foreigners in the lay parish community: the case of Sandwich' in K. French, G. Gibbs and B. Kumin (eds), *The parish in English life, 1400–1600* (Manchester 1997), pp. 203–16.

K. French, 'Parochial fund-raising in late medieval Somerset' in K. French, G. Gibbs and B. Kumin (eds), *The parish in English life, 1400–1600* (Manchester 1997), pp. 115–32.

W.G. Fretton, 'The hospital of St John the Baptist, Coventry', *Transactions of the Birmingham and Midland Institute*, 13 (1886), 32–50.

M. Frohnsdorff, *The Maison Dieu and medieval Faversham* (Faversham 1997).

L. Fullbrook-Legatt, 'Medieval Gloucester: hospitals', *Transactions of the Bristol and Gloucester Archaeological Society*, 67 (1946–8), 223–34.

A. Fuller, 'Hospital of St John, Cirencester', *Transactions of the Bristol and Gloucester Archaeological Society*, 8 (1883–4), 224–28.

— 'Cirencester hospitals', *Transactions of the Bristol and Gloucester Archaeological Society*, 17 (1892–3), 53–62.

D. Gardiner, *Historic haven: the story of Sandwich* (Derby 1954).

G.N. Garmonsway (trans. and ed.), *The Anglo-Saxon Chronicle* (1953, reprinted London 1986).★

M.McG. Gatch, 'Miracles in architectural settings: Christ Church, Canterbury and St Clement's Sandwich in the Old English *Vision of Leofric*', *Anglo-Saxon England*, 22 (1993), 227–52.

P. Geary, 'Sacred commodities: the circulation of medieval relics' in A. Appadurai (ed.), *The social life of things* (Cambridge 1986), pp. 169–91.

C. Geertz, *The interpretation of cultures* (New York 1973).

B. Geremek, *The margins of society in late medieval Paris*, trans. J. Birrell (Cambridge 1987).

— *Poverty: a history*, trans. A. Kolakowska (Oxford and Cambridge, Massachusetts 1994).

M. Gibson, 'Normans and Angevins, 1070–1220' in P. Collinson, N. Ramsey and M. Sparks (eds), *A history of Canterbury cathedral* (Oxford 1995), pp. 38–68.

R. Gilchrist, 'Christian bodies and souls: the archaeology of life and death in later medieval hospitals' in S. Bassett (ed.), *Urban responses to the dying and the dead, 100–1600* (Leicester 1992), pp. 101–18.

— 'Medieval bodies in the material world: gender, stigma and the body' in S. Kay and M. Rubin (eds), *Framing medieval bodies* (Manchester 1994), pp. 43–61.

M. Godelier, *The enigma of the gift*, trans. N. Scott (Cambridge 1999).

W. Godfrey, 'Some medieval hospitals of east Kent', *Archaeological Journal*, 86 (1929), 99–110.

— *The English almshouse* (London 1955).

— 'Medieval hospitals in Sussex', *Sussex Archaeological Collections*, 97 (1959), 130–6.

B. Golding, 'Burials and benefactions: an aspect of monastic patronage in thirteenth century England' in W. Ormrod (ed.), *England in the thirteenth century*, proceedings of the 1984 Harlaxton Symposium (Woodbridge, 1986), pp. 64–75.

R. Graham, 'Sidelights on the rectors and parishioners of Reculver from the register of Archbishop Winchelsey', *Archaeologia Cantiana*, 57 (1944), 1–12.

R. Graham (trans. and ed.), *Registrum Roberti Winchelsey, Archiepiscopi Cantuariensis AD 1294–1313*, Canterbury and York Society, 2 vols (Oxford 1952, 1956).★

The Great Rolls of the Pipe for the reign of King Henry the Second (London 1844–).★

E. Greenwood, *The hospital of St Bartholomew, Rochester* (Rochester 1962).

C. Gregory, *Gifts and commodities* (London 1982).

R. Griffin, 'The lepers' hospital at Swainestrey', *Archaeologia Cantiana*, 34 (1920), 63–78.

V. Groebner, *Liquid assets, dangerous gifts: presents and politics at the end of the middle ages*, trans. P.E. Selwyn (Philadelphia 2000).

A. Gross and A.F. Butcher, 'Adaptation and investment in the age of the great storms: agricultural policy on the manors of the principal lords of the Romney Marshes and the marshland fringe *c.*1250–1320' in J. Eddison (ed.), *Romney Marsh, the debatable ground* (Oxford 1995), pp. 107–17.

C. Haines, *Dover priory* (Cambridge 1930).

E. Hammond, 'Physicians in medieval English religious houses', *Bulletin of the History of Medicine*, 32 (1958), 105–20.

C. Harper-Bill (ed.), *Register of John Morton, archbishop of Canterbury AD 1486–1500*, Canterbury and York Society, 2 vols (Leeds 1987).★

M. Harris (trans. and ed.), *The Coventry Leet Book or Mayor's Register: containing the records of the city court leet or view of frankpledge, AD 1420–1555, with divers other matters*, Early English Text Society, 2 vols (London 1907–9, reprinted 1971).★

A. Harrison, 'Excavations on the site of St Mary's hospital, Strood', *Archaeologia Cantiana*, 84 (1969), 139–60.

B.F. Harvey, *Living and dying in England, 1100–1540: the monastic experience* (Oxford 1993).

I. Harvey, *Jack Cade's rebellion of 1450* (Oxford 1991).

P.D.A. Harvey, 'The English inflation of 1180–1220', *Past & Present*, 61 (1973), 3–30.

E. Hasted, *The history and topographical survey of the county of Kent*, 12 vols, 2nd edn (Canterbury 1797–1801, reprinted 1972).

J. Hayes, D. Williams and P. Payne, 'Report of an excavation in the grounds of St Bartholomew's chapel, Chatham', *Archaeologia Cantiana*, 98 (1982), 177–89.

P. Heath, 'Urban piety in the later middle ages: the evidence of Hull wills' in R. Dobson (ed.), *The church, politics and patronage in the fifteenth century* (Gloucester 1984), pp. 209–34.

J. Henderson, 'The parish and the poor in Florence at the time of the Black Death: the case of S. Frediano', *Continuity and Change*, 3 (1988), 247–72.

— (ed.), 'Charity and the poor in medieval and Renaissance Europe', *Continuity and Change*, 3 (1988), 145–51.

— 'The hospitals of late-medieval and Renaissance Florence: a preliminary survey' in L. Granshaw and R. Porter (eds), *The hospital in history* (London and New York 1989), pp. 63–92.

— *Piety and charity in late medieval Florence* (Chicago and London 1997).

D. Herlihy and C. Klapisch, *Les Toscans et leurs familles* (Paris 1978).

M. Hicks, 'St Katherine's hospital, Heytesbury: prehistory, foundation and re-foundation 1408–1472', *Wiltshire Archaeological and Natural History Magazine*, 78 (1984), 60–9.

— 'Chantries, obits and almshouses: the Hungerford foundations, 1325–1478' in C.M. Barron and C. Harper-Bill (eds), *The church in pre-Reformation society: essays in honour of F.R.H. du Boulay* (Woodbridge 1985), pp. 123–42.

M. Hicks and A. Hicks, *St Gregory's priory, Northgate, Canterbury: excavations 1988–1991*, The Archaeology of Canterbury New Series, vol. 2 (Canterbury 2001).

D.I. Hill, *Eastbridge hospital and the ancient almshouses of Canterbury* (Canterbury 1969).

J.C. Hodgson, 'The 'Domus Dei' of Newcastle, otherwise St Katherine's hospital, on the Sandhill', *Archaeologia Aeliana*, 3rd series, 14 (1917), 191–220.

C. Holdsworth, 'Royal Cistercians: Beaulieu, her daughters and Rewley' in P.R. Coss and S.D. Lloyd (eds), *Thirteenth century England,* proceedings of the Newcastle upon Tyne conference 1991, vol. 4 (Woodbridge, 1992), pp. 139–50.

E. Holland (trans.), *The Canterbury chantries and hospitals in 1546: a supplement to Kent Chantries*, Kent Records, vol. 12 Supplement (1934).★

M. Honeybourne, 'The leper hospitals of the London area: with an appendix on some other medieval hospitals of Middlesex', *Transactions of the London and Middlesex Archaeological Society*, 21 (1967), 1–61.

P. Horden, 'A discipline of relevance: the historiography of the later medieval hospital', *Social History of Medicine*, 1 (1988), 359–74.

T. Hugo, 'The hospital of S. Margaret, Taunton', *Proceedings of the Somerset Archaeological and Natural History Society*, 18 (1872), 100–31.

F. Hull (ed.), *A calendar of the White and Black Books of the Cinque Ports*, Kent Records, vol. 19 (1966).★

C. Humphrey and S. Hugh-Jones, 'Introduction: barter, exchange and value' in C. Humphrey and S. Hugh-Jones (eds), *Barter, exchange and value* (Cambridge 1992), pp. 1–20.

A. Hussey, 'The hospitals of Kent', *The Antiquary*, 45 (1909), 414–18, 447–50.

— 'Chapels in Kent', *Archaeologia Cantiana*, 29 (1911), 217–58.

A. Hussey (ed.), *Kent chantries*, Kent Records, vol. 12 (1932).★

A. Hussey (ed.), *Kent obit and lamp rents*, Kent Records, vol. 14 (1936).★

A. Hussey (ed.), *Testamenta Cantiana* (London 1907).★

R. Hutton, *The rise of Merry England, the ritual year 1400–1700* (Oxford 1994).

P. Hyde, *Thomas Arden of Faversham: the man behind the myth* (Faversham 1996).

E.F. Jacob (ed), *Register of Henry Chichele, archbishop of Canterbury AD 1414–1443*, Canterbury and York Society, 4 vols (Oxford 1943–1947).★

O. Jessup, 'The medieval hospital of Saint Mary Magdalene, Durham', *Archaeologia Aeliana*, 5th series, 24 (1996), 119–28.

C. Johnson (trans. and ed.) *Registrum Hamonis Hethe Diocesis Roffensis AD 1319–1352*, Kent Records, 2 vols (Oxford 1948).★

J. Jones, *The records of Dover* (Dover 1907).

W.K. Jordan, *Philanthropy in England, 1480–1660: a study of the changing pattern of English social aspirations* (London 1959).

A.V. Judges, *The Elizabethan underworld* (London 1930, reprinted 1965).

D. Keene, 'St John's hospital', *Survey of medieval Winchester*, Winchester Studies, 2 vols (Oxford 1985), pp. 813–22.

I. Keil, 'Corrodies of Glastonbury abbey in the later middle ages', *Proceedings of the Somerset Archaeological and Natural History Society*, 108 (1964), 113–31.

N. Kerling, 'The foundation of St Bartholomew's hospital in West Smithfield, London', *The Guildhall Miscellany*, 4 (1972), 137–48.

J. Kermode, 'The merchants in three northern English towns' in C. Clough (ed.), *Profession, vocation and culture in later medieval England* (Liverpool 1982), pp. 7–48.

J. Kerr, 'The open door: hospitality and honour in twelfth/early thirteenth-century England', *History*, 87 (2002), 322–35.

A. Kidd, 'Philanthropy and the 'social history paradigm'', *Social History*, 21 (1996), 176–92.

D. Knowles, and R.N. Hadcock, *Medieval religious houses: England and Wales*, 2nd edn (London 1971).

D. Knowles and R.N. Hadcock, 'Additions and corrections to *Medieval houses: England and Wales* [hospitals]', *English Historical Review*, 72 (1957), 76–85.

I. Kopytoff, 'The cultural biography of things: commoditization as process' in A. Appadurai (ed.), *The social life of things* (Cambridge 1986), pp. 64–91.

J. Latimer, 'The hospital of St John, Bristol', *Transactions of the Bristol and Gloucester Archaeological Society*, 24 (1901), 172–78.

C. Lawrence, *The friars* (London and New York 1994).

R. Lederman, *What gifts engender: social relations and politics in Mendi Highland, Papua New Guinea* (Cambridge 1986).

G. Lee, *Leper hospitals in medieval Ireland* (Dublin 1996).

R. Leech and A. McWhirr, 'Excavations at St John's hospital, Cirencester, 1971 and 1976', *Transactions of the Bristol and Gloucester Archaeological Society*, 100 (1982), 191–209.

W. Leighton, 'Trinity hospital', *Transactions of the Bristol and Gloucester Archaeological Society*, 36 (1913), 251–87.

K.J. Lewis, *The cult of St Katherine of Alexandria in late medieval England* (Woodbridge 2000).

G.M. Livett, 'West Hythe church and the sites of churches formerly existing in Hythe', *Archaeologia Cantiana*, 30 (1914), 251–62.

A. Lloyd, *King John* (Newton Abbot 1973).

T. Lloyd, *The English wool trade in the middle ages* (Cambridge 1977).

F.D. Logan, *A history of the church in the middle ages* (London 2002).

R. Luce, 'The St John's almshouse, Malmesbury', *Wiltshire Archaeological Magazine*, 53 (1950), 118–26.

J. Lyon, *The history of the town and port of Dover* (Dover 1813).

A. McHardy, 'Some patterns of ecclesiastical patronage in the later middle ages' in D. Smith (ed.), *Studies in clergy and ministry in medieval England*, Borthwick Studies in History, vol. 1 (York 1991), pp. 20–37.

M. McIntosh, 'Local responses to the poor in late medieval and Tudor England', *Continuity and Change*, 3 (1988), 209–45.

B. Malinowski, *Argonauts of the western Pacific: an account of native enterprise and adventure in the archipelagoes of Melanesian New Guinea* (New York 1922).

M. Markham, *Medieval hospitals in Oxfordshire* (Woodstock 1979).

G. Martin, 'The English borough in the thirteenth century' in R. Holt and G. Rosser (eds), *The medieval town, 1200–1540* (London 1990), pp. 29–48.

M. Mate, 'The impact of war on the economy of Canterbury cathedral priory, 1294–1340', *Speculum*, 57 (1982), 761–78.

— 'Kent and Sussex' in E. Miller (ed.), *The agrarian history of England and Wales, 1350–1500*, vol. 3 (1991), 119–36.

M. Mauss, *The gift: the form and reason for exchange in archaic societies*, trans. W. Halls, foreward by M. Douglas (1915, republished New York and London 1990).

D. Meade, 'The hospital of saint Giles at Kepier, near Durham, 1112 – 1545', *Transactions of the Durham and Northumberland Archaeological and Architectural Society*, 1 (1968), 45–55.

W. Mellows, 'The medieval hospitals and alms of Peterborough', *Reports and Papers of the Associated Architectural and Archaeological Society*, 34 (1917–18), 281–308.

E. Miller (ed.), *The agrarian history of England and Wales, 1350–1500*, vol. 3 (1991).

E. Miller and J Hatcher, *Medieval England: rural society and economic change, 1086–1348* (London 1978).

Rev. Moberley, 'St Nicholas hospital, Salisbury', *Wiltshire Magazine*, 25 (1891), 119–64.

M. Mollat, *The poor in the middle ages: an essay in social history*, trans. A. Goldhammer (Yale 1986).

P. Morgan (ed.), *Domesday Book, Kent* (Chichester 1983).★

E. Muir, 'Introduction: observing trifles' in E. Muir and G. Ruggiero (eds), *Microhistory and the lost peoples of Europe* (Baltimore and London 1991), pp. vii–xxviii.

K. Murray, *Constitutional history of the Cinque Ports* (Manchester 1935).

A.R. Myers (ed.), *English historical documents, 1327–1485* (London 1969).★

J.G. Nichols (trans.), *Desiderius Erasmus' pilgrimages to Saint Mary of Walsingham and Saint Thomas of Canterbury, with the colloquy on rash vows, and the characters of Archbishop Warham and Dean Colet*, 2nd edn (London 1875).★

A. Oakley, 'Rochester priory, 1185–1540' in N. Yates and P. Welsby (eds), *Faith and fabric: a history of Rochester cathedral, 604–1994* (Woodbridge 1996), pp. 29–56.

A. Oakley (trans.), *Calendar of the deeds of Rochester priory*, unpublished and held at Medway Local History Centre, Strood.★

A. Offer, 'Between the gift and the market: the economy of regard', *Economic History Review*, 2nd series, 50 (1997), 450–76.

N. Orme, 'Warland hospital, Totnes and the Trinitarian friars in Devon', *Devon and Cornwall Notes and Queries*, 36 (1987), 41–8.

—— 'Mortality in fourteenth-century Exeter', *Medical History*, 32 (1988), 195–203.

—— and M. Webster, *The English hospital, 1070–1570* (New Haven and London 1995).

—— 'Church and chapel in medieval England', *Transactions of the Royal Historical Society*, 6th Series, 6 (1996), 75–102.

W. Page et al. (eds), *The Victoria History of the Counties of England* (London 1900–); hospital surveys occur in:
  Bedfordshire, vol. 1 (1904)
  Berkshire, vol. 2 (1907)
  Buckinghamshire, vol. 1 (1905)
  Cambridgeshire and the Isle of Ely, vol. 2 (1948)
  Cheshire, vol. 3 (1980)
  Cumberland, vol. 2 (1905)
  Derbyshire, vol. 2 (1907)
  Dorset, vol. 2 (1908)
  Durham, vol. 2 (1907)
  Essex, vol. 2 (1907)
  Gloucestershire, vol. 2 (1907)
  Hampshire and the Isle of Wight, vol. 2 (1903)
  Hertfordshire, vol. 4 (1914)
  Huntingdonshire, vol. 1 (1926)
  Kent, vol. 2 (1926)
  Lancashire, vol. 2 (1908)
  Leicestershire, vol. 2 (1954)
  Lincolnshire, vol. 2 (1906)
  London, vol. 1 (1909)
  Middlesex, vol. 1 (1969)
  Norfolk, vol. 2 (1906)
  Northamptonshire, vol. 2 (1906)

Nottinghamshire, vol. 2 (1910)

Oxfordshire, vol. 2 (1907)

Rutland, vol. 1 (1908)

Shropshire, vol. 2 (1973)

Somerset, vol. 2 (1911)

Staffordshire, vol. 3 (1970)

Suffolk, vol. 2 (1907)

Surrey, vol. 2 (1905)

Sussex, vol. 2 (1907)

Warwickshire, vol. 2 (1908)

Wiltshire, vol. 3 (1956)

Worcestershire, vol. 2 (1906)

Yorkshire, vol. 3 (1913).

S. Painter, *William Marshal* (Oxford 1966).

C.F.R. Palmer, 'The Friar-Preachers, or Black Friars, of Canterbury', *Archaeologia Cantiana*, 13 (1880), 81–96.

K. Parfitt, 'St John's hospital reredorter, Canterbury', *Archaeologia Cantiana*, 109 (1991), 298–308.

K. Park, 'Healing the poor: hospitals and medical assistance in Renaissance Florence' in J. Barry and C. Jones (eds), *Medicine and charity before the welfare state* (London and New York 1991), pp. 26–45.

G. Parker, 'Early Bristol medical institutions, the medieval hospitals, and barber surgeons', *Transactions of the Bristol and Gloucester Archaeological Society*, 44 (1922), 155–78.

J. Parker, 'The hospital of St John the Baptist at Wycombe', *Records of Buckinghamshire*, 5 (1898), 245–48.

D. Parkin, 'Ritual as spatial direction and bodily division' in D. de Coppet (ed.), *Understanding rituals*, European Association of Social Anthropologists (London 1992), pp. 11–25.

R. Pfaff, *New liturgical feasts in later medieval England* (Oxford 1970).

C. Phythian-Adams, *Desolation of a city: Coventry and the urban crisis of the late middle ages* (Cambridge 1979).

C. Platt, *King Death: the Black Death and its aftermath in late-medieval England* (London 1996).

H. Plomer (ed.), *Index of wills and administrations now preserved in the probate registry at Canterbury, 1396–1558 and 1640–1650*, Kent Records, vol. 6 (1920).*

J.F. Pound, *Poverty and vagrancy in Tudor England* (London 1971).

E. Prescott, *The English medieval hospital, c. 1050–1640* (London 1992).

R. Price and M. Ponsford, *St Bartholomew's hospital Bristol: the excavation of a medieval hospital, 1976–8*, Council for British Archaeology Report, vol. 110 (York 1998).

B. Pullan, *Rich and poor in Renaissance Venice: the social institutions of a Catholic state, to 1620* (Oxford 1971).

— 'Support and redeem: charity and poor relief in Italian cities from the fourteenth to the seventeenth century', *Continuity and Change*, 3 (1988), 177–208.

S. Raban, 'Mortmain in medieval England' in T. Aston (ed.), *Landlords, peasants and politics in medieval England* (Cambridge 1987), pp. 203–26.

C. Rawcliffe, 'The hospitals of later medieval London', *Medical History*, 28 (1984), 1–21.

— *The hospitals of Medieval Norwich*, Studies in East Anglian History, vol. 2 (Norwich 1995).
— *Medicine for the soul: the life, death and resurrection of an English medieval hospital, St Giles's, Norwich, c.1249–1550* (Stroud 1999).
— 'Learning to love the leper: aspects of institutional charity in Anglo-Norman England' in J. Gillingham (ed.), *Anglo-Norman Studies*, proceedings of the Battle Conference 2000, vol. 23 (Woodbridge 2001), pp. 231–50.
P. Richards, *The medieval leper and his northern heirs* (Cambridge 1977).
J. Richardson, *The local historian's encyclopaedia* (New Barnet 1974).
C. Richmond, 'Victorian values in fifteenth-century England: the Ewelme almshouse statutes' in R. Horrox and S.R. Jones (eds), *Pragmatic utopias: ideals and communities, 1200–1630* (Cambridge 2001), pp. 224–41.
V.B. Richmond, *The legend of Guy of Warwick* (New York and London 1996).
S. Rigby, *English society in the later middle ages* (Basingstoke 1995).
S. Rigold, 'Two Kentish hospitals re-examined: S. Mary, Ospringe and SS. Stephen and Thomas, New Romney', *Archaeologia Cantiana*, 79 (1964), 31–69.
J.C. Robertson (ed.), *Materials for the history of Thomas Becket, archbishop of Canterbury*, 7 vols. (London 1875–85).*
S. Robertson, 'Destroyed churches of Romney Marsh', *Archaeologia Cantiana*, 13 (1880), 237–49.
— 'St Mary's church, Sandwich', *Archaeologia Cantiana*, 14 (1885), lv–lx.
J.T. Rosenthal, *The purchase of Paradise: gift giving and the aristocracy, 1307–1485* (London 1972).
G. Rosser, 'Communities of parish and guild in the late middle ages' in S. Wright (ed.), *Parish, church and people: local studies in lay religion, 1350–1750* (London 1988), pp. 29–55.
— 'Parochial conformity and voluntary religion in late-medieval England', *Transactions of the Royal Historical Society*, 6th series, 1 (1991), 173–90.
J. Rowe, 'The medieval hospitals of Bury St Edmunds', *Medical History*, 2 (1958), 253–63.
Royal Commission on Historic Manuscripts, 5th Report & Appendix (London 1876).*
M. Rubin, *Charity and community in medieval Cambridge* (Cambridge 1987).
— 'Development and change in English hospitals, 1100–1500' in L. Granshaw and R. Porter (eds), *The hospital in history* (London and New York 1989), pp. 41–59.
— 'Imaging medieval hospitals' in J. Barry and C. Jones (eds), *Medicine and charity before the welfare state* (London and New York 1991), pp. 14–25.
— 'Small groups: identity and solidarity in the late middle ages' in J. Kermode (ed.), *Enterprise and individuals in fifteenth-century England* (Stroud 1991), pp. 132–50.
— 'What did the Eucharist mean to thirteenth-century villagers?' in P.R. Coss and S.D. Lloyd (eds), *Thirteenth century England,* proceedings of the Newcastle upon Tyne conference 1991, vol. 4 (Woodbridge, 1992), pp. 47–56.
— 'The poor' in R. Horrox (ed.), *Fifteenth-century attitudes: perceptions of society in late medieval England* (Cambridge and New York 1994), pp. 169–82.
J. Russell, *The history of Maidstone* (1881, reprinted Rochester 1978).
M. Ruual, 'Monks in the world: the case of Gundulf of Rochester, *Anglo-Norman studies*, proceedings of the Battle conference 1988, vol. 11 (1989), pp. 245–60.
A. Schmidt (ed.), *William Langland's The Vision of Piers Plowman*, 2nd edn (London 1995).*
J.B. Sheppard (ed.), *Literae Cantuarienses: the letter books of the monastery of Christ Church, Canterbury*, Rolls Series, 3 vols (1887–1889).*

L. Sherwood, 'The cartulary of Leeds priory', *Archaeologia Cantiana*, 64 (1951), 24–34.

W. Shrubsole, *The history and antiquities of Rochester and its environs*, printed & sold by T. Fisher (1772).

P. Slack, *Poverty and policy in Tudor and Stuart England* (Harlow 1988).

T.R. Slater, 'The south-west of England' in D.M. Palliser (ed.), *The Cambridge urban history of England*, vol. 1 (Cambridge 2000), pp. 583–608.

H. Smetham, *History of Strood* (1899, reprinted Chatham 1978).

F. Smith, *A history of Rochester* (Rochester 1928, reprinted Rochester 1976).

G. Smith, 'The excavation of the hospital of St Mary of Ospringe, commonly called the Maison Dieu', *Archaeologia Cantiana*, 95 (1979), 81–184.

H. Smith, 'The almshouses of St George, in the town of Poole', *Dorset Natural History and Archaeological Field Club*, 47 (1926), 155–9.

L.T. Smith (ed.), *The itinerary of John Leland in and about the years 1535–1543*, vol. 4 (London 1964).★

R.A.L. Smith, 'The place of Gundulf in the Anglo-Norman church', *English Historical Review*, 58 (1943), 257–72.

R.M. Smith, 'The manorial court and the elderly tenant in late medieval England' in M. Pelling and R. Smith (eds), *Life, death and the elderly* (London and New York 1991), pp. 39–61.

R.W. Southern, *The making of the middle ages* (1953, republished London 1987)

S. Statham, *The history of the castle, town and port of Dover* (London 1899).

S. Statham (ed.), *Dover charters and other documents in the possession of the corporation of Dover* (London 1902).★

A. Strathern, *The rope of Moka: big-men and ceremonial exchanges in Mount Hagen, New Guinea* (Cambridge 1971).

M. Strathern, *The gender of the gift: problems with women and problems with society in Melanesia* (Berkeley 1988).

— 'Qualified value: the perspective of gift exchange' in C. Humphrey and S. Hugh-Jones (eds), *Barter, exchange and value* (Cambridge 1992), pp. 169–91.

W. Stubbs (ed.), *The historical works of Gervase of Canterbury*, Rolls Series, 2 vols (London 1879–80).★

M. Sturken and L. Cartwright, *Practices of looking: an introduction to visual culture* (Oxford 2001).

J. Sumption, *Pilgrimage: an image of medieval religion* (London 1975).

R. Swanson, *Church and society in late medieval England* (Oxford 1989).

— 'Urban rectories and urban fortunes in late medieval England: the evidence from Bishop's Lynn' in T.R. Slater and G. Rosser (eds), *The church in the medieval town* (Aldershot 1998), pp. 100–30.

S. Sweetinburgh, 'Supporting the Canterbury hospitals: benefaction and the language of charity in the twelfth and thirteenth centuries', *Archaeologia Cantiana*, 122 (2002), 237–58.

— 'Joining the sisters: female inmates of the late medieval hospitals in east Kent', *Archaeologia Cantiana*, 123 (2003), 17–39.

— 'Wax, stone and iron: Dover's town defences in the late middle ages', *Archaeologia Cantiana* (forthcoming).

S. Tambiah, *The Buddhist saints of the forest and the cult of the amulets* (Cambridge 1984).

N.P. Tanner, *The church in late medieval Norwich, 1370–1532* (Toronto 1984).

T. Tanner, *Saint Edmund's chapel, Dover, and its restoration* (Dover 1968)

T. Tatton-Brown, 'The history of St Gregory's priory', *Archaeologia Cantiana*, 107 (1989), 314–27.

— 'Medieval parishes and parish churches in Canterbury' in T.R. Slater and G. Rosser (eds), *The church in the medieval town* (Aldershot 1998), pp. 236–71.

J. Taylor, 'The hospital of St Mark, commonly called Billeswike, or Gaunt's hospital', *Transactions of the Bristol and Gloucester Archaeological Society*, 3 (1878–9), 241–58.

V. Thomas, 'Notes on St Margaret's chapel and hospital, Wimborne', *Proceedings Dorset Natural History and Antiquarian Field Club*, 10 (1889), xxvi–xxvii.

B. Thompson, 'Monasteries and their patrons at foundation and dissolution', *Transactions of the Royal Historical Society*, 6th series, 4 (1994), 103–23.

J. Thomson, 'Piety and charity in late medieval London', *Journal of Ecclesiastical History*, 16 (1965), 178–95.

— *The early Tudor church and society, 1485–1529* (London 1993).

J. Thorpe (ed.), *Registrum Roffense* (London 1769).★

J. Tillotson, 'Pensions, corrodies and religious houses: an aspect of the relations of crown and church in early fourteenth-century England', *Journal of Religious History*, 8 (1974–5), 127–43.

S. Townley, 'Unbeneficed clergy in the thirteenth century: two English dioceses' in D. Smith (ed.), *Studies in clergy and ministry in medieval England*, Borthwick Studies in History, vol. 1 (York 1991), pp. 38–64.

R. Tricker, *St Peter's church, Sandwich, Kent* (London 1984).

— *St Mary's church, Sandwich, Kent* (London 1985).

H. Tsurushima, 'Women and corrody in twelfth-century Kent' in *What do 'medieval documents' reflect?*, summarized proceedings of the sessions of 107 and 207 of the International Medieval Congress, Leeds University (2002), pp. 93–6,

B. Turner, 'St John's house and the commonalty of Winchester in the middle ages', *Proceedings of the Hampshire Field Club*, 19 (1955), 20–34.

G.J. Turner and H.E. Salter, *The register of St Augustine's abbey, Canterbury: commonly called the Black Book*, 2 vols (London 1915–1924).★

H.L. Turner, *Town defences in England and Wales: an architectural and documentary study, AD 900–1500* (London 1970).

T. Turville-Petre, *England the nation: language, literature and national identity, 1290–1340* (Oxford 1996).

M. Underwood, 'Index of the archive of St Mary's hospital, Ospringe, held at St John's College', Cambridge (unpublished).★

W. Urry, 'Two notes on Guernes de Pont Sainte-Maxence: Vie de Saint Thomas', *Archaeologia Cantiana*, 66 (1953), 92–5.

— *Canterbury under the Angevin kings* (London 1967).

M.G. Vale, 'Piety, charity and literacy among the Yorkshire gentry 1370–1480', *Borthwick Papers*, 50 (1976), 1–32.

J. Van Baal, *Reciprocity and the position of women* (Amsterdam 1975).

H. van der Velden, *The donor's image: Gerard Leyet and the votive portraits of Charles the Bold* (Turnhout, Belgium 2000).

M. Vovelle, *Ideologies and mentalities*, trans. E. O'Flaherty (Cambridge 1990).

M. Walcott, 'Inventories of (i) St Mary's hospital or Maison Dieu, Dover, (ii) Dover priory', *Archaeologia Cantiana*, 7 (1868), 272–80.

A. Watkins, *Small towns in the Forest of Arden in the fifteenth century*, Dugdale Society Occasional Papers, no. 38 (Stratford upon Avon 1998).

D. Webb, *Pilgrimage in medieval England* (London and New York 2000).

A.B. Weiner, *Inalienable possessions: the paradox of keeping while giving* (Berkeley 1992).

C. Wilson, 'The medieval monuments' in P. Collinson, N. Ramsey and M. Sparks (eds), *A history of Canterbury cathedral* (Oxford 1995), pp. 451–510.

W.G. Wiseman, 'The medieval hospitals of Cumbria', *Transactions of the Cumberland and Westmoreland Archaeological Society*, 87 (1987), 83–100.

A.C. Wood (trans. and ed.), *Registrum Simonis Langham, Cantuariensis Archiepiscopi*, Canterbury and York Society (Oxford 1956).★

S. Wood, *English monasteries and their patrons in the thirteenth century* (London 1955).

A. Woodcock (ed.), *Cartulary of the priory of St Gregory, Canterbury*, Camden Society, 3rd series, vol. 88 (London 1956).★

B. Woodcock, *Medieval ecclesiastical courts in the diocese of Canterbury* (London 1952).

K. Wood-Legh (ed.), *Kentish visitations of Archbishop William Warham and his deputies, 1511–12*, Kent Records, vol. 24 (1984).★

C. Woodruff, 'Some early visitation rolls preserved at Canterbury', *Archaeologia Cantiana*, 33 (1918), 71–90.

— 'Financial aspects of the cult of St Thomas of Canterbury', *Archaeologia Cantiana*, 44 (1932), 13–32.

— 'The register and chartulary of the hospital of St Laurence, Canterbury', *Archaeologia Cantiana*, 50 (1938), 33–49.

UNPUBLISHED THESES AND PAPERS

C. Burgess, 'Memory in the parish: All Saints' Bristol in the late 15th century', paper given at the International Medieval Congress, Leeds University, 1996.

A.F. Butcher, 'Hythe: indigenous knowledge', paper given at the Culture and Society seminar, Kent University, 1996.

— 'The differences between people in one community, *c*.1461–1483', paper given at the Culture and Society seminar, Kent University, 1998.

J. Croft, 'The custumals of the Cinque Ports *c*.1290–*c*.1500: studies in the cultural production of the urban record', PhD thesis, Kent University, 1997.

P.H. Cullum, 'Hospitals and charitable provision in medieval Yorkshire', DPhil thesis, York University, 1990.

C. Daly, 'The hospitals of london: administration, refoundation and benefaction *c*.1500–1572', DPhil thesis, Oxford University, 1993.

M. Dixon, 'Dover in the early sixteenth century', Local History Diploma dissertation, Kent University, 1982.

— 'Economy and society in Dover, 1509–1640', PhD thesis, Kent University, 1992.

G. Draper, 'Work, wages and earnings on Romney Marsh in the late 15th and early 16th centuries', paper given at an international conference on medieval poverty, Kent University, 1996.

S. Dimmock, 'The St George play in early Tudor Lydd', paper given at the postgraduate conference on 'Community', Bristol University, 1996.

— 'Accumulation and poverty in Lydd, *c.*1450–1550', paper given at an international conference on medieval poverty, Kent University, 1996.

B. Kumin, 'The late medieval English parish, *c.* 1400–1560', DPhil thesis, Cambridge University, 1992.

P.J. Lee, 'Nuns and parishioners in orthodox society in late medieval Dartford', paper given at the Ecclesiastical Seminar, Institute of Historical Research, London, 1997.

— 'Monastic and secular religion and devotional reading in late medieval Dartford and west Kent', PhD thesis, Kent University, 1998.

R. Lutton, 'Heterodox and orthodox piety in Tenterden, *c.*1420–*c.*1540', PhD thesis, Kent University, 1997.

M.L. Merry, 'The construction and representation of urban identities: public and private lives in late medieval Bury St Edmunds', PhD thesis, Kent University, 2000.

E.M. Phillips, 'Charitable institutions in Norfolk and Suffolk *c.*1350–1600', PhD thesis, East Anglia University, 2001.

K. Robbins, 'A new material and cultural history of the Hotel Dieu in Beaune', paper given at the conference 'Hospitals in Medieval and Early Modern Europe: Function and Form', Courtauld Institute, London, 1997.

P.Rowe, 'The customary of the shrine of St Thomas Becket, a translation of the customary with notes', MA dissertation, London University, 1990.

Y. Russell, 'Hospitals and charity in sixteenth-century Sandwich', MA thesis, Kent University, 1990.

M. Satchell, 'The emergence of leper-houses in medieval England, 1100–1250', DPhil thesis, Oxford University, 1998.

M. Seymour, 'The organisation, personnel and functions of the medieval hospital in the later middle ages', MA thesis, London University, 1946.

P. Simpson, 'Tithe disputes as a platform for inter-personal relationships', paper given at the Culture and Society seminar, Kent University, 1997.

S. Sweetinburgh, 'Care in the community: local responses to the poor in late medieval Sandwich', paper given at an international conference on medieval poverty, Kent University, 1996.

— 'The role of the hospital in medieval Kent, *c.*1080–*c.*1560', PhD thesis, Kent University, 1998.

— 'Discord in the public arena: a time of conflict in early sixteenth-century Sandwich', unpublished paper, 2002.

P. Tucker, 'The medieval hospital of St Mary Bethlehem', paper given at the Wellcome Institute, London, 1996.

J. Wallace, 'The overseas trade of Sandwich, 1400–1520', MPhil thesis, London University, 1974.

J. Zeiger, 'The survival of the cult of St Thomas of Canterbury in the later middle ages', MA thesis, Kent University, 1997.

Index of hospitals

General index